TRAINING
—FOR—
VICTORY

Titles in the Series

The Other Space Race: Eisenhower and the Quest for Aerospace Security

An Untaken Road: Strategy, Technology, and the Mobile Intercontinental Ballistic Missile

Strategy: Context and Adaptation from Archidamus to Airpower

Cassandra in Oz: Counterinsurgency and Future War

Cyberspace in Peace and War

Limiting Risk in America's Wars: Airpower, Asymmetrics, and a New Strategic Paradigm

Always at War: Organizational Culture in Strategic Air Command, 1946–62

How the Few Became the Proud: Crafting the Marine Corps Mystique, 1874–1918

Assured Destruction: Building the Ballistic Missile Culture of the U.S. Air Force

Mars Adapting: Military Change during War

Cyberspace in Peace and War, Second Edition

Rise of the Mavericks: The U.S. Air Force Security Service and the Cold War

Standing Up Space Force: The Road to the Nation's Sixth Armed Service

From Yeomanettes to Fighter Jets: A Century of Women in the U.S. Navy

Transforming War

Paul J. Springer, editor

To ensure success, the conduct of war requires rapid and effective adaptation to changing circumstances. While every conflict involves a degree of flexibility and innovation, there are certain changes that have occurred throughout history that stand out because they fundamentally altered the conduct of warfare. The most prominent of these changes have been labeled "Revolutions in Military Affairs" (RMAs). These so-called revolutions include technological innovations as well as entirely new approaches to strategy. Revolutionary ideas in military theory, doctrine, and operations have also permanently changed the methods, means, and objectives of warfare.

This series examines fundamental transformations that have occurred in warfare. It places particular emphasis upon RMAs to examine how the development of a new idea or device can alter not only the conduct of wars but their effect upon participants, supporters, and uninvolved parties. The unifying concept of the series is not geographical or temporal; rather, it is the notion of change in conflict and its subsequent impact. This has allowed the incorporation of a wide variety of scholars, approaches, disciplines, and conclusions to be brought under the umbrella of the series. The works include biographies, examinations of transformative events, and analyses of key technological innovations that provide a greater understanding of how and why modern conflict is carried out, and how it may change the battlefields of the future.

"A superbly written, extensively researched, and very illuminating examination of what most determines success in the conduct of security force assistance missions—endeavors that have become increasingly important for the American military in recent decades because, if they are done right, they can preclude substantial employment of U.S. forces on the front lines of irregular conflicts."—**Gen. David Petraeus, USA (Ret.),** former USCENTCOM Commander, former Director of the CIA, and coauthor of *Conflict: The Evolution of Warfare from 1945 to Ukraine*

"*Training for Victory* may be the most important book on military affairs to be published in recent years. The history of training and advising partner forces reveals that the United States can remain engaged in the world and advance the interests of the American people at low cost and risk. The alternative would result in high-cost wars and interventions."—**Lt. Gen. H. R. McMaster, USA (Ret.),** former National Security Advisor and author of *Dereliction of Duty: Lyndon Johnson, Robert McNamara, the Joint Chiefs of Staff, and the Lies that Led to Vietnam*

"Frank Sobchak's excellent analysis of Special Forces partner development operations goes a long way toward explaining the factors underpinning the Green Berets' well-deserved reputation as the preeminent trainers of foreign partners. It is particularly timely as the U.S. military grapples to understand its strategic failure to develop credible partners in Iraq and Afghanistan, despite an enormous expenditure in time, treasure, and lives."—**Lt. Gen. Ken Tovo, USA (Ret.),** former Commanding General, U.S. Army Special Operations Command

"An important examination of the handful of effective military units built during the 9/11 wars. Frank Sobchak's penetrating analysis and actionable recommendations are a must-read for anyone concerned about future proxy wars with China, Russia, and Iran."—**Sean McFate,** Walsh School of Foreign Service, Georgetown University; College of International Security, National Defense University; author of *The New Rules of War: Victory in the Age of Durable Disorder*

"As both a professional historian and a Special Forces officer with multiple deployments, Frank Sobchak is perhaps uniquely qualified to assess what worked and what didn't work across multiple conflicts during which U.S. Special Forces worked 'by, with, and through' local forces such as the Iraqi Special Operations Forces. *Training for Victory* is an invaluable contribution both for practitioners in the field and for those interested in the history of America's 'advise and assist' missions."—**Peter Bergen,** CNN National Security Analyst; Chairman, Global SOF Foundation; author of *The Rise and Fall of Osama bin Laden*

"An outstanding contribution to the literature on special operations and irregular warfare, one that is full of strategy and policy insights for senior leaders to consider. Bravo!"—**Michael G. Vickers,** former Special Forces officer, CIA officer, Under Secretary of Defense for Intelligence, and author of *By All Means Available: Memoirs of a Life in Intelligence, Special Operations, and Strategy*

TRAINING FOR VICTORY

U.S. SPECIAL FORCES ADVISORY OPERATIONS FROM EL SALVADOR TO AFGHANISTAN

FRANK K. SOBCHAK

Naval Institute Press
Annapolis, Maryland

Naval Institute Press
291 Wood Road
Annapolis, MD 21402

© 2024 by the U.S. Naval Institute
All rights reserved. No part of this book may be reproduced or utilized in any form or by any means, electronic or mechanical, including photocopying and recording, or by any information-storage and -retrieval system, without permission in writing from the publisher.

Library of Congress Cataloging-in-Publication Data

Names: Sobchak, Frank K., author.
Title: Training for victory : U.S. Special Forces advisory operations from El Salvador to Afghanistan / Frank K. Sobchak.
Other titles: U.S. Special Forces advisory operations from El Salvador to Afghanistan
Description: First edition. | Annapolis, Maryland : Naval Institute Press, [2024] | Series: Transforming war | Includes bibliographical references and index.
Identifiers: LCCN 2024017974 (print) | LCCN 2024017975 (ebook) | ISBN 9781682471333 (hardback) | ISBN 9781682471364 (ebook)
Subjects: LCSH: United States. Army. Special Forces—Evaluation. | Special forces (Military science)—Training of—Case studies. | Military assistance, American—Case studies. | Military assistance, American—Evaluation. | Special forces (Military science)—Evaluation. | Combined operations (Military science)—Evaluation. | Military missions—Case studies. | BISAC: HISTORY / Military / Special Forces | HISTORY / Military / United States
Classification: LCC UA34.S64 S638 2024 (print) | LCC UA34.S64 (ebook) | DDC 355.50973/09051—dc23/eng/20240628
LC record available at https://lccn.loc.gov/2024017974
LC ebook record available at https://lccn.loc.gov/2024017975

♾ Print editions meet the requirements of ANSI/NISO z39.48–1992 (Permanence of Paper).
Printed in the United States of America.

9 8 7 6 5 4 3 2 1

All figures and tables created by the author unless otherwise indicated.

*To the fallen of the
Special Forces Regiment,
who gave the last full measure
of devotion to our great country*

Contents

List of Tables and Figures   xi
List of Abbreviations   xiii
Acknowledgments   xvii

Introduction
Unravelling the Mystery of How to Create Effective Partners   1

1 "The Only War We Had"
BIRIs in El Salvador, 1981–1991   19

2 Marksmen of Death
The Light Reaction Regiment in the Philippines, 2001–2015   48

3 "The Dream Allies"
BACOA and AGLAN in Colombia, 2002–2016   76

4 "We Have Killed Many Men Together"
The Iraqi Special Operations Forces, 2003–2011   110

5 "Chasing Bright and Shiny Objects"
The Afghan Commandos, 2007–2021   140

Conclusions and Recommendations
Making Security Force Assistance Work   175

Appendix A
El Salvador Case Study,
Calculating Partner-Force-to-Advisor Ratio   195

Appendix B
Philippines Case Study,
Calculating Partner-Force-to-Advisor Ratio   200

Appendix C
Colombia Case Study,
Calculating Partner-Force-to-Advisor Ratio   206

Appendix D
Iraq Case Study,
Calculating Partner-Force-to-Advisor Ratio   212

Appendix E
Afghanistan Case Study,
Calculating Partner-Force-to-Advisor Ratio   220

Notes   227

Bibliography   271

Index   303

Tables and Figures

TABLES

Table 1	Advisory Factors	178
Table 2	Host-Nation Combat Effectiveness	179

FIGURES

1.1	Monthly ratio of partners to advisors, El Salvador	34
2.1	Monthly ratio of partners to advisors, Philippines	58
3.1	Monthly ratio of partners to advisors, Colombia	93
4.1	Monthly ratio of partners to advisors, Iraq	115
5.1	Monthly ratio of partners to advisors, Afghanistan	148

Abbreviations

AFP	Armed Forces of the Philippines
AGLAN	Agrupación de Lanceros (Lancero Group)
ANA	Afghan National Army
ANASF	Afghan National Army Special Forces
ANASOC	Afghan National Army Special Operations Command
AOB	advanced operational base (usually an SF company)
ARSOF	U.S. Army Special Operations Forces
ASG	Abu Sayyaf Group
BACOA	Batallón de Comandos Ambrosio Almeyda (Ambrosio Almeyda Commando battalion)
BIRI	Batallones de Infantería de Reacción Inmediata (Immediate Reaction Infantry Battalions)
BN	battalion
CCOES	Comando Conjunto de Operaciones Especiales (Joint Special Operations Command)
CCOPE	Comando Conjunto de Operaciones Especiales (Joint Special Operations Command)
CENTCOM	Central Command
CIA	Central Intelligence Agency (U.S.)
CIF	CINC's/Commander's in-Extremis Force
CJSOTF	Combined Joint Special Operations Task Force
CJSOTF-AP	Combined Joint Special Operations Task Force–Arabian Peninsula
COESE	Comando de Operaciones Especiales del Ejercito (Colombian Army Special Operations Command)
CONOP	concept of the operation
CTC	Counter Terrorism Command (Iraq)
CTC	Commando Training Center (Afghanistan)
CTS	Counter Terrorism Service (Iraq)

Abbreviations

DLPT	Defense Language Proficiency Test
FARC	Fuerzas Armadas Revolucionarias de Colombia (Revolutionary Armed Forces of Colombia)
FBI	Federal Bureau of Investigation
FID	foreign internal defense
FMLN	Frente Farabundo Martí para la Liberación Nacional (Farabundo Martí National Liberation Front)
FOB	forward operating base
F3EAD	find, fix, finish, exploit, analyze, and disseminate
FY	fiscal year
GAO	Grupos Armados Organizados (organized armed groups)
GCC	geographic combatant command
GWOT	Global War on Terrorism
HALO	high-altitude, low-opening
HUMINT	human intelligence
Humvee	high-mobility multipurpose wheeled vehicle
HVT	high-value target
ICTF	Iraqi Counter Terrorism Force
IED	improvised explosive device
ISIS	Islamic State of Iraq and Syria
ISOF	Iraqi Special Operations Forces
J-3	operations directorate
JCET	Joint Combined Exchange Training
JSOG	Joint Special Operations Group
JSOTF	Joint Special Operations Task Force
JSOTF-P	Joint Special Operations Task Force–Philippines
LRB	Light Reaction Battalion
LRC	Light Reaction Company
LRR	Light Reaction Regiment
MILGP	U.S. Military Group (Colombia)
MILGRP	Military Advisor Group (El Salvador)
MNLF	Moro National Liberation Front
MTT	mobile training team
NATO	North Atlantic Treaty Organization
NCO	Noncommissioned Officer
ODA	Operational Detachment Alpha (SF team)

Abbreviations

ODB	Operational Detachment Bravo (SF company)
OEF-P	Operation Enduring Freedom–Philippines
OPATT	Operational Planning and Assistance Training Team
OSS	Office of Strategic Services
PAT	U.S. Pacific Command Augmentation Team
PATT	Planning Assistance Training Team
PGM	precision-guided munition
SEAL	sea, air, and land
SF	Special Forces
SFA	security force assistance
SFG	Special Forces Group
SOAG	Special Operations Advisory Group
SOCOM	Special Operations Command
SOCPAC	Special Operations Command Pacific
SOCSOUTH	Special Operations Command South
SOF	special-operations forces
SOTF	special-operations task force
SOUTHCOM	U.S. Southern Command
SSE	sensitive site exploitation
TSOC	Theater Special Operations Command
UAV	unmanned aerial vehicle
USACAPOC	U.S. Army Civil Affairs and Psychological Operations Command
USARSO	U.S. Army South
USASFC	U.S. Army Special Forces Command
USASOC	U.S. Army Special Operations Command
USPACOM	U.S. Pacific Command
USSOCOM	U.S. Special Operations Command
USSOUTHCOM	U.S. Southern Command
UW	unconventional warfare
VSO	Village Stability Operations

Acknowledgments

I AM ETERNALLY GRATEFUL for the support, guidance, and mentorship of Professor Richard Shultz, Professor Abi Linnington, and Colonel Pat Howell. As my dissertation committee they supervised what eventually became this book and helped me make it a better product.

I also wanted to thank Padraic (Pat) Carlin at Naval Institute Press and Dr. Paul J. Springer at the Air Command and Staff College, who contributed untold hours in reviewing the proposal for this book and then helped to hone its argument and prose. Without their dedication this work would not be what it is today. Similarly I would be remiss were I not to thank the MirYam Institute and the Modern War Institute at West Point for supporting my scholarship and publishing.

This work could not have been completed without the generous assistance of over one hundred active-duty and retired Special Forces officers, warrant officers, and noncommissioned officers. They gave freely of their time and spoke frankly about their experiences. Most gave blunt assessments of their failures and mistakes as well as their successes, showing a willingness to self-critique that is often missing in oral-history interviews, especially among senior leaders. Many also shared critical documents that helped fill the gaps in information that had not yet been made available through already-released primary and secondary sources. I was especially surprised and thankful for the candor of veterans of the Afghan conflict, as their perspectives upended the existing narrative of the Commandos and correctly predicted their rapid collapse after an American withdrawal.

A friend once described writing a book as walking through the desert for a thousand years by yourself. While the first part of that statement is certainly true (or at least it certainly felt like it), the second part is not accurate, or at least it was not for me. I was incredibly fortunate to have a veritable army of friends that helped me brainstorm and find sources, reviewed my draft chapters, kept me (mostly) sane, and sometimes talked me down from the proverbial ledge. While it would be impossible to list them all here, it would be negligent of me not to highlight Karst Brandsma, Stefan Tschauko, Jeremy Gwinn, Zoltan Feher, Scott McDonald,

Acknowledgments

Meg Guliford, Faith Christie, Julie Zollmann, and Sarah Detzner. Christopher Pumford provided invaluable support by designing the charts, graphs, and tables throughout this work.

I am also grateful to my parents, Frank and Alyce Sobchak, who gave me a yearning for discovery and learning and taught me the value of discipline, hard work, and dedication. Their memories are always with me.

Most importantly I have been so fortunate to have been loved, supported, inspired, and motivated by my wife, Iris (Risa) Sobchak. She is and always has been my best partner, editor, and love. Thanks for being with me on this wild ride of life! To our kids, Josh, Nathaniel, Catherine, and William, you give me strength to sortie on and make me to want to be a better person and father. I love you all.

Introduction

Unravelling the Mystery of How to Create Effective Partners

BACKGROUND

DURING THE TWO DECADES of America's post-9/11 wars fought across a dizzying number of countries and against a rogues' gallery of opponents, there was one inviolable constant: security force assistance (SFA), where advisors help develop foreign security forces and their supporting institutions, was a cornerstone of every U.S. effort. Indeed, security force assistance was such a core component of the U.S. exit strategy in Iraq that President George W. Bush explained, "as the Iraqis stand up, we will stand down."[1] Seen as a reflection of a new way of war as well as an economical way to reduce costs and American casualties, SFA became a part of U.S. doctrine and force structure. It was also touted as a logical answer to the post-9/11 security environment ostensibly because local solutions forged by forces that spoke the language and understood the human and physical terrain were thought to produce lasting and effective results. T. E. Lawrence's fifteenth article of advice for service in the Middle East became one of the most repeated quotations across the U.S. military: "Do not try to do too much with your own hands. Better the Arabs do it tolerably than that you do it perfectly. It is their war, and you are to help them, not to win it for them."[2]

But most of the U.S. efforts to build effective partners proved catastrophic failures. In Iraq the United States committed more than $25 billion to constructing an army of 250,000 soldiers and 600,000 other security forces.[3] Fewer than ten thousand Islamic State fighters routed those troops, whose real numbers were much lower due to corruption and graft. Coalition forces spent an astounding $83 billion on training and equipping Afghan security forces, only to watch a near repeat of the Iraq experience.[4] In both cases the victors held parades with scores of captured American equipment.

Despite those colossal military disasters, however, small pockets of host-nation forces performed admirably. The Iraqi Special Operations Forces—known colloquially as the Golden Division, or simply ISOF—fought doggedly against the 2014 Islamic State offensive in Fallujah, Ramadi, Tikrit, and the critical oil refinery at Baiji.[5] At Baiji they conducted an airmobile assault, seizing the key terrain ahead of ISIS, but were then quickly surrounded. Unable to be resupplied or evacuate casualties, they continued fighting for a week, even after the Islamic State offered them free passage in exchange for withdrawing. Their retrograde operation across northern Iraq delayed Islamic State fighters enough to allow a motley coalition of U.S., Iraqi, and Iranian forces to block the militant group's advance. When the Iraqis and coalition forces counterattacked, the ISOF were at the lead of every offensive. In Mosul the unit took 40 percent casualties but continued to attack enemy strongpoints, even though that should have rendered them combat ineffective.[6] Without the ISOF, Iraq could have collapsed and might not be a unitary state today.

A similar situation played out with the Afghan Commandos. During the 2015 summer offensive fewer than two thousand Taliban fighters routed nearly five thousand Afghan government forces, whose wholesale destruction was only prevented by the timely arrival of Afghan Commandos and their advisors from among the U.S. Army Special Forces (SF).[7] In 2021 around the city of Kandahar, surrounded Commandos battled the Taliban for more than a month until their ammunition ran out.[8] As province after province fell, Commando units kept fighting to the bitter end, with some holding the perimeter around Hamid Karzai International Airport while their country disintegrated around them.

What was it that made those units so effective while the rest of the effort to build allied armies was an abject failure? One of the central puzzles was understanding why a few units performed better than nearly all the others even though their advisors' language training and cultural awareness skills seemed inconsequential. In the cases of the ISOF and the Afghan Commandos, most of the advising forces did not speak the language of the soldiers with whom they partnered. Of those who did, nearly all spoke it at a rudimentary level. That truth exposes an important riddle that challenges a core orthodoxy within the advising community: Is language training as important as we consider it to be in producing combat-effective partners? More importantly, if language training isn't critical to producing combat-effective partners, what is? This is the central question of this book, which aims to explore what factors were most important for U.S. Special Forces units to produce capable partners like the ISOF and the Commandos.

A Short History of the Green Berets

One area of consistency between the Afghan Commandos and the Iraqi Special Operations Forces was the critical guidance and instruction provided by the U.S. Army's Special Forces, informally known as the Green Berets for their distinctive headgear and considered to be among the best military advisors in the world. The historical origins of Special Forces are found in a series of elite forces employed during World War II. Its official lineage traces to the joint U.S. and Canadian First Special Service Force, a commando organization created to conduct raids behind enemy lines and made famous by the 1968 movie *The Devil's Brigade*.[9] Special Forces' more important origins draw from the Office of Strategic Services (OSS), a precursor to the Central Intelligence Agency and U.S. Special Operations Command, which performed intelligence and special-operations missions deep in occupied Europe and Asia. Especially critical to the development of U.S. Special Forces were the OSS's Jedburgh teams and operational groups, which advised partisans and guerrillas conducting unconventional warfare behind enemy lines; members of those units, like those on Special Forces teams, were required to speak foreign languages and were trained as leaders, communications specialists, demolitions soldiers, and weapons experts.[10] One final precursor is found in the U.S. Army's guerrilla-warfare campaigns against the Japanese in the occupied Philippines led by Wendell Fertig, Russell Volckmann, Donald Blackman, and others.

While the First Special Service Force, Philippine guerrilla units, and the OSS were disbanded at the end of World War II, many of their former members became influential leaders in the fledgling U.S. Army 10th Special Forces Group, which was stood up in 1952 to replicate OSS partisan warfare if the Soviet Union were to invade Western Europe.[11] Some newly minted Special Forces soldiers were also sent to the Korean War, where they fruitlessly organized guerrilla forces to infiltrate North Korea during the conflict. Seen by the conventional Army as a distraction and waste of resources, Special Forces languished until the administration of President John F. Kennedy, who sought a new way of warfare to address the burgeoning communist threat.¹² Kennedy expanded and empowered Special Forces, authorizing them to wear the iconic green beret and unleashing them across the globe in missions advising foreign forces putting down insurgencies.

Reflecting their mixed origins, Special Forces soldiers were trained to conduct a wide range of missions. From their commando roots they could carry out special reconnaissance, including high-stakes scouting operations requiring elite capabilities and equipment as well as direct action—raids, ambushes, or other specialized strike missions with or without partners. Reflecting their OSS heritage and guerrilla-warfare experience in the Philippines, Special Forces took unconventional warfare (UW) as its core mission, where they trained partisan forces against authoritarian or communist-bloc governments.¹³ Answering President Kennedy's call to adapt to emerging global threats, Special Forces could also perform foreign internal defense (FID) or security force assistance (SFA) missions that trained foreign-partner forces. Within the directives to wage unconventional warfare and conduct foreign internal defense, Special Forces were expected to operate by, with, and through local partners. Over time other assignments were added to their charge, such as counterterrorism and counterproliferation, but partnered missions such as FID and UW formed their raison d'être.

It was in security force assistance missions where Special Forces blossomed. The first and last soldiers to die in combat during the Vietnam War were Green Berets, and many of their missions there came to exemplify their approach to combat. Often a small team or detachment of a dozen or so Special Forces soldiers would establish a remote outpost partnered with hundreds of Vietnamese soldiers or tribesmen far from the reach of conventional military forces. There SF troops trained and fought shoulder to shoulder with their partners, developing long friendships and adopting enough local traditions to be often derisively accused of "going native." One of their main missions with the Civilian Irregular Defense Group program involved as much or more development work as it did combat, and Special Forces soldiers became proficient at digging wells and building schools while their medical sergeants became renowned for their skills, performing miracles in the hinterlands. Even the covert direct-action missions they performed in Cambodia and Laos as part of the Military Assistance Command Vietnam—Studies and Observations Group were partnered with indigenous soldiers, often minorities such as Cambodians, Nungs, Montagnards, or ethnic Chinese.¹⁴

While war raged in Vietnam, Special Forces teams were also deployed across Latin America and other parts of Asia to fight communist insurgencies. Long-term missions were carried out in Colombia, the Philippines, and Bolivia, a country where the Green Berets saw one of their greatest successes of the era. Che Guevara, famous for his role in the Cuban Revolution, was leading an insurgency there against government forces. Barred from accompanying Bolivians into combat, Special Forces soldiers trained a series of Army units on advanced counterinsurgency tactics and helped advise them on how best to defeat Guevara. Barely months later Guevara was captured and summarily executed by Bolivian forces, effectively putting an end to the insurgency.

U.S. military fascination with Special Forces waned as the Vietnam War drew to an end, leading to the disbanding of several units. As the Armed Forces shifted to a peacetime stance, smaller and shorter missions began to replace the large, long-term, Vietnam-style combat deployments wherein an entire SF Group would be deployed for the duration of the conflict. The new bread and butter for Special Forces became Mobile Training Teams (MTTs) and then Joint Combined Exchange Training (JCETs), which would last anywhere from a few weeks to a few months. During such missions, single teams of a dozen men deployed overseas to remote locations while their headquarters remained in the United States. There they worked under peacetime rules of engagement for the chief of mission in the local U.S. embassy and were either barred from participating in combat or deployed to areas devoid of active conflict. The short length of the missions as well as their reduced frequency made it difficult to assess long-term impact, and many saw the operations as merely a way to "keep the fires warm" and maintain some form of professional contact with allies.

By the end of the Vietnam War the organization and training of Special Forces units had more or less stabilized. The basic organizational building block, the Operational Detachment Alpha (ODA), or A team, was unlike anything in the conventional Army. Twelve men comprised the team: a commander and deputy, a senior noncommissioned officer and his deputy, two weapons specialists, two medics, two communications experts, and two engineers. Each of the eight enlisted specialists was among the best in their trade. The engineers, skilled in vertical construction and demolition, were probably the impetus for the popular *MacGyver* television character and could improvise nearly anything into items as diverse as weapons or creature comforts for their base. While most of the Green Berets' training spans a year,[15] the medics' training lasts another six months, qualifying them to do surgery, administer anesthesia, and even perform veterinary medicine. Weapons sergeants are trained to handle and maintain nearly every firearm in existence, and communications sergeants have the skills to use long-range and clandestine systems.

Structurally six ODAs make up a Special Forces company, or Operational Detachment Bravo (ODB), or simply a B team. A battalion or C team is comprised of three of those companies along with a headquarters and support troops. Finally three or four such battalions paired with logistics elements and its own headquarters made up a Special Forces Group.[16] By 1980 active-duty Special Forces Groups were regionally oriented and given language training to match where they would be deployed.[17] In 2021 that training cost more than $51 million, a sum that tracks with what was historically spent during the previous two decades.[18] Because of the significant expenditure required to train SF Groups and the belief that their specialized knowledge helped produce effective partners, before 9/11 regional orientation was often seen as sacrosanct and SF Groups were often barred from deploying outside of their area of responsibility.

While the post-9/11 wars waged, demand for Special Forces grew exponentially, so much so that some frustrated Green Beret leaders joked that their organization had become the proverbial "easy button" for policymakers to press when searching for instantaneous, low-effort solutions. Facing armed extremist groups conducting insurgencies across the globe, Special Forces became both a logical solution to that threat and a way to avoid public scrutiny because of the clandestine nature of many of their operations. Operational procedures shifted again, and a large-scale continual presence in active war zones largely replaced the episodic contact in countries at peace. Among their many other missions Special Forces units advised Yemeni counterterrorism police, Afghan militias, Somali irregulars, Philippine Commandos, and Iraqi soldiers. Tens of millions to billions of dollars were spent on different operations considered central to U.S. national strategy, heightening the need to study which operations built effective partners and which did not.

PICKING THE RIGHT NEEDLES OUT OF A HAYSTACK: CASE SELECTION

The wide variety of advisory missions makes choosing which operations to evaluate a challenging task. For much of the post-9/11 period Special Forces trained what amounted to a veritable Star Wars cantina[19] of different types of partners in dozens of countries. Evaluating all of them would be both impractical due to their scope and unreasonable because of their differences. Instead, to make a fair basis of comparison, missions would have to be similar enough to compare proverbial apples to apples but also different enough so that from one case to another variations in the missions could be used to evaluate what caused one unit to be effective and another not.

To meet these requirements I have chosen to focus on missions that involved U.S. Army Special Forces training a special-operations, elite, or commando partner force created during the time of the advisory effort. Such a case selection excludes efforts with police or paramilitaries (such as Village Stability Operations in Afghanistan or the Sunni Awakening[20] and Hillah SWAT in Iraq) as well as missions advising conventional partner forces or training surrogates in unconventional warfare (as was done in Syria with the Kurdish YPG, or People's Protection Units). While there could be some debate on the semantics of what constitutes a special-operations, elite, or commando partner force, in practicality there are often clear delineations in partner-force armies between those forces and other units. Such elite units are clearly identified by the partners themselves and receive more training and greater budgets, and their makeup is often composed primarily of volunteers rather than conscripts. Focusing on these forces reduces variance in the quality of the host-nation forces, a factor that could skew the outcome of how effective they became after being trained.

To add further consistency I have decided to study host-nation elite units that were stood up through U.S. assistance during an ongoing insurgency. Because the pressures of combat affect all elements of the construction and employment of host-nation units, it would not be fair to compare a unit built under such conditions with one built during peacetime. Furthermore, organizations that were in existence before the advisory effort began are excluded from the study. It would not be reasonable, for example, to compare an elite unit in one country that had been in existence for a decade and had considerable combat experience with an elite unit that had just been assembled from scratch in another country.

Finally I have chosen to study only security force assistance conducted by U.S. Army Special Forces in major operations where their presence was sustained and continuous. Each of the missions under review spanned nearly a decade or more and constituted a strategic priority for national decision-makers. Such conditions establish a fair basis of comparison and focus on the most important and costly missions in terms of budgetary expenditure and human casualties. Evaluating these engagements against the more episodic Joint Combined Exchange Training (JCET) program or shorter missions would not make sense.

Based on these criteria I have chosen to evaluate five Special Forces missions— four that were carried out after 9/11 and one that occurred at the tail end of the Cold War: El Salvador from 1981 to 1991, the Philippines from 2001 to 2015, Colombia from 2002 to 2016, Iraq from 2003 to 2011, and Afghanistan from 2007 to 2021. Before moving on it would be worthwhile to provide a brief overview of each mission.

Introduction

Fearing a communist takeover of El Salvador, as had happened in neighboring Nicaragua, the United States supported government forces against Marxist insurgents for the last decade of the Cold War. A large portion of that support involved the training of Salvadoran Army units, which was done by conventional advisors as well as Green Berets from the Latin American regionally oriented 7th Special Forces Group. Discovering that conscript units were being systematically destroyed by guerrilla forces, American advisors ordered the creation of elite units named BIRIs (Batallones de Infantería de Reacción Inmediata, or Immediate Reaction Infantry Battalions, as they were known in English). Due to a combination of congressional opposition and sovereignty concerns from El Salvador, only fifty-five advisors were permitted in country at one time, and they were forbidden from accompanying their partners into combat. Because of those limitations, advisors had many responsibilities across the brigades with which they partnered, and engagement with the BIRIs was often episodic rather than the intense partnerships of other missions.

Before the terrorist attacks of September 11, 2001, the United States had offered to help build an elite counterterrorism force for the Philippines, named the Light Reaction Company, with the regionally aligned 1st Special Forces Group in charge of the advisory effort. As the World Trade Center's Twin Towers still smoldered, the two nations decided to expand the advisory effort to counter local militant groups allied with al-Qaida. By 2005, however, demands from the Afghan and Iraqi theaters drew 1st Group soldiers out of their assigned region, and the advisor impact in the Philippines waned considerably. Philippine law prevented U.S. forces from engaging in combat, and other global commitments kept the footprint of deployed soldiers relatively small, especially in comparison to troop presences in Iraq and Afghanistan.

In the late 1990s the United States began an extended advisory mission in Colombia to help government forces combat insurgents and stem the flow of the coca trade. As in the Philippines, after the September 11th attacks this mission was expanded and refined to fall under the broader aegis of the what the George W. Bush administration termed the Global War on Terrorism (GWOT). The regionally aligned 7th Special Forces Group, which had previously stood up the BIRIs in El Salvador, was tasked with helping to create two new elite forces, the BACOA (Batallón de Comandos Ambrosio Almeyda, translated as "Ambrosio Almeyda Commando battalion") and AGLAN (Agrupación de Lanceros, translated as "Lancero Group"). Global commitments caused fluctuations in the number of advisors, who were barred from assisting Colombian forces in combat.

After the U.S. invasion of Iraq and dissolution of its army, Special Forces were called upon to organize elite units for the new government. The Middle East–oriented 5th Special Forces Group stood up a mixed-ethnicity commando battalion, which was quickly followed by the Iraqi Counter Terrorism Force (ICTF). Together the two units became the basis for the Iraqi Special Operations Forces (ISOF). Because of the substantial personnel requirements for the mission, 10th Group, which is normally oriented on Europe, was tasked with assisting 5th Group, but even that proved to be insufficient, and eventually every Group contributed to the advisory effort. Unlike as in El Salvador, the Philippines, and Colombia, U.S. advisors in Iraq had nearly carte blanche to construct the units as they wished after the decapitation of Saddam Hussein's regime and were allowed to accompany their partners into combat. Considerable resources were committed to ensure sufficient advisors were available to train the fledgling forces.

Special Forces leaders in Afghanistan recognized the value provided by the ISOF to Iraq and decided to stand up a similar force, which they named the Afghan Commandos. Because the unit that normally would have responsibility for Afghanistan, 5th Special Forces Group, was committed to Iraq, two Groups that had neither language training nor cultural connections to Central Asia were assigned instead. Those units, 3rd and 7th Special Forces Groups, proved insufficient to meet the personnel demands of the war in Afghanistan and, as in Iraq, every Group contributed forces to the advisory mission. Also reflecting similarities to postregime-change Iraq, advisors in Afghanistan accompanied their partners into battle and had considerable influence on the construction of the units they built.

WHAT MAKES ADVISORS EFFECTIVE? DECIDING WHAT TO EXAMINE

Having established the cases to be evaluated, the next issue to be resolved is perhaps the most important one. This book aims to determine what conditions are most important for U.S. Army Special Forces to build a combat-effective partner force. What was done differently during the advisory efforts for the Afghan Commandos and the ISOF that made those units and units like them successful? Unfortunately thousands of different factors could have contributed to those outcomes, and it would be utterly impossible to try to evaluate all of them. But after careful evaluation, five factors stood out as more likely to be impactful than others: (1) the advisors' language training and cultural awareness, (2) the consistency in advisor pairing, (3) the partner-to-advisor ratio, (4) the advisors' ability to organize the host nation's unit, and (5) the advisors' ability to advise host-nation forces during combat. As these five factors form the foundation of this study, I will explain each in detail and clarify the reasons they were selected.

Advisor Language Training and Cultural Awareness

Conventional wisdom holds that advisors with language training and cultural awareness matching the area to which they are deployed are better able to help their partners become combat effective. The famous Lawrence of Arabia once dictated that an advisor learn everything possible about the partner culture and its family groups and, beyond merely learning the language of the host nation, learn local dialects as well.[21] Yet exactly how language and culture impact the advisor-advisee relationship is unclear—at least considering the interventions in Iraq and Afghanistan.

Language training and cultural awareness are at the very core of Special Forces concerns, shaping their very identity and origin. Indeed, soon after the geographic combatant commands (GCCs) had been stood up, each SF Group was affiliated with one of the commands and its soldiers trained in languages specific to that region. 7th Special Forces Group, for example, was oriented toward U.S. Southern Command (USSOUTHCOM), which concerns itself with Central and South America and the Caribbean, so its members learned Spanish and Brazilian Portuguese. Since then considerable funds have been spent building and maintaining these capabilities. So much credence was given to the belief that knowing the host-nation language and understanding the culture make a difference in training partner forces that before 9/11 an orthodoxy developed that SF units would rarely be deployed outside their regional orientation. This rigidity often resulted in an imbalance of deployments, with some Groups exceedingly busy while others struggled with boredom. Inflexible regional alignment is once again *en vogue* among some SF leaders, and the notion of regional alignment is even being implemented by the conventional Army as part of its new force-generation model; thus it is timely and even critical that we study the underlying assumptions about such a policy.[22]

During the post-9/11 wars, the exceedingly challenging troop-to-task demands for SF advisors made it impossible to match their skills to the areas they deployed. For example, 1st Group soldiers speaking Mandarin and Tagalog trained Afghans and Iraqis—which allowed me to assess the actual importance of matching advisor language training and cultural awareness with their partners. Because each of the five active-duty Special Forces Groups under study is regionally oriented, it is relatively easy to determine the degree of a match between their language ability and cultural awareness and the region to which they are deployed. In each case under review, if multiple Groups contributed to a particular advisory mission, I have calculated the amount of time there was a matching orientation and compared it to the amount of time that there was not, creating a variation of *high*, *moderate*, *low*, or *no match* in language skills and cultural awareness.

Consistency in Advisor Pairing

There is a prevailing belief that consistent contact between Special Forces advisors and their host-nation partners is important to the mission. Proponents of the position argue that it creates interpersonal bonds with the advised force and can lead to long-term relationships that pay dividends. Personal memoirs written by Green Berets almost always include discussions of those relationships and highlight their importance.[23] Despite the considerable anecdotal support for this position, no scientific study has examined the impact of consistency in advisor pairing.

Historically it has been easier said than done to consistently pair the same advisors with the same host-nation forces. Some of the challenge stems from the long duration of most SF advisory missions, meaning it is impossible to deploy the same personnel for the entire mission. Soldiers need time to rest and recover between missions, and other operations and training compete for each unit's available deployment time. The global nature of the United States' post-9/11 wars made it especially difficult to return the same advisors to work with the same partners as demand from Iraq and Afghanistan fluctuated, necessitating adding personnel with little experience to a theater in need of a surge of troops or experiencing a crisis. Commanders also contributed to the problem by changing priorities and shifting advisors from one mission to another. However, by either luck or design some efforts had the same set of advisors return to train the same partner forces multiple times for the duration of the mission, allowing me to measure and assess its impact.

Partner-to-Advisor Ratio

According to U.S. military doctrine, one Special Forces detachment of twelve soldiers should be paired with one host-nation battalion (which is comprised of roughly six hundred to nine hundred soldiers)—equating to a ratio of sixty or seventy-five partners to one advisor.[24] The Special Forces community holds this belief as strongly as original canon is held by fans of the *Star Wars* and *Star Trek* universes. People become oddly agitated and even irate when the principle is challenged.

Though the anointed ratio is held as sacrosanct, little study has been carried out to formally confirm its efficacy, whether, in fact, it accurately depicts what is happening in the field and what is most effective. Fortunately, that ratio is purely mathematical and can be easily calculated. The general principle, however, is that a lower ratio produces more-effective partners, a theory with parallels to the intense education debate over the importance of student-to-teacher ratios.[25] The belief is that a lower ratio allows advisors to interact with trainees more frequently and establish personal connections that build trust and cohesion.

Advisor Ability to Organize the Host-Nation Unit

One of the thorniest challenges facing advisors involves convincing reluctant host-nation forces to make necessary changes that would improve their combat effectiveness. While some allies accept recommendations relatively easily, in many cases effecting change is a torturous slog as advisors butt up against cultural, economic, and institutional challenges. Shame-and-honor societies prefer not to be corrected, and corrupt officers eschew any change that would take money out of their pockets. Among the different theorists who directly or indirectly explain the challenges of security force assistance at the macro level, Douglass North, John Wallis, and Barry Weingast posit in *Violence and Social Orders* that the host nation maintains its power and strata through blocking change to its prevalent social structures.[26]

Others use variations of principal-agent theory to explain why it is so difficult for countries providing security force assistance to get countries receiving assistance to make necessary changes.[27] The theory holds that the agent, or host-nation country, possesses an information asymmetry over the principal, or the advising force. Stated another way, the host nation simply knows more about their own capabilities, actions, and objectives than the advisors. Acting to further their own interests rather than those of the country providing assistance, the host nation can control the amount of information the advisors receive, thereby skewing the advisors' understanding of the situation and making it difficult for them to alter host-nation behaviors. Taken a step farther, if the host nation, for whatever reason, does not want progress to be made, it is nearly impossible for a foreign power to impose an external solution.[28]

While principal-agent theory helps us understand the inherent challenges of SFA at the macro level, it does little to explain why some units can overcome those barriers and become militarily effective. For example, why did the Iraqi Special

Operations Forces and the Afghan Commandos become capable fighting forces while the rest of the SFA effort failed in Iraq and Afghanistan? Principal-agent theory helps explain the overall collapse of security forces but fails to explain why there are wide variations in effectiveness between different host-nation units in the same country.

To address this seeming contradiction I opted to subjectively quantify advisors' organization of host-nation units. *Organization* in this case refers to the degree to which host-nation forces implement the recommendations of SF advisors. Those recommendations could include decisions relating to personnel, force structure, equipping, and employment, among other considerations. *Personnel* decisions involve the selection, promotion, and replacement of host-nation leaders as well as the selection and pay process for the unit's soldiers; for example, if Lieutenant Abbas is incompetent, will the host nation follow the recommendations of the advisors and cashier him? Decisions regarding *force structure* and *equipping* address how the unit is organized and what kit it is provided. *Employment* decisions include command-and-control structures for the units and tactical decisions determining how the units are used.

In some cases, as in Iraq and Afghanistan, regime change initially led to what was effectively a "reboot" of the nation's military forces, giving foreign powers nearly carte blanche to organize the units being trained as sovereignty issues could be ignored. Other cases had more traditional advisor/partner relationships affected by national sovereignty wherein SF soldiers had to build rapport in the hope that the host nation would implement their recommendations. Although the degree to which advisors were allowed to organize host-nation units changed over the duration of a mission, it is still possible to subjectively assess that overall impact.

Combat Advising

Special Forces folklore holds that partnering while in actual combat is the gold standard of advisory. Many look back longingly at the Vietnam War as the ultimate example of what SF soldiers can accomplish when allowed to fight shoulder to shoulder with their host-nation partners; SF leaders thus often desire to expand authorities to bring advisory efforts as close to the sound of the guns as possible. Historical accounts of other advisory efforts also tend to highlight the importance of combat advising.[29] However, like many Special Forces legends, the scant evidence that combat advising is essential or even has an impact has not been given sufficient scrutiny.

This book will correct that deficiency and assess combat advising not as a binary but as a spectrum influenced by a variety of factors. Some of those factors include how far forward Special Forces soldiers were allowed to accompany their host-nation partners into battle and whether SF soldiers were allowed to engage the enemy with their individual weapons. In some cases where advisors were prohibited from accompanying their partners on combat missions—whether due to national-sovereignty issues, legal issues, or risk avoidance—they trained their partners at remote bases but waved goodbye as the host-nation forces went off to fight. In the other extreme, Green Berets trained their partner force and accompanied them into combat where they continued their advisory efforts. In between those two extremes exist a multitude of degrees of risk U.S. leadership was willing to take and an equally wide degree of sovereignty the host nation was prepared to cede.

IT'S MORE THAN JUST KILLING: DEFINING COMBAT EFFECTIVENESS

In order to assess what factors were most important for U.S. Special Forces units who ultimately trained capable partners, we must first understand what is meant by *combat effectiveness*. Since the dawn of warfare quantifying military effectiveness has been a challenge, and military officers, political leaders, their staffs, and theorists have struggled to ascertain what makes one organization or army effective while another is not. As with the study of principal-agent theory, much of the literature focuses on the strategic or national level of combat effectiveness, which provides little value when studying of the effectiveness of individual units.

To assess military effectiveness at the micro or unit level, however, I decided to rely on the literature of counterinsurgency, because each case study we examine here involves SF support to host-nation forces conducting a counterinsurgency campaign. Therefore, I will define a combat-effective partner as a unit that is capable of (1) fighting without advisors present, (2) fighting at night, (3) conducting multiday combat operations, and (4) consistently defeating enemy forces in combat. The first three focus on skills that are used to conduct counterinsurgency, while the fourth pertains to performance and the outcome of combat. Examining all four ensures that an assessment of the partner force reflects the challenges of measuring combat performance where one unit could be highly trained but facing an extremely skilled enemy that is difficult to defeat while a unit in another country could be only marginally trained but facing an inept enemy that is easier to defeat.

Fighting without Advisors Present

A host nation's ability to fight without the aid of advisors is a self-evident criterion for success, as most advisors consider it their objective to work themselves out of a job. Indeed, the U.S. counterinsurgency manual describes the final phase of such operations as a "movement to self-sufficiency."[30] Counterinsurgency theorists also posit that this movement to self-sufficiency reflects a need to minimize and eventually eliminate foreign involvement, which itself is thought to be a potential driver of insurgency. The Army's manual on security force assistance deems the goal of independently operating host-nation forces so essential that it underscores the point no fewer than eleven times.[31]

To fight independently a host-nation force should be able to conduct intelligence-driven operations in which the unit generates its own organic intelligence, plans missions based on that intelligence, conducts the operation, and then processes intelligence garnered from that target to generate additional new targets. This cycle was named *F3EAD* by U.S. special-operations forces during the post-9/11 wars, with the letters of the acronym identifying the different phases of the cycle: finding, fixing, and then finishing the enemy, exploiting intelligence recovered from the target, analyzing that information, and then disseminating that information to begin the cycle again.[32] In a way F3EAD is the pinnacle of intelligence-driven operations as the units that can do it may be able to seize the initiative by conducting operations that kill or capture insurgents faster than they can be replaced. This strategy was pioneered in Iraq by Gen. Stanley McChrystal and has since been copied extensively by other U.S. and allied forces.[33] Therefore a partner force truly capable of fighting without advisors must be able to conduct the F3EAD intelligence-driven operations cycle without U.S. advisors present.

Night Fighting

Defining the second element of combat effectiveness is fairly easy: successfully fighting at night simply means that the military organization can continue to conduct combat operations at night with or without technological equipment such as night-vision devices. Many military experts argue that this skill is a key differentiator for military effectiveness, especially in counterinsurgency operations where guerrilla forces often move and fight under the cover of darkness. In his counterinsurgency opus *Modern Warfare*, Roger Trinquier says that, "except in rare cases of emergency," missions should be carried out after nightfall to gain surprise and minimize civilian casualties.[34] The Army and Marine Corps manual on counterinsurgency is replete with calls to conduct operations at night, and the U.S. Joint Forces manual echoes its importance.[35]

Conducting Multiday Combat Operations

The third element I am using to ascertain combat effectiveness requires some explanation: Nearly any unit can conduct a raid that lasts for an hour. Being able to fight for multiple days implies that a military organization is proficient in logistics and has sufficient cohesion to take casualties and keep fighting.

It has long been said that "amateurs talk tactics; professionals talk logistics."[36] While effectively supplying, maintaining, supporting, and moving military forces does not guarantee success, logistic ineptitude can often doom otherwise-successful military efforts. Counterinsurgency operations are no different, as consistently resupplied food, ammunition, and fuel are imperative to remaining in contact with stealthy insurgents consistently on the move. The chapter on assessments in the U.S. Army's *Security Force Assistance Brigade* manual focuses extensively on the importance of logistics, noting that a host-nation unit should not only be able to sustain itself in combat after American forces depart but should also be able to manage their own equipment throughout its lifecycle from procurement to disposal.[37]

Cohesion is likewise critical to conducting multiday combat operations. It steels a unit to absorb casualties and keep fighting and is the sinew that holds a unit together despite long marches, horrible conditions, and lack of sleep. Numerous scholars and practitioners have emphasized the importance of cohesion to military effectiveness, whether in conventional warfare or conducting counterinsurgency.[38]

But how long exactly is "multiday" combat? From a standpoint of logistics and cohesion, a good yardstick would be seventy-two hours. Few commando or special-operations units could carry enough ammunition, food, and water to sustain themselves for that long while engaging in intense fighting; although soldiers can often get by on less food for a short period of time, there are no workarounds for the requirements of water and ammunition.[39] Thus an outfit capable of sustaining combat for at least seventy-two hours has sufficient cohesion to not break under prolonged assault, even in the face of casualties, running low on supplies, and witnessing evacuations of the wounded. It is only when units are nearly out of food and ammunition, exhausted, and under intense emotional and physical strain that their true level of morale and cohesion can be measured.[40]

Performance against the Enemy in Combat

This final element of combat effectiveness is widely accepted as one of the basic building blocks of military capability as a whole. While repeated defeat of insurgent forces in battle at the tactical level could still result in operational or strategic failure of the partner force, without tactical battlefield success it is impossible to achieve progress in other fields critical to counterinsurgency. As former U.S. secretary of state Henry Kissinger once put it, "the guerrilla wins if he does not lose; the conventional army loses if it doesn't win."[41] Victory on the battlefield buys time for political reconciliation, economic development, and civil society to build, as well as for establishing other elements necessary for strategic success.

"Above all," says counterinsurgency theorist David Galula, "we must loose the guerrilla's hold on the population by systematically destroying his combat organization."[42] Speaking from the guerrilla's perspective, Mao Zedong emphasized that insurgents should dodge decisive battle at all cost to avoid being destroyed—even calling on his forces to withdraw when faced by a superior enemy.[43] It follows then that, if a counterinsurgent force can force a guerrilla element into combat and defeat them, they are challenging core principles of guerrilla strategy.

OVERALL ASSESSMENT OF COMBAT EFFECTIVENESS

For each case in the following study I will award a value between *low* and *high* to quantify the host-nation force's ability to (1) fight without advisors present, (2) fight at night, (3) conduct multiday combat operations, and (4) consistently defeat enemy forces in combat. To assess each mission's *overall* combat effectiveness, I will make a subjective assessment of the impact of those four factors combined and, likewise, award a value between low to high. It is important to reiterate that this assessment is not related to the overall success of the larger mission or whether U.S. policy goals were met at the strategic or macro level. Instead I am measuring only the tactical-level combat effectiveness of the partner-force unit because there are important lessons to be learned from such a microstudy that have been previously unexplored. Some cases examined in this book were overall strategic failures and U.S. policy objectives were not met—including constructing capable host-nation security forces. Still, at the same time we were able to build some capable units, specifically special-operations partner forces at the tactical level. That paradox lies at the heart of what I will be exploring.

Introduction

GOING FORWARD

This book aims to determine why U.S. Army Special Forces have been able to produce highly effective partners in some missions and not in others. More specifically, it aims to ascertain what factors are most relevant to achieving that goal of combat effectiveness. Finding those answers has relevance to the larger debate about security force assistance as lessons from building individual units could be scaled up to improve larger missions. Within the Special Forces community that information would help inform questions roiling leaders about the importance of regional orientation as well as debates about future structure, doctrine, and missions.

To answer this question, in each case study we will explore five of the most important factors that determine whether advisors are effective: language training and cultural awareness, consistency in advisor pairing, partner-force-to-advisor ratio, advisor ability to organize the host-nation units, and ability to combat advise host-nation forces. Those inputs will then be compared to the results of their efforts: how effective their partners became. Only then will we be able to assess which of those five factors is most important to producing combat-effective partners. Now that the road map has been laid out, we will move on to our first case study—El Salvador.

– 1 –
"The Only War We Had"
BIRIs in El Salvador, 1981–1991[1]

BACKGROUND

EL SALVADOR'S economic disparities, military governance, and lack of representation were dry kindling for insurgency and revolution. The fraudulent election of General Humberto Romero in 1977 provided the spark that ignited armed insurrection. Salvadoran military forces responded to protests against Romero by opening fire on crowds of civilians, killing hundreds. A state of emergency, suspension of civil rights, and government-sponsored death squads followed. Moderate Salvadoran Army officers partnered with civilians overthrew Romero in yet another coup in 1979, only to have their proposed reforms blocked by reactionary elements. The capital's archbishop, who had been openly critical of the government's oppression and human-rights abuses, was assassinated while celebrating mass, and four Catholic nuns from the United States were kidnapped, raped, and then murdered by Salvadoran security forces. Tens of thousands of civilians were killed in politically motivated violence between 1977 and 1981, the majority at the hands of government forces.[2] Such abuses strengthened rebel forces, which unified under the banner of the Frente Farabundo Martí para la Liberación Nacional (FMLN, or the Farabundo Martí National Liberation Front).[3] Recognizing an opportunity to win propaganda and military victories, the Soviet Union began supplying military assistance and training to the Salvadoran insurgents. Soviet proxies Cuba and

Vietnam also provided military advisors, and Nicaragua offered a sanctuary for the FMLN to train and recuperate.

Worried that another Cold War domino might fall and concerned with the domestic political ramifications of "losing" El Salvador like the United States had "lost" Nicaragua and Iran, the newly elected administration of U.S. president Ronald Reagan decided to increase military assistance and boost the U.S. advisory effort. Not even a decade after the withdrawal of U.S. troops from Vietnam and barely five years since the Fall of Saigon, they faced considerable domestic opposition. Seeing parallels between El Salvador and Vietnam, many in Congress sought to avoid getting drawn into a similar conflict. After extended negotiations, administration and congressional officials agreed on a limit of fifty-five advisors, who would be barred from engaging in combat operations.[4]

As the mission unfolded, U.S. political leaders tasked the military with assessing the situation. In 1981 a commission headed by U.S. Army brigadier general Frederick Woerner completed what proved to be a brutal evaluation of the Salvadoran military's capabilities and prospects. The fall of the government was deemed a distinct possibility, with the report noting, "the Salvadorans couldn't win the war with what they were doing."[5] Other members of the commission described the country's armed forces as "a militia of 11,000 that had no mission" and spent most of its time "sitting in garrisons abusing civilians."[6] Defeat could be staved off by tripling the size of the Salvadoran Army combat forces, professionalizing its officer corps, instilling respect for human rights, and training it to conduct counterinsurgency operations.[7] The Woerner report provided three alternatives: (1) a lengthy and costly "strategic victory" option, (2) a slightly less-expensive offensive strategy that would aim to gain the initiative, and (3) the least expensive "survival" option that aimed to merely prevent an FMLN victory. Shocked by the price tag of the first two options and fearful of the political headwinds they would face in the wake of the Vietnam War,[8] the Reagan administration selected the survival option.[9]

Armed with a plan, the U.S. advisory effort in El Salvador split into two phases: a mobile training team (MTT) period from 1981 to 1984 and a brigade-advisor phase from 1984 until the end of 1991. During the MTT phase, units from 7th Special Forces Group trained and advised host-nation forces in El Salvador, neighboring countries, and the continental United States for periods ranging from one to six months. Their focus was growing the Salvadoran armed forces from its peacetime strength of around 11,000 troops to a wartime complement of 42,000 men; during this phase, more than 40 Special Forces MTTs were deployed to El Salvador.[10]

In 1984 the effort shifted from growth to increasing the effectiveness of newly fielded units. Rather than training during episodic MTTs for mere months, each Salvadoran brigade was assigned two to four U.S. advisors who would work with them for an entire year. The program was dubbed the Operational Planning and Assistance Training Team (OPATT), and the acronym became synonymous with the brigade advisor program. A standard complement included one SF or combat arms officer, one noncommissioned officer (NCO), and one intelligence officer, with each member of the team generally chosen by an Army-level selection process.[11] In addition to OPATT, rotating MTTs continued to provide training that Salvadoran units needed, such as a local noncommissioned officer school, or mortar, and scout training. At least three to four MTTs deployed per year, a stark reduction from the initial MTT phase.[12]

Creation of the BIRIs

As noted in the Woerner report, the Salvadoran military was poorly suited for the type of warfare it would have to conduct. It was organized and trained to fight a conventional conflict in a repeat of the last war they had fought—the 1969 Football War against Honduras. Few units could conduct offensive operations, and Army forces mostly performed static defense at checkpoints and critical infrastructure locations.[13] It was not prepared or equipped to fight guerrillas, and Army officers understood little about counterinsurgency tactics.

Because it would be difficult to train and equip existing Salvadoran Army units to that capability, U.S. advisors decided it would be best to create new units modeled on what had been successful against insurgents in Bolivia, Colombia, and Venezuela: small, lightly armed and equipped, but highly mobile *cazador* (hunter) battalions of 250 to 350 conscripts.[14] U.S. and Venezuelan advisors trained the units in a compressed six-week program like what had been used by 8th Special Forces Group trainers in the 1960s with the original Venezuelan *cazador* battalions and Bolivian Ranger units responsible for finding and killing Marxist revolutionary Che Guevara.[15]

Unfortunately the situation and terrain were different in El Salvador, and the FMLN units had progressed far beyond small patrols of guerrillas hiding in the jungle. By 1982 the insurgents had formed organized and well-armed battalions of six hundred or more fighters that included crew-served machine guns, snipers, and mortars. One advisor later observed that the *cazador* battalion "was a good concept for the Orinoco River Valley, Venezuela, vintage 1962, against that threat, on that terrain, and in that type of vegetation. This concept was not completely translatable to the Central American conflict, vintage 1983."[16] When facing the larger and more-capable FMLN battalions, the *cazador* units were torn to pieces.

To address this problem, the Salvadoran military needed elite forces that were much more highly trained than the *cazador* units but also larger, extremely mobile, and aggressive. The answer was the Batallones de Infantería de Reacción Inmediata (quick reaction infantry battalions), commonly known as BIRIs. A total of five were stood up, and rather than six weeks, each BIRI was to receive six months of intensive training by SF advisors. BIRIs had six to nine companies and nine hundred- to twelve hundred soldiers and functioned like U.S. Ranger units in practice.[17] They were under the control of the Salvadoran General Staff, the Estado Mayor, but in practical terms they were based within the area of operations of the six Army brigades, often at the same base as the brigade headquarters.[18] BIRIs acted as firefighters, checking in and operating under the command of the military zone or district requiring assistance, then returning to their original base to refit once the danger had abated.

Survival and Peace

The November 1989 fall of the Berlin Wall signaled the beginning of the rapid downfall of the Soviet Union and its Eastern Bloc allies. Accompanying that dizzying collapse was the evaporation of support for Marxist insurgencies worldwide, without which the FMLN had no hope of achieving victory. At the same time the United States considered suspending funds to its ally, surprised by FMLN success in their 1989 offensive and embarrassed by seemingly never-ending human-rights abuses committed by Salvadoran government forces.[19] The war had been fought to a standstill in El Salvador, and both sides were exhausted. The country's infrastructure and people had been devastated, with nearly a million people out of a population of 5.4 million displaced and hundreds of thousands of homes destroyed.[20]

Both adversaries were enthusiastic to end the conflict, which was completed by the signing of the Chapultepec Peace Accords in January 1992. The terms required the FMLN to disband and transition to a political party, the Salvadoran Army to shrink to half its size, and the judicial and electoral systems to undergo significant reform. As part of the accords all the BIRIs were forced to demobilize. Despite the devastation and the inability of government forces to defeat the insurgency, the United States had achieved its strategic objective and prevented the fall of the Salvadoran government.

THE ADVISORY EFFORT

Consistency in Advisor Pairing: "Living the Dream"

Overall there was a medium level of consistency in advisor pairing across the span of the mission in El Salvador. Even though there were two very distinct phases of the advisory effort, many of the same officers and NCOs returned for numerous deployments.[21] Indeed, many advisors completed three or four rotations, coming to know the country and its peculiarities to the point that they would openly complain to their comrades upon reassignment, "El Paraiso again? I hate that place!"[22]

This occurred for a variety of reasons. First, a vast majority of the advisors came from 3rd Battalion, 7th Special Forces Group (hereafter 3/7), which was stationed in Panama.[23] Because of the unit's location, the commander in chief for U.S. Southern Command (USSOUTHCOM) had operational control of 3/7 and could task it without having to go through Army bureaucracy in Washington. In essence he "owned" the unit and could—and did—assign it to missions within his theater at will. Furthermore, because U.S. Special Operations Command and the Theater Special Operations Command (TSOC)—Special Operations Command South (SOCSOUTH)—played almost no part in the selection process, assigning 3/7 members to the advisory effort in El Salvador was relatively streamlined.[24] "To put it into context," noted one former officer in 3/7, "we have to realize that not only did we not have theater SOCs [theater Special Operations Commands], we had no USASOC [U.S. Army Special Operations Command], we had no USACAPOC [U.S. Army Civil Affairs and Psychological Operations Command], we had no USSOCOM [U.S. Special Operations Command]. . . . [As such] the commander of the 3rd Battalion, 7th Special Forces Group, in Panama informally wore the hat of the UW [Unconventional Warfare] advisor to the CINC SOUTH."[25] Because of that role the 3/7 commander had considerable influence in the assignment of units and individuals to El Salvador.

When possible taskings across USSOUTHCOM were circulated, 3/7 leaders consistently picked El Salvador first since they saw it as the most dangerous, challenging, and important mission within their area of responsibility. Other missions were simply bypassed and handed down to sister battalions in 7th Group. Honduras demanded a commitment of an entire company of advisors, and with 3/7 dodging that mission, it meant that the pool of personnel focused on El Salvador was further reduced.[26] One advisor recalled that the 3/7 battalion commander gave his operations officer a verbal directive to never turn down any El Salvador mission.[27] Another remarked, "3/7 was very parochial about who went to El Salvador. They didn't want any 1st or 2nd Battalion [7th SF Group] guys there."[28] Combined, these factors resulted in a near monopoly on 3/7's provision of advisors to the mission, with one officer recalling that thirty-five of the fifty-five advisors during the OPATT phase were consistently from 3/7.[29]

Another factor in consistency was that for most of the mission only three Special Forces Groups existed: 1st and 3rd Groups were reactivated in 1984 and 1990, respectively.[30] This meant that the pool of potential advisors was 20 to 40 percent smaller during the conflict in El Salvador when compared to the post-9/11 period. It also meant that the three active-duty Groups, including 7th Group, also had to split responsibilities for Asia and Africa (which became the geographic purview of the two new Groups). As a result, elements of the other two battalions in 7th Group (1st and 2nd) were regionally focused on Korea, the Caribbean, and parts of Africa, which further centered 3/7 on Central America.[31]

Consistency also arose because advisors saw the mission in El Salvador as personally rewarding. Many advisors returned time after time because what they did "in country" was exactly the reason they had volunteered to join the SF regiment. Day in and day out advisors lived, ate, and sometimes fought shoulder to shoulder with the host-nation forces they advised. There was no dedicated air support, no transportation, and no U.S. mess hall. If they came under attack, support would have to come from Salvadoran forces. In the era before email and mobile phones, advisors might not see or hear from their higher headquarters for weeks or even months. By default they had considerable autonomy in decision-making.[32] News from the embassy would take at least two days to arrive, as did mail—both personal and official. Due to travel challenges advisors were only allowed rest and recuperation once every thirty days—and then for a single weekend in the capital. Years later one advisor nostalgically described El Salvador as "living the dream."[33]

An assignment to El Salvador was also especially attractive because it was seen as an opportunity to deploy to combat, even though it wasn't formally sanctioned as such by the U.S. government. When advisors returned from their deployments they passed on tales of being engaged by enemy fire, calling in artillery support, and rallying Salvadoran soldiers during combat. Those events represented the ultimate professional achievements for nearly all Special Forces personnel—being tested by the crucible of warfare. As such, numerous SF personnel leapt at the opportunity presented in El Salvador, and many volunteered multiple times to return as advisors. Describing this influence, one advisor noted, "It was the only war we had."[34] Another relayed that during the 1980s deploying to combat in El Salvador was "a big deal. It was the only war in town."³⁵ Another described his intense desire to join the effort in El Salvador because he had been too young and had "missed" the Vietnam War; his deployment to El Salvador ended up being the only time during his military career that he carried a loaded weapon every day of the mission.³⁶ Others described contemporaries assigned to other SF Groups (such as 10th, which was focused on Europe) who taught themselves Spanish in their spare time so as to be able to join the mission and go to combat.³⁷

The missions in El Salvador were so sought after by individuals and units that it created competition within the SF battalions to be chosen to deploy. Commanders often published careful selection criteria to determine who would be picked for the mission, and individuals and units fought to prove themselves worthy of the assignment. Language training often was a criterion, and test scores or oral interviews or pre-mission briefings in Spanish were frequently part of the process. Unlike other U.S. advisory efforts, one was not selected haphazardly for the mission to El Salvador.³⁸

Demonstrated language skill also played a part in increasing the consistency in advisor pairing. There was not a large pool of Spanish-speaking officers, and the initial language requirement had to be lowered to qualify a sufficient number of advisors.³⁹ Because so few officers met even the reduced requirement, many of those that did returned for multiple tours. A similar shortage of Spanish speakers did not exist among NCOs, but consistency was seen as important by the leadership who assigned them to the mission, and many returned year after year.⁴⁰

Conversely, several factors hampered consistency. First, while the mission was nearly universally seen as personally rewarding by SF officers and NCOs, there was a consensus that it was not professionally rewarding. For officers in particular, the U.S. Army's centralized promotion system deterred some advisors from coming back to serve multiple tours. During the OPATT phase most positions were for majors or senior captains (frocked as majors). In order for officers of those ranks to be promoted, they had to serve in tactical units and hold key positions such as the battalion executive officer or operations officer as well as attend the Command and General Staff College at Fort Leavenworth. That meant that they would have to leave their advisor duty and "punch their ticket" by filling those positions.⁴¹ Worse, within the Army system, serving as an advisor was not considered a key position that would accelerate promotion. As one interviewee observed, if you wanted a successful career and sustained promotions, you couldn't go to El Salvador and serve as an advisor for a couple of years. The Army promotion system was neither flexible nor set up to recognize the importance of consistency. More bluntly he noted,

"People who sit on promotion boards did not do those [advisory] jobs."[42] Serving repeated tours was somewhat easier for NCOs as their career paths generally had more flexibility; but some officers avoided serving as OPATT advisors for fear of hurting their careers. Some of those who did choose to return for multiple tours were able to successfully navigate the system carefully and still get promoted, while others simply chose to not worry about their own promotions.

A much larger challenge to maintaining consistency in advisor pairing came from the Salvadorans themselves. Across the span of the war, their military had two-year conscription, and in many cases entire units were drafted at the same time en masse. This included even the elite BIRIs, which received better equipment, more training, and additional advisory focus. When the two-year obligation concluded, often nearly the entire organization mustered out of the service at the same time. Some officers and, in rare cases, a handful of NCOs remained past their commitments, but in general entire units simply dissolved. The process was so consistent that the FMLN knew when certain units were to demobilize and planned their offensive operations around those dates, knowing those units would have shifted from veteran status to new and inexperienced.[43] El Salvador's conscription procedure dramatically affected consistency because, even though many of the same U.S. soldiers returned for rotation after rotation, compared to other cases fewer of the same host-nation forces remained in the BIRIs to be their partners. As one example, when BIRI Atlácatl was formed, 1,383 soldiers participated in training, but after the two-year period of mandatory service, only 250 remained.[44]

Assessment

Advisors universally agreed that there should have been more consistency between them and host-nation forces, with the yearlong rotations seen as insufficient. Ambassador Thomas Pickering believed that because it took considerable time for new advisors to become familiar with the environment in El Salvador long and repeated tours were the only solution to the challenges the mission faced. During a retrospective interview he observed the mission "had an enormous problem with . . . longer tours for military personnel. I felt that we were constantly running people through there who had to relearn. The one-year tour did not become effective for four to six months, and it was a tragedy that we did this. . . . In a sense, we were constantly relearning old lessons."[45] To Pickering and many others, if the advisor did not return for a second rotation, their replacement would likely be starting over again and wasting time learning the basics of the mission and the unit with which they worked.

Other advisors reiterated this point, noting that as a rule the longer an advisor served in El Salvador the more effective they were. "An advisor who is only there once doesn't see the entirety of the picture, and it is easy to get frustrated or discouraged. They don't know where the unit has come from."[46] Multiple tours allowed advisors to understand unit organization, the terrain, and how the FMLN fought, and more importantly it allowed them to connect with key Salvadoran officers. As some observed, the familiarity built over multiple missions helped advisors develop the trust necessary to have difficult conversations with their partners about problems with their units. At the same time, some advisors noted that consistency also had a continuum where on the other side of effectiveness some advisors went native and stopped focusing on U.S. objectives, instead focusing on the goals of the host-nation leadership.[47]

At times consistency not only paid dividends during the advisory effort but also generated returns far in the future. Near the beginning of his career Maj. Gen. Simeon Trombitas served as a brigade advisor in El Salvador and became friends with many of the unit's officers and NCOs. More than a decade later one of those lieutenants had become the commander of El Salvador's solitary airborne battalion during its deployment to Iraq—by happenstance while Trombitas was the senior advisor to the Iraqi Counter Terrorism Service. Several years later the officer had risen to commanding general of the Salvadoran Army at a time when Trombitas was commander of U.S. Army South (USARSO).[48] The interpersonal relationship built during the advisory effort helped Trombitas quickly reestablish connections with his friend that bypassed bureaucratic challenges.

Advisor Language Training and Cultural Awareness

There was a consistent and complete match between the regional orientation of the advisors with the mission in El Salvador. Robust Spanish-speaking skills and an understanding of Latin American cultures were a baseline requirement for all advisors, and interpreters were not provided. No SF unit other than 7th Special Forces Group, the regionally affiliated unit, contributed forces in any significant amount.

During the first phase of the war when advising was conducted primarily by mobile training teams every Special Forces unit that conducted the mission came from a Latin American–oriented battalion within 7th Group. As previously noted most of those units were part of 3rd Battalion, which was forward deployed in Panama, a fact that further strengthened the SF operators' language skills and cultural awareness. The monopoly was in part because El Salvador was considered the closest a soldier could get to combat, and 7th Group carefully guarded the assignment of its units to such an opportunity and blocked other units from participating. Mission size was also a factor. With an imposed cap of only fifty-five advisors, SF leaders were able to be more selective and ensure those involved had the appropriate language and cultural-awareness skills. There was no need to "spread the wealth" among other SF Groups that did not speak the language to give advisors a break.

During the OPATT phase of the advisory effort when individual advisors were assigned to brigades, demonstrated Spanish proficiency on the Defense Language Proficiency Test (DLPT) was a mandatory prerequisite. Initially the requirement was for advisors to have scored at the 3/3 level,[49] which equates to general proficiency, and be "able to speak the language with sufficient structural accuracy and vocabulary to participate effectively in most formal and informal conversations in practical, social, and professional topics."[50] With a relatively large population of native Spanish-speaking personnel within Special Forces, ensuring that advisors had the requisite skills was generally attainable, especially among noncommissioned officers. However, the requirement proved more difficult for officers, and the prerequisite was changed in 1983 so that it would allow those who attained a minimum score of 2/2 (limited working proficiency) to be accepted as advisors with a waiver.[51] That skill level could "satisfy routine social demands and limited work requirements . . . but has some difficulty understanding native speakers in situations that require specialized or sophisticated knowledge."[52] There was no evidence that anyone under a 2/2 level was accepted as an advisor.

Even past the formal testing requirements, organizations added informal conditions for selection as an advisor during both phases of the mission. Within 7th Special Forces Group, units underwent intense language preparation before deploying. Detachments trained as a unit for four months practicing Spanish, and only units that performed the best were slated for MTT missions.[53] Even after completing the training the assessment continued. Leaders at all levels mandated that deployment briefings be conducted in Spanish, and if a soldier's Spanish was not deemed strong enough they simply were dropped from the mission.[54]

Upon arriving in El Salvador, units selected for the MTT mission and individuals assigned to the OPATT effort were evaluated yet again by Military Advisor Group (MILGRP) leadership. Several advisors reported firsthand knowledge of individuals rejected and returned to their home station upon failing that assessment. "The MILGRP were real sticklers for people being able to speak Spanish. . . . They would go check you out, and if your Spanish was not up to par before you could even unload your bags they sent you back."⁵⁵ One advisor recalled that his predecessor had only lasted for two days before being redeployed because although he had scored well on the proficiency exam, the Salvadoran leaders he worked with could not understand him.⁵⁶

Assessment

There was little disagreement among advisors about the importance of Spanish-speaking skills and cultural awareness, with several observing that "to be able to advise, you have to be able to talk to them,"⁵⁷ and "to properly advise, you have to know who is who and to be able to speak the language and know the culture."⁵⁸ Without proper communication skills "you could talk to guys and they would nod their head, but then when you asked questions they didn't understand a thing you said."⁵⁹ Many advisors warned that in the heat of combat, when seconds mattered, immediate communication with the host nation was essential. Others commented that speaking Spanish had additional advantages because, "the better your Spanish skills, the more you were able to get inside the head of the officer that you are advising so that you could think the same way they would, which allows you to understand and anticipate needs."⁶⁰

There were few English-speaking Salvadoran soldiers, thereby making Spanish skills among U.S. advisors essential. "If I tried to talk to my brigade commander through an interpreter, that would have been the end of me simply because he would not have put up with it."⁶¹ Another advisor noted that, "you couldn't communicate in English. There might be someone in the brigade who spoke a few words of English, but if you didn't speak Spanish, you were dead in the water."⁶²

Dissenters pointed out that individual skills, knowledge, and experience mattered as much as being able to speak Spanish. "It is a handicap not to speak the language. But most places are worried about what you can show them and what you can do for them more than the language."⁶³ Others observed that because so few of the host-nation forces spoke English, advisors were immersed and forced to consistently speak Spanish. As a result, even if advisors had only workable knowledge of Spanish at the beginning of the mission, over the duration of their deployment their Spanish improved significantly.

Partner-to-Advisor Ratio

At first glance, calculating the ratio of the partner force to advisor would appear to be relatively straightforward. Theoretically the denominator, representing the number of advisors present, should be fixed at fifty-five, based on the force cap.

Because of intense political and media pressure, considerable effort was made to ensure that number was not exceeded. One advisor noted that during his rotation three SF advisors were asked to leave the country for several days so that three other advisors could be brought in to conduct specialized training. Those in El Salvador were put on leave, packed their bags, and were then quickly flown out of the country. As soon as the new set of advisors completed their task and left, the original advisors were flown back in to resume their mission.[64] There was exceptional congressional oversight, and one MILGRP leader recalled that whenever lawmakers visited the politicians inevitably asked to see the list of advisors and counted them to make sure the fifty-five-person limit had not been exceeded.[65]

While the official requirement was clear that there should be only fifty-five U.S. advisors in El Salvador, some ambiguities often allowed more than two times that number to be present.[66] During the interagency process in El Salvador, embassy and military leaders agreed upon a set of arcane rules to determine who would count against the fifty-five-person ceiling. First, some soldiers who were in the country on short temporary duty assignments were not counted against the advisory effort. There is conflicting information regarding exactly how long an assignment would need to be in order to be counted,[67] but strong enough evidence indicates this rule was in place.[68] Second, soldiers who were conducting humanitarian or noncombat training did not count against the advisor cap. Under that interpretation, SF medics training Salvadoran troops on casualty treatment and first aid were not counted.[69] Similarly, SF engineer sergeants training on minefield detection and clearance did not count. While the fifty-five-person cap did not stop a stretching of the original intent of the rule, it did serve to prevent those numbers from becoming so large that they would trigger congressional intervention.

The rules associated with what counted toward the number of in-country advisors was not the only factor that made calculating the partner-force-to-advisor ratio so complex. Any training conducted outside El Salvador did not count toward the force cap, a loophole that the U.S. military recognized and exploited. Several advisors noted that the cap specifically led to decisions to conduct training outside the country, and several BIRIs benefitted from having more advisors during their initial training as a result.[70]

The first BIRI, Atlácatl, trained with Special Forces MTTs in El Salvador from March to August 1981. As a result the force cap greatly limited the number of advisors who could train the battalion, and most SF leaders concluded that conducting training inside El Salvador was not the best option. With this in mind the second

BIRI, Ramón Belloso, was trained by 7th SF Group in the United States at Fort Bragg, North Carolina, from January to June 1982 with a massive effort in personnel and cost. In addition to being a way to circumvent the fifty-five-advisor cap, BIRI training was shifted to the United States because constant conflict inside El Salvador made training complicated. During the standup of the first BIRI, Salvadoran officers had halted training to take "everyone with a rifle" straight into combat operations, leaving the SF advisors temporarily unemployed.[71] Recruits were sent into battle with little training, the equivalent of "sending an armed mob out to fight well-trained and disciplined guerrillas" with the expected disastrous results.[72]

But training in the United States was not without controversy. An entire SF battalion with considerable augmentation conducted the mission, altogether more than 220 advisors.[73] The training cost the United States more than $8 million, which if it had been spent in El Salvador could have trained six to eight battalions for the same price.[74] Additionally many advisors believed that training in the United States offered too many distractions, such as alcohol, movies, and other temptations.[75] As a result of all these factors, military leaders decided not to repeat BIRI training in the United States.

Under pressure to create another BIRI in time to protect national elections in April 1982, the third BIRI, Atonal, had its training abridged to only ten weeks rather than the normal six months.[76] To compensate for the rushed training effort, a full company in 3rd Battalion, 7th Special Forces Group—which at the time was five Operation Detachment Alphas (ODAs)—was dedicated to the effort.[77] The next BIRI, Eusebio Bracamonte, was trained in Honduras. Like the first two BIRIs, its training lasted six months, from June to December 1983, and involved a considerable advisory element from 7th SF Group. Training was conducted in Honduras both because doing so meant these advisors were not counted against the El Salvador fifty-five-person cap and also because leaving El Salvador meant the soldiers could work in a relatively relaxed environment without having to worry about being attacked during exercises. A reinforced Special Forces company of seven ODAs led the mission, amounting to roughly ninety SF trainers.[78] The final BIRI, Manuel José Arce, was formed from October 1983 to March 1984.[79] A company from 3rd Battalion, 7th SF Group, was committed to the effort—approximately eighty advisors—and the training lasted for six months.

Other types of training were also conducted outside El Salvador to avoid cap limitations. Special-skills training such as mortars and scouts was given to small groups taught at bases in the United States, and individuals from the BIRIs went to leadership and specialized training at Fort Bragg, Fort Benning, and other locations across the United States on a consistent basis.[80] ODAs trained BIRI leaders in RECONDO (light infantry long-range reconnaissance) tactics, and groups of thirty handpicked BIRI soldiers attended SF-led Ranger courses in Panama.[81]

Salvadoran literacy rates, which nationally stood at 74 percent in 1992, and baseline education levels were a significant problem during the training mission.[82] Advisors recalled that lack of schooling affected all types of training and that for more technical training, such as for radio operators or mortar crew members, U.S. advisors had to administer a pretest to see if trainees could read or do math.[83] Screening candidates delayed training, especially when illiterate soldiers had to be unexpectedly replaced.

To determine the number of advisors working with BIRIs, all advisory efforts must be totaled: those in El Salvador, the United States, and other countries. Altogether a good estimate of that sum is 130 advisors a month, which spikes higher when new BIRIs were trained by additional personnel outside of El Salvador.

Salvadoran Personnel Strength

While most sources agree that the authorized strength of the BIRIs was in the range of one thousand soldiers, there is considerable debate about the number of Salvadorans who were present for duty on a regular basis.[84] The Salvadoran Army did not have a generous leave policy like the Afghan and Iraqi militaries, though its soldiers were granted passes to visit their families, and did experience some desertion. Soldiers who snuck off to be with their families or girlfriends were known as "iguanas," but they usually returned after a day or two.[85] Also a problem were "ghost soldiers" who were supposed to be present for duty according to official rolls but did not in fact exist; although the problem in El Salvador was not as great as it would be in either Iraq or Afghanistan. There was a consensus among advisors that Salvadoran officers generally overreported their personnel statistics because it offered an opportunity to pocket the additional funds and because if a commander reported actual strength he might not be allocated necessary funds to run his base. It was common enough that two terms were used to describe the practice: *ficticiosos* (fictitious ones) and *fantasmas* (ghosts).[86] Interviews of twenty different advisors produced estimates of the present-for-duty strength of BIRIs in the eight hundred– to nine hundred–soldier range. For simplicity I used an average of 850.

Unlike the other case studies in this book, SF advisors in El Salvador during the OPATT phase were not just responsible for one BIRI; their mission was to advise an entire Salvadoran Army brigade. As a result the amount of time OPATT advisors worked with the BIRIs varied from advisor to advisor and brigade to brigade. Because the BIRIs were the most elite unit based in the brigade sector, some advisors gravitated toward them and spent a considerable amount of time working with them. Others, in the words of one advisor, "loved everyone equally" and spent similar amounts of time with each unit in their area.[87] Many others—perhaps most—focused on the brigade staff or other brigade units and peripherally worked with the BIRIs. Some barely worked with the BIRIs at all during their rotations. To reflect this challenge the number of soldiers being advised will reflect not only the personnel strength of the BIRIs but also the personnel strength of the brigades to which the advisors were assigned.[88] As the Salvadoran Army grew from 11,000 soldiers to 56,000 in the span of 1981 to 1984, each brigade also grew proportionally.[89] At the beginning of the war each brigade comprised roughly 900 troops and at the end approximately 4,500 troops.[90] Rather than reflect monthly growth, at the beginning of each year from 1982 to 1985 an additional 900 troops were added to each of the six brigades (for a total of 5,400) because Salvadoran conscription was conducted once annually rather than on a rolling basis.

Assessment

To determine the partner-force-to-advisor ratio over the entire span of the mission, I first calculated each month's ratio (see figure 1.1). Those monthly ratios were then averaged to calculate an overall ratio, which was radically higher in El Salvador than in any other case study examined in this book, hitting a whopping 189.6 to 1.[91] Rather than an ODA advising a battalion of host-nation forces, in El Salvador a quarter of an ODA advised a full brigade of host-nation forces.[92] In terms of the anecdotal impact of this difference, many advisors argued that the three-person OPATT advisory teams were wholly insufficient to properly train their forces. Rather than try to do the impossible, they made the best of a difficult situation and focused on one battalion or a specially recruited "strike" company, or else on the most capable leaders, where efforts could pay dividends.[93] A small minority disagreed that the small teams were problematic and posited that the fifty-five-advisor cap was of great value because it prevented the conflict from becoming a United States–centered mission and forced the Salvadorans to take agency for the conflict.[94]

Advisor Ability to Organize Host-Nation Unit: "Money Talks"

Many advisors noted that the ability to affect host-nation decisions depended mostly on the relationship between the advisor and the host-nation partner. For the advisor

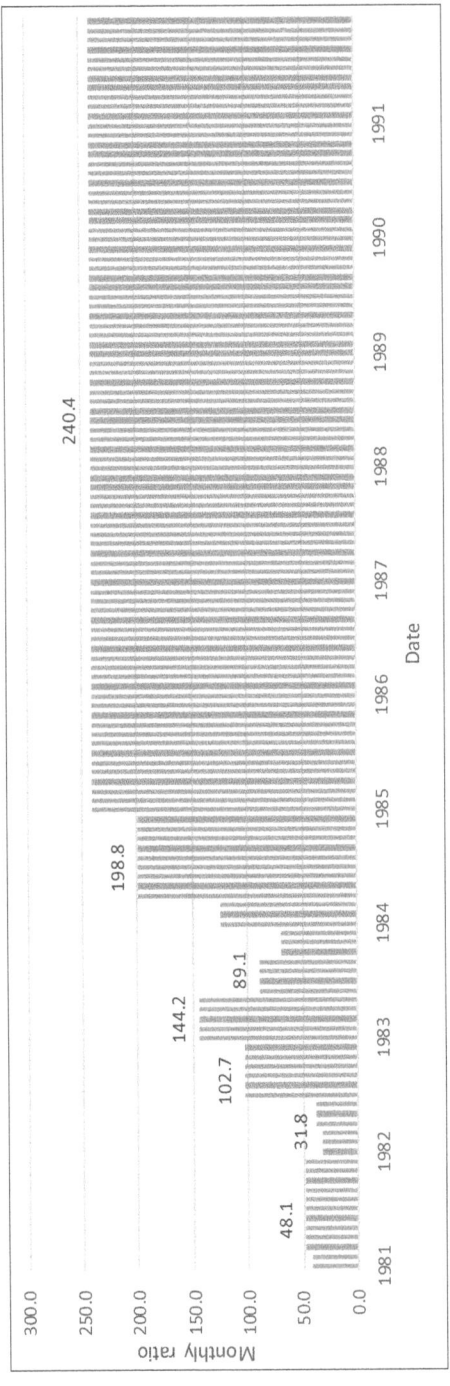

FIGURE 1.1 Monthly ratio of partners to advisors, El Salvador

to be able to influence the Salvadoran unit to the degree that they could organize them tactically or administratively, two factors had to be present. First, the host-nation commander had to be receptive to foreign advice. Some commanders were very receptive while others had no interest in listening to their U.S. partner. Second, the advisor had to build and retain rapport with the Salvadoran counterpart. This came easily to some, while others were unable to earn the trust of their partner even though they were receptive to U.S. advice overall. Generally the best advisors lived with their counterparts, ate Salvadoran food, and connected on a personal level.

For some the ability to influence came over time and once the Salvadorans grew to respect their U.S. advisors' skills and the value of their recommendations. One advisor noted that when he initially arrived his counterpart, who outranked him, was leery of taking any advice from a U.S. soldier who lacked combat experience. That changed after the Salvadoran officer disregarded the advisor's recommendations and his unit maneuvered into a tragic ambush that resulted in multiple casualties.[95] A similar crisis led to another officer suddenly earning the trust of his Salvadoran brigade commander. During the 1989 offensive in Santa Ana, one advisor noticed that the brigade operations officer had refused to leave his bunker when the *cuartel* (base) was in danger of being overrun. After the advisor passed this information to the Salvadoran commander, the operations officer was fired, and the commander told the American, "You are my new operations officer."[96] Such a situation, where U.S. advisors were asked by Salvadoran leaders to temporarily take charge until imminent danger had passed, occurred sporadically.[97]

Another advisor made subtle changes by showing that his recommendations were sound. The brigade commander believed there should not be socialization between officers and conscripts, always ate in the officers' club, and rarely interacted with his soldiers. His advisor, after building rapport with the colonel, talked him into eating with his troops for a meal, knowing well that the dining facility's contractor was corrupt and the food barely edible. When the colonel suffered a bout of food poisoning after just one meal, he replaced the contractor, drastically improving his soldiers' morale and willingness to fight.[98]

For other advisors, influencing their partner was purely transactional. Several interviewees noted that money and resources played a factor in whether a Salvadoran officer listened to advice. Upon meeting his partner at the beginning of his tour, one advisor was told he would have nearly carte blanche to do whatever he wanted with the unit. When he humbly noted that he didn't deserve such influence, the Salvadoran bluntly told him that he did because, "when we get advisors, funds will come later."[99] In another case an SF advisor gained the trust of his partner simply by consistently supplying the brigade headquarters with replacement cartridges for the xerox machine.[100] As one advisor noted, "money talks."[101]

Lack of combat experience did not seem to affect the host nation's willingness to accept advice. This seems to be because El Salvador's conscription policy and low retention rate meant that most host-nation soldiers left the military after two years of service and there was a constant cycle of brand-new soldiers for the U.S. advisors to train. In addition, Salvadoran initial training was so rudimentary that some soldiers did not even fire weapons. As a result, while many advisors lacked combat experience, they were still seen as a valued asset because of the resources and training experience that they brought.[102]

Other advisors disagreed that possessing tactical skills and knowledge was enough to persuade Salvadoran officers of their value. They noted that U.S. captains were seen as not senior or experienced enough to work alongside a brigade headquarters, which managed both tactical- and operational-level activities. Advisors had to be able to understand U.S. domestic politics and explain decisions made in Washington and how they affected the war effort, and many captains were not mature enough to assess and interpret the strategic situation.[103] Even U.S. advisors holding the rank of major or lieutenant colonel were seen by some Salvadoran officers as too junior to contribute to command decisions.

Some relationships were purely negative, and advisors had little influence on the decisions made by Salvadoran officers. One SF captain observed that the brigade officers "didn't see the need for us. They [felt that they] were perfectly capable of training their own units."[104] Another advisor opined that for his position, "Observer would be a far more accurate term than 'advisor' or 'trainer.' Those latter two terms require either a willingness of the host nation to accept advice/help or, lacking that, some sort of power base from which to implement change in spite of local resistance. Neither of those conditions existed for me, and so during almost my entire tour I was strictly an observer."[105] In one particularly caustic demonstration of an inability to influence, an SF NCO observed a string of lights stretching down a nearby mountain at night and asked the unit commander what it was. The commander nonchalantly commented that it was FMLN guerrillas. When the advisor responded that they needed to go attack them, the Salvadoran officer flatly refused, dryly observing that if they attacked the FMLN, the FMLN would attack them back.[106]

In cases where the Salvadorans were not receptive to change, rather than push back directly they often would be subtle and delay a proposal until the U.S. advisor left, which effectively prevented change from occurring. But on issues that the

United States saw as nonnegotiable, such as human rights, most advisors agreed that the Salvadorans would toe the line, at least in front of the Americans. The threat of advisor assistance being removed for violations, either for a specific unit or the country writ large, was significant enough to ensure compliance, at least when U.S. advisors were present.[107] Often, however, if SF advisors were not physically present Salvadoran units would drift back to their default practices.

U.S. advisors made no attempt to stand up a Salvadoran special-operations command. Indeed, USSOCOM had only been authorized by Congress in 1987 and was still in its functional infancy at the end of the conflict. Special Forces itself did not even become a separate branch in the Army until 1984 for enlisted personnel and 1987 for officers. Until then many of those serving in SF did so in a part-time functional area and their careers were controlled by their original branch.[108] Regardless, even if SF advisors had recommended the creation of a Salvadoran headquarters for special-operations forces (perhaps to spite their own system), it is unlikely that it would have been stood up due to structural complexities of the Salvadoran military system. Two of El Salvador's other elite units, the Airborne Battalion and the Patrullas de Reconocimiento de Alcance Largo (or Long Range Reconnaissance Commandos) were functionally controlled by the Salvadoran Air Force. Neither unit could conduct true special operations during the war, and interservice rivalry at times made synchronizing their efforts with Army forces challenging. Without a parent headquarters for special-operations forces, the BIRIs never benefited from having an independent command that protected their budgets and oversaw their operational employment like each of the other case studies enjoyed.

Assessment

At the macro scale, constraints on the number of U.S. advisors and their ability to combat advise limited their impact on improving the performance of Salvadoran units in battle. Instead the most significant influence they had was on the culture of the Salvadoran Army in the fields of civil-military relations and human rights. Advisors put considerable effort toward these two areas, with one senior officer noting, "Up and down the chain of command human rights was an important issue for us."[109] Without a doubt far too many war crimes were still being committed despite the advisors' efforts, and the Salvadoran record was marred by numerous abuses, such as the 1981 El Mozote massacre carried out by the Atlácatl Battalion and the 1989 murders of Jesuit priests and civilians at Central American University by members of the same battalion.[110] At the same time, over the course of the war improvements were made in the Salvadoran military culture, which was inherently linked to endemic corruption, brutal repression, and utter disregard for civilian oversight, albeit less than advisors wanted. Compared to where the Salvadoran military had been in 1981, advisors celebrated that some progress had been made.

Different strategies were employed to achieve this objective, ranging from refined to coercive. For example, the United States called FMLN fighters either insurgents or guerrillas, while initially the Salvadoran military had called them terrorists. Insurgents have significantly more rights under the Geneva Conventions, and American insistence on using that terminology resulted in many Salvadorans adopting the same vernacular. Advisors mandated that the Salvadoran military treat the population and captured guerrillas respectfully and in accordance with the laws of land warfare, making it clear that violations would mean an end to U.S. money and advisory efforts. One advisor recalled that by his second rotation in 1984 he started seeing change because civilians were beginning to enter the base and provide information on guerrillas. One of the *campesinos* (a peasant farmer) told him that the FMLN "used to come up to the house and ask about food, water, and intelligence. They rarely do that anymore because soldiers are often there. In the past soldiers used to steal watermelons and oranges. They are much better behaved now."[111]

Another strategy focused on how Salvadoran Army leaders treated their own soldiers. If SF advisors prevented Salvadoran NCOs and officers from mistreating their own troops, that positive treatment could have a trickledown effect that would impact how soldiers treated civilians. Abusing soldiers could also produce infiltrators or informants, and good treatment provided an inoculation against this threat. While advisors noted it was more difficult to train senior leaders, junior officers were often open to learning, and by the end of the ten-year U.S. mission many of those junior leaders had been promoted to positions of responsibility.[112]

Perhaps the most effective strategy involved advisor threats to remove U.S. support if the Salvadoran military did not clean up its human-rights record, or at least reduce the number of abuses. As one SF officer observed, respect for human rights "wasn't a religious conversion; it was a self-interest conversion."[113] U.S. advisors served as conduits to report human-rights violations directly to the embassy through military channels. Nearly every advisor noted that they had warned Salvadoran leaders that any incident of abuse would be reported immediately and could result in the recall of advisors and a drop in military-assistance funds. "We made it crystal clear that the U.S. would not tolerate it."[114] An unfavorable report from an advisor regarding human rights would result in U.S. efforts to retrain or even sack the Salvadoran commander.¹¹⁵ When one advisor suspected that his partner was involved in abuses, he was blunt: "I can't tell you what you can do, but I can tell you what I will do, and we [the advisors] are leaving in the morning."¹¹⁶ His partners came to understand that if the Americans saw or heard anything that looked like a human-rights violation, the Salvadorans would lose training, logistics support, and funds. Consequently, at least in the U.S. advisor's presence or around other advisors, the commander restrained himself and his men. As perhaps the most convincing evidence that the U.S. advisors had an impact on the Salvadoran military's human-rights record, among the provisions to the peace accords that ended the war was an insistence by FMLN leadership that the advisors stay for at least another year after the cessation of hostilities. When asked why they had made such a request, the FMLN leaders stated that the advisors would guarantee that the Salvadoran military would behave and at least not commit human-rights abuses in their presence.¹¹⁷

A second area where U.S. advisors had a strategic impact was in changing the Salvadoran military's perception of civil-military relations. Prior to the war, coups and military juntas had been common, and the armed forces had little respect for civilian leaders. Over the course of the war, through example, coaxing, and threats, the Salvadoran military came to gradually accept civilian leaders' authority.

Several key points stand out during the war's termination. As part of the Chapultepec Peace Accords, El Salvador's security forces, which had ballooned to more than 56,000 troops, were forced to drop to less than half that strength. All the BIRIs were ordered to disband en masse. Such a massive demobilization would have been challenging for any country, much less one without a robust record of military leadership respecting elected civilian officials. This sharp reduction in forces meant armed young men would lose their jobs and have to be retrained into a civilian profession, a risky endeavor that could easily lead to disaster. Defense budgets, at least some of which were being skimmed by corrupt officers, would drop dramatically. Despite these challenges, El Salvador's military demobilized peacefully and professionally, with little friction or pushback against elected civilian officials. Many times in the past the military had seized power because it did not like the policies being implemented; this time was different. While there was still military interference in the affairs of elected civilian officials, ultimately the fragile new deference for civil authority held. Barely two years after the end of the war the military respected the results of a free election—one that even included a party representing their erstwhile enemy, the FMLN.¹¹⁸ When combining all these factors, the advisor ability to organize host-nation forces should be rated as medium.

Combat Advising

In reaction to the Vietnam War, U.S. policymakers put considerable restrictions on what advisors in El Salvador could and could not do in the execution of their mission. At a fundamental level, advisors were explicitly barred from combat. Theoretically they were supposed to only serve as trainers and not as advisors, owing to the negative connotation of advisors in Vietnam; but in practice the distance between training and advising in El Salvador blurred.[119] Advisors were to principally supervise training on Salvadoran military bases, and if they planned to be involved in activities away from that facility they were to obtain permission from the MILGRP. To further emphasize their defensive posture, advisors were initially only allowed to carry pistols and at times were required to conceal them both to prevent negative reactions among the Salvadoran population and to make it harder for them to respond to challenges in an aggressive way. Although the prohibition on carrying rifles did not last long, the restriction remained that advisors were only allowed to fight to protect themselves or other Americans.[120]

To keep them away from the front lines, advisors were allowed to accompany their senior counterpart, the Salvadoran brigade commander, but not lower-ranking officers.[121] One advisor recalled that the embassy regional-security officer told a group of new advisors that if they made contact with the enemy they were to fall back to the rear of the unit and call for extraction. Such a suggestion was completely impractical—even ludicrous.[122] Because the mission was not officially sanctioned as combat, advisors were prohibited from receiving combat awards, such as right-shoulder sleeve patches that designated wartime service, valor awards, and the combat infantryman's badge.

Despite the relatively unambiguous rules, there was considerable gray space in what actually happened as advisors went about their day-to-day activities. The gray space existed for a variety of reasons. First and foremost, in the violent Salvadoran Civil War there was no semblance of a front line or rear area; advisors could be and were frequently attacked at any time. Nearly every interviewee experienced this personally, and some were swept up in combat multiple times.

Recognizing the advisors' importance to the conflict, the FMLN explicitly targeted U.S. soldiers.[123] As one advisor noted, U.S. troops did not go looking for trouble but the war often came to them. When Salvadoran base camps were attacked the advisors had few options, and in the words of one advisor, "if we didn't fight, we would have been killed. There was no quick-reaction force coming for us."[124] One interviewee remembered having dinner poolside in downtown San Salvador at the Hotel Presidente while watching firefights in the hillsides all around him, knowing that he could be engulfed in combat unexpectedly at almost any time.[125]

Advisors were frequently drawn into combat, and one SF NCO, Sfc. Gregory Fronius, was killed while trying to rally Salvadoran troops under FMLN assault.[126] Fronius was not the only advisor to die during the mission; a total of twenty-two U.S. military personnel perished while conducting their duties.[127] Recognition that the advisors were involved in combat was forbidden until 1998, when the U.S. Army relented amid pressure from the media and Congress. Within 7th Special Forces Group's advisors, a total of one Silver Star, twenty Bronze Stars (Valor), four Army Commendation Medals (Valor), fifty-one Combat Infantryman's Badges, and four Combat Medical Badges were finally awarded.[128]

Some of the rules of engagement also created room for interpretation. For example, the rule on being able to accompany their partner created confusing guidance. If the Salvadoran brigade commander was going into combat, should the advisor accompany him? The rule had assumed that a brigade commander would not be near the front lines, but some host-nation commanders were willing to take more risks than others, and the counterinsurgency environment led to situations where rear areas were consistently at risk. Even when an advisor did accompany their partner, the general rule created still more questions: If a Salvadoran commander was leading his forces from the operations center and chose to move forward, exactly how far forward was the advisor allowed to travel? Last terrain feature before the enemy? Mortar range? Small-arms fire? There were no easy answers to what was allowed, and in some cases guidance shifted when new leaders took charge of the embassy's regional security office or the MILGRP.[129]

Even transiting from one location to another while accompanying their partner was dangerous. At least one advisor was shot down while flying with their brigade commander in his helicopter. In that case a Salvadoran reconnaissance team had been compromised and was being pursued by FMLN forces and faced imminent destruction. When confronted with the decision to either try to rescue his unit immediately or take the U.S. advisor accompanying him back to base first, the Salvadoran brigade commander chose to try to evacuate his team, and the helicopter was shot down in the process.[130]

The gray space also occurred because of the time when the conflict occurred. In the 1980s and early '90s there was little technology to follow the whereabouts of the advisors. There was no blue force tracker that a headquarters could use to observe where advisors were at any time, and social media, cell phones, and even global-positioning systems simply did not exist or were not yet in widespread use. In addition, because of a lack of resources, senior personnel in the embassy were rarely able to visit the advisors on their partners' bases.

The ambiguity also put advisors in a challenging moral position, and many felt it necessary to interpret or even stretch the rules to be effective. To them the only way to properly advise was to accompany their partners on operations as far forward as possible so they could observe the Salvadoran units and report ground truth to U.S. and Salvadoran leadership. One advisor told his partners, "If I go out and something bad happens to me, drag my body back to the *cuartel* [base] and tell them I got shot here."[131] Several recalled witnessing fellow advisors not report wounds sustained because doing so could impact the overall mission.[132] Still another reported that some advisors wore Salvadoran uniforms to conceal their presence on operations.[133] Altogether these factors result in a medium rating for combat advising.

Assessment: "Coaching a Basketball Game from the Locker Room"

Nearly all interviewees bristled at the restrictions and felt they would have been more effective if they had been allowed to fight shoulder to shoulder with their partners. "We were expected to coach a basketball game from the locker room," quipped one advisor, describing the challenges created by not being allowed to accompany their partners into battle.[134] Advisors also noted that not being able to consistently observe their partners in combat limited their ability to assess performance, thereby impeding their ability to produce combat-effective partners.

In addition advisors argued that the prohibitions affected their ability to establish and maintain rapport. Showing that they were willing to share the same risks as the troops they advised was critical in the minds of many interviewees. One commented, "Advising was so much easier when you are part of the combat action. It shows that you are willing to die for them . . . it completely trumps the importance of language and culture."[135] Another observed, "There is no substitute for being there and sharing imminent danger with those you advise. If an advisor shows one of his soldiers something, he should be willing to do it also."[136]

EVALUATING COMBAT EFFECTIVENESS

Night Fighting

There was a general consensus that Salvadoran night-fighting skills improved slowly over the span of the conflict.[137] At the beginning of the war, Army units avoided fighting at night and would return to camp and build large fires to wait out the cycle of darkness.[138] One advisor noted that they had to train officers on night land navigation and most would not venture farther than one hundred meters from their base as they were not comfortable maneuvering their units in the dark.[139] Even after considerable training and effort by U.S. advisors, by the end of U.S. involvement most Salvadoran units were still unwilling or incapable of conducting night operations.[140] The sole exceptions were some of the BIRIs, which benefited from a longer initial training period as well as having better equipment. By the end of the war at least BIRI Belloso and BIRI Atlácatl were conducting night patrols and ambushes.[141] While advisors debated the extent of their skills, some felt that the Salvadorans were able to conduct offensive operations against the FMLN at night and best them in combat.

Assessment

Salvadoran units began with absolutely no night-fighting skills and without a military culture steeped in the practice. Limited by numbers in what they could affect and in authority in what they were allowed to do, U.S. advisors focused mostly on other baseline soldier skills. As a result only a few of the BIRIs were able to generate night-fighting capabilities, and those that did had varying levels of skills, equating to an overall low rating.

Conducting Multiday Combat Operations: "It Wasn't Enough Just to Have Boots on the Ground; You Also Had to Have Boots"

When the BIRIs were organized, they were designed to function within the Salvadoran Army logistics system.[142] Each battalion had a small internal-logistics organization but was expected to get long-term support from other logistics units within the military district to which it was assigned. As such, the BIRIs suffered from the institutional logistics challenges of the Salvadoran military.

Advisors provided mixed opinions as to whether the BIRIs could conduct operations longer than seventy-two hours. Some noted that because the Salvadoran logistics system was so unreliable, units had no expectation that the military could resupply them. To counter this challenge, they would pack everything they could into rucksacks and operate based on what the unit could carry. Operations were often carried out near major roads where vehicles could potentially bring resupplies of ammunition to mitigate the risk of running out.[143] Because El Salvador was relatively small geographically speaking, operations could generally be conducted close to a road or a village, meaning units could purchase water or food.[144] U.S. advisors also tried to augment logistics capability by adding a maintenance and supply unit at each brigade headquarters.[145]

Others disagreed and argued that the Salvadoran Army was incapable of conducting tactical resupply of units in contact and even struggled with performing long missions that did not involve resupplying during combat. Salvadoran military culture focused on the combat arms branches, and many officers looked at logistics with disdain. Units often had difficulty anticipating their true needs in combat, and commanders frequently failed to order a resupply until it was too late, when the organization had already run out of a critical need. At times SF advisors intervened to prevent crises by personally ordering supplies to make sure that ammunition and food were sufficient for engagements.[146] Several advisors noted occasions when it had been necessary to resupply units via U.S.-organized paradrop.[147] At the same time, other advisors noted that by the end of the war the Salvadorans—especially BIRIs—were using UH-1 helicopters or even their own airdrop for resupply.[148] Some observed that while the BIRIs were probably not capable of supporting themselves through seventy-two hours of sustained combat, very few fights lasted that long because much of the combat was hit-and-run guerrilla warfare.[149]

Medical evacuation of casualties was especially problematic. At the operational level, for example, in 1985 the United States purchased six helicopters specifically designed for casualty evacuation. Before then a wounded soldier would have had to remain in the field until evacuated by truck, and many died from their injuries before they could receive proper care. Even after the helicopters' fielding, medical issues were still challenging and evacuation inconsistent, especially at night, because aviators did not have the ability to evacuate wounded during darkness.[150]

Corruption within the logistics system severely hampered the BIRIs' ability to conduct extended operations. Numerous advisors told stories of ill-equipped soldiers even when headquarters had warehouses full of supplies. Despite storerooms with shelf after shelf stocked with boxes of new magazines for M-16 rifles, the soldiers in one advisor's unit each had a single magazine for their weapons. When advisors tried to issue the items to their partnered units, the logisticians would not budge.[151] Other units had soldiers training with wooden sticks instead of guns and lacked boots, uniforms, and cleaning kits—all of which had been provided as part of military assistance but either had been sold on the black market or were sitting on warehouse shelves.[152] One advisor noticed that his partners were carrying broken night-vision goggles on their missions and asked them why they were packing them along. The Salvadoran officer responded that the logistics officer had refused to issue replacements even though there were ten new goggles on the shelf.[153]

Assessment

Advisors provided mixed opinions on whether BIRIs could operate for seventy-two hours in combat. In some ways knowing that their logistics system was dysfunctional helped the units, which compensated by packing more supplies along on missions. The relatively compact El Salvador, even with its poor but sufficient infrastructure, made resupply easier than other cases under study. Salvadoran units were generally able to pay for the resupply of water and food from local villages. By contrast medical evacuation was limited, and corruption made for dysfunctional theater-level logistics. Altogether these factors result in the BIRIs scoring a medium rating.

Fighting without Advisors

Methodologically, to be able to fight without advisors a host nation's forces had to be able to conduct intelligence-driven operations. As previously noted, this means they would have to organically generate their own intelligence, action those targets, conduct sensitive site exploitation, and then use that information to repeat the cycle. Most BIRIs displayed limited ability to conduct intelligence-driven operations. When one advisor first began working with his partnered unit he asked the commander where the tactical operations center was located. The Salvadoran officer took out a map from his pocket and tapped it, meaning effectively that he and the map were the operations center; his unit had no intelligence analysts and made no effort to collect intelligence. After several months the advisor was able to establish a rudimentary headquarters that included operations, intelligence, and logistics cells. With those in place they were able to conduct basic intelligence activities but were still unable to carry out intelligence-driven operations by the time the advisor returned home.[154]

Other advisors noted that initially the most likely way that Salvadoran units gained intelligence was not through human intelligence and informants but by conducting a movement to contact patrol in search of enemy forces.[155] In most cases BIRIs could plan a single operation but could not process intelligence from one mission quickly enough to make it of value to conduct a follow-on operation.[156] Salvadoran units such as the BIRIs were culturally more attuned to intelligence that was issued by a higher headquarters rather than generating their own intelligence.[157]

BIRIs were inconsistent in their ability to generate human intelligence. Some units had moderate to good informant networks while others had not invested at all in developing the appropriate connections and capabilities. Some advisors noted that units that had internalized U.S. lessons on human rights often treated the civilian population better, which resulted in more consistent and trustworthy informants.[158] Salvadoran abilities to generate signals intelligence were rudimentary, and only a few units had handheld signals-intercept devices that could overhear the FMLN conversations. When using them, officers frequently recognized the voices of the FMLN leaders, as they had known each other before the war.[159] At times the United States provided recordings or transcripts of radio intercepts when intelligence was deemed important. Imagery intelligence was limited to U.S. capabilities as the Salvadorans did not have an organic capability.[160]

Assessment

While the BIRIs were the most capable Salvadoran units they could rarely conduct intelligence-driven operations, the standard for being able to fight without advisors present. Given the extremely basic starting point of many units, most advisors prioritized teaching other skills. Eventually some BIRIs developed basic human- and signals-intelligence capabilities, but few could gather and process intelligence quickly enough to conduct back-to-back operations. Such factors result in a low rating for being able to fight without advisors present.

Performance against the Enemy in Combat

The BIRIs consistently performed capably in combat even when other Salvadoran units did not. During the 1989 FMLN offensive the BIRIs fit prominently in the government's response, shifting from one crisis to the next to root out guerrillas. On December 4, 1990, FMLN forces attempted a night ambush of BIRI Atonal. The unit counterattacked so effectively that the FMLN was forced to flee the battlefield, taking more losses than did the unit it ambushed.[161] Unlike other Salvadoran Army units, which advisors at first described as "not much more than an armed mob" conducting static defense at fixed checkpoints, BIRIs were aggressive, patrolling off roads and conducting operations such as ambushes and raids to kill guerrillas.[162] Also unique to the Salvadoran military, the BIRIs conducted combined operations and pursued FMLN guerrillas regardless of the situation, even across unit boundaries despite fear of political reprisal or danger of fratricide.[163] The FMLN feared and hated the BIRIs, singling out only these units to be disbanded as part of the 1992 peace accords.

Assessment

One advisor recalled that a fellow U.S. soldier who was a Vietnam veteran had disparagingly said that if the Salvadorans were fighting the Vietcong, "these guys would have a problem." Noting that performance in battle against your opponent is what matters more than raw effectiveness, the advisor responded, "if they were fighting the Vietcong, they probably would [have a problem], but they are fighting other Salvadorans."[164] U.S. leaders had chosen a strategy that aimed to prevent El Salvador's military from being defeated and ultimately achieved their goal.[165] The BIRIs were an important part of that effort and had helped fight the FMLN to a standstill. With that in mind a medium rating is appropriate for the BIRIs' performance in battle.

INITIAL ASSESSMENT

The BIRIs were seen as the most effective force U.S. advisors helped build during the war in El Salvador, albeit with considerable shortcomings. BIRIs lacked the ability to conduct intelligence-driven operations, and only some could carry out limited night operations.[166] They had difficulty with resupply operations while in contact, and the larger logistics system that supported them was abysmal. Only because of their mental and physical toughness and their ability to pack along most of what they would need could they meet the standard of fighting for seventy-two hours. In combat they fought the FMLN to a draw. All these factors combined results in a low-moderate effectiveness rating for the BIRIs.

After the peace accords had been signed, then–brigadier general Joseph Stringham, who had served as the MILGRP commander from 1983 to 1984, met with one of the former commanders of the FMLN. The one-time guerrilla bluntly told his opponent, "If it wasn't for your men, we would have won the war."[167] In the end the United States' relationship with El Salvador's military would persist long after the country's civil war came to a close. El Salvador later contributed forces to U.S. efforts in Afghanistan and Iraq, with their service in Iraq being particularly exceptional. During an especially intense battle in April 2004 Salvadoran forces fought until they ran out of ammunition and then engaged in hand-to-hand combat, repulsing insurgents and earning a rare nomination for six U.S. Bronze Star Medals.[168]

In the next chapter we shift focus to the beginning of the Global War on Terrorism, choosing for our case study a similar operation that faced parallel host-nation and U.S. constraints—the effort to build the Light Reaction Regiment in the Philippines.

− 2 −
Marksmen of Death

The Light Reaction Regiment in the Philippines, 2001–2015

BACKGROUND

IN THE LATE 1990S many U.S. and Filipino military leaders had grown eager to revive a relationship that had been adrift for nearly a decade since the Senate of the Philippines had forced the United States to leave Naval Base Subic Bay and Clark Air Base. A spate of terrorist actions by Philippines-based Islamic terrorist groups provided the impetus for rapprochement. The foiled 1995 Bojinka plot, which had aimed to blow up eleven airliners and assassinate Pope John Paul II, had been planned in Manila by eventual 9/11 mastermind Khalid Sheikh Mohammed and by Ramzi Yousef, who had led the 1993 bombing of the World Trade Center.[1] Then in May 2001 the al-Qaida–linked Abu Sayyaf Group (ASG) kidnapped several hostages, later beheading one of them, U.S. citizen Guillermo Sobero.

Recognizing little capability existed to address these sorts of threats, U.S. Army attaché Maj. Joseph Felter crafted a plan to assist the Armed Forces of the Philippines (AFP) in forming a national-level counterterrorism unit. Felter had served in 1st Special Forces Group before becoming a foreign-area officer and was familiar with Philippine military leaders and capabilities.[2] After a short period of negotiations the United States agreed to help stand up the Light Reaction Company (LRC), which would serve as the Philippines' tier-one counterterrorism unit.[3] Members of 1st Special Forces Group began conducting instruction in January 2001 that was to continue through July at Fort Magsaysay on Luzon, the most populous island of the Philippines.[4]

A Brave New World: The Post-9/11 Relationship

Initially modest U.S. support for the LRC blossomed exponentially after the May Abu Sayyaf Group kidnappings in Honda Bay and the September 11 terrorist attacks in the United States. In particular, the seizing of two U.S. hostages during the kidnappings all but guaranteed the creation of a second front in the global war against al-Qaida and its allies. As part of that mission, named Operation Enduring Freedom–Philippines (OEF-P), in 2002 Special Operations Command Pacific (SOCPAC) stood up a six hundred–person Joint Special Operations Task Force centered around Green Beret advisors from 1st Special Forces Group. The decision to link the global war on terrorism to support for the Philippines proved to be a financial windfall, and U.S. foreign military financing jumped from $1.4 million in 2000 to $23.4 million the next year.[5] It continued to grow, and through 2010 annual U.S. military assistance never dropped below $34 million.[6] While creating and later expanding the LRC to regimental size was only a small portion of the larger mission, the elite unit was seen by many advisors as the pinnacle of their efforts.

The OEF-P mission lasted until February 2015, when it was replaced by a smaller advisory team based at the embassy in Manila. Like 1984's Operational Planning and Assistance Training Team in El Salvador and the Planning Assistance Training Team that would be assembled in Colombia, the new office was uncreatively dubbed the U.S. Pacific Command Augmentation Team (PAT).[7] U.S. Special Forces' partnership with the Light Reaction Regiment (LRR) continued, albeit on a dramatically smaller scale with more episodic intervention.[8]

THE ADVISORY EFFORT

Advisor Language Training and Cultural Awareness

1st SF Group, which was regionally oriented to Asia and the Pacific, was tasked to stand up the first Light Reaction Company in March 2001. Such an assignment was common because before September 11th deploying a Special Forces unit outside of its assigned geographic area was sacrosanct: it rarely happened due to the bureaucratic pressures exerted from regional stakeholders. After 9/11 more than 80 percent of the demand for SF soldiers was in the U.S. Central Command (CENTCOM) area of responsibility, so there was little competition from other SF Groups wanting to join the Philippine advisory mission, and working with the LRR became a near monopoly for 1st Group.[9] If anything the tremendous troop requirements facing CENTCOM created pressure to draw 1st Special Forces Group teams out of their theater to contribute to the wars in Iraq and Afghanistan.

During the entire tenure of the advisory effort in the Philippines only one other SF Group contributed forces. Starting in October 2006 and spanning the next six months the mission was led by a battalion from 19th Group, a National Guard unit itself regionally oriented to U.S. Pacific Command (USPACOM, or PACOM).[10] Every other mission was composed of 1st Special Forces Group units, resulting in a complete match between the regional orientation of the Groups assigned to the mission and the region where they were deployed.

Assessment

Despite the complete match between the regional orientation of the units deployed and the region to which they were deployed, SF personnel of all ranks reported the mixed importance language training and cultural awareness had toward producing a combat-effective partner—something of a counterintuitive finding. One would expect those who deployed extensively to the region and knew local languages to underscore the importance of those skills. Instead they explained that the extreme heterogeneity of PACOM's area of responsibility, with its hundreds of languages and cultures spread across the region, made it difficult to match language training to the diverse assignments SF soldiers could face. As a result 1st Group trained in multiple languages, including Mandarin, Korean, Thai, Hindi, and Tagalog. Even within the Philippines itself over 170 languages and even more dialects are spoken, further complicating communication between U.S advisors and host-nation forces.[11] This meant few soldiers who were deployed to the Philippines had been trained in Tagalog or Filipino.

In addition the long association between the Philippines and the United States meant many of the Filipino soldiers spoke English. One Special Forces officer recalled a public-relations event on Mindanao where the American speaker began in Tagalog only for the local participants to stare at him in confusion because they only understood Tausug and Maguindanao. When the speaker switched to English the attendees were finally able to understand.[12] Because it seemed a common denominator most advisors conducted training with the LRR in English, either directly or through one of the LRR soldiers who served as an informal translator. None of the advisors who spoke Tagalog or Filipino indicated they used those skills consistently. Interviewees gave a variety of reasons for this decision, many said their limited linguistic skill weren't sufficient to adequately relay complex subject matter.[13] Others found the English skills of the host-nation forces to be a large factor. For some, speaking in English made it easier to conduct training as they did not have to deal with the mental exhaustion of speaking a foreign language for hours at a time and worrying about erroneous translation. Others noted that Filipinos relished the opportunity to practice their English skills, with many insisting that advisors speak English rather than their domestic languages.[14]

Many argued that knowing one of the specific languages spoken on the Philippines was not critical to making the LRR combat effective. However, they felt that the broader skills of knowing a language and having a general awareness of how to function effectively while working with other cultures were critical.[15] In addition they remarked that what seemed to be more important than the knowledge of a specific language or culture were adaptability, flexibility, patience, and respect of other cultures—the skills on which Special Forces candidates are evaluated during their assessment, selection, and initial training.

Consistency in Advisor Pairing: "Repeat Offenders"

For the first six years of the advisory effort most of the training for the LRR was provided by 1st Battalion, 1st Special Forces Group, which was based in Okinawa. This monopoly was because the unit was the PACOM Commander's in-Extremis Force. The CIF, as it is known, was a company-sized element in each SF Group that focused on hostage rescue and direct-action missions.[16] It was kept on alert to respond to regional crises that other U.S. forces could not reach in time or were incapable of executing due to other priorities. To be able to accomplish such a complicated mission the members of that company received additional sniper and assault-force training.

While the CIF companies rarely performed hostage-rescue missions, having those skills enabled them to provide first-rate training to foreign counterterrorism forces such as the LRR. As such Operation Detachment Alphas were repeatedly provided by C Company, 1st Battalion, 1st Special Forces Group, the PACOM CIF, to train the LRR. When the requirements of the mission became too much for one company, a second company in 1st Battalion was trained in the CIF mission and began assisting in advising the LRR. Because CIF training was so long (nine weeks for a single course), soldiers in those companies moved to other assignments much less frequently, thereby creating an additional pathway for consistency.[17] Only in 2006, when the 1st Group CIF began to help train the Iraqi Special Operations

Forces, were ODAs from non–CIF-trained companies committed to the LRR mission.[18] Such conditions produced a high level of consistency in pairing between SF advisors and members of the LRR.

Across the OEF-P missions working with the LRR, commanders at all levels across 1st Special Forces Group exerted great effort to ensure ODAs would pair with the same host-nation units they had worked with during previous rotations. They were nicknamed "repeat offenders" or "OEF-P alumni" to highlight the importance of returning the same individual to the same mission.[19] One Special Forces ODA had worked with the LRR on so many occasions over the course of a decade that a soldier who had started on the team as a junior communications sergeant eventually became the team's warrant officer, the second in command. That continuous contact provided a wealth of knowledge for those working with the LRR as well as important interpersonal connections.[20]

In some cases those connections had been built not only during 1st SF Group's assignment with the LRR but also during previous advisory efforts and training programs with the Philippines. Numerous officers and NCOs provided myriad examples of the consistency and the trust and depth of personal relationships flowing from the shared history. At the first planning conference for the stand-up of the LRC in 2000, in addition to the larger delegation of senior officers led by PACOM commander Adm. Dennis Blair, two Special Forces officers and a senior NCO were chosen to act as subject-matter experts. Some among the PACOM officers had unsuccessfully tried to rescind the SF sergeant's invitation believing it inappropriate for such a low-ranked servicemember to attend a meeting with the Philippine General Staff. Much to the chagrin of these officers, when the meeting started the Philippine generals perfunctorily greeted their U.S. counterparts before quickly moving to warmly embrace the NCO and ask him about his family. Those generals had immediately recognized the NCO, Sfc. Joe Morley, with whom they'd trained multiple times nearly two decades earlier when they had been junior captains.[21] As the planning session progressed, Philippine generals frequently sought the advice of the NCO over that of the U.S. delegation's more senior members.[22]

Then–lieutenant colonel David Maxwell filled the critical role of SF battalion commander, overseeing the initial LRC stand-up, and later commanded the special-operations task force. He recalled that upon landing in the Philippines in October 2001 he was met at the aircraft's ramp by a Filipino commander with whom, it turned out, he had attended the Infantry Officer Advanced Course in 1985. That officer, Colonel Yano, had eventually been promoted to general and served as chief of staff of the Philippine Army and later commander of its Armed Forces. When Maxwell returned to the advisory effort in a different role he reconnected with the Philippine general, tapping into a deep reservoir of trust and rapport filled over decades.[23]

Other advisors reported similar experiences. Lt. Col. Leo Liebreich had sponsored an LRC officer while both were attending the Special Forces Qualification course and later helped advise that officer's unit in the Philippines.[24] Maj. Noel Sioson worked with the LRR four times from 2010 through 2017. The connections he had built over the course of those rotations included a personal friendship with Danilo Pamonag, who as a colonel was first LRR commander during Sioson's first rotation. In 2017 the two were having coffee when Pamonag, who had by then been promoted to two-star general, received the call notifying him of the failed LRR assault in Marawi that was to kick off five months of intense fighting.[25]

Assessment: "You Can't Surge Trust"

Maintaining consistency in advisor pairings made deciding what type of training to conduct much easier, preventing the long learning curve that often occurs at the start of a mission. According to one officer, when advisors who had worked with the LRR on previous rotations were once again paired with the unit, they already understood what type of training worked and what did not. This reduced start-up time allowed advisors to focus training far more effectively than if they had been new advisors unfamiliar with the LRR.[26]

Consistency also built personal relationships that engendered rapport and trust, a process always requiring time and effort. As one advisor observed, "You can't surge trust."[27] Repeatedly pairing the same advisors with the LRR allowed them to skip the time-consuming initial phase wherein soldiers got to know one another, instead allowing them pick up where they had left off on the last rotation. Maj. Noel Sioson noted that trust built over multiple rotations often allowed him to bypass much of the Philippine military bureaucracy. Rather than shepherding paperwork through a complicated and unfamiliar process, his relationships allowed him to go directly to senior leaders and get immediate approval.[28]

Although the U.S. teams were not allowed to accompany the LRR into combat, they provided advice and shared intelligence and mission enablers such as contracted rotary wing aircraft. Deciding what intelligence to provide is often subjective, and personal connections sway decision-making.[29] When considering whether or not a particular set of images would be provided or whether or not to disclose how a particular piece of human intelligence had been obtained, more often than not the decision would hinge on the personal relationships of those involved.[30] Trust was reciprocal, and Filipino leaders who trusted their U.S. counterparts were more willing to listen to advice and implement recommendations.

Partner-to-Advisor Ratio: Growth of the LRC into the LRR

In 2003 the original Light Reaction Company consisted of approximately one hundred soldiers but by year's end had expanded into a three-company battalion. One new company was created while training with 1st Special Forces Group advisors from May to August and a second company from July to December.[31] U.S. military assistance for the growth, including new equipment and training, totaled $5.25 million.[32]

The decision to expand the elite force reflected both the recommendations of Special Forces advisors and recognition by the Philippine Army that a single company was insufficient to meet operational needs. Adding two companies allowed a cycle wherein one company would be training, a second conducting operations or on standby to conduct operations, and a third on leave or resting. The Light Reaction Company was thus expanded to the Light Reaction Battalion (LRB).

In 2014 the Philippine government chose to further expand the LRB into a regiment after the unit's impressive combat performance during the Zamboanga City Crisis of 2013, when rebel forces took hostages and occupied parts of that coastal city. The unit was renamed the Light Reaction Regiment (LRR), and the number of companies doubled from three to six. However, this time around augmentation proved extremely challenging. Even before the decision had been made to grow from battalion to regiment, the unit had barely been able to muster 40 percent effective strength,[33] and finding new quality candidates had been problematic, reinforcing received wisdom that special-operations forces cannot be created quickly or as the result of a crisis.[34]

Central to the issue of expansion was resistance from conventional-force commanders to the new elite force. Paralleling the opposition to special-operations forces (SOF) in the U.S. military before the creation of U.S. Special Operations Command, many conventional commanders in the Philippine Army argued that giving up their best soldiers to serve in the LRR weakened their units, and some even refused to send their troops to the LRR's selection course. This recruiting challenge was compounded because the Philippine military had initially decided against standing up an institutional special-warfare training center, thereby further slowing the flow of new operators into the unit. Making matters worse, a gradual loss of personnel occurred through casualties and dissatisfaction resulting from misuse of the LRB in roles more suited for conventional forces, such as reconnaissance patrols and daylight assaults against well-defended positions.[35]

Personnel Strength of the LRR

From its inception in 2001 until August 2003, the size of the advised force can be estimated to have been one hundred soldiers.[36] At that point with the stand-up of the second company, the strength increased to two hundred soldiers. In December 2003 the strength increased to three hundred soldiers with the activation of the third company. A small battalion headquarters was added of roughly thirty commandos. From that highwater mark of 330 soldiers a gradual decline occurred, with a loss of approximately nineteen personnel each year. This estimate is drawn from the fact that in September 2013, during the siege of Zamboanga, the three LRCs had 47, 44, and 48 operators, for a total of 139 Commandos.[37] Their performance during that battle resulted in an accelerated training schedule such that by the end of the U.S. advisory mission in 2015 the original three companies were back to full strength but only one new company activated, totaling four hundred soldiers.[38]

Advisor Commitment

At the inception of the mission in the Philippines an SF company with three full-strength ODAs—a total of forty-five advisors—was committed to standing up the first LRC.[39] Training began in January 2001 and concluded that July, after which the larger mission withdrew and left behind only a residual force.[40] During the transitional period from that August until January of the following year, only two SF advisors were working with the LRC.[41]

As a part of the post-9/11 effort to counter al-Qaida and its allies across the globe, the U.S. commitment in the Philippines blossomed again in February 2002, skyrocketing to 1,300 personnel.[42] It included every branch of the armed services, a Special Forces battalion headquarters, and nine ODAs, with the total SF commitment consistently in the range of 160 troops.[43] While the majority of those troops focused on other Philippine military forces, one overstrength ODA of fourteen soldiers was paired with the LRC.[44] That August, 1st Special Forces Group stood up the Joint Special Operations Task Force–Philippines (JSOTF-P), which expanded the SOF footprint to 226 personnel by increasing the number of headquarters and support personnel while maintaining one company and four ODAs as advisors, one of whom remained paired with the LRC.[45]

The pairing of one ODA with the LRC stayed constant until May 2003, when the LRC was expanded to a three-company LRB and the advisory effort swelled to support its growth.[46] To accomplish that mission, two and a half ODAs (thirty SF advisors) assessed and trained new candidates for the LRB through December 2003.[47]

After that surge the advisory commitment dropped substantially, partly because of a changed focus from the new SOCPAC commander and partly due to extended negotiations over the scope of the U.S. mission. Those negotiations had been upended by the political blowback from media revelations of U.S. Marine Corps proposals to conduct domestic combat operations paired with Philippine military forces. During that phase, which lasted across all of 2004, the entire OEF-P mission totaled fifty to eighty personnel and reverted to caretaker status.[48] Even though the overall U.S. commitment was small the LRB remained a priority because of its tactical importance and the connections that SF advisors had made with unit personnel. Yet with such a small footprint only a half of an ODA (six advisors) could be paired with the LRB.[49] Following that low point the JSOTF-P and OEF-P mission grew to 273 personnel in 2005, but the number of advisors working with the LRB remained the same.[50]

In October 2006 the troop footprint increased considerably, and a battalion headquarters, a Special Forces company headquarters, and seven ODAs deployed for the JSOTF-P mission.[51] With such growth, an entire full-strength ODA was able to be paired consistently with the LRB.[52] The JSOTF-P continued to grow over the next few years, eventually reaching 607 personnel at its highwater mark in early 2010, but still only one ODA advised the LRB.[53]

That same year PACOM decided that the OEF-P mission should begin to incrementally close, which led to a gradual reduction in advisors working with the LRB.[54] By July only two SF advisors were nominally paired with the LRB, living and working at the LRB's higher headquarters, the Joint Special Operations Group at Fort Magsaysay on Luzon, and only advising the unit part time. The advisory effort again shifted in February 2011 after it was recognized that two SF NCOs were insufficient, and an entire ODA took on the shared mission.[55]

That pairing ratio was maintained until August 2013 when Col. Robert McDowell became commander of 1st Special Forces Group and was able to successfully lobby to take command of the JSOTF-P mission and temporarily increase its footprint. Some officers under his command believed that the desire to deploy additional forces was not part of a strategic reassessment of U.S. objectives but instead reflected a belief that increasing the scope of the mission and being personally involved in commanding the deployment could be professionally beneficial. While most of the increase in forces worked with other AFP elements the growth temporarily increased the number of SF advisors working with the LRB to three ODAs (approximately thirty-six personnel) until May 2014.[56]

During McDowell's deployment the political winds shifted again, and it was announced that the mission would conclude in 2015. To reflect this reality, as his forces redeployed, they left behind half of an ODA to work with the LRR.[57] That ratio remained until the JSOTF-P guidon was furled and the mission's conclusion in February.

Assessment

To determine the ratio of partners to advisors I first calculated each month's ratio. Those monthly ratios were then averaged to calculate an overall ratio of 28.7 soldiers per one U.S. Special Forces advisor. Please see appendix B for further details on that process and figure 2.1 for the monthly results. Advisors generally noted that decreasing the partner-force-to-advisor ratio had a positive impact on the combat effectiveness of the unit they trained.

Advisor Ability to Organize Host-Nation Unit

The Philippines' unique history with the United States had considerable impact on the ability of the SF advisors to organize the LRR. The long relationship had led to deep bonds forged between the two militaries that in turn led to Filipino officers trusting the recommendations and judgment of U.S. advisors. That said, the shared history and the Philippines' identity as the United States' only de facto colony made the host nation particularly sensitive to sovereignty issues. Indicative of the tensions in such a bipolar relationship was the christening of the Light Reaction Regiment as Tiradores de la Muerte, or "marksmen of death." That nickname had originally been used in the Philippine-American War by a Filipino guerrilla unit whose sharpshooters were responsible in 1899 for the death of the most senior U.S. officer killed during the conflict, Gen. Henry Lawton.[58]

Early Successes

Despite these sensitivities the Philippines ceded considerable sovereignty during the stand-up of the LRC. The Armed Forces of the Philippines lacked a national-level counterterrorism capability, and the United States offered to not only train Philippine forces but also provide $2.2 million to equip the new unit. Almost all the kit

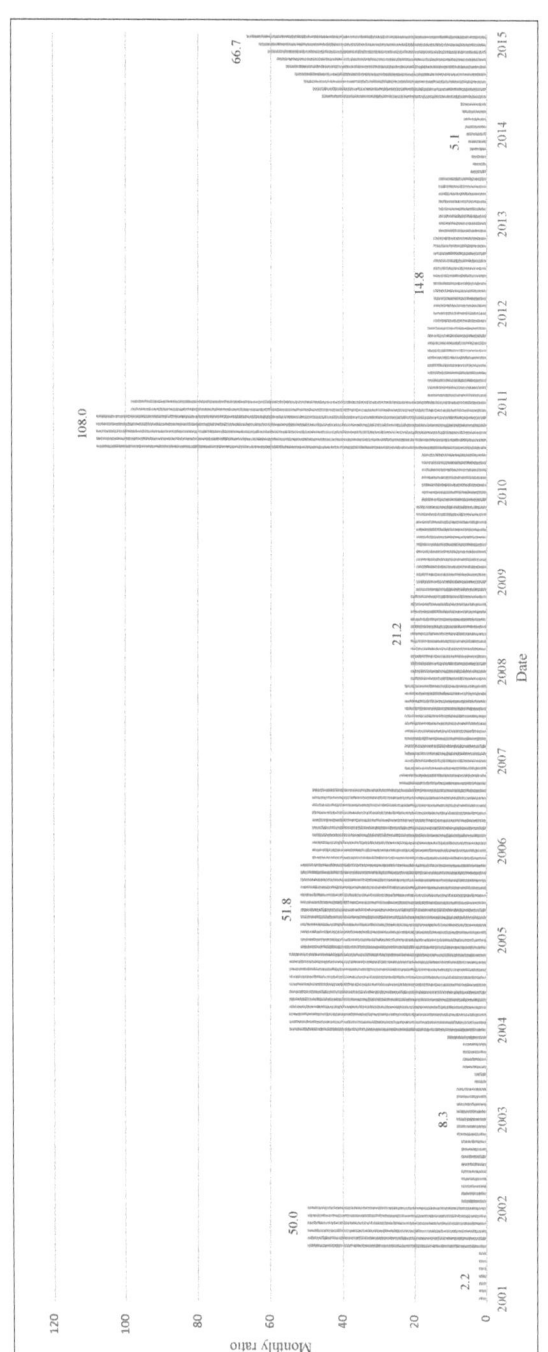

FIGURE 2.1 Monthly ratio of partners to advisors, Philippines

provided was brand new, still wrapped in its shipping containers and plastic, and some Philippine leaders compared receiving the tactical gear to "opening gifts during Christmas."⁵⁹ Potentially buoyed by the considerable grants and free training, the Philippines initially gave U.S. SF advisors substantial leeway in the unit's formation.

The Philippine officers who oversaw the creation of the LRC were content to let the United States pick out the equipment for the new unit. Special Forces NCOs from 1st Group tried to copy the equipment of their own unit, the PACOM Commander's in-Extremis Force (CIF), and spared no expense on the weapons, night-vision apparatus, and other equipment they chose.⁶⁰ The SF advisors even chose the sidearm the LRC operators would carry, selecting .45 caliber pistols rather than the 9mm used by U.S. forces because the Philippines produced .45 caliber ammunition indigenously.⁶¹

Although the Philippines ordered a complete basic airborne class comprised of Scout Ranger and Special Forces companies to begin the LRC training, the AFP let U.S. advisors determine who would pass the course.⁶² In the words of one of the soldiers involved, "It was like a [Special Forces] selection.... We had the ability to send home the ones we didn't want."⁶³ Every advisor emphasized that if a Filipino officer or NCO did not meet the standards of their training they would be failed and sent back to their unit. That said, around 70 percent of initial trainees passed the rigorous process.⁶⁴

Although Philippine officers were generally willing to subvert their sovereignty concerns in most cases, they insisted on maintaining control of the size of the advisory force. Concerned with the optics of a large U.S. military footprint and its political impact, Philippine leaders set a force cap of 1,300 total U.S. personnel for the broader OEF-P mission, which equated to only 160 Special Forces personnel, fewer than the Americans had wanted to deploy.⁶⁵ Of that total only six hundred Americans would be allowed into the southern operating area where most of the nation's Muslim population lived and the Abu Sayyaf Group operated.⁶⁶ Excepting the force cap, during the heady early days of the mission U.S. advisors had considerable control over the organization, training, and equipping of the LRR. Past that initial period several factors impeded U.S. advisors from having such an impact.

Used and Abused: Resistance to Creating a Philippine SOF Headquarters

One challenge was the decision to keep the LRR under the command of conventional commanders and not stand up a special-operations headquarters that could oversee funding and operational use. Although the U.S. advisors were allowed to control the stand-up of the unit, operational control was not ceded to them. Advisors quickly realized that, "while the Philippines' government could develop a tactically proficient counterterrorism force, the Armed Forces of the Philippines (AFP) did not have a command-and-control structure to properly employ the LRC or to integrate it with other forces and current operations."[67] Instead the LRC and later the LRB fell under the regional conventional-force commander where the unit was deployed, and many of those officers did not understand how to properly employ or logistically support special-operations units. At its worst, Marine and Army officers often did not trust one another and refused to cooperate, resulting in the LRR being used—over the protests of their U.S. advisors—as a sacrificial force or on a mission for which neither a Marine nor an Army commander would risk their own forces.

Such practices began even before the first LRC completed its training. Faced with the political-relations nightmare caused when the ASG took American hostages in May 2001, the Philippine government pushed to curtail the unit's training and commit them to the hunt. Unfortunately the SF advisors were unable to persuade Philippine leaders that the unit needed more preparation, and the LRC was deployed a mere two days after completing training.[68] Instead of being used on missions for which it had been prepared—namely, hostage-rescue operations based on precision intelligence—the LRC was ordered to conduct zone reconnaissance in jungle areas based on guesses where the hostages might be held, missions a conventional unit could have performed more effectively. Despite nearly continuous patrolling, the LRC only succeeded in exhausting its members during the fruitless search.

Such misuse continued for years against the advice of U.S. mentors. Desperate to contain the ASG and under considerable pressure to recover European and U.S. hostages, the Armed Forces of the Philippines sent the LRC into the jungle throughout 2002 and 2003. In the words of then–JSOTF-P deputy commander Lt. Col. Dennis Downey, the LRC was "ordered it to patrol endlessly without intelligence, mobility, or supply chains to track the ASG on their home turf. It was not a great plan."[69] Rather than take advantage of the elite counterterrorism training the LRC had received, they were deployed ahead of conventional AFP elements, beating the bushes in a hammer-and-anvil approach to flush out ASG elements. This led to several perilous encounters between large groups of ASG on terrain with which they were intimately familiar and small numbers of LRC troops, nearly resulting in disaster.[70]

Similar problems occurred in 2006 during the AFP's Operation Ultimatum on the island of Jolo. During that effort Philippine joint forces conducted an amphibious landing aimed to catch ASG elements by surprise while other ground forces served as blocking or deception elements.[71] Over the objections of SF advisors, two LRCs were used as part of the cordon force, a complete misuse of their capabilities. Unsurprisingly the ASG were able to push past them and disappear into the jungle.[72]

As a result of the persistent misuse of the LRC and LRB, Special Forces advisors assisted by U.S. embassy staff and leadership at PACOM and SOCPAC lobbied to create a proper command-and-control mechanism for the LRC.[73] As had happened on many other Special Forces advisory missions, the creation of this host-nation special-operations headquarters was slow to launch. In late 2003, at the behest of the JSOTF-P, the Armed Forces of the Philippines stood up the Joint Special Operations Group (JSOG), which would oversee the LRC and Philippine Navy and Air Force special-operations elements.[74] JSOG was independent of the Philippines' regional commands for institutional support, falling under AFP chief of staff. But those conventional regional commanders could request elite forces from JSOG, which would deploy and fall under the tactical command of the regional headquarters as JSOG units were not allowed to operate unilaterally.[75] Over the objections of U.S. advisors, the Philippine government chose to station JSOG at Camp Aguinaldo, located in a dense urban environment on the outskirts of Manila, a suboptimal location. Aguinaldo had limited command-and-control, logistics, and maintenance facilities, and mobility was problematic as the base did not have an airfield with a dedicated airwing, meaning units had to travel through the capital's notorious traffic to deploy. Some advisors speculated that the headquarters had been placed near the capital to reassure worried civilian leadership who wanted constant oversight of the organization's forces and plans.[76] Standing up other SOF headquarters and training elements, long a desire of SF advisors, was a long and arduous process. An Army component headquarters was added first, followed by a self-sustaining special-warfare school to train candidates for the elite units, and finally in 2018 a joint headquarters, Armed Forces of the Philippines Special Operations Command. Even after their creation, the various organizations were slow to gain institutional control over disparate SOF elements.[77]

Coup-Proofing and the Oakwood Plot

Another factor that affected the ability of SF advisors to control or organize the LRR came from the involvement of unit members in an attempted coup in 2003. At that time, President Gloria Arroyo had been in office for only two years, having replaced President Joseph Estrada after his impeachment and subsequent resignation. President Estrada was well respected within military circles and in the early part of his term had led a successful military campaign against the Moro Islamic Liberation Front, a separatist group based on Mindanao. Arroyo's election to the presidency provoked concern from military who perceived her to be "soft" on the domestic Islamic threat, and eventually several units revolted.[78]

From late 2002 through 2003 coup plotters recruited the popular commander of the first LRC, who was then helping stand up the second LRC. This officer in turn convinced four other members of the LRC to join the coup attempt, which began on July 27, 2003, with the takeover of the Oakwood Hotel in Manila. Though the coup was short-lived it left a permanent stain on the LRC.[79] After the revolt ended the elite unit was under intense scrutiny by President Arroyo and other elected leaders who were on the lookout for threats from the organization. Senior civilian leaders questioned equipping the unit with the best gear and personnel, fearing the danger it could pose to any duly elected government.[80] More importantly, in the immediate aftermath of the coup attempt the unit's leaders had been carefully staffed with officers whose loyalty to the civilian administration was impeccable. Allegiance to elected officials and respect for proper civil military relations became the primary qualities for selection rather than military proficiency. Fortunately those skill sets were not always mutually exclusive, and several superb officers rose to command the unit. At times, however, the LRR suffered under leaders seemingly placed only for the likelihood that they would prevent the unit from becoming a threat to the government.

Several U.S. advisors believed that the resistance from the Philippine government affected the combat effectiveness of the LRR. Fearing the LRR would become too powerful for its own good, the government at least temporarily stunted the unit's capabilities to prevent another coup. Over time those fears gave way to appreciation for the LRR's fighting prowess—especially evident during the five-month Battle of Marawi in 2017, after which it received considerable attention and accolades from President Rodrigo Duterte. Those successes seemed to prove the unit's value to the government, which reversed curbing the unit's advancement—albeit after the completion of the SF advisory mission.

The Duration of the Mission

In some ways the duration of U.S. advisory efforts in the Philippines worked against the Green Berets. In the early days of the mission, members of the LRR were exceedingly impressed with U.S. Special Forces accomplishments at the beginning of the wars in Iraq and Afghanistan. Over time members of the LRR gained enough combat experience that they began to consider themselves peers or even more capable than some U.S. advisors.[81] By 2010 the LRR had been in combat more than a decade and some of its members had more experience than some of the younger SF advisors. This led to more pushback against U.S. suggestions, leaving American advisors less able to organize the unit.[82]

Assessment

Likely because of a "honeymoon period" stemming from renewed U.S.-Philippine relations as well as the considerable amount of military assistance provided, SF advisors' ability to organize LRR elements was initially high. Philippine military forces gave advisors considerable leeway in organizing and equipping the LRC as well as the selection of its operators. Philippine concerns over national sovereignty were often sublimated to the perceived experience of U.S. advisors and the advantages of access to an open American purse. Before long, however, Philippine concerns reemerged. This coupled with the damage done to LRR relations with civil authorities in the wake of the Oakwood coup attempt led SF advisors to fear that the LRR would never be allowed to meet goals set for them by U.S. advisors lest it endanger the government.

Additionally, because the LRR had been placed under the operational control of conventional units that often misunderstood their unique capabilities and limitations, U.S. recommendations were watered down or often ignored. Calls from U.S. Special Forces elements to resolve this by putting the unit under a special-operations headquarters were often slow to be implemented, limited in application, or even altogether unheeded. The shift from a substantial ability to impact the organization of the LRR to a considerably reduced impact leads to the assumption that a "sovereignty clock" existed, whereby the longer the mission lasted, the more concerned a host nation would grow with sovereignty issues. Eventually the clock ran out, resulting in significantly less influence for the advisors. Because of all these factors the overall rating for how much U.S. advisors were able to organize the LRR will be rated as low.

Combat Advising

The Constitution of the Philippines explicitly prohibited foreign forces from engaging in domestic combat operations.[83] This meant U.S. advisors were unable to offer the same kind of combat advising as was possible in Iraq or Afghanistan. The separation between offering counsel and combat assistance was considered so critical that commanders issued guidance noting that "*any perception* of U.S. or unilateral operations equals U.S. strategic failure in the Philippines and Pacific Region."[84] Despite that prohibition, considerable variation existed regarding what type of advising was permitted, and that variation changed over time.

An example of how this sensitivity played out occurred during the first deployment to the Philippines after the September 11 attacks. JTF-150, SOCPAC's standing Joint Task Force, had been committed to the mission, but military and political leaders in the Philippines balked, concerned that the term *Joint Task Force* could imply that U.S. forces were conducting combat operations.[85] To alleviate these worries, both countries agreed to publicly refer to the first deployment of forces as Balikatan 02-1 ("shoulder to shoulder" in Tagalog). Since the closure of U.S. bases in the Philippines the two nations have conducted Balikatan, annual military exercises meant to cement the relationship between the respective armed forces. Thus senior military leaders believed that cloaking this new operation with familiar and accepted terminology would generate less negative media attention and national concern.[86] Similarly Philippine military leaders cautioned U.S. SF advisors to avoid being photographed with their military forces in an operational setting for fear of possible political repercussions as well as the potential that the images could be used as propaganda material by the ASG or other insurgent groups.[87]

Despite these attempts to minimize perception of a U.S. colonial return or disruption of Philippine sovereignty, the ensuing sizeable U.S. deployment resulted in considerable political oversight. The Philippine Senate opened investigations and conducted hearings, eventually holding a vote on the mission's legitimacy. That resolution, approved in a hair's breadth vote, required that U.S. forces not engage in combat except in self-defense and prohibited them from operating independently or from establishing permanent bases. Total U.S. forces were capped at six hundred personnel of all types, including guards, doctors, pilots, and SF advisors, which meant deployment of civil-affairs and psychological-operations personnel was limited.[88] Philippine leaders also set a geographical restriction for the mission to the island of Basilan and to the Zamboanga Peninsula on Mindanao, which was interpreted as a way to limit U.S. presence and thereby visibility to domestic news media.[89] Even those terms were so controversial that the Philippine Supreme Court heard a case related to the prospective deployment, eventually ruling that the mission was legal.[90]

When in 2003 U.S. Marine Corps leaders were given responsibility for the third rotation of Operation Enduring Freedom–Philippines, they announced their desire to expand the mission to over one thousand personnel and to conduct combat operations paired with Philippine military forces against al-Qaida–affiliated groups. This triggered such significant sovereignty concerns within the Philippine government that then-president Gloria Arroyo canceled the conventional-force portion of the mission altogether, citing the constitutional ban on U.S. military engagement on Philippine soil. The ensuing fallout left only a small 1st Special Forces Group caretaker force deployed from March 2003 until 2005, which itself maintained an extremely low profile.[91]

In addition to changing the name of the mission to protect political sensibilities, U.S. and Philippine leaders also put operational restrictions on the movement of SF advisors to ensure they remained out of combat. At the start of the mission in January 2002 the Green Berets had to obtain permission from the JSOTF-P headquarters to participate in any type of operation, restrictions that proved incredibly cumbersome. To resolve the issue, the JSOTF-P negotiated blanket permission for its advisors to deploy with Philippine battalion headquarters. That rule was largely interpreted as preventing advisors from getting closer to combat than the physical location of the battalion commander; it remained in place for the first six months of the mission.[92]

In practice, SF advisors found the rule to be problematic because in the jungles of the Philippines there was no front line and the battalion commander's position could easily be in range of the enemy. U.S. forces retained the right to defend themselves, which created a fine line for advisors who wished to respect Philippine sovereignty and avoid combat but also be situated to offer their best advice.[93] The rule was also awkward because during the early phases of the mission the LRC had no battalion headquarters. To resolve the conundrum, some advisors reinterpreted the guidance to mean they were not to venture beyond the last covered and concealed position before the objective, which was theoretically outside of small-arms range and therefore outside of combat.[94] Other SF advisors simply made the best of the situation by interpreting the restriction to allow them to go wherever the battalion commander moved, even if the commander moved forward to the front lines.[95]

JSOTF-P leadership felt pairing with the battalion level was suboptimal, so they actively campaigned for SF advisors to be permitted to accompany company-level units on operations.[96] Gaining such approval was particularly challenging as Secretary of Defense Donald Rumsfeld had consistently blocked previous requests, with some senior leaders hypothesizing that his opposition stemmed from an old grudge with the Philippines over their 1991 decision to close the U.S. Navy base at Subic Bay. But an opportunity materialized in June 2002 when Deputy Secretary of Defense Paul Wolfowitz visited the mission and asked how he could help. The

1st SF Group Commander, Col. David Fridovich, said that he really needed his advisors to work at company level and indicated they were being creative in their approach to working with the Philippine military. Wolfowitz noted that Rumsfeld was on vacation for the next few days and that as the acting secretary he would approve the decision.[97] Still, some missions—such as the LRC attempt to locate U.S. hostages—were deemed so risky that SF advisors were barred from accompanying Philippine Commandos.[98]

The rule changed yet again in 2006 when U.S. Pacific Command authorized troops to be in a "combat environment" so long as they were in locations where they would not encounter the enemy. Such nebulous wording gave leeway to LRR advisors, but most commanders interpreted it conservatively due to the potential repercussions should U.S. forces became embroiled in conflict.[99] Despite the care that U.S. advisors took to avoid combat, three were killed by hostile action. Reflecting the paradox of the inherent dangers of the mission paired with rules that aimed to bar combat operations, the Philippines advisory effort ranks as a medium degree of combat advising.

Assessment

The prohibition on accompanying the LRR and other Philippine military forces into combat was disparaged by most U.S. advisors. While they understood and accepted the limitations, they expressed frustration at the restriction's perceived impacts. Many argued that had they been able to accompany Philippine forces into combat they would have made much more rapid, consistent, and meaningful progress. Specifically they believed that combat advising would have allowed them to assess LRR performance firsthand rather than rely upon Philippine after-action reports, which U.S. advisors considered untrustworthy.[100] As noted by Col. Erik Brown, final JSOTF-P commander, "Combat advising gives you much better situational awareness of your training program . . . because everyone looks good in the shoot house and [on the] parade ground."[101]

Additionally advisors argued that the ban on combat advising damaged their rapport with their host-nation counterparts, making them less willing to take U.S. recommendations.[102] Rules of engagement prohibiting U.S. soldiers from sharing the same dangers as LRR members inherently created frictions in the advisory relationship. Lt. Col. David Maxwell, battalion commander of the first LRC advisory effort, noted further complications in a 2002 report to his headquarters: "Rapport with the AFP (Armed Forces of the Philippines) is going to wane because there is a perception that the US forces are not willing to commit to advising and assisting at the lowest levels. Furthermore, until US SF conducts advisory operations at the lowest tactical levels, [AFP] operations will never be sufficiently improved to get the job done."[103]

EVALUATING COMBAT EFFECTIVENESS

Night Fighting

The LRR was outfitted similarly to the CIF Special Forces companies that conducted their initial training. Each LRR member was equipped with PVS-14 or -15 night-vision goggles and laser pointers for their rifles.[104] This equipment gave them significant technological advantage over the Islamist insurgent groups they faced.

Despite that imbalance the LRR was rarely willing to engage in night actions. Some U.S. advisors believed a cultural reluctance to fight at night showed LRR soldiers were "solar powered"—when the sun went down they ceased operations. Others hypothesized that the seemingly endless conflict with Islamic militants played a role in the reluctance to fight at night. That struggle had spanned generations, and U.S. advisors recalled being told stories by Philippine officers that the AFP had already killed two generations of men in some families and was fighting the third.[105] Because of that reality, many had come to see fighting at night as an unnecessary risk since the extra effort would be unlikely to have an impact; if you had to "mow the grass" of insurgency every few years, there was no reason to put yourself in the way of additional peril.[106]

Another advisor described disinclination to engage in night combat as part of a daily progression established over years of fighting:

> Everything stopped at about 1700 every day [because] it's a tropical area and equatorial. The sun goes down . . . and nobody fights at night. It was a civilized way of warfare because you could have a cold beer by about 1800 every day. Both sides would . . . text each other in the evening and brag about how many they killed on each side, and the other ones would refute, "No, you did not kill us, we killed you." And so over beer and pasta and noodles they would heckle each other before the next day's event. But they wouldn't fight at night.[107]

Others argued that the lack of willingness to fight at night came from the weakness of the casualty-evacuation system. When the LRC was first organized there was not a single helicopter crew in the AFP capable of extracting wounded at night.[108] Knowing that if they were wounded after nightfall they would have to wait until the sun rose to be evacuated—and potentially bleed to death—led many LRR members to dismiss night combat as an unacceptable risk.[109] This issue was so significant that the JSOTF-P worked with the embassy to improve the capability of Philippine helicopter pilots, a project only partially realized. Recognizing those limitations, USPACOM granted permission for the JSOTF's civilian contract helicopters to perform night evacuations so long as Philippine forces were not in direct combat.[110]

Another set of advisors believed the terrain caused the LRR's reluctance to fight at night. Night vision technology was not remarkably effective in triple canopy jungle, and without sufficient ambient light to function effectively the efficacy of the LRR's night-vision goggles was reduced.[111] The jungle terrain was so complicated, some advisors noted, that even the United States with its advanced technology would not have been able to perform well.[112]

A smaller group of advisors disagreed, believing the LRR to be one of the best forces in Asia at night fighting.[113] They pointed to LRR response to the 2013 Zamboanga City Crisis and again to LRR effectiveness in the 2017 Battle of Marawi, during which media reports and advisor commentary noted that the LRR had routinely conducted operations at night.[114] But both battles were fought in urban settings, meaning state-of-the-art trauma centers were close by and accessible by road and night-vision equipment functioned better than in the jungle.

Assessment

Putting all these perspectives together, a medium rating most accurately reflects the LRR's night-fighting skills.

Conducting Multiday Combat Operations

Few thought that the LRR could withstand casualties, logistically sustain itself, and conduct casualty evacuation to a standard supporting multiday operations. The most glaring challenge came from the AFP's failure to emphasize proper logistics procedures and equipment maintenance.[115] U.S. advisors tried to inspire cultural change but were unable to make significant headway. Many newly fielded systems such as night-vision goggles and long-range Harris high-frequency radios were soon falling into disrepair, and with the AFP showing little interest in their upkeep advisors were forced have the embassy set up contracts for servicing the highly technical gear.[116]

Unfortunately the negligence extended to the entire logistics system: conducting preventative maintenance, ordering replacement parts, getting those parts where they were needed, and repairing damaged equipment.[117] Ammunition and fuel resupply suffered from poor quality and distribution that created systemic challenges.[118]

One of the root causes of the problem was that the Philippine military simply did not have funds sufficient to pay, arm, equip, and properly supply all of its forces. The situation was so dire that some soldiers stole ammunition and sold it on the black market to help feed their families.[119] Recognizing the depth of the problems, advisors often bent the rules to prevent catastrophic failure. One SF officer noted that before their deployments some U.S. units often ordered extra supplies, such as batteries and replacement parts for night-vision goggles, knowing that if they were not all used the excess would be left behind with the LRR.[120]

Executing a logistics resupply in the middle of a mission was challenging for the LRR unless it occurred near a logistics hub. The AFP logistics structure was unreliable and LRR internal capabilities could not fill the institutional gap. As in many other special-operations forces U.S. advisors have helped train and build, the primary focus was on tactical combat skills, meaning logistics capabilities were often an afterthought receiving little funding or focus.[121] The compound effect was that the LRR would rarely conduct operations longer than twenty-four hours. Knowing that resupply was unlikely, they usually planned a mission that would hit a single target or series of targets in one night after which they would return to base for refit and resupply.[122] In some ways the LRR's logistical horizon was limited by what the troops could carry with them on their backs.[123]

While many advisors expressed frustration at the logistics capabilities of the LRR, they also noted that after more than a decade of collaboration the LRR's logistics culture was far better than the rest of the Philippine military's. They maintained their weapons and other equipment more carefully, and levels of corruption—as measured anecdotally through the amount of "disappearing" or lost equipment—were far below those in any other unit with which they had worked.[124]

Assessment

U.S. advisors made it clear that the LRR could rarely conduct combat operations for seventy-two hours or longer. Therefore the LRR is assessed as having a low capability to conduct extended combat operations.

Fighting without Advisors

To be able to genuinely fight on their own, host-nation forces must be able to generate their own organic intelligence, successfully action targets generated by that intelligence, conduct sensitive site exploitation of those targets, and then use that information to repeat the cycle. Despite providing advice, financial assistance, and even some equipment, the United States was unable to develop organic signals-intelligence or imagery-intelligence capabilities in the LRR across the decade and a half mission. Instead the LRR relied on U.S. resources such as the ScanEagle unmanned aerial reconnaissance vehicle, sensors on a P-3 Orion surveillance aircraft, forward-looking infrared radar capabilities on Navy SH-60 helicopters, and some signal-intercept gear organic to 1st Special Forces Group.[125] Although the AFP was unwilling to enhance their extremely limited signals- and imagery-intelligence capabilities despite U.S. prodding, they embraced the concept of fusion centers that blended their own human intelligence with tactical reconnaissance and U.S. resources. In most cases the centers were permanently established at the Philippine combatant command level but at times were set up ad hoc for the LRR on a mission of significant importance and duration.[126]

By contrast the Philippine military had a robust but erratic human-intelligence capability and the LRR ran its own agent networks. These networks benefited from extensive family connections among LRR officers as well as the long periods its leaders had served in the same areas, giving them a deep roster of sources. LRR officers were skilled at recruiting and developing contacts, training them on basic tradecraft, and evaluating intel to determine what was bogus and what was valid.[127]

The LRR's human-intelligence capabilities also had significant flaws. Rather than run their contacts through the unit intelligence staff, most Philippine officers personally managed their own human-intelligence networks. This is because the U.S. and Philippine systems provided individuals—not organizations—financial incentives for killing or capturing high-value targets. Aiming to cash in on the rewards and incentivize efforts, many Philippine officers set up agreements with their contacts so that they would split the proceeds. Sharing information with other units or even within their own intelligence cells rarely happened as it would diffuse the rewards into smaller portions. What resulted was a systemic inability to corroborate intelligence and a reluctance to provide intelligence to other units for fear that someone else would earn the reward.[128]

These problems were not limited to the LRR but were endemic to the Philippine military. When the LRR shared battlespace with conventional Philippine Marine or Army units, intelligence sharing was always a major issue that hamstrung operations.[129] Those units would rarely disclose information they had obtained not only because of the bounties placed on ASG leaders but also because of the prestige that could be earned from such a capture. One advisor noted bluntly, "You throw money around an area that is really impoverished and needs money, and people will tell you whatever you want to hear.... You really had to confirm their HUMINT [human intelligence] through multiple sources."[130]

Across the fifteen-year mission, SF advisors made dedicated attempts to train the LRR in sensitive site exploitation (SSE). Advisors taught their counterparts the importance of SSE for intelligence gathering and collecting evidence, and the JSOTF-P even set up training sessions led by the U.S. Federal Bureau of Investigation and other government intelligence organizations.[131] Despite these efforts the LRR's ability to conduct proper SSE was inconsistent after the advisory mission concluded. A major problem was that there was no way to exploit documents or electronic media in a timely manner either by moving the intel to a location where it could be evaluated quickly or by analyzing it near the point of capture.[132]

In some cases military cultural challenges had to be overcome to conduct proper SSE. Due to the endemic poverty in the Philippines, some LRR operators were known to take computers and cell phones from objectives to keep for themselves.[133] While this practice was mostly suppressed with training, at times it resurfaced. Despite the LRR's inability to conduct technical SSE, most advisors noted that the unit learned how to conduct basic tactical SSE by questioning prisoners and could perform it effectively after the advisory mission had concluded.[134] On multiple occasions during the battles of Zamboanga in 2013 and Marawi in 2017 LRR members performed limited tactical SSE that generated follow-on targets.[135]

Zooming back out to the macro perspective, most of the successful missions the LRR conducted against high-value targets before the closure of the JSOTF-P mission in 2015 required extensive U.S. support, indicating that the unit was not able to conduct unilateral intelligence-driven operations. After ASG leader Abu Sulaiman ordered a series of bombings that killed scores of Muslim Filipinos in 2007 an informant—either angered by the deaths or hoping to earn the $5 million reward—began filtering information to Philippine intelligence officers. A search ensued, supported by both the LRB and other Philippine elite forces, but it was unsuccessful. When the informant provided Abu Sulaiman's cell phone number, the AFP shared it with the United States, which quickly located the insurgent. Philippine Special Forces Commandos and the LRB then launched a raid that surrounded and killed him when he tried to escape.[136] This mission demonstrates the received wisdom across the LRR experience that while the Filipino human-intelligence capabilities could be effective, deficits in other capabilities made it impossible to conduct real-time intelligence-driven operations.

Chapter 2

Assessment

Because the LRR lacked organic signals and imagery intelligence and had a capable but erratic human-intelligence capability, their ability to carry out unilateral intelligence-based operations without advisors present was marginal. Additionally their sensitive site exploitation skills were inconsistent, making it difficult to generate follow-on targets from successful missions. Combined, these factors result in a low rating for the ability to fight without advisors present.

Performance against the Enemy

Although the LRR engaged in countless smaller operations, the 2013 Zamboanga City Crisis and the 2017 Battle of Marawi provide the best opportunities to assess their capabilities. Both operations were long, complex, and fought against a determined enemy. While shorter engagements have some value, an operation planned over a few hours and executed over mere minutes simply doesn't compare to one that requires logistical resupply, intelligence-driven operations, and casualty evacuation. In such battles the LRR produced mixed results.

The siege of Zamboanga City began on September 9, 2013, when 500 fighters from a splinter element of the Moro National Liberation Front (MNLF) attempted a takeover of the Philippines' sixth most populous city with over 800,000 residents. The MNLF force took hostages and occupied sections of the city and outlying towns, declaring the region to be independent from the Philippines. The Armed Forces of the Philippines rushed troops to the besieged city, including the LRB, which had received extensive training on hostage rescue. Unfortunately the unit expansion and inability to recruit new operators meant it was massively understrength, with only 40 percent of its assigned personnel during the fighting.[137]

During the initial phases of the battle, MNLF fighters took more than two hundred hostages and barricaded themselves in dense urban areas.[138] Initial assaults by the Philippine military were quickly repulsed as the siege in urban terrain represented a significant change from the jungle fighting to which they were more accustomed. AFP forces also exhibited overconfidence, expecting to quickly vanquish the MNLF, and as a result at times did not plan or prepare properly before initiating operations.

All three companies of the LRB were ordered into the twenty-one-day maelstrom. When logistical resupply quickly became a problem, some units had to rely on the local population for food and water.[139] The LRB's ability to collect intelligence was similarly challenged, as its agent networks in the area were poorly developed and the LRB lacked its own unmanned aerial vehicles. Making matters worse, the JSOTF-P was technically prohibited from helping the mission because the MNLF was not officially recognized as an al-Qaida affiliate. But SF leaders found a loophole because the fighting was near their base at Camp Navarro, determining that they could provide intelligence to help protect themselves.[140] As such, the JSOTF-P launched its organic intelligence, surveillance, and reconnaissance assets and provided real-time intelligence to the LRB.[141]

The LRB's expertise in hostage-rescue and counterterrorism missions meant it was well suited for many of the tasks it was given in Zamboanga, and they were credited with saving 96 hostages and capturing 99 and killing 116 MNLF fighters.[142] The unit also excelled in sniper and countersniper missions, recording a stunning fourteen confirmed kills on the first day of operations alone.[143] The LRB also performed relatively well at night, using night-vision goggles and sniper scopes to put continuous pressure on MNLF forces. However, when the unit had to perform traditional assaults on defended objectives, they were less successful and on several occasions had to disengage under fire, losing nine operators. All things considered, the LRB's performance was commendable during the Zamboanga City Crisis.

Despite having several years to hone their skills and to expand from three companies to six, the LRR struggled during the 2017 Battle of Marawi. The unit's informal historian described the opening phase of the battle as the Philippine's Gothic Serpent redux, indicating it was on par with the disastrous Battle of Mogadishu spanning October 3 through 4, 1993, memorialized in the book and movie *Blackhawk Down*.[144] As combat in Marawi dragged on, the LRR suffered losses on a scale like those taken by U.S. elite forces in Somalia, which was one of the worst days for U.S. special-operations forces since the inception of USSOCOM. Lasting nearly five months, the conflict in Marawi became the longest urban battle in the Philippines' history: four times longer than the U.S.-led effort to liberate Manila in World War II.[145]

At the outset of the battle, the JSOTF-P had been closed and the mission reorganized into the small U.S. Pacific Command Augmentation Team (PAT) principally operating out of the U.S. embassy in Manila. The LRR still had Special Forces advisors attached to the unit, but, as in the battle of Zamboanga, U.S. soldiers were prohibited from accompanying the unit into battle. Like in that battle, advisors were authorized to share U.S. intelligence and offer material support where possible. Because of those similarities, the U.S. reorganization was not a significant factor in the LRR's performance.

The battle opened like the fateful operation in Somalia, as LRR Commandos had planned a mission to kill or capture Isnilon Hapilon, leader of the Abu Sayyaf Group and ISIS emir of Southeast Asia. Expecting a mission that would be concluded in minutes if not hours, many LRR operators were unprepared for extended battle. When the initial assault force suffered three killed and became bogged down, other elements of the LRR as well as conventional forces scrambled to help.[146] The LRR's quick-reaction force blundered into an ambush and became encircled, itself requiring rescue. In the ensuing chaos Hapilon escaped. As the fighting expanded and the situation for the trapped force became more dire, it became clear that there were hundreds if not thousands of fighters in the nearby area, highlighting the gross inaccuracy of the LRR's intelligence estimate.[147] Rather than executing a surprise strike to snatch the terrorist group's leader, the mission unexpectedly uncovered the ASG's efforts to declare an ISIS affiliate on Mindanao, kicking over the proverbial hornet's nest.

Copying tactics that had worked effectively during the Battle of Zamboanga, ASG fighters took hundreds of civilian hostages as human shields, barricaded themselves in the city, and placed belts of IEDs (improvised explosive devices) along likely avenues of approach. The guerrillas included foreign fighters from across the globe and employed skilled snipers, primitive night-vision goggles, and commercial drones to conduct reconnaissance.[148] When the fighting finally concluded, 165 Filipino soldiers had been killed, including twelve members of the LRR.[149] Dozens of other LRR operators had been wounded, many to the point of being unable to serve.

Incapable of digging out the entrenched insurgents, the LRR was forced to revert to softening up targets through sniper teams and airstrikes or artillery before assaulting—taking grievous casualties in the process.[150] LRR snipers again helped save the day, eventually killing the top three ASG leaders, including Hapilon.[151] The unit used its night-fighting capabilities to its advantage and crossed obstacles and conducted some assaults at night that had been deemed too dangerous to carry out during the day.[152] But in general the LRR struggled to overcome the defensive advantage held by the ASG, and the fight dragged on for months. Those delays highlighted the logistical Achilles' heel of the LRR, and some offensives stalled when operators ran out of ammunition or fuel.[153] By the time the city was finally retaken, it was a ruined shell from airstrikes and artillery, and hundreds of thousands had been made homeless.[154]

Assessment

The LRR's performance against the enemy in battle is mixed. It generally fought well across those two major battles, but the unit was also sporadically repulsed by determined enemy fighters. Logistics confounded the unit, and it had to rely on the JSOTF-P for some of its intelligence, showing that even near the end of the advisory mission it was not able to operate fully independently. Altogether those factors indicate a medium rating would be most appropriate.

INITIAL ASSESSMENT

There is always considerable debate over how military forces stack up against one another. Much ink has been spilled touting the capabilities of the U.S. Navy SEALs, real or imagined, for example. But where does the LRR fit in the pecking order? In 2020 the magazine *Business Insider* ranked the LRR as one of the top five non-U.S. special-operation forces in the world, beating out even the legendary Israeli Sayeret Matkal, the national mission-force unit famous for conducting the daring Entebbe rescue mission in 1976 and other storied operations.[155]

But the *Business Insider* article used little rigor in its methodology, if any at all. Looking at the factors we identified in this book's introductory chapter to evaluate combat effectiveness, the LRR received low ratings in ability to conduct combat operations for seventy-two hours and in ability to fight without advisors present and received medium scores in performance in combat and night-fighting skills. This results in an overall rating of low-moderate effectiveness for the LRR, on par with the performance of the BIRIs in El Salvador.

The next chapter focuses on two elite units in the National Army of Colombia that were established shortly after the LRR—BACOA and AGLAN. Like the LRR, these two units were advised exclusively by the regionally oriented Special Forces Group but saw very different outcomes.

– 3 –
"The Dream Allies"

BACOA and AGLAN in Colombia, 2002–2016

BACKGROUND

COLOMBIA, LIKE THE PHILIPPINES, has had a long history of cooperation with the U.S. military, but without the colonial baggage. What has resulted is a deep reservoir of goodwill and strong connections between the two American nations. Indeed, Colombia was the only South American nation to answer the U.S. call to assist United Nations forces during the Korean War, sending an infantry battalion and a frigate. Those forces engaged in combat, and of the more than 4,300 that deployed, 141 were killed, 448 wounded, and 69 listed as missing in action.[1] By all accounts the Colombian performance was exemplary, and during the 1953 Battle of Old Baldy their battalion fought ferociously, preventing a Chinese attack from encircling the U.S. 7th Infantry Division.[2] One U.S. war correspondent observed of the Colombian unit, "They are the bravest men I have ever seen."[3] By the end of the war, the United States had awarded a Presidential Unit Citation—the highest unit award—as well as eighteen Silver Stars and twenty nine Bronze Stars for valor to individual Colombians.[4]

That cooperation continued across the internal conflict known as La Violencia (the violence), a civil war lasting from 1948 to 1958, when at Colombia's request the United States sent both CIA and Special Forces teams to help.[5] Colombia especially wanted to establish a program like the U.S. Ranger School, and in 1956 U.S.

advisors helped a cadre of Korean War veterans and recent Colombian Ranger School graduates found Lancero school. Named after the elite Colombian "Lancer" cavalry force that supported General Simón Bolívar's army during the nineteenth-century South American wars of independence from the Spanish Empire; the course soon became known as one of the most difficult commando schools worldwide.[6] The three-month-long program has a graduation requirement to lead troops in combat for Colombian personnel and includes sleep deprivation, insufficient food, difficult conditions, and constant leadership tests. Losing twenty pounds is not uncommon for soldiers completing the training, and one U.S. graduate from 2011 lost 48 pounds.[7] Over time Lancero school developed into a course that soldiers from across the globe sought to attend.

The second U.S. advisor to Lancero school was Gen. John Galvin, who served as the commander in chief of U.S. Southern Command (USSOUTHCOM) during the U.S. advisory effort in El Salvador.[8] One of the company commanders for BIRI Belloso was the honor graduate from his Lancero course and returned to El Salvador to fight the FMLN using the skills he had learned.

Despite military cooperation with the United States, Colombia struggled to contain different rebel factions, especially the Fuerzas Armadas Revolucionarias de Colombia (Revolutionary Armed Forces of Colombia). The FARC, as they are known, originally espoused a Marxist-Leninist liberation ideology but chose to engage in narcotrafficking in the 1980s. With access to abundant finances from the drug trade, they shifted from being a threat to Colombia's well-being into a menace to the nation's survival.[9]

Plan Colombia

By the late 1990s Colombia was at a breaking point. Ambassador Kevin Whitaker, who held the post in Bogotá from 2014 to 2019, later observed that during this era "Colombia was on the verge of becoming a failed state."[10] One U.S. Army officer with extensive experience in Colombia posited that "in the '90s, the FARC was an existential threat to the Colombian state. They had beaten the Colombian Army multiple times in combat, defeating battalion-sized units in horrific ambushes. It looked as if, at a minimum, the FARC would bring down the government, forcing them to sue for peace and create a FARC-controlled autonomous zone."[11] Indeed, the FARC had surrounded and destroyed an elite counterguerrilla battalion at the 1998 Battle of El Billar, with two-thirds of the unit's soldiers killed or captured in three days of combat.[12]

U.S. officials issued a series of grim warnings. Clinton administration appointees cautioned that the Colombian government could collapse, the U.S. ambassador in Bogotá assessed that the Colombian military would be unable to stabilize the security situation, and the U.S. Defense Intelligence Agency concluded that if the FARC was not properly countered, the central government would collapse within five years.[13] In a retrospective article, the *Washington Post* noted that in the early 2000s comparing Colombia to Afghanistan would have been reasonable, with each having their share of bombings and kidnappings, but with Colombia edging out Afghanistan for the highest murder rate in the world.[14]

The grave situation spurred action within Colombian military and civilian leadership. Andrés Pastrana was elected president in late 1998 on a reform platform, and he and his senior generals decided to work more closely with the United States.[15] Officials on both sides were excited at the prospect of reenergizing bilateral connections, which had sunk to a low point across the 1994–1998 presidency of Ernesto Samper. During Samper's tenure the United States had declared the Colombian government too corrupt and tainted by human-rights abuses to effectively fight drug cartels and cut off economic and military assistance valued at over $1 billion.[16] Once taking office President Pastrana lobbied Washington to support his Plan Colombia, a massive infusion of foreign assistance aimed at defeating the FARC and funding development projects and counternarcotics efforts. After its approval by the U.S. Congress, the program's allocations exceeded all aid packages other than those given to Israel and Egypt.[17]

In exchange for renewed support the United States demanded that Colombia execute massive internal reforms and clean house. Due in part to that pressure and in part due to President Pastrana's desire to reset his government in light of the ongoing crises, many senior Colombian military leaders including division commanders and the Army chief of operations were cashiered.[18] A cascading impact ensued, with new senior leaders firing midgrade officers for incompetence and corruption and appointing more competent and upright replacements.[19] With those changes in place, U.S. support began flowing again, with $959 million allocated in FY 2000, nearly ten times what had been appropriated only two years prior.[20] At the same time, considerable limitations were placed on those funds, including a bar on using counternarcotics funds for counterinsurgency or counterterrorism missions, even though there was considerable operational overlap. Those limitations led to significant consternation, and it was not uncommon to hear Colombian Army commanders begging in vain to use U.S.-supplied counternarcotics helicopters to reinforce troops in contact who would be doomed without the additional support. The United States also made a sizeable troop commitment to help advise and assist the Colombian military, a large portion of which came from 7th SF Group.[21]

Expanding Colombia's Special Operations Forces

In the earliest days of Plan Colombia only one true special-operations unit existed in the nation's armed forces, and its primary focus was urban counterterrorism. Other high-caliber units could carry out large-scale offensive operations, but few had the ability to conduct high-value target (HVT) or hostage-rescue operations in rural environments. The Colombian Army was unwilling to retrain any of their elite units or reassign them to those missions, as they were the only forces that could go on the offensive against the FARC. As happened in El Salvador, the vast majority of the Colombian Army was a conscript force capable only of territorial security: guarding roads, bridges, pipelines, and other fixed sites.

In 2002, the commander of the U.S. Military Group (MILGP), Col. Ken Keen, recognized the capability gap and offered to help develop a force similar to the U.S. Ranger Regiment that could conduct kill/capture missions against HVTs, rescue hostages, and carry out long-range reconnaissance in rural settings.[22] Even though powerful factions of the Colombian military opposed the creation of such a unit, Keen's proposal was met warmly by General Jorge Enrique Mora, commander of the Colombian Armed Forces, whose campaign plan included killing or capturing FARC senior leadership.[23] The ability to rescue hostages was also highly lucrative to other Colombian military officials, who recognized it as an important morale issue and means to undermine FARC finances. At any time there were at least five hundred military hostages as well as untold civilian hostages, including Íngrid Betancourt, a dual French-Colombian politician who had run for the Colombian presidency.[24] Across the long conflict the FARC kidnapped more than 24,000 Colombians.[25]

The unit that would carry out those hostage-rescue missions was the Batallón de Comandos Ambrosio Almeyda (Ambroseo Almaeda Commando battalion, or BACOA), which began to form in early 2002.[26] As the plan moved from idea to reality, SF advisors decided to model BACOA after elite South Vietnamese and Salvadoran reconnaissance units that could locate enemy encampments and leaders and then destroy them through airstrikes. To provide the stealth necessary to accomplish that, the battalion was designed to break down and function as platoon- or squad-level units, a capability that no other Colombian unit then possessed. It would also have the skills to perform hostage rescues, although the unit would not focus on the precision-shooting skills central to such high-risk missions. Training consisted of a three-week assessment course, and many candidates had already completed the Lancero course or Colombian Airborne School.[27] Experience in combat was a prerequisite to acceptance into BACOA, as were good conduct, superb physical fitness, strong marksmanship, and passing a psychological exam.[28]

While BACOA was concluding its training, senior Colombian military leaders, including Colombian Army commander general Carlos Ospina Ovalle, decided that they needed another battalion with similar capabilities and began to organize a unit named Agrupación de Lanceros (Lancero Group, or AGLAN).[29] AGLAN was focused on operationalizing the skills taught in Lancero school, which itself was modeled on the U.S. Army Ranger program. Lancero companies had previously served in the Colombian Army during the 1950s and 1960s, which made AGLAN's stand-up more straightforward as organizational blueprints only needed to be updated and expanded.[30] It was decided that AGLAN core missions would be reconnaissance and HVT kill/capture missions, mirroring the capabilities of BACOA and providing depth and redundancy for the Colombian campaign plan. U.S. Special Forces advisors helped in the selection and training process, and the battalion was fully operational by the end of 2003.[31] Selection lasted for three weeks, and, paralleling the U.S. Ranger Regiment, most of the unit's soldiers would attend Lancero school after serving in the battalion.

This chapter assesses the combat effectiveness of those two new units, BACOA and AGLAN.

Changes in the American Commitment: The Dream Authority, Operation Willing Spirit, and Afghanistan

Across the span of the U.S. mission the degree of Special Forces commitment and the authorities associated with it experienced several significant changes. One massive turning point occurred in 2002 when, in response to the 9/11 attacks, the U.S. Congress erased the regulatory line between counternarcotics and counterterrorism that had caused friction during Plan Colombia. One scholar later described that congressional action as "the dream authority" because it allowed a broad variety of counternarcotics activities with few restrictions.[32] While engaging in combat was still barred to U.S. soldiers, the changes opened significant funding streams and added so many new authorities that amounted to a complete change to the mission in Colombia.

A second change occurred unexpectedly in February 2003 when a U.S.-contracted aerial-surveillance aircraft involved in coca eradication efforts developed engine trouble and crashed in FARC-controlled territory. FARC guerrillas executed one wounded American contractor and took three others hostage. In a parallel to the Philippines when the Abu Sayyaf Group kidnapped two U.S. citizens, the taking of U.S. civilian hostages in Colombia caused a visceral reaction out of proportion to the number of civilians held.[33] Perhaps related to historical scar tissue from the Iran hostage crisis, the U.S. government quickly authorized expanded authorities that allowed its soldiers to participate in missions related to the rescue of the American contractors. To that end, and with the approval of the Colombian government, Operation Willing Spirit was organized, and additional forces were deployed to share intelligence and prepare for potential operations. Those authorities lasted until the hostages' rescue by a unilateral Colombian operation in 2008.

One final change occurred gradually. When the United States decided to invade Iraq in 2003 it became clear that 5th SF Group, the unit regionally assigned to the CENTCOM area of responsibility, could not handle that mission and operations in Afghanistan simultaneously. As a result, the special-operations mission in Afghanistan was retasked as a shared responsibility between 7th Special Forces Group and 3rd Special Forces Group. The considerable commitment there drew forces away from the mission in Colombia, and the vast difference between missions made it challenging for advisors to adapt.

Victory

The success of Plan Colombia led to a parallel effort under newly elected President Álvaro Uribe. Plan Patriota, as it was dubbed, perpetuated massive U.S. military assistance but also included significant domestic reforms. Colombia's defense budget was doubled from 2 to 4 percent of gross domestic product, and the size of the Army was increased by 60,000 troops. Even more importantly, mandatory conscription began to end, and the Army slowly became a volunteer force.[34]

In addition, Colombian military leaders—some of whom had trained at the School of Advanced Military Studies at Fort Leavenworth, Kansas—crafted a new campaign that focused on area control, continuous-offensive operations, and killing or capturing FARC high-value targets (HVTs).[35] Area control aimed to reestablish government control over FARC-held or ungoverned territory. Offensive operations employed conventional forces to keep the FARC off-balance through constant pursuit, preventing them from resting or training. Colombian special-operations forces, including BACOA and AGLAN, were given responsibility for the final leg of the campaign plan by hunting FARC high-value targets.[36]

The HVT campaign blended GPS precision bombing with SOF ground forces to kill or capture FARC senior leaders.[37] From July 2007 through November 2013, sixty-five senior FARC leaders were killed by SOF elements or precision-guided munitions (PGMs), or a combination of both where SOF elements provided terminal guidance to the PGMs.[38] The U.S. ambassador at the time, Kevin Whitaker, later recalled that the HVT strategy of the Colombian military "put the idea into the minds of senior FARC leadership that their time on this Earth was limited. That they may be under continuing threat of ending up on the wrong end of a precision-guided munition at some point."[39] Combined with conventional forces' continuous-offensive operations, the kill/capture campaign put FARC leaders under constant pressure. Thousands simply gave up. After surrendering, the FARC 47th Front commander told government interviewers, "Everywhere we went, the Army was there. We couldn't sleep in one place for more than one night."[40] Exhausted and fearful for their safety, in 2015 senior FARC leaders announced a unilateral cease-fire, and the next year the two sides agreed on a peace deal. During the negotiations the FARC splintered and a handful of dissident groups, mainly lower and midgrade leaders, decided to continue fighting. But for the most part Colombia was at peace for the first time in more than half a century.

THE ADVISORY EFFORT

Consistency in Advisor Pairing: "La Familia"

Of the U.S. advisors interviewed, six had served in both El Salvador and Colombia, even though the two conflicts were separated by more than a decade.[41] They brought considerable lessons from El Salvador, such as morphing the Operational Planning and Assistance Training Team concept to fit the conflict in Colombia, renaming it the Planning Assistance Training Team (PATT).[42] Such consistent regional relationships resulted in many Special Forces leaders referring to the SOUTHCOM-focused 7th Group as "La Familia" (the family). They saw working in Latin America as a family business with their host-nation partners as extended family members.[43]

Despite their regional experience, advisors were matched to the same units only moderately consistently. Before 7th Group began to deploy to Afghanistan, the sheer size of the U.S. commitment in Colombia meant that SF advisors had to work with many different host-nation units. While there was always an SF presence with Colombian SOF units, Green Berets also worked with regular Army forces, police, and even pipeline security forces. Working with SOF elements was seen as the best mission by far, while working with infrastructure security forces was often viewed as drudgery. Because of that vast disparity in perceived quality of assignment, some of the Group's commanders purposely rotated their forces through different host-nation units to more fairly allocate "good" and "bad" missions.[44]

Other commanders believed that consistency in advisor pairing was important in an immature relationship but over time became less vital. Having a habitual unit-to-unit relationship was valuable, noted one commander, but he believed that by 2008 nearly everyone in 7th Group knew who the BACOA were and their capabilities. He also believed that if a Colombian saw an SF shoulder patch and a red 7th Group beret flash, the advisor had instant credibility.[45] In essence, different leaders had conflicting priorities on the value of pairing the same advisors with the same host-nation units.[46]

As a result of the lack of command emphasis, to some advisors attaining consistency in advisor pairing seemed purely coincidental. With each new SF leader, Colombian units fell in and out of favor, impacting whether or not they paired with the same advisors. At least one officer noted policies seemed to change every two years, which, not coincidentally, matched the command tenure for group leaders. Such turnover, he observed, created "relationships built only by happenstance."[47]

The lack of consistency was noted by the Colombians, who pointed the issue out to U.S. embassy officials. The lack of consistency, the Colombians felt, manifested itself in redundant training, where newly assigned SF advisors repeated what the previously deployed advisors had already covered. General Alberto Mejía Ferrero—who would later become Colombia's Joint Special Operations Command (CCOPE) commander—told one U.S. officer in the MILGP, "I love your SF guys, but they always seem to teach the same thing. They pull out the same program-of-instruction folder they have done before, and off we go."[48] The lack of consistency also resulted in conflicting recommendations for equipment supplied as part of the military-assistance program. As different U.S. units rotated through, each provided a new list, often with completely different priorities that either ignored the previous list published only months earlier or even requested cancellation of previous decisions.[49]

After 7th Group began to deploy to Afghanistan in 2004, the ability to consistently pair advisors with the same Colombian SOF units became even more difficult.[50] There were simply not enough soldiers available to complete all the missions SF units had been tasked with performing, and some commanders saw the less-dangerous environment in Colombia as an opportunity to provide a break for their forces from the strains of combat in Afghanistan. One senior NCO felt leadership without previous regional experience was a liability; he recalled that on a particular rotation the two senior members of one ODA had never before deployed to SOUTHCOM and thus lacked perspective on the Colombia mission. He felt "Afghanistan and Iraq were distractions from what we were trying to accomplish in Central and South America."[51]

Those combat deployments, some of which focused on unilateral operations without a partner force, were diametrically opposite to the environment in Colombia, where teams were barred from combat, under the authority of the embassy, and paired with host-nation forces. At times, switching between the two distinct environments caused ODAs to forget the rules of the road and the cultural nuances of Latin America. Recognizing this phenomenon, one senior SF leader observed that, counterintuitively, when 7th Group had fewer advisors assigned to SOUTHCOM on deployments, there usually were more significant problems and scandals.[52] Deployments to Afghanistan also meant that when SF personnel were newly assigned to Colombia they did not know the important people there—the "key belly buttons" that needed to be touched to make things happen.[53] In Colombia the informal power dynamics often did not match formal positions, and the decrease in consistency caused each rotation to have to relearn who was crucial in making the mission function efficiently.

The demands of the Afghan theater also resulted in shorter deployments to Colombia, a reduction from six to three months, which further diluted consistency.[54] A 2014 USSOCOM study reported the dilemma thus: "Most team [ODA] members observed that three months afforded too little time for understanding the operational environment and building relationships with Colombian personnel."[55] Because of the pressures of Afghanistan and other military commitments, advisors noted that on average the same ODA would only return to the same host nation unit 25 to 50 percent of the time in a two-year period.[56]

While maintaining consistency at the organizational level was challenging, on numerous occasions soldiers from 7th Group had regular deployments to Colombia that over time resulted in deep personal connections with the host nation's military. Several advisors noted that across a twenty- or thirty-year military career they partnered with many Colombian officers who, like them, had been junior officers or NCOs at the beginning of the relationship but by the time of their retirement had gone on to become some of the most senior leaders in the Colombian military. Command Sgt. Maj. Amil Alvarez had dozens of deployments to Colombia and became command sergeant major for both 7th Special Forces Group and SOCSOUTH. "Some Colombians you met in the 1990s later became general officers," he said, "and even if you didn't see them for a couple of years due to Iraq and Afghanistan, you still had a relationship."[57]

One junior officer advised BACOA as it was created and became friendly with many of the unit's officers. A decade later one of the platoon leaders had become the BACOA battalion commander and recognized the 7th SF Group officer when he returned as a more senior advisor.[58] Another more senior SF officer who served three tours in Colombia noted that because he had worked as a captain with the Colombian forces in the 1990s, by the 2010s he had personal relationships with all the senior leaders of the Colombian military, including the commander of the Armed Forces.[59] Perhaps the best example of such sustained interaction is of Brig. Gen. Sean Mulholland, who attended Lancero school as a captain and was the honor graduate. In the 1990s he returned as the U.S. exchange officer at Lancero school, living in Colombia for two years. He led 7th Group at all levels, including as its commander, and later headed SOCSOUTH. His decades of experience and extensive personal connections in Colombia helped him in his duties, especially in the stand-up of AGLAN.[60]

Recognizing the importance of consistency and the challenges deployments to Afghanistan created toward maintaining it, several innovative leaders implemented policies to improve stability. In 2008 then-colonel Sean Mulholland was 7th Group's commander; he helped establish a system wherein officers and NCOs assigned to the one-year unaccompanied PATT mission in Colombia would receive credit for serving at the U.S. Army John F. Kennedy Special Warfare Center and School. Such an arrangement was highly lucrative to SF personnel, as it would allow them to stay on an operational deployment but also get credit for a schoolhouse training assignment, an important requirement for promotion. It would also allow their families to remain at Eglin Air Force Base, home of 7th Group, rather than having to uproot them and move to Fort Bragg, where the Special Warfare Center was based.[61]

Other advisors leveraged technology to offset some of the lack of consistency, using the communications program WhatsApp to make free text, voice, and video calls to their Colombian partners between rotations. Through the app, advisors stayed connected with the personal and professional lives of Colombian SOF NCOs and officers, albeit virtually.[62]

While there was significant turbulence on the U.S. side of the advisory effort in maintaining consistent pairing, there was considerable stability on the Colombian side. Unlike the U.S. experience in El Salvador, Colombian SOF personnel—especially those in BACOA and AGLAN—spent long careers in their parent unit. One RAND study shows that nearly 70 percent of Colombian SOF personnel were career soldiers.[63] Because the Colombian Army and Joint SOF headquarters were organized almost in tandem with the creation of the two units, their soldiers usually did not transfer to other Colombian units and were able to stay within the broader SOF organization without negatively impacting their careers. There was so much personnel stability within the units that the Colombian soldiers would often tell their departing U.S. advisors, "See you in six months."[64]

Assessment: "Operating at the Speed of Trust"

Even though there were challenges with ensuring consistency in advisor pairing, there was a consensus as to its importance. Command Sgt. Maj. Amil Alvarez called it "absolutely critical." He said, "If you were worried about the long-term impact you had, consistency in pairing matters."[65] General Carlos Ospina Ovalle, who served as the commander of the Colombian Armed Forces, took a pragmatic view: "Consistency is very important but not always possible.... I knew that there was great appreciation from the Colombians to the advisors and that some of them were especially trusted because they had deployed several times to Colombia."[66]

Interviewees pointed out that consistency was important because the most significant tactical growth occurred after long and extended contact, which was essential to building the trust necessary to asking difficult questions or accompany host-nation forces on sensitive operations. In the absence of consistency, U.S. advisors were perceived as temporary help by the Colombians.[67] Personal relationships that developed from consistency were seen as critical because those connections made it easier to get things done when bureaucracy intervened. Strong relationships allowed advisors to "operate at the speed of trust."[68] In addition, the knowledge and familiarity that came from having worked with the same host-nation forces minimized or precluded the requirement for a pre-deployment site survey, saving taxpayer funds. Experience would "jump-start" a mission, allowing advisors to pick up where they had left off and produce better results than had they started from scratch.[69] When the same 7th SFG teams worked with AGLAN across multiple rotations, one U.S. advisor concluded that planning had been easier because they already knew the unit they were working with, knew the people in it, and knew what training would be required to advance their capabilities.[70]

Advisor Language Training and Cultural Awareness

As with the advisory missions in the Philippines and El Salvador, there was a complete match for the regional orientation of the SF Groups assigned to Colombia, resulting in a high rating. The Latin America–oriented 7th Special Forces Group essentially had a monopoly on the mission.[71] While the demands of the post-9/11 wars drew 7th

Group to Afghanistan, at no time was the organization's regional affiliation changed. Before the terrorist attacks of 2001, nearly all the Group's units spoke Spanish, even though a few individuals and detachments were trained in Brazilian-Portuguese. As the war in Afghanistan dragged on, some individuals were trained in Dari and Pashto, but the Group maintained its regional affiliation and linguistic focus.

Early in the mission emphasis was placed on making sure that advisors were proficient in Spanish. "At the beginning of the Colombian mission, if you weren't a skilled Spanish linguist your value to the team was diminished.... There was a tremendous amount of pressure on the ODAs to maintain and improve their language because the most challenging missions in the 7th SFG most often went to teams with strong language skills."[72] Any SF soldier scoring below a 1/1 on the Defense Language Proficiency Test faced disciplinary action in the form of counseling statements, prohibition from attending advanced-skills training, or worse and was often forced to spend their free time conducting remedial training in Spanish.[73] Money did not exist to pay for interpreters, so some teams hired local tutors to help train their nonnative speakers. Like in El Salvador, it was common for ODAs deploying to the Colombia mission to give their premission briefings to their chain of command in Spanish. To improve their language skills some 7th Group organizations even spent the entire month before deployment conversing in Spanish for all military duties.[74]

Assessment: "You Have to Have the Language to Communicate"

Advisors described the importance of language training and cultural awareness in a variety of ways. They reiterated the point, made in other cases studied in this book, that language is part of friendship and is a critical component to building trust. "Spanish was really important to building rapport. Even knowing some slang could help get a team in the door in tough times."[75] Some advisors argued ODAs that did not focus on language or culture were not as effective, and SEAL (sea, air, and land) units, because of their poor linguistic skills, did not seem to be received as well or have as much of an impact as SF ODAs.[76] Others posited, "If you don't understand the host-nation history and culture, you could create an international incident.... You need to know both the national culture and subcultures."[77] General Carlos Ospina Ovalle, commander of the Colombian Armed Forces, agreed: "I think that the combination of language and culture is very important to advise troops in a foreign country.... Many of them [advisors] were sons of immigrants, and that is very helpful—what they call 'second generation'—because they were aware of the difficulties they would have to face."[78] Another advisor noted, "If you're really trying to build capacity or work with partners . . . you have to have the language to communicate and to pick up all the nuances, whether they are social or cultural. You cannot do that through an interpreter."[79]

Some argued that because the Colombian military's skills had grown so advanced, language training and cultural awareness became even more important for U.S. advisors. "Language skills are paramount to building a combat-effective partner force. At the tactical level they have value but are not essential. But once you get into the operational and strategic levels of advice for a partner like Colombia, where they have made the jump and are doing tactical [operations] in their sleep, language becomes more and more important. Understanding logistics, building SOF institutions, [and] building intelligence-sharing processes across the host-nation interagency—all of those require precise language skills and cultural understanding."[80]

At the same time, a decline in the capability of 7th Group Spanish speakers provides reason to question the general importance of language skills. Even though advisors stressed the importance of language skills, if those same advisors deployed with less-than-proficient Spanish skills then perhaps other factors were at play in the creation of combat-effective Colombian SOF elements. Quantitative and qualitative data show a drop in language skills across 7th Group's decade of deployments to Central Asia, which likely made it difficult to find time to practice Spanish.

This degradation in language and cultural skills was noted by officers within the SF regiment and by embassy personnel. Some noted that by 2006 the deployments to Afghanistan had resulted in powerful command emphasis for some 7th Group soldiers to learn Central Asian languages, to include Pashtu, Uzbek, and Urdu, even though the Group was still regionally oriented to Latin America. Others noted that some of the new soldiers arriving from the SF training pipeline spoke Central Asian languages rather than Spanish.[81] In 2016 the 7th Group command sergeant major was shocked to learn that the organization had been assigned a battalion commander and battalion command sergeant major who had never deployed to Latin America but had been to Iraq and Afghanistan numerous times.[82]

Embassy personnel provided an even grimmer perspective on the language skills of 7th Group. While the Spanish of some SF operators was phenomenal, owing to the fact that they were native speakers, others had limited to no skills.[83] One MILGP officer observed that in the 2006 time frame some ODAs had only a few soldiers who could speak Spanish effectively. In one particularly striking vignette a 7th SFG team sergeant—the senior NCO on the ODA—was evaluating a group of Colombian SOF leaders as they conducted mission planning. The U.S.

embassy official asked him how he thought the Colombians had performed, and he responded that he didn't know because he didn't speak Spanish. That team sergeant had spent most of his career in 3rd Special Forces Group, where French was the target language because of the unit's focus on Africa.[84] Such assignments were not uncommon as individuals crossed between Groups to follow mentors or fill key leadership positions important for promotion.

A 2014 SOCOM report noted that most SF personnel deploying to Colombia were able to score a 1/1 on the DLPT, the minimum level necessary to deploy to the USSOUTHCOM area of responsibility, but few had higher levels of proficiency.[85] Although the requirement to graduate the training pipeline and become a qualified Special Forces operator was generally 1/1,[86] at times that standard was waived to a 0+/0+ level in order to provide teams sufficient personnel to deploy to Afghanistan.[87] Several officers interviewed noted that even the 1/1 score was insufficient to be an effective advisor. Criticizing such approaches, one advisor reasoned, "True cultural awareness requires sustained study and academic rigor, something that comes from a graduate-level education in regional studies or at least four months of immersion in-country."[88]

Back-to-back deployments to Afghanistan not only degraded Spanish-language skills but also had implications for cultural awareness. When 7th Group had been entirely focused on Latin America, its members understood the cultural nuances of the environment and how to advise even when they were barred from combat. Over time continuous combat deployments redirected some of the Group's teams toward focusing on leading during combat operations and not advising.[89] Switching from a mindset of guiding partnered combat operations to a mentality of an advisor invited by the host nation and unable to lead their partners in battle was challenging and affected rapport.[90] "Early on we did everything for the Afghans. They didn't even have uniforms or equipment. We would direct them and lead them everywhere. Then we would deploy to Colombia with its well-established and experienced military and SOF commands, and there was little need for an E-7 [sergeant first class] to advise a colonel or a general in counterguerrilla tactics."[91]

Echoing comments made by El Salvador advisors about the importance of personality in building rapport, several advisors in Colombia noted that language skills and cultural awareness were only two pieces of the puzzle. "If it was just about language training and a little bit of culture you could take twenty-five Hispanic drill sergeants from Fort Benning and give them two days of classes and deploy them. They [the U.S. Army] tried to do that, multiple times, and it was an unmitigated disaster."[92]

Another SF advisor who later served as a foreign-area officer noted the quirkiness of the relationship between language and good advising. In some cases Puerto Rican officers and NCOs who were native Spanish speakers were fired and sent back to the United States while others from West Virginia who struggled to achieve a 2/2 on the DLPT and spoke Spanish with a thick Southern accent were highly successful. In those instances personality mattered more than language skills and having the right character traits and temperament were critical. Language helped, but an advisor had to be able to gain trust and provide value through training, advising, and delivering what they had promised.[93] Humility, respect, honesty, professionalism, and interpersonal-relations skills seemed to matter as much as language skills.

Partner-to-Advisor Ratio: Making the Best of It

The Colombian component of the equation to calculate the partner-to-advisor ratio is relatively straightforward. The BACOA battalion was composed of a headquarters company, two line companies, and one reconnaissance company of scouts and snipers—altogether approximately three hundred Commandos.[94] AGLAN was a battalion-sized element made up of five fifty-man companies, for a total of 250 Lanceros.[95] Like other SOF elements partnered with U.S. forces in the post-9/11 era, both the BACOA and AGLAN units adopted a red/amber/green cycle with one-third of the unit conducting combat operations, one-third conducting training, and one-third on leave.[96] This put the number of BACOA soldiers being actively advised closer to two hundred Commandos and the number of AGLAN soldiers closer to 170.[97] There was no evidence of "ghost soldiers" or other corruption endemic to nearly all the other case studies, and desertions were simply unheard of in either unit. Casualties and retirements were replaced almost immediately, especially in AGLAN, which used the preexisting Lancero school to screen for new candidates. As a result of these factors both units' strengths wavered little.

By contrast the size of the advising force varied considerably, and while advising BACOA and AGLAN was exclusively the domain of Special Forces, they were only a small portion of the overall advisory effort in Colombia. During its rotations in 2002 and 2003, 7th Special Forces Group dedicated two companies supported by a battalion headquarters and staff, equating to ten ODAs and approximately one hundred advisors.[98] Of that element, one full-strength ODA was committed to the stand-up of BACOA and later to the creation of AGLAN, each of which lasted six months.[99] After the initial training of AGLAN and BACOA was concluded, only fifteen advisors were directly involved in training Colombian SOF elements.[100]

When 7th Group was assigned shared responsibility for the SOF mission in Afghanistan, the unit's commitment to Colombia dropped precipitously. As it became clear that the mission in Afghanistan would require two battalions from 7th Group for each rotation, SOCSOUTH pressured the Group leadership to continue to commit a battalion to Colombia to assist in the effort to rescue the American hostages. After being briefed on the location of every deployed ODA, the SOCSOUTH commander acknowledged that the Group did not have the ability to meet the request. Thus for the span of 2004 only a single advanced operational base remained with seven ODAs.[101] Despite the overall reduction in advisors, because of the importance that U.S. commanders put on maintaining relationships with AGLAN and BACOA, an ODA was assigned to each of those elite units, resulting in a net increase in the number of their advisors.[102] Reflecting on the troop-number constraints, then–brigadier general Charles Cleveland, SOCSOUTH commander, later commented, "We were the economy-of-force theater; you made your case, took what was given, and made the best of it."[103]

In 2005 the troop commitment was again cleaved in half, to only three ODAs. Of those, one ODA was dedicated to Colombian SOF elements, one trained national-police units, and one worked with the conventional Army.[104] Rather than completely abandon the partnerships that they had forged, SF leaders assigned split teams (half ODAs) to work with BACOA and AGLAN.[105] Group-level guidance focused on "keeping the lights on" to maintain a long-term relationship with Colombian SOF.[106] At perhaps the lowest advisory point, the summer 2006 rotation had three advisors each with AGLAN and BACOA before 7th Group was again able to pair split ODAs with the units.[107]

As U.S. forces began to draw down in Afghanistan, more SF teams became available for the mission in Colombia. By 2013 the 7th Group presence had notched up to four and a half ODAs conducting a variety of missions.[108] Approximately one detachment (ODA) and a half (eighteen troops) were paired with the Colombian Joint Task Force Omega interagency headquarters as it planned the FARC HVT mission. AGLAN and BACOA were considered important enough to each warrant a consistent partnership with an ODA, which 7th Group classified as a "persistent presence."[109] Little change occurred until 2016, when the Colombian government and the FARC agreed to end the conflict.

In addition to these cyclical advisors, USSOCOM sent several advisors to Colombia on permanent-change-of-station orders, which allowed them to live in Colombia with their families for two to three years. Of the units studied in this case, BACOA was authorized an exchange officer while the Lancero school—the training pipeline for AGLAN—was authorized one NCO.[110] In addition, each key division—including Colombian SOF headquarters—had a four-person PATT[111] embedded within it, which was supposed to be led by a major but often was led by a captain as Colombia was lower in priority than Iraq and Afghanistan.[112] Because these more-permanent advisors worked directly with AGLAN and BACOA, a net total of six personnel was added to the monthly total: four for the PATT and two for the exchange officers.

Assessment

Please see appendix C for the partner-to-advisor calculations and figure 3.1 in this chapter for the monthly results. At 17.5 to 1, the overall partner-force-to-advisor ratio in Colombia far exceeded the doctrinal ratio.[113] In terms of the anecdotal impact of that ratio, there was general agreement that the number of advisors working with host-nation forces was at the appropriate level. Some advisors felt it made sense to have more advisors present when host-nation units were first being stood up but that over time as the units gained capabilities and skills fewer advisors were needed.[114] Such an observation could also be related to the fact that after the first few years of advisory work, in both AGLAN and BACOA, Colombian leaders began to assign their own instructors to conduct training when advisors were not present. Other advisors, however, posited that rapport was damaged by the rapid and significant decrease in advisors that occurred as 7th Group teams were diverted to the conflict in Afghanistan.[115]

Advisor Ability to Organize Host-Nation Unit: "Acompañado"

Most advisors were particularly pleased with how accommodating the Colombians were to U.S. recommendations. One simply noted, "Colombians were great partners: they appreciated the United States, were very forgiving, and were easy to work with."[116] Some speculated that their receptiveness was because the Colombians were enamored of the U.S. military and respected the United States as a country. Others described the Colombian desire to emulate SF advisors and follow their advice almost in the way that a younger brother looked up to an older sibling. Advisors noted that Colombians often looked to the United States for affirmation even when they knew what they wanted to do and understood that it was the right choice. This Colombian desire for American approval was described by some advisors as *acompañado*, which literally translates as "accompanied" but more accurately describes a yearning to stand shoulder to shoulder in partnership with their U.S.

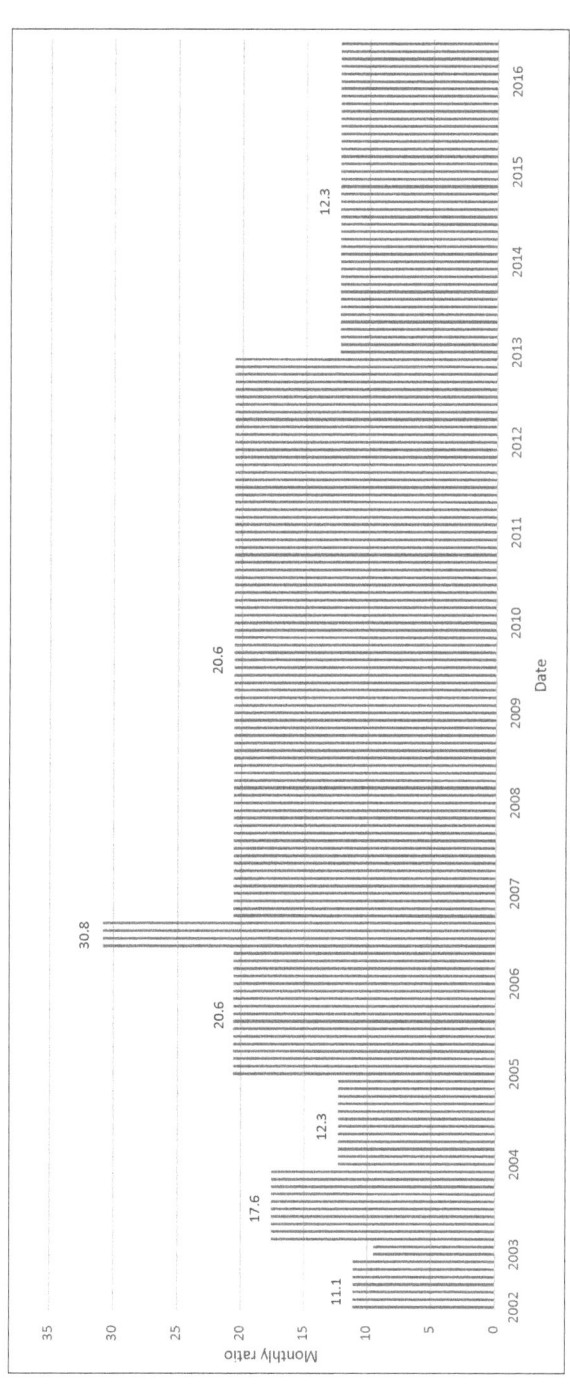

FIGURE 3.1 Monthly ratio of partners to advisors, Colombia

friends.[117] This desire to please was so strong that one U.S. advisor described the Colombians as "receptive to a fault."[118] Another posited that the Colombians "would never do anything to damage the U.S.-Colombian relationship, even if it meant tolerating bad American actors."[119] One journalist who served as an advisor to the U.S. MILGP simply described them as "the dream allies."[120]

In practice, a desire to please their partners and friends translated into the Colombians often going out of their way to accommodate American requests. One advisor noted that during the selection process for BACOA commandos if he told the Colombian commander that someone was not a good candidate, the soldier would be removed from the unit without debate.[121] Several commented that the Colombians were much more willing to accept U.S. tactical recommendations than were Afghans. Colombians were also particularly adept at recognizing how U.S. ideas could be adopted and then adapted, or "Colombianized," to match the conditions in their country.[122]

Perhaps one of the best examples of Colombian willingness to adopt American ideas was the creation of the various SOF headquarters. Like their mentors, the Colombians stood up not just an element to lead the Army Special Operations component (Comando de Operaciones Especiales del Ejército, or Colombian Army Special Operations Command) but also a joint force command (Comando Conjunto de Operaciones Especiales, or Joint Special Operations Command) designed to command special-operations forces in combat as well as provide for their institutional needs by organizing, training, and equipping them.[123] First commanded by a colonel, the headquarters was later led by a one-star general and then a two-star general, which put it on even footing with Colombian conventional regional commands. In another parallel with the United States, by 2019 the Colombian military had also created a special forces branch for its officers and special skill identifiers for its NCOs.[124]

These elements were created mainly because, like in the American experience, after the various Colombian SOF elements were formed they were misused by conventional Colombian officers.[125] Colombia's national counterterrorism force was routinely tasked with performing personal-security-detachment missions for Colombian civilian and military VIPs and was even ordered to perform static defense guarding airfields.[126] BACOA and AGLAN initially experienced similar mismanagement as they were repeatedly railroaded by conventional commanders and given inappropriate missions.[127]

Another reason for the creation of the SOF headquarters was that Colombia had been divided into different military zones, each commanded by a two-star general.

Those regional commanders had considerable power and were reluctant to cede control of units that operated within their battlespace.[128] Such a construct made it difficult to flow forces from one region to another as the FARC or other enemy forces moved seamlessly between regional commands. The various SOF commands helped address this challenge by giving national leaders forces that could quickly deploy anywhere in the country and match the flexibility of their opponents.[129]

There is some dispute as to whether the United States convinced the Colombians to form their own SOF headquarters or the Colombians recognized the challenges they were experiencing and decided to do it on their own. Most involved in the process noted that there was a two-way communication on the stand-up of the organizations, and at least one U.S. officer described the process as "pushing on an open door," in that the Colombians did not require any convincing and immediately took to implementing the idea.[130] On the Colombian side, Generals Alberto Jose Mejia Ferrero and Carlos Ospina Ovalle were both particularly committed to the creation of new SOF units and headquarters. Others argued that it was more U.S.-driven and based on a desire to remake Colombian SOF forces in the U.S. image to prevent the mistakes of the pre-SOCOM area where SOF was misused and underfunded.[131] Either way, it represents a significant divergence from the other cases wherein U.S. efforts to create domestic SOF headquarters were poorly supported by host-nation forces.

Most advisors believed that the long military partnership greatly helped them influence Colombian decisions. The nearly continuous SOF presence, which began in the 1960s, built a deep reservoir of trust, connections, and friendships. While U.S. presence was not always robust, it was consistent and became the foundation upon which later success was built.[132] An integral part of that connection was sending SF NCOs and officers to Lancero school, which was a de facto requirement to become a senior leader in the Colombian military, and 7th Special Forces Group went to great pains to ensure their Lancero graduates always returned to work in Colombia. One such graduate observed, "I went to Lancero school to better understand the Colombians and how their military works, and it gave me instant credibility with them.... Because of the course, whatever I said was gold [and] I could do no wrong as soon as they found out that I had attended the Lancero course."[133]

Another factor that affected Colombian willingness to accept U.S. suggestions was combat experience, which in Colombia provided intense credibility. Until 2004 American advisors were at a disadvantage because few had been in combat. Once 7th Group was assigned Afghanistan as its primary focus, that calculus changed quickly, and many Colombians wanted to mirror U.S. capabilities and become part of the U.S. global SOF network.[134] U.S. skill conducting kill/capture missions of high-value targets were particularly admired, and many Colombians wanted to learn them, considering those capabilities relevant for dismantling the FARC. As was noted by General Carlos Ospina Ovalle, "the experience in Iraq and Afghanistan . . . provided both parties with common language and a common mentality of soldiers battling against terrorists and terrorism. In the same way, combat experience brought together two very distant worlds. . . . Firefights, ambushes, and close combat in the Colombian jungles can be compared with the situation in Iraq and Afghanistan and is part of that common language."[135]

Despite the extremely positive relations, there were limits to what Colombians would accept from their U.S. advisors. When Colombians felt that a request was not in their best interest or not well thought-out, they would respectfully decline to implement it. Simply put, while the Colombians generally loved and respected their U.S. partners, they were not going to make a bad decision for the sake of friendship. This led more than a few advisors to conclude that most successes in Colombia were due to the Colombians themselves, especially their knowing when to say no to the U.S. advisors.[136] One went as far as concluding that the United States was "relatively successful, often quite in spite of ourselves," because "a superb Colombian senior team not only understood its war better than we did but also understood how best we could fit in."[137] Another commented of the Colombians, "In some ways, they put up with U.S. advisors who weren't qualified to do the job."[138]

There were numerous such anecdotes. Early in the advisory effort a set of American contractors believed that providing rubber boots would help the Colombians better move about in the rainy season when rivers swelled and roads became nearly impassable. But the Colombians didn't need the boots, and even though they accepted them to appease the Americans, they never took the boots on missions.[139] When initially building BACOA, a set of military advisors had called for the Colombians to have psychological-operations loudspeaker teams, high-mobility multipurpose wheeled vehicles that could be sling loaded by helicopters, and Carl Gustaf recoilless rifles so that they would be equipped like a U.S. Army Ranger unit in a classic case of mirror imaging. Rather than tell the U.S. advisors no, the Colombians accepted the assistance but set the loudspeakers up around their base as a public-address system and left the sling-load equipment and recoilless rifles in storage.[140]

Similar disconnects occurred at the operational level. In the early days of Plan Colombia, the SOUTHCOM director of operations, J-3, was livid because the Colombian Army would not focus its main effort on Putamayo, where plantations of coca were located. He was particularly incensed because he felt the Colombians had walked back on an agreement. But his anger was unjustified because he failed to appreciate which officer had the authority to make the decision. Even though Colombian politicians and senior generals had agreed to the U.S. focus (likely to placate them), a more-junior general had command of the units that would be involved and simply ignored the request.[141] Other advisors noted that some senior U.S. leaders neither appreciated nor understood General Carlos Ospina Ovalle's strategy, but he was clear and unwavering in his objectives—which proved to be key to successfully winning the war against the FARC.[142]

Overall the relationship "was much more an arrangement of equals."[143] The Colombians were very willing to push back on U.S. desires, frequently telling them, "That's not something we are going to do." But the Colombians were also willing to accept U.S. ideas and recommendations when they realized that the concepts were sound and advantageous to their situation. Furthermore they rarely let national pride or sovereignty impede what could help them in the fight against the FARC even if it meant accepting an idea that was not the most beneficial to them at a personal level.

Assessment

During the advisory effort that exceeded a decade, there was not any significant shift in Colombian willingness to accept recommendations from their U.S. advisors. The "sovereignty clock" so prevalent in other cases never even started ticking. Why this happened is not clear but is likely related to the warm long-term relations that have existed between the two countries.

There is little doubt that the advisory effort had considerable impact, especially on the creation of Colombian SOF. The development of those organizations was far deeper and broader than the special-operations forces created in all the other cases examined in this book. The Colombians wholeheartedly embraced creating an SOF enterprise and stood up not only units but also headquarters designed to lead them in combat and to care for their institutional needs. The creation of Colombian SOF was so complete and matching U.S. recommendations that several advisors noted Colombia lacked only the legislative equivalent of the Nunn-Cohen Amendment to the Goldwater Nichols Defense Reorganization Act, which in 1987 had provided a dedicated funding stream to U.S. Special Operations Forces.[144]

With this in mind, it would not be an exaggeration to say that the United States changed the very culture of the Colombian military. Indeed, General Carlos Ospina Ovalle observed, "I think the most important contribution was the transfer of military culture. The way American soldiers understand their duty, the way they understand what is to be a true professional, the way they handle difficult human-rights situations in the field, as well as their discipline were important practical lessons for their Colombian counterparts."[145] Without question, in Colombia the advisor ability to organize host-nation forces was high.

Combat Advising

Considerable restrictions were put on SF advisors in Colombia, and as in El Salvador, advisors were explicitly barred from engaging in combat. At various times, however, changes to the rules of engagement allowed SF personnel to get closer to the fighting and even assist in reconnaissance missions. But the prohibition on combat advising was explicit and invariable. Unlike in El Salvador, technology had developed sufficiently that advisors to Colombian SOF were rarely out of contact with their headquarters or the embassy and it was impossible for them to skirt the rules as had been done back in the 1980s. Ubiquitous mobile phones with cameras and twenty-four-hour media embedded with Colombian military units and FARC guerrillas changed the environment such that any violation of the rules was likely to be quickly discovered and punished.

Before the FARC capture of U.S. contractors in 2003, rules restricting what SF advisors could and could not do were even more stringent than in El Salvador. In many cases advisors could not leave the base of their Colombian partners and were not allowed to accompany them if they moved forward to plan an operation.[146] Advisors were required to use an armored vehicle to transit from domicile to duty because the FARC realized their impact and hoped that killing, wounding, or capturing one would create enough political drama to lead to at least a partial U.S. withdrawal.[147] Embassy officials even prohibited U.S. forces from returning fire if they inadvertently came in contact.[148] For example, in February 2003 a Special Forces ODA that was partnered with a Colombian police unit monitored the distress call from the U.S. contractor aircraft as it went down; they were not allowed to respond even though their partners were less than thirty minutes' flight time from the crash site.[149]

After the capture of the U.S. contractors, the rules of engagement became a point of intense frustration and dispute. SF leaders tried desperately to convince the embassy and Department of Defense to permit advisors to go forward with Colombian units in limited numbers and under certain constraints. Working with embassy personnel, SF advisors reviewed threat assessments to gain preapproval for potential areas where they could deploy to a forward operating base with their partners.[150] When such approval was given, advisors could then accompany Colombians to the staging area as they moved forward.[151] Some recalled that midlevel leaders, such as the SF company commander and sergeant major, could go forward with their partnered Colombian commander and the command-and-control element, effectively shadowing where he went.[152]

In June 2005 the authorities expanded slightly during Operation Willing Spirit, allowing U.S. SOF elements to conduct sensitive site exploitation (SSE) of recently captured FARC camps while paired with Colombian SOF.[153] Although such operations only occurred after combat had ended, they were a significant change as they allowed U.S. forces to enter FARC-controlled territory—a risky proposition. Over the next year, U.S. SF leaders obtained approval to pair with Colombian SOF reconnaissance teams looking for the American hostages.[154] At first the authority was limited to three U.S. soldiers per mission but was later expanded to a full ODA.[155] Still, even at its apogee of June 2008, when recovery of the hostages appeared imminent, the number of advisors allowed to accompany Colombians forward only reached thirty-three personnel.[156] Even then U.S. forces were still barred from combat, and some interpretations held that they had to remain at the last covered and concealed location.[157]

As soon as the hostages were freed the expanded authorities evaporated quickly. By the end of 2008 restrictions were again so tight that advisors were generally not permitted to leave the installation where their host-nation partner was based. If they wanted to move with their partners to a different location, either for operational or training purposes, they had to put together a request in the form of a concept of the operation (CONOP) for embassy approval.[158] Even then the rules held that advisors could not accompany the Colombians tactically. Instead advisors travelled to the town closest to where the operation would be conducted and stayed in a hotel where they could assist with final mission preparations but go no further forward.[159]

Several interviewees noted that at times the rules—or the interpretation of the rules—changed depending on personalities in the embassy, leadership at SOC-SOUTH, or even the Colombians themselves. Some leaders were more willing to accept risk than others, and if either the senior SF officer in Colombia or the MILGP commander had good relations with the U.S. ambassador or the Colombians, it was possible that certain restrictions would be made less onerous.[160] Like in El Salvador, but to a lesser degree, at times the nature of the conflict put SF soldiers in contact with enemy forces regardless of the rules of engagement. Explaining why he had engaged in combat despite the prohibitions, one advisor quipped, "I'm coming home alive."[161]

Advisors often struggled with the contrast in rules between Afghanistan and Colombia. Transitioning from the intense combat of Afghanistan to strict rules of engagement was challenging, and some ODAs failed dramatically and were ordered to leave. In Colombia advisors had to be comfortable negotiating with both the Colombians and the embassy about what they could do, an environment entirely different from Afghanistan.[162] Altogether combat advising rates as low for SF operations in Colombia.

Assessment: "Good Luck on Your Mission"

Advisors provided mixed opinions on the impacts of limitations to combat advise host-nation forces. A slight majority vociferously argued that not being able to combat advise impeded their ability to make progress with Colombian SOF elements. "We're only using 20 percent of our capabilities under the current rules of engagement," offered one SF officer.[163] A slightly smaller group noted that restrictions on participating in combat were simply inviolable and might have provided some advantages but there was no way to tell for certain.

Most important among those who argued that the limitations hurt their effectiveness was the sense that U.S. advisors would lose credibility and damage rapport if they were not subject to the same dangers as their Colombian partners. One senior advisor noted, "When you pat them on the back and say good luck [on your mission], you lose credibility. If you don't share the same risks they do, you can't really build rapport."[164] Others perceived that it became a friction point when advisors could not accompany their partners. "Because we are not in the field, the Colombians think that they know better than us," remarked one senior MILGP officer.[165]

Not being able to accompany the Colombians on operations also limited an advisor's ability to observe and critique their partner's performance when it mattered most. Command Sgt. Maj. Chris Zets served as 7th Group's command sergeant major and had numerous deployments to Colombia. He felt seeing the partner troops in action was critical for evaluating their ability: "As soon as you send people out the gate and they leave, you have no idea whether they're doing what you told them to do or not. You have no idea whether they're using fire discipline, and you have no idea whether they're following any kind of human-rights considerations. The way you do that is by presence."[166] Not being able to accompany partners often meant what actually happened was lost in translation due to cultural differences between how Colombians would describe events or was impeded by language skills insufficient to understanding the technical details and jargon in a report.

Those who argued to the contrary often emphasized that the political realities in Colombia and the United States would never have permitted combat advising. Colombia was a sovereign country, and the United States was not at war with Colombia or with the FARC. Because of that, they said, while combat advising was important, there should still be limits on what U.S. forces could do. The fight was Colombia's, and U.S. soldiers should not be first through the door in battle.[167] Echoing this sentiment, another advisor noted that if the host nation only fights because the United States is there next to them in combat—like in Afghanistan—then combat advising is actually counterproductive.[168] One senior MILGP officer went so far as to argue, "one reason that we are successful is that we are not involved in combat."[169]

EVALUATING COMBAT EFFECTIVENESS

BACOA and AGLAN played an integral role in the Colombian campaign to kill or capture FARC high-value targets, and nearly all observers rated them as being true special-operations forces—not just elite infantry.

Night Fighting: "Night Freefall Combat Operations"

As in the Philippines, the terrain in Colombia impacted night fighting. Triple-canopy jungle made U.S.-style operations reliant on night-vision goggles nearly impossible because of the lack of ambient light on the jungle floor.[170] One advisor noted that some conventional Colombian units chose to stop moving at sunset and build fires rather than try to maneuver in such inhospitable terrain.[171] But nearly every advisor noted that Colombian SOF units had much stronger night-fighting skills and the jungle was only a hindrance for them during periods of darkness. With equipment, training, and will, those elements could move at night, even through dense jungle, but it was very deliberate with an average movement rate of around one kilometer per hour.[172]

In terrain that was not as restrictive, Colombian SOF elements performed superbly at night.[173] Some advisors noted that due to their culture of aggressiveness and machismo they were not afraid of taking risks and their night-fighting prowess rivaled the United States'.[174] Several recalled that the Colombians conducted multiple unilateral military freefall operations at night, using goggles and oxygen and performing their own jumpmaster safety inspections.[175] That alone was a capability out of reach of most NATO countries, with then–chief of staff of the Army Gen. Mark Milley observing that it was a skill set possessed by only six armies in the world.[176] On one such mission they landed at night on a very small landing zone in dangerous jungle terrain within eight hundred meters of the target. The unit set up hide sites and then shot and killed a renegade FARC commander in darkness and then successfully exfiltrated.[177] Colombian SOF had also developed—through U.S. advisory and financial assistance—a highly capable aviation unit comparable to the U.S. 160th Special Operations Aviation Regiment, capable of flying anywhere in the country at night under goggles to conduct infiltrations, exfiltrations, casualty evacuation, and logistics resupply.[178]

Assessment

Colombian SOF units, such as BACOA and AGLAN, had the proper equipment, skill, and willingness to perform night-combat operations in challenging terrain. They were supported by rotary wing assets and maintained other skills that gave them capabilities matched by few armies in the world. Without a doubt their night-fighting skills deserve a high rating.

Conducting Multiday Combat Operations: "They Are Tough and Hard"

Although the Colombian SOF headquarters did have a logistics battalion, most units relied on the conventional military logistics system.[179] Unlike many of the other case studies examined in this book, the logistics system in Colombia was developed and functional by 2003, at least in part through U.S. financial support and advisor assistance. One advisor noted that as BACOA and AGLAN were stood up, their soldiers first received basic items through the Colombian supply chain, such as boots, web gear, body armor, and other individual equipment. Only then did the United States provide SOF-specific equipment to those forces.[180] Not a single advisor offered observations of significant corruption within the Colombian logistics structure, an endemic factor in every other case study.

With that foundation, Colombian SOF units were consistently able to conduct multiday sustained-combat operations, often far in excess of seventy-two hours. Such feats were even more noteworthy given the challenges of the Colombian environment. Dense jungle labyrinths made ground resupply challenging, and even aerial resupply relied on finding an appropriate drop zone or landing zone. Because of those conditions, the Colombians frequently chose to pack as much ammunition and food as was humanly possible into their gear. Nearly every advisor praised the mental and physical toughness of the Colombians, who stoically conducted missions for up to thirty days.[181] During such missions, soldiers either lived off the land or simply did without proper nourishment. One advisor witnessed Colombian SOF troops deploying on ten-day special reconnaissance missions with only a foot-long brick of sugar to eat for the entire operation. Rather than rely on a precarious resupply system for water, the Colombians drank stream water without filtration or purification, something that would likely kill a U.S. soldier, if not make them incapacitated and mission ineffective.[182] Some technological advances did help, with dehydrated rations especially appreciated among AGLAN Lanceros.[183]

On dismounted missions, Colombian SOF units would often pack a pot and bags of rice and beans, which they would cook in a patrol base. Because it matched the way that local *campesinos*, or farmers, prepared their meals, the fire and cooking would not necessarily alert the FARC or other enemy forces to their presence. One advisor noted that if the mission went long, the Colombians simply made do with less food or even without food for days. "The Colombian military doesn't need much gear; they are tough and hard and more comfortable suffering and taking risks than American forces are."[184]

Colombian SOF elements routinely conducted combat resupply and casualty evacuation for units in contact and included logistics in mission planning. They performed these functions during night and day as well as during adverse weather conditions.[185] One advisor recalled a BACOA element conducting an air assault into the FARC autonomous zone in 2006 at night and then fighting for several days. During that time, the unit required a combat resupply of ammunition and conducted airmobile casualty evacuation at night under night-vision goggles while in contact. During other long missions, the unit conducted resupply via parachute, recovered caches emplaced specifically for the mission, or bundles kicked out of the side doors of helicopters.[186]

During Operation Willing Spirit, U.S. SF personnel were paired with their Colombian counterparts to conduct reconnaissance as part of the hostage-rescue effort. Those combined forces conducted operations for over a month—the longest U.S. patrol in hostile territory since the Vietnam War. The U.S. soldiers struggled with the physical challenges of the operation, losing an average of twenty-five pounds per person, resulting in the SOCSOUTH commander's dry observation that after the mission "We had a new appreciation for our Colombian counterparts."[187]

Assessment

There was nearly universal agreement that BACOA and AGLAN could consistently conduct combat operations for more than seventy-two hours. Many advisors marveled at the toughness and skill of the Colombian SOF units in conducting long combat missions, and some noted that their logistics skills were as good as those of U.S. forces.[188] Their institutional logistics system functioned well, and they could conduct resupply and casualty evacuation of units under fire. With such capabilities, assigning a high rating is easily warranted.

Fighting without Advisors

Because of the operational-level problem that the Colombians faced in their objective to decapitate the FARC leadership through relentless kill/capture missions, they were enthusiastic to learn the F3EAD cycle—find, fix, finish, exploit, analyze, and disseminate—used by U.S. SOF elements in Iraq and Afghanistan and adapt it to their needs. The Colombians proved excellent students, and there was near universal consensus that BACOA and AGLAN could consistently conduct intelligence-driven operations. Colombian SOF units developed organic first-world intelligence-gathering capabilities anchored by especially strong human intelligence with tradecraft skills learned from SF advisors.[189] Colombian signals- and imagery-intelligence capabilities were less developed but included UAVs (unmanned aerial vehicles) with full-motion video, aircraft with high-resolution ground radars, and various types of signals intelligence capable of intercepting and geolocating communications.[190]

SF advisors also trained BACOA and AGLAN in sensitive site exploitation, which the Colombians consistently used on missions. They were extremely proficient at battlefield interrogation and could conduct basic document exploitation on the objective.[191] While they did not have the same problems with corruption that the Philippines had with captured computers and cell phones being stolen, they did have similar challenges at not being able to exploit computers and other media in a timely manner because they lacked the resources to process them at their forward operating bases. Almost all electronic devices had to return to Bogotá to be analyzed, and as a result follow-on missions, rather than happening the same night, were likelier to be conducted two or three nights later.[192] Because many of the operations were in rural environments, such a delay did not dramatically affect the success rate of subsequent missions.

At the same time, there was agreement that those skills developed over time and as a direct result of U.S. military assistance.[193] During Operation Willing Spirit, the United States ran a fusion center in the embassy that shared copious amounts of intelligence with their Colombian partners.[194] The Colombians also generated a considerable amount of intelligence themselves: a typical scenario would begin with the Colombians getting indicators through their organic signals intelligence that a FARC leader was becoming a viable target. Colombian human intelligence would confirm the signals intelligence, and only then would the Colombians inform the U.S. Embassy Intelligence Fusion Center of their activities. From there, the United States would refocus its own intelligence capabilities on the target to help refine the intelligence picture for the Colombians.[195]

As the United States provided those resources, the Colombians worked to develop their own parallel domestic capability, and by 2010 they had constructed a system that rivaled the U.S. capability to conduct the F3EAD process. Central to that system was a Colombian fusion cell that linked Colombian SOF headquarters with Colombian police, intelligence, and conventional military elements. With analysts from across the country's intelligence communities operating under one roof, they built combined target lists of FARC leaders and often tasked resources collaboratively. Ironically, by that point the Colombian experience mirrored some of the same challenges the U.S. intelligence community had faced several years prior, when organizations had sometimes shared their proprietary intelligence based on the personalities of their principal leaders and their relationships with those in other organizations.[196]

Between 2009 and 2011 the Colombian ability to carry out intelligence-driven operations was so effective that it began to profoundly affect key FARC leaders. The FARC's existential threat to the state dissipated, and the dominant agency for domestic intelligence gathering and target prosecution shifted from the military to the police. As a functioning democracy no longer facing dire circumstances, the Colombian government wanted to return to the rule of law. Except in rare circumstances, the police were considered the only agency with the authority to arrest Colombian citizens, which led to an increase in interagency operations at the tactical level.[197] If the military wanted to kill a Colombian citizen, a judicial process had to be followed and civilian authorities had to approve the operation. Restrictions were also placed on military collection of domestic intelligence against fellow Colombians. Because of the importance of gathering evidence to support criminal trials against captured enemy leaders, the conduct of SSE changed to ensure that a proper chain of custody was maintained. In nearly all cases, the military began to have to hand over anything captured to police elements or have a police representative on the mission to collect it firsthand. It became illegal for the military to "crack" a confiscated cell phone to search it for other connections or intelligence. Such requirements slowed down the F3EAD cycle but were a critical component of returning to a state of normalcy.[198]

Chapter 3

Assessment

By 2016 BACOA and AGLAN could conduct intelligence-driven operations to a degree unrivaled among the other cases examined in this study. One interviewee noted that the processing of high-value FARC targets rivaled the pace set by U.S. national forces in Iraq and Afghanistan, killing or capturing senior and midlevel leaders so often that it became difficult for the insurgent group to replace them.[199] That degree of competence earns the Colombians a high rating for ability to fight without advisors present.

Performance against the Enemy in Combat: Bringing the FARC to Heel

Echoing a trend, there was widespread agreement that BACOA and AGLAN performed extremely well against the FARC, their principal enemy.[200] One U.S. officer commented, "The Colombians brought the FARC to heel and pushed them to the negotiating table mostly through their own efforts."[201] In addition, nearly every advisor admired the Colombian willingness to take risks, something they considered important for conducting successful special-operations missions. Several noted that many of the Colombian operations would not have been approved by U.S. SOF leaders, who are generally more risk averse.[202] Those advisors also relayed numerous anecdotes of Colombian SOF performance in battle, often in the conduct of true special-operations missions.

On one occasion, BACOA commandos received domestic intelligence revealing when and where a FARC commander would be moving a mere five days later. They planned and rehearsed quickly and then conducted a night air assault into a small helicopter landing zone. After walking across mountains for two days, they set up a surveillance and overwatch position and waited another two days. When the FARC HVT appeared on horseback on the fifth day, the sniper team engaged and killed him and his escorts at a range of one thousand meters, extremely impressive shots for any army. After searching the bodies, the commandos exfiltrated without taking casualties. A comparable mission profile resulted in disaster for U.S. special-operations forces in Afghanistan during Operation Red Wings.[203]

After the war, a former FARC guerrilla offered his personal recollections of being hunted by AGLAN and BACOA from 2004 to 2007, noting that the arrival of those counterguerrilla units on the battlefield shocked the FARC leadership with their discipline and skill. In particular, one AGLAN unit had infiltrated deep into FARC-held territory and remained undetected for a dozen days while waiting for their prey. When their targets did not arrive, the Lanceros exfiltrated without detection, leaving their hide sites as the only evidence they had been there. When those sites were found, it terrified the FARC because that territory had been a complete sanctuary for them from Colombian military units. "Nobody expected such a raid, [and] . . . the details left the bloc's commanders astonished."[204] Sometime later, twenty-six guerrilla leaders were conducting a reconnaissance to set up an ambush of a Colombian Marine unit, but unbeknownst to them the Colombian SOF leadership had been alerted to their movement and ordered an AGLAN counterambush. A dog accompanying the FARC leaders warned them just before they walked into the kill zone, and in the chaos the FARC sent several mobile companies to pursue the Lanceros, who escaped without any losses. Stunned by the fierceness of the government unit's fighting as it successfully extricated itself, the FARC leaders mistakenly estimated that the 38-man unit had been one made up of over 1,800 soldiers.[205]

In 2008 Colombian SOF succeeded in killing the FARC's second in command, Raúl Reyes, who had been hiding just across the border in Ecuador.[206] After detecting his location through an informant and confirming it through an intercepted satellite phone call, Colombian SOF elements had infiltrated covertly and placed beacons to assist in a precision-guided-munition airstrike. After the strike, those forces conducted a nighttime sensitive site exploitation to recover proof that they had killed Reyes. Intelligence gathered there was later described by the *Washington Post* as "the most valuable FARC intelligence find ever."[207]

Over time Colombian SOF systematically dismantled FARC leadership, and in 2011 they were successful in killing FARC supreme leader Alfonso Cano. He had long been a target of the HVT campaign, and considerable pressure had kept him on the run, eventually drawing him out of the mountainous Tolima Department into Valle del Cauca, where it was easier to find him. In November of that year Colombian intelligence located Cano, and Colombian SOF units briefly surrounded him before he was killed in a firefight.[208] Over the next year, the Colombian military killed nineteen senior FARC leaders and captured another through a combination of precision-guided munitions and SOF raids, and in 2013 they killed another thirteen and captured five.[209]

Operations continued even after the peace accords with the FARC because the organization had splintered when some elements that came to be known as organized armed groups (Grupos Armados Organizados, or GAOs) rejected the armistice and decided to keep fighting. In 2017 GAO fighters kidnapped five international kayakers, including two U.S. citizens. One of the kayakers was able to send a surreptitious note that he was being held, which triggered FBI and U.S. national-level military hostage-rescue elements to plan a rescue. But before those forces were able to deploy to Colombia, Colombian SOF commander General Luis Fernando Navarro Jiménez called and promised that his forces would resolve the crisis if the U.S. shared intelligence.[210] U.S. officials agreed, and Colombian SOF elements began planning and moved forward to the region. When an aircraft began circling over the GAO position, the leaders of the insurgent group panicked and chose to release the kayakers that same day rather than face a commando raid.[211]

In 2018 Colombian SOF elements targeted one of the GAO's most-senior leaders operating in an area that was both difficult to access and had challenging terrain. Domestic Colombian intelligence identified a route that the GAO leader would be using, and Colombian special operators hid in a swamp for nine days because it was the only area that provided concealment along the target's path. On the final day, the target appeared for a total of five minutes, and a sniper killed him with his first shot. They then successfully exfiltrated the area without taking casualties.[212]

Assessment

Colombian SOF units performed extremely well against the FARC, and over time they systematically disemboweled the organization's leadership. Conducting true special-operations missions, they killed and captured senior commanders at a pace that rivaled the best American SOF units' efforts in Iraq and Afghanistan. Unable to replace its leaders as quickly as they were being eliminated, the FARC became vulnerable to conventional Colombian units and eventually faltered. Taking all of that into consideration, a high rating of combat effectiveness is appropriate.

INITIAL ASSESSMENT: "AS GOOD AS U.S. SOF AT THE TACTICAL LEVEL"

AGLAN and BACOA received high ratings across every measured assessment. They even consistently conducted combat operations for longer than seventy-two hours, a logistics challenge for many first-world militaries. Such unwavering performance earns an overall effectiveness rating of high; this evaluation is backed up by anecdotal comments from former advisors and embassy personnel, nearly all of whom had worked with other foreign units evaluated in this study.

One U.S. advisor offered that "Colombian SOF is as good as U.S. SOF at the tactical level. . . . We beat them in resources and technology, but Colombian SOF is even better than many 'first world' SOF."[213] The Colombians were so proficient by

2014 that when an embassy official asked a Special Forces team sergeant partnered with Colombian SOF how they were performing, the NCO responded that he did not know why they were being deployed to Colombia anymore because the Colombian units were as capable as his own team.[214] That expertise has played out in Fuerzas Commando, the grueling nine-day military competition sponsored by the United States that is open to militaries within USSOUTHCOM. Of the fifteen events held through 2019 the Colombians won an astounding ten competitions.[215] That year the United States decided to get serious about trying to win and put their competitors on a special duty status so their only job was to train and prepare for the competition. They still lost to the Colombians.[216]

Indeed, Colombia progressed from needing U.S. assistance to helping the United States assist other militaries and from being an exporter of coca to an exporter of security assistance. In 2009 they offered to deploy SOF elements to Afghanistan in support of the U.S. Combined Joint Special Operations Task Force, but the plan ultimately was scuttled for political reasons.[217] By 2017 Colombian SOF units had begun to deploy to conduct foreign internal-defense missions with other nations' military and police forces in coordination with SOUTHCOM goals. At that stage, when U.S. SOF elements deployed to Colombia the expectation that they would conduct tactical training was dropped and they were placed on equal footing with the Colombian SOF so that each element would learn from the other.[218]

While U.S. assistance undoubtedly helped lead to such impressive outcomes, the Colombians themselves were predominantly responsible for their own success. In the words of one advisor, the Colombian commandos "never lost what we gave them. They honed it and improved upon it, using every TTP [tactics, techniques, and procedures] we trained them in. They soaked it up."[219] Another concluded, "The Colombian SOF were capable even before the U.S. advisory effort began. We just made them better. When you engage so heavily in terms of manpower and funds, it is almost inevitable that they will get better. Using a baseball analogy, Colombian SOF was a Double-A Minor League team at the time U.S. SOF began to engage them in earnest; through our persistent engagement they became a Major League team."[220]

The next chapter addresses the Iraqi Special Operations Forces, an elite unit built under very different circumstances than those in Colombia.

– 4 –
"We Have Killed Many Men Together"
The Iraqi Special Operations Forces, 2003–2011

BACKGROUND

Operation Iraqi Freedom and Regime Change

THE UNITED STATES' involvement in Iraq was limited and fleeting before the Gulf War of 1990 and 1991. That conflict, which aimed to eject Iraqi forces from Kuwait and preserve the flow of oil, destroyed most of the military but left its authoritarian leader, Saddam Hussein, in power. After the war Iraq remained a central part of U.S. foreign policy, and a long period of hostilities persisted, often punctuated by U.S. airstrikes. For his part, Saddam brutally repressed minorities that had risen up against him in the final days of fighting, resulting in the establishment of no-fly zones in northern and southern Iraq. The northern zone eventually grew to become a de facto Kurdish autonomous region, and many Green Berets from 10th Special Forces Group assisted in the initial humanitarian mission, Operation Provide Comfort, while the zone was being established.

The terrorist attacks of September 11, 2001, fundamentally altered U.S. policy toward Iraq. No longer content to pursue the status quo of containment, the administration of George W. Bush opted for a strategy of regime change followed by occupation and democratic elections. U.S. special-operations forces played an outsized role in the 2003 invasion, with the Middle East–oriented 5th SF Group conducting unilateral operations and supporting U.S. conventional forces, and the European-oriented 10th SF Group pairing with Kurdish Peshmerga fighters. While the invasion quickly crushed the ramshackle Iraqi Army and dissolved all central authority, its insufficient troop force and poorly planned reconstruction phase left the country without viable replacements. A capable insurgency quickly filled the void. Coalition errors that included disbanding the Iraqi security forces and banning Saddam's Ba'ath Party accelerated the growth of that resistance.

Creation of the Iraqi Special Operations Forces

In the aftermath of the catastrophic Coalition Provisional Authority Order 2, which disbanded the Iraqi security forces in their entirety, the United States and its allies were faced with the daunting task of completely rebuilding the Iraqi police, military, and intelligence services. While the U.S. Army began building Iraq's new army, the Combined Joint Special Operations Task Force–Arabian Peninsula (CJSOTF-AP) initially focused on kill/capture missions to round up the principal leadership of the Saddam regime. But in October 2003 the CJSOTF was tasked with forming the new army's 36th battalion after leaders of Iraq's five top political parties complained that they were being sidelined in U.S. efforts to rebuild the Iraqi security forces.

Rather than a regular infantry battalion, the CJSOTF decided to build an SOF partner force and named the unit the 36th Commando Battalion. The Commandos were patterned after the U.S. Ranger battalions in organization, equipment, and missions and would operate as a platoon or company but muster all the companies together for larger missions. Operations would occur at night and target top-tier threats. As the Commandos were being recruited, trained, and organized, in parallel the CJSOTF organized the Iraqi Counter Terrorism Force (ICTF), which would have similar capabilities to the U.S. Army Special Forces Commander's in-Extremis Force (CIF) companies. Over time those two units grew from a modest assemblage of soldiers into a division-sized force known as the Iraqi Special Operations Forces (ISOF).[1] Special Forces from every active-duty group were involved in the advisory effort, although 3rd (which focused on U.S. Africa Command), 5th, and 10th SF Groups carried most of the burden. The ISOF became the centerpiece of the SOF advisory effort and was resourced intensively from its inception in 2003 until December 2011, when U.S. forces were withdrawn from Iraq.

Chapter 4

THE ADVISORY EFFORT

Partner-to-Advisor Ratio

The ISOF experienced considerable growth over its development. At first the elite Iraqi forces comprised two disparate battalions, the 36th Commandos and the ICTF, but they were combined into a brigade in August 2004 to share common headquarters and support elements even while they maintained their distinct organizational identities and missions. A support battalion was added to fulfill logistics needs and a recce (recon) squadron was created to handle human intelligence and urban reconnaissance. To ensure force regeneration as the organizations took losses and soldiers retired, an Iraqi-led training center, later named the Iraqi Special Warfare Center and School, was also stood up.[2] In total, the elite forces were authorized 1,600 personnel, inclusive of operators and support elements, from late 2005 until mid-2007.[3]

In May 2006 the CJSOTF and Iraqi government agreed that the ISOF should be expanded by forming a second commando battalion that would include regional companies in Anbar, Basra, Diyala, and Mosul provinces.[4] With all the elements of the 1st ISOF Brigade garrisoned in Baghdad and recognizing Iraqi forces would not always be able to rely on U.S. aircraft to move around the country quickly, CJSOTF advisors believed that regional companies would allow the ISOF to react quickly to threats across Iraq. This change resulted in dramatic expansion of the ISOF to 4,800 authorized personnel, but the Iraqi Special Warfare Center was incapable of meeting the demand to grow that quickly. As such, actual growth was extremely slow, and only the Basra and Mosul companies were activated by January 2008.

Near the end of 2007 U.S. and Iraqi SOF leaders decided that the regional companies would be expanded to battalions and that those units would form the 2nd ISOF Brigade, which was activated in July 2009. That growth propelled the ISOF to 8,500 personnel, but that size was purely hypothetical as the stand-up of the regional companies was still not completed.[5] Despite pressure from Iraq's political leaders, both U.S. and Iraqi SOF officers were reluctant to mass-produce the elite forces, and actual ISOF personnel strength hovered at around 59 percent. By the time of the U.S. withdrawal in 2011, each regional battalion was in actuality closer to a company-sized unit.

Advisor Commitment

The SF advisor ratio in Iraq was relatively constant, and as the ISOF expanded the advisor commitment grew to match it. This was likely because Iraq was considered the United States' main effort in the larger global war on terrorism. That consistency makes it easier to explore the commitment to each of the two main components of the ISOF and then normalize that over time to reflect an overall ratio.

Iraqi Counter Terrorism Force

The ICTF was made up of three operational troops; a support element with vehicle drivers, gunners, and mechanics; a headquarters section; and one "recce" or reconnaissance troop. Each of the operational troops was assigned twenty-two Iraqi soldiers, and they followed a red-amber-green cycle with one troop in each phase. Phases lasted ten days, allowing ICTF members to go on leave (red), train (amber), and then conduct combat operations (green). Advisors mirrored the Iraqi cycle, and when an ICTF troop entered the leave phase, their partnered ODA either took time off or assisted advisors of other troops as required.

Each ICTF troop was paired with an ODA of SF advisors, a substantial commitment.[6] This was accomplished by having a U.S. CIF troop (which was composed of three ODAs) paired with the ICTF battalion.[7] Only CIF units advised the ICTF. It is worth noting that this ratio is roughly 1.83 to 1, massively larger than the doctrinal ratio of between 50 and 75 to 1. The ratio might have been even higher during the initial stand-up of the organization, reaching or exceeding a 1-to-1 ratio, but interviews I conducted with many officers and noncommissioned officers who worked with the ICTF during this period were not able to corroborate this data.[8]

Commando Battalions

When the Commandos initially stood up as the 36th Commando Battalion, an SF company headquarters (AOB) and two full strength SF ODAs—approximately thirty-four personnel—served as advisors. That initial phase lasted from approximately October 2003 until June 2004, when an additional ODA was added to support the battalion as it became fully operational (with advisors increasing to forty-six personnel).[9] The new ratio was short-lived as the demands of the wars in Iraq and Afghanistan as well as the missions in the Philippines, Colombia, and elsewhere far exceeded the number of SF soldiers in the Army. The additional troop requirements dropped by the end of 2004, when the partnership stabilized to two ODAs working with the battalion.

Such a pairing allowed the SF advisors to match the cyclical leave-training-operations cycle of the Commandos with one ODA paired with the company conducting training while the second paired with the company conducting operations. Because one Commando company was always on leave, this resulted in a ratio of one ODA paired with an Iraqi Commando company of 120 soldiers, a matching that persisted throughout the remainder of the conflict.[10] That ratio (ten to one), is considerably higher than the doctrinal SF ratio of one ODA advising a host-nation battalion.

As each regional Commando company was stood up, an ODA was assigned to advise it. Such a commitment matched the ratio already in place and reflected the opinion of CJSOTF leaders that they should duplicate the pattern for continued success. However, the actual ratio of Commandos to advisors was slightly smaller than the original assignment because the regional companies had one platoon of soldiers always on leave, with their other two platoons in a training-and-operations cycle. Based on the documents detailing numbers of active troops and interviews with advisors, none of the regional Commando units expanded much beyond company size before the U.S. withdrawal in 2011.[11]

Assessment

The overall partner-to-advisor ratio for the Iraq case study calculates as 6.2 ISOF soldiers per SF advisor (see figure 4.1 for the monthly averages).[12] In terms of assessing that impact, there were advisors who had served on other missions studied in this book, and they observed firsthand the effects of different partner-to-advisor ratios.[13] Of those, there was near-universal agreement that decreasing the ratio had a positive impact on the combat effectiveness of the unit they trained, and not a single advisor thought that a higher ratio was better.

Consistency in Advisor Pairing

There was considerable consistency in advisor pairing with the ISOF. For the ICTF, only two SF companies advised the unit for the first three years of its existence. The decision to minimize the number of advisors was centered on the fact that the ICTF was considered Iraq's national-level counterterrorism force. As such, it should be paired only with an equivalent capability within the U.S. effort: the Special Forces Commander's in-Extremis Force (CIF) companies. B Company, 2nd Battalion, 3rd Special Forces Group, stood up the organization and served as their sole advisors for the first eighteen months of the unit's existence. As a CIF, the company's organization differed slightly from regular SF companies and was instead based around two troops of roughly thirty-six SF operators each. For those eighteen months the two troops of the company did back-to-back rotations, switching out every 120 days. Such a cycle was quickly deemed to be too grueling, and the 5th Special Forces

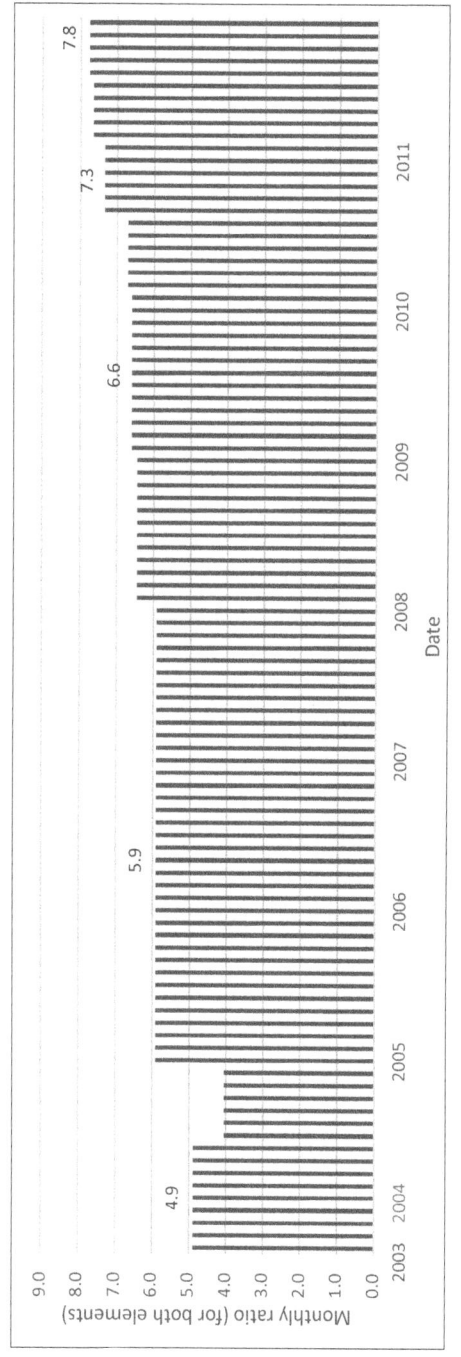

FIGURE 4.1 Monthly ratio of partners to advisors, Iraq

Group CIF, A Company, 1st Battalion, was added to the rotational cycle in March 2005. Each one of the two troops in those two companies cycled through 120-day rotations for the next year.

Even though the rotations were shorter than conventional yearlong rotations, they were physically and emotionally brutal for the advisors.[14] One advisor noted that he submitted 118 combat operations for approval during an average four-month rotation, leaving only two nights without a mission. Each operation was complex, with multiple structures to be assaulted and almost always follow-on operations conducted the same night. One atypical fifteen-hour combat cycle in 2005 involved the rescue of an Iraqi Army general who was an al-Qaida hostage and then four follow-on missions, including the capture of Number 11 on the theater high-value target list. Thus in March 2006 even the two-Group cycle was determined to be too arduous, and all the other CIFs in U.S. Army Special Forces Command (C Company, 1st Battalion, 1st Special Forces Group—which stood up the LRR, C Company, 1st Battalion, 10th Special Forces Group, and C Company, 3rd Battalion, 7th Special Forces Group) were added to the rotation. Even then, however, the 3rd Group and 5th Group CIFs were considered the primary advisors, and each company would deploy once in the annual cycle. One of the other three CIFs would deploy for the other four months of the year so that each of those companies would deploy once in a three-year cycle.[15] This rotation persisted for the remainder of the conflict.[16]

Like in the Philippines, the assignment of the CIF to the ICTF advisory effort greatly increased the consistency of advisor pairing for a variety of reasons. First, because there were only five CIF companies across the entire U.S. Army, there was an extremely small pool of personnel to pull from to serve as advisors. Second, those companies had an extremely stable set of assigned personnel. Individual advisors would often stay within the same CIF company for years, some never conducting a permanent-change-of-station move. The relative stability occurred because CIF companies were designed to be kept on call to respond to regional hostage crises or similar missions, and the members of each company received considerable specialized training.[17] An SF soldier without that training could not be assigned to those companies.

The Iraqi Commando battalions in the ISOF, first the 36th and then the regional battalions, experienced a similar consistency in advisor pairing. A vast majority of the ODAs that served as advisors to the Commandos came from 5th and 10th Special Forces Groups, the two organizations that provided the headquarters for CJSOTF-AP. For the first three deployments, 5th Special Forces Group worked with the Commandos: initially teams from 1st Battalion, then 2nd Battalion, and then the same teams from 1st Battalion returned as advisors on the third rotation.[18] Only when the SF soldiers on those ODAs started to become burned-out by back-to-back rotations were other SF Groups added to the mix.[19] During that phase considerable effort was made to pair the same advisors with the same Commando unit, rotation after rotation.[20]

Although initially there were no special qualifications for an ODA to pair with the Commandos, in 2006 Special Forces CIF companies and teams became the primary set of advisors.[21] Like in the ICTF, this greatly increased the consistency in advisor pairing because the CIF requirement vastly limited the potential advisory pool. There was also considerable personnel stability within the ISOF, and many Iraqis stayed within the organization for the duration of their careers. At times new Iraqis were brought in to imbalance the sectarian equilibrium of the ISOF, but the organizational culture minimized those impacts and personal and professional factors motivated those already part of the unit to stay.

There are numerous anecdotal reports about how frequently the various elements of the ISOF were paired with the exact same advisors. One advisor noted that an SF teammate had served on four different ICTF rotations and then retired. After his retirement, he returned as a contractor to continue working with the ICTF, supporting them in their fight to recapture Mosul in 2016.[22] Another participated in eight combat tours in Iraq, acting as direct advisor to ISOF units during four of them, while during the other tours he supported and interacted with the ISOF. This meant the same advisor worked with the same Commando battalion for thirty-two months (nearly three years) out of a possible eight years.[23] One advisor, whose exploits became legendary in the SF community, served with the ISOF for three years on five straight rotations during assignments to both 5th and 10th Special Forces Groups. He worked with the ISOF so often that other teams joked that they had to sign for him as part of the property handover as they changed out in between missions.[24] Such consistent pairings were more common than not, and one SF company worked with the same ISOF unit for more than seven years. Their only breaks from the coupling were when they returned to the United States, allowing the SF advisors to see their Iraqi partners mature from their positions as captains commanding companies to generals leading the entire organization.[25]

Because of how consistently many advisors were paired with the ISOF, deep friendships often developed with the soldiers and officers they advised. Maj. Gen. Patrick Roberson, who completed four advisory rotations with the ISOF, noted that he had first met Fadhil Jalil al Barwari, the unit's future commander, in 1996. This time distortion occurred because Roberson commanded an ODA during Operation Provide Comfort, which delivered humanitarian and military assistance to Kurdish factions after the first Gulf War.[26] At that time, Barwari was serving in a Kurdish Peshmerga militia and met numerous SF soldiers rotating through northern Iraq. During Roberson's deployments, his long-term connections with Barwari helped him pick up where he had left off on prior rotations, greatly facilitating growth in unit capabilities.

Assessment: "We Have Killed Many Men Together"

Nearly all the SF soldiers who worked with Iraqi Special Operations Forces believed there were considerable advantages to consistently pairing with the same Iraqi forces. It reduced the start-up time of each mission, allowing the advisor to pick up where they previously left off rather than start anew.[27] One advisor noted that for the first two years of his work with the ISOF his unit did four-month rotations. That meant he knew that when he finished each deployment, he would be back working with the same Iraqis in eight months at the most. "Because it was the same face coming back, they knew who you were, they trusted you, they've been in a room with you in a gunfight before. You just picked up where you left off. There was no dogs-sniffing-each-other's-butts."[28] Within a few days they were back on track, executing complex missions.

Another advisor pointed out the differences between the SF effort with the ISOF and the advisory effort with the rest of the Iraqi Army. To him the ISOF consistency created a coherent campaign plan but the conventional-forces effort building other Iraqi forces was akin to fighting the war in Iraq with a different plan each year. "Every single year was just start over. It is all new Americans, and most of them have never been there. [Meanwhile] the Iraqis haven't gone anywhere, and they knew how to navigate that environment."[29]

Consistency also created personal relationships and trust that made it easier to work through issues that impeded progress.[30] Sgt. Maj. Ron McDaries served as an advisor during three rotations and transitioned to contractor work after he retired. In 2014 he was still in Iraq as a contractor with the U.S. State Department as ISIS marched toward Baghdad. His supervisors were alarmed that there was no formal security where they were based and asked him if he could help. McDaries said that he knew General Barwari and asked for his supervisor's phone to set up a meeting. Much to his supervisor's surprise, Barwari invited them to his home, and when they arrived the general walked past the higher-ranking U.S. embassy official and gave McDaries a big hug, saying, "This is my brother. We have killed many men together and drunk many beers." Even though it had been several years since the two had seen each other, Barwari did not hesitate to offer McDaries whatever support he needed, including providing an ISOF element for security.[31]

A few dissenting voices noted that while they agreed in principle that consistency was important there could be exceptions when that pairing ought to be broken. Consistency could be a double-edged sword: if an ODA was not skilled at teaching and training or individuals on the team were bad at establishing rapport, then pairing that unit with the same host-nation forces would likely have adverse effect.[32] Others posited that some ODAs had life cycles, wherein team members would have personal issues or became burned out after multiple rotations and their performance would drop.[33] In such exceptional cases it made sense to break the bond of consistency.

Overall, consistency in advisor pairing with the ISOF was high. Across multiple rotations the efforts of CJSOTF leaders and assignment of the CIFs to work with the ISOF greatly limited the pool of advisors and resulted in frequent return pairings. As one advisor noted, "continuity is better than gold. [It] is absolutely how you shape a force and ensure that they are responsive to our requirements and our objectives. . . . It is instant trust, credibility, and, most importantly, influence."[34]

Advisor Language Training and Cultural Awareness

The demand for Special Forces operators in Iraq far exceeded what the Middle East–oriented 5th Special Forces group could provide. As one former Group commander noted, even if the entire group had been deployed for the duration of the war and its members never returned home, it still could not have met the needs of the theater commander.[35] Because of its connections with the Kurds after the first Gulf War, 10th SF Group, which was officially regionally and linguistically oriented to Europe, was selected to assist 5th Group in Iraq. The two groups shared roughly even responsibility as the CJSOTF-AP headquarters and contributed similar amounts of forces. Yet even those two units were not sufficient to the task, and every other active-duty SF group provided forces to help alleviate exhaustion from back-to-back rotations. Of all those groups involved in the mission, only 5th Group was officially oriented to the Middle East, focused its training on regional languages, and had extensive cultural experience.

While 5th and 10th Groups took the lion's share of troop commitments to Iraq, when examining the contribution toward the ISOF—only a portion of the

CJSOTF-AP mission—the assessment becomes more complicated. The 3rd Group CIF, regionally and linguistically oriented toward Africa, stood up the ICTF and had a monopoly on pairing with the organization for its first eighteen months of existence. After that the 3rd and 5th Group CIFs shared equally in pairing with the ICTF until mid-2006, when the other three CIFs were added to the rotational cycle. Rather than share the advisory responsibility equally among the five CIFs, 3rd and 5th Groups were each given one-third of the partnership while the other three CIFs shared in the other third of the deployment time. At the macro level this means that 5th Special Forces Group, the only regionally oriented organization, advised the ICTF for less than a third of its existence.

The history of the Commandos' partnership is similar. While they were stood up by 5th Group, 10th Group rapidly fell in on the advisory cycle, and the two groups worked nearly equal amounts of time with the Commandos. By 2006 operational pressures resulted in the Baghdad-based Commando battalion being rotated primarily between CIF units on a ratio that matched the ICTF. As a result the Middle East–oriented 5th Special Forces Group advised that Commando battalion for roughly a third of its existence. Because the regional Commando companies (later battalions after the organization grew again) were not advised by CIF elements, they were shared in approximately even proportions between 5th and 10th Group teams.

When consolidating this data it should be noted that even though the ICTF was technically a battalion its personnel size was much closer to company strength. The regional companies, when combined, came close to the personnel strength of the Baghdad-based Commando battalion. Altogether the driving force on determining the degree of match with language training and cultural awareness was driven mostly by the Baghdad-based Commando battalion because it had the largest number of personnel. As noted, that meant a regionally oriented SF unit with matching language training and cultural awareness was only paired with the ISOF for approximately a third of the advisory effort. This leads to an overall assessment that the degree of match for language training and cultural awareness of the SF advisors to the ISOF was low.

Assessment: "None of Us Spoke the Language in the Early Days"

Interviewees provided many different opinions regarding the importance of language training and cultural awareness. Although members of 5th Special Forces Group generally noted that they believed their regional orientation to the Middle East and knowledge of Arabic contributed positively to the development of the ISOF, this opinion was by no means universal, and few argued it emphatically. One SF soldier who spent most of his career in 5th Group and was trained in Arabic but later transferred to the non-regionally affiliated 10th Special Forces Group noted that there was little difference between the two groups. Across three years of deployments, he could recall only one occasion on which someone from another Group made a significant cultural error that affected operations.[36] Another advisor who started his career in 5th Special Forces Group, which was regionally oriented to the Middle East, but served in other groups as well observed, "Regional orientation only matters for the first trip. Once you have an advisor pool of special-operations forces that have deployed and built a relationship with that partner force, it doesn't take long for special-operations forces to regionally orient [themselves]. That doesn't mean that they are 3/3 in a language [test], but you can take a unit from 1st Group and put them in Iraq, and very quickly they understand the cultural, tribal, political, and social aspects of that environment and are able to operate effectively."[37]

Those that downplayed the importance of language training and cultural awareness provided various explanations. Some noted that even from its early days all ISOF units were fortunate to have many interpreters. Rather than relying on their own skills, U.S. advisors trusted interpreters to translate for them in training and in combat. Many also noted that over time the Iraqis came to take on many Western habits, traditions, and processes, which made it easier to communicate and work together.[38] By the middle of the eight-year mission, many of the Iraqis had learned conversational English and taken to wearing uniforms with pockets on the shoulders, replete with Velcro, and even copied the way the Americans would wear their Oakley sunglasses. They wore American baseball caps backward like the Green Berets did (and that, likewise, had annoyed conventional U.S. military leaders), carried the same flip knives as their advisors, and basically looked like mirror images of their U.S. partners.[39] Some had even picked up American vices, such as dipping tobacco—a far cry from the more common Iraqi habit of smoking cigarettes or shisha (water pipes).

Others noted that the duration of the mission, coupled with consistently pairing with the same ISOF units, resulted in close personal contacts that went beyond a simple capacity to communicate in Arabic. While the lack of language skills might have impacted the first rotation, by the second it was negligible. By the third or fourth rotation, some advisors had worked with the same Commandos so often that they knew how their Iraqi partners would react or behave in a certain situation, which effectively precluded the requirement for verbal communication.[40]

Some senior advisors noted that the ability to build rapport—which they argued was critical to having a positive impact on a host-nation unit—is a personal skill that was not always correlated with language training or cultural awareness. They posited that the two skills were completely independent from one another and from rank. In fact, some leaders paired a more-junior SF soldier who had strong interpersonal skills and ability to build rapport with important host-nation elements rather than more-senior operators.[41]

Another poorly kept secret was how few SF operators in 5th Group, the regionally oriented unit, were professionally proficient in Arabic. During the decade that SF soldiers advised the ISOF, the requirement to graduate from the U.S. Army John F. Kennedy Special Warfare Center and School language program was a 1/1 rating on the DLPT, which equates to elementary proficiency with only "sufficient comprehension to read very simple connected written material." However, because of the complexity of some languages such as Arabic and Mandarin Chinese, that graduation requirement was frequently waived to 0+/0+, where one can "read some or all of the following: numbers, isolated words and phrases, personal and place names, street signs, office and shop designations. The above [are] often interpreted inaccurately."[42]

The 2012 U.S. Special Operations Command Language Regional Expertise and Culture Strategy Report noted that only 66 percent of Special Forces students could attain the 1/1 level, a statistic matched by anecdotal evidence gathered from interviewees and my personal experience.[43] During my four years in 5th Special Forces Group no more than a dozen SF operators at any given time had scored at the 2/2 level of limited working proficiency and no more than one or two had scored at the 3/3 level of general professional proficiency across the entire group of 54 ODAs (approximately 650 SF qualified personnel). As of April 2021, across *all* of Special Forces command, inclusive of the five active-duty and two National Guard groups and the headquarters, schoolhouse, and support elements, there were only 57 SF personnel who had scored at the 2/2 level or above on the DLPT or Oral Proficiency Interview on an Arabic dialect.[44]

These scores show that the vast majority of those in the regionally oriented 5th Special Forces Group had only elementary proficiency in Arabic and led some advisors to posit that their language training did not significantly contribute to the mission because it was impossible to train to the level necessary to operate without interpreters. Even an SF linguist at a DLPT level of 3/3 in Arabic, they argued, would not be able to understand critical nuances, subtleties, and tone and would require the skills of a native speaker, such as an interpreter, to operate effectively.[45] Six months of perfunctory Arabic training for five hours a day simply did not provide sufficient experience for functional proficiency.

Those who were less proficient in Arabic, such as one advisor who scored 0+/1 on the DLPT, noted that only a small subset of words were critical in the thick of combat. "None of us spoke the language in the early days. I went to school for Farsi. But by the end we could say the important stuff like *Put the machine gun over there* or *You are our prisoner*."[46] Another advisor noted that he did not know any Arabic when he began advising the ISOF and instead spoke French and Serbo-Croatian.[47] However, simply knowing the situation and the desired end state allowed communication because he could memorize the most important words and phrases. Such a perspective matches what other SF advisors in the Philippines observed—that while the specific language does not matter, knowing any language adds to one's willingness and ability to learn other languages more easily and also gives the patience and cross-cultural communication skills important to advisors.

Advisor Ability to Organize Host-Nation Unit

Across the span of the partnering effort with the ISOF, the ability to organize the host-nation unit changed significantly. After regime change and the disbanding of the Iraqi security forces under Coalition Provisional Authority Order 2, rebuilding the Iraqi security forces started from scratch. During that initial phase U.S. advisors had nearly carte blanche to organize the ISOF in whatever way they saw fit. Over time Iraqi leaders asserted more and more sovereignty, and by 2008 operational control of the ISOF had been returned to the Iraqi government. Once that occurred the ability of the SF advisors to organize and influence the unit decreased appreciably, even though the unit maintained much of the identity and organizational culture that the Americans had built.

Regime Change: "We Work for President Bush"

When the ISOF were first organized as the 36th Commando Battalion and the ICTF, their SF advisors had almost total control over all the important decisions. The Americans chose the organization's equipment, leadership, and training standards. The unit's list of authorized equipment and even the ethnosectarian makeup of the force were dictated by SF advisors as well—with little to no input from the Iraqis. One Iraqi officer who started with the ICTF in 2003 and rose to become a brigadier general in charge of the unit's schoolhouse noted that during that phase the ISOF were "controlled 100 percent by the U.S. forces at the time, and especially the U.S. Special Forces. They had the ability to adjust, change, and modify any kind of organizational layout that we had within the unit."[48]

Many advisors believed that much of the long-term success of the ISOF came about because early in the mission they had handpicked Iraqis to serve in key leadership positions within the organization.[49] For the first several years, SF advisors could hire and fire leaders at will and executed that authority frequently. Advisors noted that they had relieved an ISOF company commander for stealing, a sergeant major for corruption, and another leader for having an accidental discharge with his weapon.[50] Such a hands-on approach helped prevent corruption and sectarianism from spreading within the organization and contributed to a culture of competence. Many of the leaders picked by SF advisors in the ISOF's early days later became battalion and brigade commanders or command sergeant majors, perpetuating the virtuous cycle.

One of the most important early decisions made was when SF advisors chose Fadhil Jalil al Barwari to lead the 36th Commando Battalion. Barwari replaced an ineffective officer and became the unit's second commander. Iraqi leaders had little to no input in the decision, and Barwari was chosen for his professionalism, leadership ability, bravery in battle, and personal gravitas, as well as his connection with 10th Special Forces Group after working with them in a Kurdish militia during Operation Provide Comfort.[51] He methodically climbed the ranks, earning promotion to major general and selection to command the 1st ISOF Brigade from 2004 until his death in 2018.[52] Reflecting on the importance of being able to select organizational leaders, Maj. Gen. Patrick Roberson remarked, "A lot of it goes to in the beginning . . . [when] we had a lot of control. If you have a lot of control over an organization, the most important thing you can do whether you're in the American Army or whether you're controlling a partner force is to pick the leadership. If you're able to pick the leadership, that matters the most, because picking the best leaders in a meritocracy-type organization usually works out the best for you in the long run."[53]

SF advisors also designed and implemented the unit's organizational and equipping structure. The troop structure of the ICTF mirrored the SF CIF units that advised it, and the composition of the Commando battalions was conceived to match U.S. Army Ranger battalions. The set of equipment those units employed was also designed and issued by U.S. advisors. In what would later become a controversial decision, the ISOF were equipped with U.S. special-operations gear to match that which their advisors carried. Designed to make them more interoperable with their SF partners, it had the unintended consequence of not matching the logistics system of the rest of the Iraqi security forces, which used Soviet Bloc equipment.[54] Some senior SF advisors later commented that with similar equipment and unit design, the only way one could tell the Iraqis from Americans on the full-motion video of unmanned aerial vehicles was that the SF soldiers were usually slightly taller than their ISOF partners.[55]

Another key decision that advisors made at the unit's inception and enforced while they had control was to require that the unit be nonsectarian. Unlike most units in the Iraqi security forces, which were nearly homogeneous, the SF advisors mandated that the ISOF's ethnosectarian makeup roughly match Iraq's demographics.[56] When the unit was first formed, it was comprised of elements of the five largest militias in Iraq, each of which represented major ethnosectarian identities. The Kurdistan Democratic Party provided approximately 28 percent of the troops for the unit; Ahmed Chalabi's Shia Iraqi National Congress, 22 percent; the Patriotic Union of Kurdistan, 20 percent; Ayad Allawi's secular Shia Iraqi National Congress, 15 percent; and the Supreme Council for the Islamic Revolution in Iraq, 15 percent.[57] Not only was the general makeup of the unit prescribed by the U.S. advisors, but the leadership too was carefully selected to ensure that no ethnic or religious group had more than its fair share of command and responsibility.[58] In the words of one advisor, this resulted in the unit "policing itself," with Iraqis of different sects regulating each other's behavior and preventing corruption. Another described the effect of this dynamic: "When Shia and Sunnis are out on a target, they're saving each other's lives and fighting side by side. Over time it erodes prejudices and they become more loyal and beholden to each other than to whatever tribe they came from."[59] The nonsectarian identity of the unit became a point of pride for ISOF soldiers and a self-sustaining part of the organization's culture that persisted even after the U.S. advisors left. In 2014 Arabs, Sunnis, Shia, Kurds, Christians, and Turkmen still comprised the ISOF in rough approximation to Iraq's population.[60]

Special Forces advisors also carefully organized and controlled the rigorous selection and training pipeline to ensure that only quality recruits would serve in the unit. To become part of the ISOF, Iraqis had to volunteer and then pass a three-week selection and assessment course. Advisors weeded out candidates who were not physically fit and those who were incapable of working together. The advisors had ultimate authority to eliminate from the training pipeline any candidate not up to standard regardless of political connection or position. In the initial group of applicants only 389 of 508 Iraqis passed, a far cry from the limited screening process administered to the remainder of the Iraqi Army.[61] As the unit's accomplishments grew in renown and screenings became even more stringent, the attrition rate soared to between 40 and 50 percent.[62] The high standard set by SF advisors still persisted in 2020, when the pass rate for selection was only 60 to 65 percent.[63] Those who passed selection were sent on to either an eight-week commando course or three months of ICTF training.[64] Advisors removed additional candidates in each phase, further ensuring the quality of graduates.

The pay for the ISOF units was also initially controlled by U.S. advisors. Believing it to be an issue critical to recruitment, retention, and trust, they authorized an incentive pay that nearly doubled or tripled the income of a similarly ranked soldier in the Iraqi Army.[65] To ensure there was no corruption, many advisors held formal "payday activities," during which the ISOF lined soldiers up to distribute salaries.[66] Initially these funds came directly out of U.S. coffers; but as Iraq's sovereignty was restored, the Iraqi leadership in the ISOF slowly took control of the system. This additional pay of $800 a month was perceived by some Iraqis to be quid pro quo for their service.[67] Once, after a difficult mission had domestic Iraqi political repercussions, a U.S. advisor asked a group of ISOF soldiers what they thought the operation's fallout would be. One responded, "We don't care about that; we work for President Bush."[68] Another advisor noted the importance of ensuring that his partners were well compensated. "When he is taking home enough cash to feed all four generations of his family and provide housing... that is a game changer. You've got loyalty, and you are definitely hitting on all cylinders with that individual."[69]

In addition to the extensive screening ISOF hopefuls underwent, U.S. advisors insisted the recruits receive special protections. Prospective candidates were vetted with a polygraph as well as a counterintelligence review. In addition many of their families were moved into on-base housing where they could not be targeted, manipulated, or corrupted.[70] At least partly because of this, there was not a single green-on-blue fratricide by the ISOF against a U.S. advisor, and Americans operating alone with them in training rarely wore body armor. The conditions starkly differed in Afghanistan, where most units required an armed "guardian angel" during training whose function was to be ready to kill an infiltrator in the partner force.[71]

One CJSOTF commander noted that his advisors initially had almost complete control over the ISOF to organize and reorganize them at will: "We created them with the equipment, the training, and the work ethic. It wasn't like we're going to the range for forty minutes and, *inshallah*, taking a nap and calling it a day. We inculcated and instituted a work ethic that these guys really just took on."[72] This nearly complete control over the ISOF was only formally changed in September 2006, well past the June 2004 transition of sovereignty, which should have returned control of the ISOF to the Iraqi government. Despite signing a memorandum of agreement that ratified the 2006 change, the CJSOTF ignored the directive and continued to exert control over the ISOF until January 2008. Only then was a new agreement created that resulted in shared control between the government of Iraq and the CJSOTF.[73] During that evolutionary period as the SF advisor's level of control waned, a domestic Iraqi SOF headquarters was formed.

Institutionalizing the Iraqi Special Operations Forces: The Counter Terrorism Command and Counter Terrorism Service

Iraqi political and military leadership offered no resistance to U.S. SF recommendations to establish an SOF headquarters to command, manage, and resource the various elite forces. Similarly, because the elite forces had fallen under the direct control of the CJSOTF since their inception, there was little friction with Iraqi conventional commanders, as they were not in the ISOF's chain of command. Demonstrating how much ability to organize the Iraqi elite forces they still had, in 2007 U.S. advisors drew up plans to create a military headquarters and civilian ministry to command and provide oversight for the ISOF.

In some ways, U.S. advisors fought among themselves more than with Iraqi leadership over the creation of the new organizations. One perspective held that the new headquarters should resemble U.S. counterterrorism forces and therefore ought to be an organization outside the typical government and military bureaucracy that answered directly to the head of the executive branch. In crisis situations such a construct would allow Iraq's elite counterterrorism forces to react nimbly and quickly.[74] A second perspective argued that the ISOF should fall within traditional military structures because Iraq's political and military institutions and their respect for civilian authority were not mature enough to create an elite force outside the military chain of command. They feared the ISOF would become a Praetorian Guard for the prime minister and that political targeting would follow.[75] Indeed, Prime Minister Nouri al-Maliki had long sought to obtain direct control over the elite force, even issuing an executive order in January 2007 that would place the unit under his own Office of the Commander in Chief, a shadow military organization run out of the prime minister's office.[76] Faced with two conflicting recommendations, senior U.S. leaders opted to support the first proposal. It is worth noting that the entire process of the creation of the headquarters elements reflected how much the U.S. advisors could organize the Iraqi SOF elements, as the discussion and decision cycles were almost entirely within U.S. circles.

The decision resulted in the creation of the Counter Terrorism Service (CTS) and the Counter Terrorism Command (CTC). The CTS was created as a standalone ministry-level organization led by a civilian that handled the strategic, institutional, and force-management affairs of Iraqi SOF elements. Critical functions such as acquisition, medical care, communications, finance, logistics, and personnel management were to be performed by the CTS.[77] Meeting Prime Minister Maliki's desires, the CTS was completely independent of the Iraqi Ministry of Defense and reported directly to Iraq's chief executive. The CTC would be a military organization led by a two-star general that served as an operational headquarters performing command and control for ISOF combat operations.[78] The goal of civilian leadership for the CTS dissipated quickly as Maliki assigned as the organization's first director a three-star general known to be loyal to him.

Fedayeen Maliki: "You Taught Us Better than This"

After that assignment by Prime Minister Maliki, SF advisors gradually lost control of the unit. Over time the leadership of the organization changed from the demographically mixed ratios that matched the population to ratios favoring Shia leaders. The shift occurred slowly, as the U.S. advisors still had some control over the unit and much of the unit's culture and identity that had been instilled persisted in the face of Shia partisanship. At times entire groups of Shia soldiers who had not completed ISOF training arrived unannounced to the unit, with instructions to integrate at all levels of the organization. SF advisors tried but were not always able to shut down such sectarian infiltration.[79] In parallel, it became much more difficult for SF advisors to influence the selection of key leadership at the battalion level and above. Some of those positions fell to Maliki supporters—often to officers unqualified to fill special-operations leadership positions. Below that level, however, the long-term relationship U.S. advisors had with Major General Barwari, the ISOF commander, enabled them to still have a say.[80] Any newly appointed ISOF officer deemed incompetent or sectarian but politically connected was sidelined by Major General Barwari, who would assign the appointee a noncombat role or prevent him from making important decisions.[81]

Loss of control over the ISOF's personnel system was not the only change that occurred after Prime Minister Maliki gained control of the ISOF. More ominously, the unit's targeting shifted considerably. Missions against Shia targets were rarely approved, and those that were seldom succeeded in killing or capturing their objective. The situation became so acute that SF advisors, in coordination with loyal ISOF officers, decided to conduct a test. They put together what they described as "near perfect" target requests for Shia objectives, which were rejected forthright. When they submitted similar or even less-detailed requests for Sunni targets, they were immediately approved.[82] Even when Shia targets were approved, several advisors believed that elements within the CTS or CTC were tipping off the targets to prevent their capture.[83]

Most jarring was the political targeting. In August 2008 the prime minister's office, via the CTS, ordered the arrest of the governor of Diyala Province, a prominent Sunni politician. Although the governor avoided capture, two other Sunni politicians were arrested in what was a clear case of sectarian political intimidation.[84] This began a long series of politically driven operations U.S. advisors believed had more of a goal to terrify and coerce Maliki's political opponents than to kill or capture insurgents. The SF advisors denounced the operations and refused to participate but were nearly powerless to stop them from happening. Over time the politicization of the ISOF grew to the point that the CJSOTF began conducting more combat-advisory missions with other Iraqi units such as the National Police's Emergency Response Unit. The ISOF became unpopular and was known as "the dirty brigade" or "Fedayeen Maliki" by Iraqis who remembered the violent paramilitary force Saddam Hussein had used as political enforcers.[85] ISOF Commandos recognized the malignant influence but were unable to stop it, commiserating with their advisors and telling them, "You taught us about being Iraqis. . . . You taught us that our ethnicity is not part of it, [that it should be] Iraq first. . . . You taught us better than this."[86]

The Post-Maliki Renaissance

Despite Maliki's political malfeasance, many key Iraqi leaders remained in the ISOF and worked to minimize his long-term impact on the unit. U.S. advisors also served as a brake, slowing Maliki's worst impulses until most departed in December 2011. Even then, a small element of soldiers and civilian contractors remained, many of them former SF advisors, and they were also able to degrade malicious influences. Although Maliki was able to put some of his allies into key positions and temporarily unbalance unit demographics, in many ways the core identity and culture of the unit remained. The founding ethos persisted, outlasting Maliki's eight years in power: a multiethnic and multisectarian identity; a dedication to excellence; recruitment, selection, and retention of quality individuals; and a commitment to difficult, challenging, and realistic training.[87] Those characteristics were maintained even though the ISOF expanded to 13,000 personnel with each of the regional battalions growing into a brigade-sized unit.[88] The ISOF's ethos was preserved because those who disagreed with Maliki and dragged their feet on his initiatives were able to wait him out.

The 2014 assault by the Islamic State of Iraq and Syria (ISIS) almost destroyed Iraq as a unitary nation but was something of a catharsis and cleansing. Prime Minister Maliki rightfully absorbed much of the blame for the disaster and was ignominiously forced out of office in August of that year. In the aftermath of his resignation the ISOF bore the brunt of the fight against ISIS, serving as one of the only Iraqi military institutions that did not crumble. Acting as a bulwark against ISIS, the organization was perceived by many as the savior of Iraq, buoying ISOF popularity and support. Its multiethnic identity and dedication to the nation proved particularly important, with one scholar noting the ISOF and CTS "gave Iraqis confidence in their country's unity, and without it, some believe Iraq would today be a failed state. All in all, the CTS is now widely regarded as loyal to Iraq and not to any one person."[89]

Assessment: Racing against the Sovereignty Clock

At the start of the U.S. mission in Iraq, advisors enjoyed complete control over every aspect of the ISOF's creation and existence. They controlled who joined the unit and who led it, and they established and upheld the standards for assessment, training, and retention. SF advisors chose the unit's organization, weapons, demographic makeup, and pay. At first they controlled the unit directly in combat. When change came, it arrived gradually, and the United States still exerted considerable influence over the force. For all these reasons the advisors' ability to organize host-nation forces is rated as high.

The United States stood up the ISOF and held absolute dominion over it for four years until ceding control back to Iraq. That uninterrupted period helped U.S. advisors establish a culture that persisted through Prime Minister Maliki's abuses of power and ISIS' brutal offensive. It was almost as if the ISOF required a certain amount of time to "cure" or "set" before they would be resistant to negative influences. Like in the Philippines, this seems to indicate the extreme importance of the sovereignty "clock," that short period when host-nation forces are prone to allowing the most change by foreign advisors.

Combat Advising: "You Were Killing with Them"

Advisors to the Iraqi Counter Terrorism Force and Commandos were involved in every aspect of daily life with their host-nation partners and across their entire life cycle, from recruitment to selection to initial training to advising them in combat. Often the Iraqi schoolhouse mission was assigned to a team that had many newly assigned personnel, and over time that ODA would "graduate" to advising ISOF soldiers in combat. That way they would forge personal bonds with the Iraqis during weeks or even months of training together that later could be called upon in combat. There were no American mess halls on the camps where the ICTF and Commandos were located, and the SF advisors ate at the Iraqi dining facilities. One advisor noted, "You were training with them, you were eating next to them in the mess hall, and you were killing with them."[90] Few if any restrictions were put on SF advisors' ability to accompany their partners in combat.

There were, however, minor variations between SF Groups concerning what U.S. advisors would and would not do. For example, during missions, some 3rd SF Group teams would not allow Iraqis to serve as drivers or operate the vehicle-mounted heavy machine gun for fear of a green-on-blue fratricide. By contrast, 5th SF Group teams allowed Iraqis to fill both of those roles.[91] But in general, ISOF soldiers and their SF advisors lived, fought, and sometimes even died shoulder to shoulder.

Some advisors did note that even though they were deeply involved in combat advising the ISOF, at times it was difficult to assess how much risk was acceptable. Returning rotation after rotation contributed to the perception that risk built up over time and that some missions might be so difficult that advisors would need to decide if the operation was worth losing the life of one of their friends and comrades. In those cases, advisors might adjust whether or not they would accompany the first group of Iraqi assaulters through the door or let the ISOF conduct the initial clearing before entering the building.[92]

Assessment: "You Had to Have Skin in the Game"

During the entirety of the ISOF advisory mission, there was little to no restriction on what type of advising SF soldiers could do with their partners. Any limitation put in place was usually at the behest of the advisors themselves based on their personal risk assessment or their own preferences. With the dissolution of the Iraqi government in 2003 and the installation of generally compliant institutions in their place, coalition forces met little resistance when implementing their preferred advising policies, and issues of national sovereignty simply did not affect what was allowed. Even as Iraq gradually regained its sovereignty, SF advisors consistently accompanied them on combat missions. Based on these factors, the degree of combat advising with the ISOF is rated to be high.

U.S. advisors universally touted the importance of combat advising and its impact on the ability to produce a combat-effective partner force. As noted by one advisor who had also served as commander of the Joint Special Operations Task Force–Philippines, "You had to have skin in the game. You have to share danger and adversity with your partner force to be successful. You can shower millions of dollars [on them] and have a yearslong relationship like in the Philippines, but if you're not out there on operations with them in the fight, leading by example and sharing that, then you would never reach anywhere near the same level of effectiveness."[93] Others pointed out that, unlike other missions, the U.S. advisors lived in the same buildings as their Iraqi partners and basically were with them almost every day, all day. Advisors accompanied the ISOF onto the objective and fought as partners but also spent time with them between missions and got to know their families. This considerable proximity of day-in and day-out contact built trust and helped erase some cultural reluctance to admit mistakes, but it also made errors easier to spot because advisors were present to evaluate their partners' performance in combat.[94]

EVALUATING COMBAT EFFECTIVENESS

Several vignettes provide interesting insight into the ISOF's combat effectiveness. In 2005 a high-value target the unit had been chasing for months suddenly showed up at the Commandos' doorstep and surrendered. He said that once he had learned the ISOF were chasing him, their reputation struck such fear into him that he felt it better to give himself up and avoid getting killed or possibly having his family hurt as collateral damage.[95] Another story stems from the unit's successes in the 2014 war against ISIS. After the conflict, many Iraqis considered the ISOF the saviors of the nation. Songs and poems were written to honor their battlefield successes, and college students and children wore T-shirts with the unit's logos.[96] Unfortunately these are merely anecdotal assessments, so to properly evaluate the ISOF's combat effectiveness I will review the same factors assessed for other case studies.

Night Fighting: Solar Powered to Black Coveralls

The Iraqi Counter Terrorism Force was equipped to match the capabilities of the Special Forces CIF companies that advised them. While the Commando battalions had slightly less capability, each soldier was still equipped with night-vision goggles and laser pointers for their rifles. Standard equipment included PVS-7, -14, and -15 goggles, which gave them considerable advantages over almost all their opponents.

When SF advisors first formed the Commandos and the ICTF, they had to overcome Iraqi military cultural habits that avoided training and fighting at night. One advisor—unwittingly echoing the same metaphor used by another advisor to describe LRR troops—quipped that at first the Iraqis were "solar powered" and that at night operations seemed to cease.[97] But through training and mentorship the Iraqis overcome those barriers relatively quickly. By mid-2004 the ISOF operated almost exclusively at night and conducting several raids in a single period of darkness. One U.S. advisor noted that by 2005 the Iraqis had grown so proficient operating at night that he felt like he was working with a U.S. unit.[98]

Because their night capabilities so overmatched their opponents', the ISOF switched to a reverse-cycle operation wherein it carried out missions at night and slept during the day. The ISOF then painted their vehicles black and changed their uniforms to black Nomex coveralls, further allowing them to take advantage of darkness.[99] Over time those capabilities became more and more honed, and one CJSOTF commander noted that no military within the CENTCOM area of responsibility matched the ISOF's night-fighting skills.[100]

After the U.S. withdrawal in 2011, the ISOF's night-fighting skills decayed somewhat. Misuse by Iraqi government forces desperate for a unit that would stand up to ISIS in 2014 meant the ISOF were thrown into combat more as shock infantry rather than in their SOF role. Such dire straits caused ISOF elements to often fight during the day, an environment for which they were not prepared and that they did not prefer. After ISIS' advance had been halted, the ISOF returned to the offensive where they were able to take advantage of their night-fighting capabilities, conducting operations such as offensives, raids, and ambushes in darkness during the 2016–2017 Battle of Mosul.[101] Media reports from 2021 also show that as the conventional threat from ISIS ebbed, the ISOF returned to kill/capture operations, which they primarily conducted at night using night-vision equipment, performing capably and successfully.[102]

Assessment

The Iraqi Special Operations Forces had and still have considerable night-fighting skills. Even after the withdrawal of U.S. forces, the ISOF routinely conducted operations in darkness, both on traditional kill/capture missions and during sustained combat against ISIS in a role more akin to that performed by elite infantry. Taking all those influences into consideration, a high rating is warranted.

Conducting Multiday Combat Operations: "Not as Sexy as Kicking Doors, but Just as Critical"

While the ISOF consistently demonstrated that they can conduct multiday combat operations, as evinced by their performance against ISIS from 2014 to 2020, at times they have struggled with logistical resupply, maintenance, and long-term sustainment. Most U.S. advisors noted that the individual-level maintenance performed by ISOF soldiers was acceptable or even good but the organization faced challenges with unit- and depot-level maintenance programs. In some ways this was a self-inflicted wound caused by early advisor decisions. Rather than arm the ISOF with Eastern Bloc weapons such as the AK-47, which were relatively easy to maintain and matched the logistics system of the rest of Iraqi security forces, advisors provided equipment matching their own. Individual ISOF troops used the model of the M4 rifle employed by U.S. Special Operations Command with its high-end optics and night vision, along with M9 pistols, .50 caliber M2 heavy machine guns, and U.S. sniper rifles. This decision created challenges with ammunition resupply, as the ISOF had to requisition something completely different from what was normally available to other Iraqi units. It also created challenges with maintenance for the same reasons, and the units even lacked appropriately trained armorers at times.[103]

Another challenge stemmed from the organizational flow: Because the ISOF fell outside the traditional Iraqi Ministry of Defense construct, obtaining immediate resupply in the heat of battle was challenging. Advisors had assumed that the ISOF could obtain critical resupply of water, food, and fuel from nearby conventional Iraqi Army units.[104] However, the Counter Terrorism Service functioned as its own ministry-like department, and when the ISOF were placed under the CTS and not in the Defense Ministry, local military commanders sometimes refused to resupply them because the ISOF were not funded by the same ministry. In some instances ISOF units waited for resupply until the CTS headquarters transferred funds to the Ministry of Defense to cover their resupply from the Iraqi Army. This challenge was alleviated somewhat by the establishment of interdepartmental agreements and the creation of a CTC-level logistics command, but at times conventional units delayed ISOF resupply and institutional lapses occurred when the Defense Ministry delayed paying ISOF soldiers.[105]

At the same time, the ISOF successfully established a baseline in critical institutional logistical functions. Before U.S. advisors left, Iraqis conducted their own assessment and selection courses and training for both the Commandos and ICTF. This gave them the ability to replace combat losses and keep the organization functional at the institutional level as the force took casualties—capabilities that became critically important in the battle against ISIS. One advisor noted how consequential this aspect of unit management is to the overall organization. "As important as being effective out on operations is, their ability to regenerate combat power and to sustain themselves, conduct administration, intelligence, logistics, and communications—it isn't sexy, certainly not as sexy as kicking doors, but it is just as critical."[106] The ISOF were able to perform all those functions, and even though they were not to the standard of the U.S. military, they were capable.

Although the ISOF's logistics system has struggled to meet the demands of high-intensity combat, it has rarely failed. Unlike many other partner-force units built or assisted by Green Berets, building a logistics component for the ISOF began nearly in parallel with construction of its tactical forces. Even before the first brigade was officially stood up, a support battalion had been organized in March 2004 to meet the logistics needs of the disparate Iraqi SOF elements.[107] At least in part due to this, the historical record of the unit was exemplary during its fighting with ISIS and there were numerous examples of ISOF units fighting for more than seventy-two hours. During the Battle of Baiji in July of 2014, a small group of ISOF Commandos, outnumbered five to one by ISIS fighters, held out for over a week, refusing to surrender even when given the offer of safe passage.[108] In the Battle of Mosul, ISOF units took 40 percent casualties yet fought on consistently for months on end with little to no relief. The Najaf regional Commando battalion went from 350 soldiers to fewer than 150 in ninety days of combat.[109] During the fighting, ISOF logistics elements were able to provide hot meals to their soldiers and conduct recovery and repair of their vehicles in contact, returning damaged high-mobility multipurpose wheeled vehicles to the front within days.[110] Such feats were repeated in Ramadi, Fallujah, and Tikrit: when the ISOF's system was called upon to provide water, ammunition, fuel, and food in the height of intense urban combat, it delivered.

Assessment

ISOF logistics capabilities are mixed. While they were generally able to conduct local resupply or organically resupply their own units, at times those capabilities broke down. Compared to the Iraqi Army, which has its own logistics challenges, the ISOF's resupply capabilities are not robust. Although there are support elements at every level of command from battalion through CTC level, those capabilities are rarely sufficient to conduct long-term resupply and are challenged when ISOF units operate far away from either their Baghdad headquarters or one of the four regional hubs. There is ample evidence, however, that the ISOF consistently met the standard of fighting independently in sustained combat for seventy-two hours or more. Therefore the ISOF are assessed as having a medium capability to conduct extended combat operations—although at the high end of that rating.

Chapter 4

Fighting without Advisors

The ISOF proved eager students when learning how to conduct intelligence-driven operations, the foundation of fighting without advisors present. Both the ICTF and the Commandos had recce units organic to the battalion level. These units were not typical tactical-reconnaissance forces or scouts but instead were urban-reconnaissance forces that had been trained in human-source operations and tradecraft by highly skilled Special Forces operators. Those human-intelligence cells were functioning independently as early as 2004 and generating their own target sets.[111] ISOF recce personnel could manage source operations as well as conduct close-target reconnaissance out of uniform and in civilian vehicles.[112] It was a robust capability that ranged across the entire geographical and ethnosectarian span of the country, and they could communicate between elements via a secure electronic server.[113] The recce force was well trained, employing their own control elements as well as counterintelligence capabilities. Women were recruited for the force without limitations to collect intelligence and infiltrate terrorist networks.[114] While ISOF recce units successfully generated their own intelligence, at times Iraq's political leadership was unwilling to carry out missions based on that intelligence.

The impact of that capability meant that ISOF were able to effectively carry out intelligence-driven operations. Unlike any other Iraqi unit, they could conduct multiple kill/capture operations in the same night using information gained from one operation to build the next target set. Their process was not slowed even when the Iraqi government established a requirement that warrants be issued before any mission could be carried out; the unit accordingly recruited civilian judges to pair with their intelligence fusion cells, facilitating rapid approvals.[115]

At the same time, the ISOF were somewhat challenged when conducting high-end, intelligence-driven operations. The force only had rudimentary signals intelligence and imagery intelligence and had relied on U.S. forces to provide those capabilities. Like many developing countries, Iraq lacked the financial resources to purchase such expensive equipment. After the withdrawal of U.S. forces, the CTC slowly developed a baseline capability.[116] Similarly the ISOF did not have the budget to acquire technical capabilities that could conduct real-time sensitive site exploitation. Instead, a standard battle drill was to immediately obtain a warrant from an Iraqi judge to enable the search of captured mobile phones. Warrant in hand, they brought the phone to the appropriate Iraqi mobile provider and had them unlock the phone and provide stored and frequently contacted names and phone numbers. This procedure often took up to twelve hours, although at times it was done more quickly.[117] The ISOF also routinely collected documents from the battlefield and attempted to benefit from them in real time, but more often than not documents were brought to rear areas for later exploitation.[118] In addition to those challenges, sometimes elements within the CTC were reluctant to share intelligence with one another, fearing compromise of the intelligence as well as desiring to take credit for successful missions.[119]

Assessment

The ISOF made the most of their budget constraints and had extremely effective human intelligence and some ability to perform sensitive site exploitation on electronic devices and documents. Their human-intelligence operators were well trained and motivated and fit into a system that generated targets. However, the ISOF had limited signals intelligence and intelligence, surveillance, and reconnaissance capabilities in addition to certain institutional challenges. Even with these limitations the ISOF had the ability to conduct timely and effective intelligence-driven operations wherein the first target generated follow-on missions, even if this capability was inconsistent at times. All combined, these factors result in a medium rating for ability to fight without advisors present.

Performance against the Enemy in Combat

There is considerable acclaim for the ISOF's performance in battle. Whether fighting Shia militias such as Jaysh al Mahdi or Kata'ib Hezbollah or fighting Sunni terrorist groups such as al-Qaida in Iraq or ISIS, Iraqi Special Operations Forces consistently defeated their enemies. At times the fighting was brutal, drawn out, and costly, resulting in many casualties, but in nearly every case they prevailed. Their performance was steady whether in sustained kill/capture operations or large set-piece battles such as in Mosul and Fallujah. Only when they were vastly outnumbered did the ISOF retreat, and even then it was after holding out far longer than any other Iraqi unit. Many such engagements, particularly those after 2011, happened without the help of U.S. advisors or enablers, providing a critical perspective of the ISOF's unilateral capabilities.

As ISIS marched across Iraq in 2014, nearly every Iraqi unit crumbled in front of the onslaught. The ISOF by contrast remained cohesive and fought determined delaying actions across the country—even when significantly outnumbered. At Baiji a small detachment held out for more than a week before retrograding on their own to safety. The ISOF's only defeat—albeit temporary—was in Ramadi in 2015 when CTC forces that had been defending the city for sixteen months were hit by a well-planned ISIS offensive led by nearly two dozen car bombs in immediate succession, causing the force to withdraw and abandon the city to regroup. The attack had been extremely well planned and used sleeper cells dressed in police uniforms for surprise as well as car bombs in dump trucks and bulldozers armored with welded-on steel plates.[120]

As the tide against ISIS turned, the ISOF led the effort to liberate captured towns and cities, often succeeding where other Iraqi forces had failed, such as during the April 2015 Battle of Tikrit. The organization was often the first unit to enter ISIS-held cities and was present at every major battle. At the Battle of Mosul they demonstrated adept combat performance and were instrumental in the city's liberation.[121]

At times the ISOF faced challenges, forced to use tactics for which it had not prepared in the fight to save Iraq. Instead of the deliberately planned offensive operations such as raids, ambushes, or kill/capture missions formed on a foundation of actionable intelligence, the ISOF had to fight as a conventional infantry unit.[122] When pushed into conducting defensive operations, most elements were challenged to adapt. In traditional infantry-style offensive operations, some of the more-recently formed brigades stumbled and demonstrated poor tactics, lack of fire discipline, and reluctant use of body armor. Other units tended to rely on their vehicles too much and eschewed dismounted operations. Often the ISOF had to rely on U.S. or coalition airstrikes to help rout ISIS forces, as in Ramadi where the ISOF called in over six hundred aircraft, most of them not from the Iraqi Air Force. Many of these problems were tied to overuse of the unit by senior Iraqi leaders as well as to the appalling casualties the ISOF took as a result.[123] After the defeat of ISIS, the ISOF gradually reverted to its traditional intelligence-driven kill/capture operations and was generally successful in breaking up the terrorist group's stay-behind cells.[124]

Assessment

Evaluating the ISOF's performance in battle is relatively straightforward as they were involved in every major engagement against ISIS. Despite being thrown into a situation for which they were not prepared, organized, or trained, the ISOF performed quite well. With the exception of a few battles, the ISOF either held their own against ISIS or defeated the militant group outright. Success came at a cost, and the unit endured considerably high levels of casualties and was forced to rely on coalition air support during some battles in order to achieve victory. After the fall of ISIS, the unit transitioned reasonably well back into its more-traditional SOF role of conducting counterterrorism missions. Considering all these factors, a high rating—albeit at the low end of the scale—would be most appropriate.

INITIAL ASSESSMENT

On the macro level, when assessing combat effectiveness the Iraqi Special Operations Forces received medium ratings in conducting multiday combat operations and fighting without advisors present and received high scores in performance in combat and night-fighting skills. When looking at those components holistically, the ISOF rate an overall ranking of high-moderate effectiveness. The ISOF proved to be a highly capable and adaptable force that bore the brunt of ISIS' assault on Iraq from 2014 to 2017 and is still leading that fight today, albeit against the terrorist group's underground cells rather than in set-piece battles. The ISOF proved to have a competent and skilled human-intelligence capability that could generate multiple target sets in the same twenty-four-hour cycle, if inconsistently. Logistically the unit could engage in extended battles, but due to some institutional-level shortfalls it frequently faced real challenges in performing at the highest levels. At night the ISOF have few equals and overall are the most capable force built in Iraq by coalition forces, retaining many of the skills and organizational values instituted by SF advisors long after they withdrew.

In the next chapter we will assess these same factors relating to U.S. advisory efforts with the Afghan Commandos, a case that shares many similarities with the mission in Iraq.

– 5 –
"Chasing Bright and Shiny Objects"
The Afghan Commandos, 2007–2021

BACKGROUND
September 11 and Operation Enduring Freedom

HAD AL-QAIDA not attacked the United States on September 11, 2001, Afghanistan probably would have remained forgotten by the world. Owing to the country's role as a haven for the terrorist group, mounting a U.S. response there was a foregone conclusion. Like in Iraq, special-operations forces played an outsized role in the initial invasion, with the Middle East–oriented 5th Special Forces Group working hand in hand with CIA paramilitary officers. ODAs assisted Afghan militias representing various ethnic and political groups, providing them little training but a direct link to U.S. and coalition airpower. Guiding punishing airstrikes, less than four hundred U.S. soldiers, a vast majority of whom were SF operators, proved to be decisive to the Afghan conflict. After a lightning-fast defeat of the Taliban, the fundamentalist Islamic militia ruling most of Afghanistan with an iron fist since the mid-1990s and allied to al-Qaida, Hamid Karzai, a Pashtun, was selected to become Afghanistan's interim president.

As the George W. Bush administration pivoted to face Iraq in 2003, resources and personnel quickly exited Afghanistan, which was reduced to a supporting theater in the global war effort. 5th Group ceded the Afghanistan mission to a series of non–regionally oriented Groups as it began to prepare for Iraq. Even greater numbers of conventional forces, which had been in supporting roles and small numbers during the toppling of the Taliban, flowed into the country as they took command of the mission from special-operations forces. Yet many parts of the country still had been untouched by coalition forces. One SF NCO noted the bewilderment on the part of some Afghans during this period: "We showed up at one village and they thought we were Russians."[1]

The mission, dubbed Operation Enduring Freedom, was initially schizophrenic. Political efforts attempted to unify the disparate Afghan population and provide legitimacy to the Karzai government. As the U.S. presence changed from expeditionary to long-term and logistics-intensive, its strategy vacillated widely: from pursuit of al-Qaida to stability and support of the Afghan government and then to counterinsurgency against the Taliban. The mission itself also morphed from one led by the United States and a small coterie of allies to one that included a parallel effort with a vast constellation of coalition forces under NATO auspices named the International Security Assistance Force. Despite determined efforts to destroy them, the Taliban and other insurgent and terrorist forces seemingly only gained strength over time.

Creation of the Afghan Commandos

Unlike in Iraq, in Afghanistan U.S. advisors made no immediate effort to build elite partners. From 2001 until 2007 Special Forces ODAs either operated unilaterally, with whatever local militia forces they could find, or, when they could, with Afghan National Army (ANA) conventional forces. That began to change in late 2006, when the head of Special Operations Command Central tasked the Combined Joint Special Operations Task Force (CJSOTF) to determine whether or not they could build an Afghan Special Forces unit. The CJSOTF determined that the ANA could neither build nor sustain such a unit and that doing so would probably be unnecessary. Instead the CJSOTF recommended that an elite light-infantry Ranger-style force be assembled to serve as an SOF partner force as well as "shock troops" to deal with tactical challenges that the ANA was unable to handle on its own.[2] That unit would be the ANA Commandos.

Up to that point, the CJSOTF had been spending $1.2 million a month on local tribal militias to guard the bases of U.S. Special Forces ODAs.[3] Although Afghan governments traditionally provided local security using tribal militias, doing so became fiscally untenable and not consistent with the goal of disbanding irregular forces and replacing them with a centralized Afghan national military force. As such, there was considerable pressure to stop working with the militias, giving further impetus to stand up the Commandos quickly.[4]

Lessons learned from standing up the Iraqi Special Operations Forces were considered but did not directly influence the creation of the Commandos. Senior CJSOTF leaders believed the situation in Afghanistan was so different that it required a distinct solution from what had worked in Iraq. Afghan leaders modified the U.S. plan slightly based on their experience with the previous Afghan Commando unit that had been created by the Russians during their occupation in the 1980s. Major General Sher Mohammad Karimi, who had graduated the U.S. Special Forces Qualification course before the Soviet invasion and was serving as ANA chief of operations, was particularly instrumental in shepherding the proposal so that it quickly gained approval.[5] Over time the Commandos grew into a division-sized force and became the primary Afghan military instrument.

Operation Freedom's Sentinel

By 2015 the war in Afghanistan had ground on for more than a decade yet produced little more than strategic equilibrium. A democratically elected, coalition-supported government sputtered along in Kabul and the main population centers, but the Taliban and other insurgent groups continued to survive. With little sign of forward progress and domestic war-weariness growing, U.S. president Barack Obama moved to draw down forces and adjust the mission. The impetus to change also reflected shifts in sovereignty, as Afghans had tired of night raids, civilian casualties, and airstrikes and pushed to decrease the amount of U.S.- and coalition-led offensive operations.

After a period of negotiations, the U.S. troop commitment was reduced to around ten thousand personnel—less than half of the year before—and those forces were consolidated on fewer bases. In addition, the core mission shifted from conducting combat operations to training and assisting Afghan forces as well as counterterrorism. Apart from the Commandos and a few other organizations, most of the coalition's security force assistance shifted to building institutional capabilities rather than advising combat forces. Reflecting these changes, Operation Enduring Freedom was concluded and replaced with Operation Freedom's Sentinel.

Afghan military forces took the lead for the country's security and proved unequal to the challenge. In some districts, Taliban forces came to openly control significant population centers, and in others they expanded their control of the countryside. Attacks in Kabul escalated, giving rise to concerns about the survival of the government. U.S. president Donald Trump decided that the United States would leave Afghanistan completely, only to see the withdrawal stretch into the administration of his successor, President Joe Biden. As the final U.S. soldiers were preparing to leave, the situation imploded, and province after province quickly fell to the Taliban. Many Commando units fought to the end while their country disintegrated around them, holding out until the Taliban capture of Kabul put an official end to the conflict. A brave few Commandos even helped hold the perimeter of the Kabul International Airport as the United States and its allies conducted a final evacuation.

THE ADVISORY EFFORT

Partner-to-Advisor Ratio

Expansion of the Afghan Commandos: Special Operations Forces Cannot be Mass-Produced

Echoing a trend in U.S. efforts during its post-9/11 conflicts, the Afghan Commandos grew significantly over the span of the SF advisory mission.[6] To begin the mission, advisors trained an Afghan cadre and helped them stand up the Commando Training Center (CTC) at Camp Morehead, which would serve as the training center for all forces under Afghan National Army Special Operations Command (ANASOC).[7] Ironically, the base at Camp Morehead was the same location the Soviets had used to train their version of Afghan Commandos.[8] The first Commando *kandak*, or battalion-sized unit, graduated from the CTC in July 2007 and reported for duty that August.[9] Each kandak originally had three Commando companies and one headquarters and service company—920 to 950 soldiers all told.

The initial plan for the Commandos aligned one kandak to support each of the five regionally oriented Afghan Corps headquarters and based one additional kandak in Kabul to provide national-level counterterrorism capabilities.[10] Such an orientation put a battalion near Afghanistan's major population centers to respond to local crises. Two battalions were stood up in 2007, three in 2008, and the last in 2009.[11] As the final battalion came online, Brig. Gen. Ed Reeder, then commanding general of Combined Forces Special Operations Component Command–Afghanistan, ordered the construction of four additional battalions, which when completed would put the total number of Commando kandaks at ten.[12] Two of those new kandaks were produced in 2010, one in 2011, and one in 2015.

One U.S. advisor observed that during this period nearly every Commando who began training passed and that Afghan Commandos were being "mass-produced to meet the need," in contravention of core SOF principles.[13] Another senior NCO noted that he considered the Commandos more of an elite infantry force though for Afghanistan they were considered SOF.[14] A third was even more explicit: "They just took an infantry battalion and said, *Hey, you're going to be Commandos.* Iraq was a quality program; Afghanistan was a quantity program. I literally think the assessment must have been, *Hey, give me a roster.* There was no assessment criteria. There were no true standards that were established, or if there were they weren't followed."[15]

In 2017, the ANA General Staff, supported by U.S. leaders, decided to double the size of the Commandos by 2020, from 10 battalions and 11,700 soldiers to 20 battalions and 23,300 personnel.[16] As the directive was passed down the chain of command, leadership at the Commando Training Center insisted this kind of growth was impossible. The Commando school was already struggling to maintain the existing force structure due to casualties, desertions, and soldiers completing their terms of service. Instead of creating additional battalions, the CTC recommended adding a company to each battalion, which they saw as both feasible and meeting the intent of the General Staff. While following this recommendation would not double the size of the Commandos, it would add more combat power at the tactical level without creating additional bureaucracy or headquarters.

To accomplish this growth, the CTC was forced to greatly expand throughput and reduce the quality of the candidates even further. Regular ANA units were ordered to Camp Morehead, tasked with attending training, and "reflagged" as Commando units. While they had technically completed the required twelve-week Commando course, few candidates failed the training, raising questions about quality control. New buildings, ranges, and training areas had to be built, and obtaining equipment for the additional units was particularly difficult. The tenth kandak still did not have its entire complement of weapons by 2017, further slowing growth of the force.[17] Yet on the eve of the U.S. withdrawal from Afghanistan in 2021, ANASOC made up one-fifth of all Afghan security forces.[18]

Advisor Commitment

When the Commandos were first organized, a single ODA was paired with each battalion-sized kandak to match doctrinal requirement.[19] This partnering remained relatively constant for the first few years of the mission because of a global shortage of ODAs from commitments to Iraq and other missions worldwide.[20] The ratio also remained constant as additional Commando kandaks were created and then sent into combat.[21] The only exception to this general rule was that after the 6th Kandak was stood up, it was paired with two ODAs because it was considered the national counterterrorism force.[22]

In practice, because the Commandos followed a red-amber-green operations cycle, the pairing would be more accurately described as an ODA advising two companies. In this cycle, of the three fighting companies in each kandak, one conducted combat operations (green), one conducted training (amber), and one was on leave (red), which allowed its soldiers to travel across the country to visit family and bring their pay back home. Because Afghanistan did not have a developed banking system, Commandos were paid in cash, and many physically delivered their pay to their families for either safekeeping or financial assistance.[23]

At several points during U.S. involvement in Afghanistan, the CJSOTF obtained more troops, allowing two ODAs to pair with each Commando kandak. The increase was in part due to a realization that a single ODA was insufficient to advise a battalion-sized element, a finding also noted in a 2015 RAND study. Nearly every advisor interviewed echoed the same sentiment. One noted, "It takes more than twelve guys. Just mentorship alone with commanders, we don't have enough bodies to do the mentoring."[24] These more-robust pairings occurred from March 2011 to February 2012 and from June 2013 to October 2014.[25] Even though the pressure on the SF institutional force had been relieved somewhat by the 2011 withdrawal of U.S. forces from Iraq, the rise of ISIS in 2014 made such a large commitment to Afghanistan untenable, and by October the enhanced pairing ratio concluded.[26]

The pairing ratios shifted again in November of that year due to changes associated with the end of Operation Enduring Freedom and preparations for the beginning of Operation Freedom's Sentinel. The CJSOTF, which had been made up of a Group headquarters and two or more SF battalions, was stood down in October 2014 and replaced with a single reinforced battalion. The significant reduction in SF advisor presence resulted in some kandaks having an ODA assigned for the duration of the deployment, other kandaks having a sporadic presence, and some kandaks going without a partner ODA entirely. When one ODA was paired with two or three kandaks per rotation, the ODA would travel to one of the kandaks, spend four or five days with them, and then travel to the next kandak.[27] Other advisors noted that for some kandaks, support from an ODA only occurred if requested or if the tactical situation warranted support, meaning ODAs came and went as needed across the battlefield.[28]

Evaluating the Personnel Strength of the Commandos

Endemic desertion and AWOL status made assessing Commando personnel strength a major challenge. Even though each kandak was doctrinally between 920 and 950 Commandos, in actuality unit strength hovered at around 60 to 70 percent.[29] At the company level, authorized strength was 118 Commandos, and several interviewees noted that units worked to keep as many soldiers present for duty in the operations or "green" company by shifting soldiers from the headquarters unit.[30] One advisor from the Center for Army Analysis estimated annual desertion rates for the Commandos to be between 20 and 25 percent, something that rapidly depleted ability and willingness to fight.[31] To keep up with these astronomical rates, the Commando school had to conduct two to three classes a year, producing a total of roughly one thousand new Commandos annually.[32] During some surge periods, production tripled to an astounding three thousand Commandos a year.[33]

Like other Afghan soldiers, Commandos deserted or went AWOL for a variety of reasons. Sometimes the soldiers or their family members were threatened. Sometimes they could not get home on leave and were desperate to give a portion of their pay to family members or just see their relatives and families after long absences. Due to the size of Afghanistan and the state of its infrastructure, getting from one side of the country to the other was a daunting task that could take a week or more. Recognizing how important it was to Commandos to be able to get home during leave, at times the CJSOTF tasked one of their C-130 Hercules aircraft to fly to various Commando outposts and bring soldiers who were due to take leave to the transit hub in Kabul. This solution was not sustainable given the Afghan logistics system, and as U.S. forces drew down, the practice was discontinued, leading to increased AWOL rates.

Other Commandos apparently left due to stagnant and dysfunctional Afghan military personnel practices. Many Afghan soldiers believed that career progression from enlisted to NCO was difficult to impossible, a perception U.S. advisors attempted to change with minimal success. Moreover, the Afghan National Army did not have a functional system to move soldiers from one duty station to another, either for personal reasons, such as wanting to be closer to family members, or professional, like obtaining important postings. Because going AWOL or deserting was such a common cultural practice, perhaps a trait the ANA adopted from their militia precursors, it did not incur a significant penalty or punishment.

Calculating the Partner-to-Advisor Ratio

The starting point for calculating the number of Commandos being advised was the doctrinal strength of a company (118), because most of the ODA focus was at the company level due to the red-amber-green cycle. Most ODAs advised two companies, although at times a single ODA was paired with a single company. Appendix E reflects those calculations, with matching advisor and partner additions at each point that a new Commando kandak was organized. It should be noted that I only measured the monthly ratios through December 2019 as the data for 2020 and 2021 were not reliable because the increasingly smaller set of advisors made it difficult to cross-reference. The data also reflect a best estimate of Afghan personnel strength based on desertion and AWOL rates. As each new Commando unit was created, its strength was rated at 100 percent, reflecting that the unit began its life cycle with a full complement of Commandos. To match the reported 25 percent desertion loss rate, a monthly reduction of 2 percent is imposed on those new units until they reach 75 percent strength, which many advisors reported was the sustainable personnel strength. After conducting those calculations, the overall monthly average is calculated to be 16.4 soldiers per advisor (see figure 5.1 for the monthly ratios).

Assessment

Calculating the partner-to-advisor ratio reveals that the doctrinal standard where one ODA advises one battalion was not practiced because it was deemed insufficient. Instead an ODA advising a company was common and informally considered a requirement. Like in Iraq, advisors I interviewed were adamant that the ratio of partners to advisors mattered significantly and that the lower that ratio was, the better chance of producing combat-effective partners. One Green Beret who served in Iraq and Afghanistan noted that because of the higher ratio in Afghanistan, each advisor's span of control was wider, meaning they simply couldn't accomplish the same tasks because there were not enough advisors.[34]

Advisor Language Training and Cultural Awareness

The 2001 invasion of Afghanistan was led by 5th Special Forces Group, which was regionally oriented toward the Middle East and Central Asia. The Group was soon pulled out of Afghanistan to prepare for the looming 2003 invasion of Iraq, where

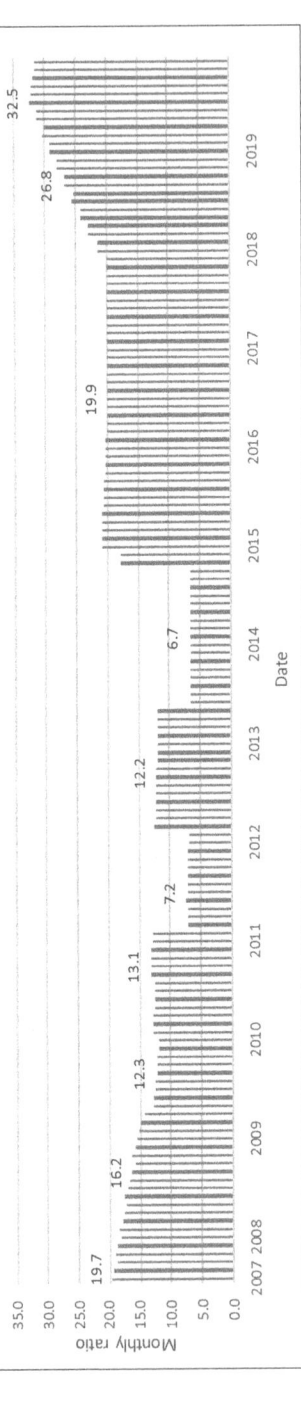

FIGURE 5.1 Monthly ratio of partners to advisors, Afghanistan

it became fully embroiled along with 10th Group. As a result, 3rd Special Forces Group, which was regionally oriented toward Africa, and 7th Special Forces Group, regionally oriented toward Latin America, were assigned shared responsibility for the Afghanistan mission and provided the majority of the ODAs advising the Commandos. Due to the duration of the conflict and the intense personnel requirements in Afghanistan, every other Group also contributed forces, although to a lesser degree. 5th Group was especially hard-pressed to provide a contingent, because less than three years after formally withdrawing from Iraq, they returned to help fight ISIS and soon after that were tasked with advising Kurdish and other paramilitary forces in Syria. As a result, from 2007 to 2009, when the Commandos were first stood up, the Special Forces Groups advising them were not regionally oriented to central Asia and did not speak the appropriate languages.

In August 2009 the regional alignment of the five active-duty Special Forces Groups shifted. Recognizing that 5th Group was overtasked with other responsibilities in the Middle East, 3rd Special Forces Group was given responsibility for Afghanistan and Pakistan. Pashtu language training started at the U.S. Army Special Warfare Center and School in parallel with the shift, but given the length of the training program, few of those who learned the language deployed to Afghanistan until 2010. By 2012, a limited number of Pashtu speakers had arrived but few, if any, Dari speakers. Language training was slow to adapt to the needs in Afghanistan because there had been a continuing assumption that the United States would be withdrawing from the country soon, and as a result there was a reluctance to reengineer the focus of the institutional schoolhouse.[35] Changing languages would require letting go current instructors, finding and hiring new instructors, and rewriting programs of instruction and syllabi—a slow and drawn-out process that caused many leaders to resist any shift.

The 3rd Group's responsibility for Afghanistan only lasted until 2016, when the unit was refocused back to Africa and responsibility for Afghanistan and Pakistan was returned to 5th Group. Some SF NCOs noted that even though their unit had been assigned Afghanistan for seven years, by the time 3rd Group was switched back to Africa fewer than half of the operators had been trained in Dari or Pashtu.[36] During that window, from 2009 to 2016, teams from 3rd Group were technically regionally oriented to Afghanistan, resulting in an orientation match around less than half of the time, even though many of those ODAs had never been fully trained in the local languages. The calculation reflects the split of the Commando mission roughly evenly between 3rd and 7th Group but reduced slightly by the participation of other non–regionally oriented groups in the advisory effort. From 2016 until 2019 the match again dropped to near zero as the regionally oriented group (5th) was still extensively deployed to Iraq and Syria while 3rd and 7th Groups usually still led the mission in Afghanistan. Overall this puts the degree of match in language training and cultural awareness of the SF advisors for the Afghan mission as low.

Assessment: "It Is Good to See You Are Training Your Men in the Language of the Enemy"

Echoing a trend, most of the SF advisors in Afghanistan believed that knowing the local language had little impact on their ability to produce a combat-effective partner force. One significant factor was that in Afghanistan, like in the Philippines and completely unlike in Iraq, multiple languages were spoken. Even though there were at least twelve widely spoken languages in Afghanistan and three official languages, roughly 90 percent of Commandos spoke Dari.[37] This demographic was far outside the country's norm, for roughly half of Afghanistan was Pashtun. That disparity created some challenges, with many Pashtuns feeling that Tajiks, who usually spoke Dari, were occupying their homelands in Afghanistan.[38] A small number of Commandos also spoke some of the other languages of Afghanistan, further complicating which languages SF soldiers should learn. Knowing which Commando spoke which language was often challenging and caused confusion among interpreters and advisors.[39]

Each language often represented a completely different ethnic group, creating cultural communications challenges. For example, one advisor recalled the CJSOTF's judge advocate teaching the laws-of-land warfare to a group of Commandos of mixed ethnicities. Most of the Tajiks and Hazaras accepted the guidance on treatment of civilians and prisoners with little conflict, but many Pashtuns had difficulty understanding some of the basic concepts. Several of the Pashtuns asked why they could not search the property of female household members to ensure they did not own "illegal" Western-style clothing and were further dismayed when they were told that they could not physically strike those civilians if they discovered anything they deemed "salacious."[40]

Another advisor who served on four SF and one contractor rotations to Afghanistan highlighted the complications of understanding the connections between culture and language. During one deployment he was speaking with a senior Commando officer when a U.S. logistics officer approached who was part of the Afghanistan-Pakistan Hands Program, which focused on language and culture training and consistently returned those soldiers to Central Asia. When he greeted the Afghan senior leader in Pashtu, the Afghan officer grunted and ignored him. After the logistics officer walked away, the Afghan, who was Tajik and preferred to speak Dari, quipped, "It is good to see you are training your men in the language of the enemy."[41]

Many of those languages were difficult for English-speakers to learn, further complicating communication. Dari, Urdu, and Farsi were all rated category III languages by the Defense Department, and Pashtu was a category IV—the most difficult.[42] This convinced many leaders that trying to learn all the nuances of an Afghan language was not an effective use of time. Maj. Gen. Ed Reeder commanded the CJSOTF and deployed six times to Afghanistan; he posited, "You're never going to master the language well enough to be able to have a decent conversation with a minister or with a general, much less a peasant."[43]

Advisors nearly universally noted that even if they did not speak whatever Afghan language their partners spoke, they were able to find ways to work around the barrier. Many SF soldiers either relied on interpreters or spoke English and enlisted the help of one of the Commandos to translate. One NCO noted that he could almost always find someone who liked American movies enough to be able to communicate and use them as a de facto interpreter.[44] Others believed that advisors absolutely required interpreters so as to ensure that what was relayed to the Commandos was accurate and could be delivered quickly in crisis situations, such as the heat of battle.[45] Another advisor bluntly opined, "Language was not important. . . . The key thing was finding the right interpreter that could teach me about the cultural stuff. . . . I needed to know how they think and why they [Afghans] made the decision they are making. That's what is important. I need to understand that, not how to say hello."[46]

Like in Iraq, some advisors noted that over time, those who did not speak host-nation languages caught up by learning the most important vocabulary. "Experienced guys who had been to Afghanistan before and knew right and wrong was what mattered most."[47] Other advisors argued that perhaps language mattered on the first rotation but not on later rotations. Across multiple deployments advisors learned what they needed to know about culture as well as bits and pieces of important vocabulary.[48] As one NCO noted, an SF soldier with a penchant for languages who hears the same word enough times on multiple rotations will soon learn the most important words and phrases.[49]

Advisors also noted that when Americans tried to speak and learn Afghan dialects, Commandos almost always went out of their way to help them. One advisor noted that "cultural awareness works both ways" and that the interpreters and Commandos, after several rotations working with Americans, began to get to know what their advisors meant and began to understand what they were implying even if it had not been explicitly stated.[50] Over time the Commandos would often learn broken English, at least enough to function in tactical operations, learning key phrases such as *Take the left door* or *Search him* or *Set up a base of fire here*.

In the words of one advisor, "knowing Dari or Pashtu was not mission essential; it was mission enhancing. Not knowing the specific language where you operated was not limiting."[51] Understanding the environment was essential, however, as was being aware of critical cultural sensitivities, such as Islam and the impacts of Ramadan. Many advisors felt most of this could be learned over time.

There were few dissenting voices. Of those, some noted that knowing a host nation's language was not as important as having solid cultural awareness. Maj. Gen. Ed Reeder once asked a senior Afghan general what he should do to best understand the culture and language. The Afghan replied, "Read the Qur'an. I live for the Prophet and make all of my personal and professional decisions in the name of the Prophet." Reeder provided another anecdote that some advisors would see Afghans stop fighting and drop to their knees and pray in the middle of battle. If the advisors did not understand the culture, they might call the soldiers cowards to try to shame them into returning to battle, which would almost certainly destroy any chance of building rapport: they were praying not because they were afraid but because they were religiously devout.[52]

Other advisors emphasized the importance of culture: "Teams that were good at building rapport didn't have problems, while teams that didn't get it had problems. The cultural aspect of it is huge; it is probably the biggest thing. . . . It is only through cultural awareness that you can talk someone into doing something that you want them to do."[53] Some advisors who had served in 7th Group—which is oriented toward Latin America and the Caribbean—noted that Afghan culture often parallels Hispanic culture: Both have male-dominated societies where masculinity and projections of strength matter and where honor and families are a key part of life. Although Islam and Christianity have myriad differences, the importance of faith in daily life is central to both. This meant that it was "not a giant leap" for 7th Group to shift from understanding and building rapport with soldiers in Latin America to soldiers in Afghanistan.[54]

Others observed that while language and cultural awareness were important, interpersonal skills were critical. Some advisors noted that the SF assessment and training process identifies and selects for traits of empathy and respect for others, which are critical for effective advising. They said a classic example is the Robin Sage guerilla-warfare exercise, the culminating event of the SF qualification course. During the exercise students must demonstrate they are able to build rapport and develop trust with the guerrilla chief and are invariably asked to eat some odd food or another in order to help achieve that goal. As one senior SF leader noted, when the guerilla chief brings out an earthworm and says it is a delicacy, you must eat the earthworm; you need to eat it with a smile to build rapport, and if you do not eat it or pretend to eat it, you will never earn your partner's trust.[55]

Some advisors theorized that not everyone on the advisory team had to be able to speak a host-nation language but it was important that at least some know it. As an example, one noted that during her deployment one SF advisor who had been in the Afghanistan-Pakistan Hands Program spoke Dari fluently. The Afghans respected and feared him because he understood everything that was said, even making jokes in their language, and the Afghans could not conceal anything.[56]

Consistency in Advisor Pairing: "Chasing the Latest Bright and Shiny Object"

Unlike in Iraq and the Philippines, in Afghanistan advisors were not consistently paired with the same host-nation forces. A 2015 RAND study harshly noted, "U.S. special-operations commanders have not instituted a policy of routinely returning the same SOF teams to partner units."[57] Even though the problem was identified, little was ever done to correct it. One senior NCO said he deployed three times to Afghanistan but never went to the same location or worked with the same partner force. "The same detachment rarely went to the same location. It just didn't happen.... It was infuriating."[58] Another officer noted that after six or seven rotations, statistically some ODAs ended up in the same place out of sheer luck, but there was not a concerted effort to pair them with the same Commando unit.[59] "We thrive off partnership, [but] there is no effort to get guys back to the same location."[60] Some advisors even requested that they be matched with the same partners on subsequent deployments, but little changed rotation to rotation.[61] Together, these factors result in a low rating for consistency in advisor pairing.

This problem occurred for a variety of reasons. First, there were no specific requirements for an ODA to partner with Commando kandaks. This differed from Iraq and the Philippines where leaders established policies that prioritized pairing Commander's in-Extremis Forces (CIF) companies with elite partner forces. As a result, the pool of ODAs that could match with Afghan partners was much larger. Instead of five companies from across the entire SF enterprise, each of the two primary units committed to the mission (3rd and 7th Groups) had eight available companies.[62] All the other groups also contributed forces, further expanding the pool of potential advisors.

Some advisors believed that the lack of consistency stemmed from a desire to ensure everyone had a chance to deploy to combat—which was necessary for promotion to senior levels.[63] One senior SF planner said, "There is no plan. We keep going there [Afghanistan] because no commander wants to be the first one to not have a combat rotation."[64] The shift of 3rd Group's area of responsibility from Afghanistan back to Africa was viewed as particularly illogical and counterproductive. To some the decision struck a chord of, "Everyone gets a trophy, and everyone has to play," which ignored expertise hard-won across a decade.[65] Adding SEAL platoons and Marine Special Operations Command detachments to the pool of potential advisory forces further decreased the likelihood of consistent pairings. Senior officers, however, denied such thinking was behind the lack of consistency and countered that the intense global demands on Special Forces required them to rotate the combat missions among all of the groups and add other forces to the advisory pool to prevent SF soldiers from burning out.

Another cause for inconsistency was the nearly constant shift in advisory priority between one Afghan partner force or another. At different times the focus would be trained on Afghan National Army regular forces only to move to the Afghan National Police, the Afghan Highway Police, the Afghan National Army Special Forces, the Afghan Local Police Program, the Ministry of the Interior's Provincial Response Companies, or the Village Stability Operations program—among multiple other elements.[66] In some ways, as each senior U.S. theater and SOF leader rotated through Afghanistan, ODAs were pulled from the Commandos and put on whichever program the new commander prioritized.[67] Frustrated NCOs and officers referred to this lack of unified effort as "chasing the latest bright and shiny object."[68]

Particularly jarring was the stand-up of the Afghan National Army Special Forces (ANASF)—created to help provide human intelligence for ANASOC, perform foreign internal defense, and train and advise Afghan army units.[69] When Faiz Wafa, command sergeant major at ANASOC, learned that the United States would be standing up the ANASF, he was surprised and concerned. "I was like, *Hey, let's complete the Commandos first, then worry about the [ANA] Special Forces....* The Commandos are the best unit right now in Afghanistan, and everybody wants to become a Commando. When you say, like, *Hey, there's another unit that is above them*, the Special Forces, which is higher than the Commandos, guess what? Everybody wants to become Special Forces. Now you cannot complete the Commandos."[70] Recruiting for ANASF from the Commandos set their combat effectiveness back because they lost capable personnel and had to rebuild key skills. One Special Forces NCO observed this impact directly, noting that even though his partnered Commando force was far from ready to fight unilaterally, when the ANASF were stood up he was directed to send some of those Commandos back to Camp Morehead to be retrained as ANASF.[71]

Similar prioritization problems emerged with the stand-up of the Village Stability Operations (VSO) program—a local defense initiative aiming to copy the Vietnam War program that had placed Special Forces ODAs in Nung and Montagnard villages. One SF officer noted that during his 2011–2012 rotation, the VSO mission was given precedence and ODAs that had traditionally been paired with Commandos were moved to support VSO. SEAL platoons replaced the ODAs working with the Commandos because, as one SOTF commander concluded, "there were holes to fill" and so he assigned what he believed to be the best suited forces to the important VSO mission.[72]

Assessment: "It's like Seeing Your Relatives Again"

Even though it was difficult to pair the same advisors with the same Commando units, there was a clear recognition that consistency in advisor pairing paid generous dividends. One advisor commented, "for an Afghan, relationships were everything."[73] Being able to work with the same individuals built trust and confidence on both sides, allowing each to take risks they would normally avoid. Consistency and the personal relationships that came along with it also helped units progress more quickly. Another senior NCO observed that going back to the same area and partner force allowed a soldier to understand the physical and human terrain, which made a huge difference on achieving success for a rotation. Advising the same unit would be "plug and play" because advisors would know the unit leaders and NCOs and who could be trusted.[74] Maj. Gen. Jim Linder, who served as commanding general for the Special Operations Joint Task Force–Afghanistan, believed that advisors were ten times more effective on their second rotation as they were on the first one. To him, relationships were critical, beginning as transactional processes but, as an advisor built the relationship across rotations, over time shifting to personal.[75]

Command Sergeant Major Faiz Wafa, former senior NCO for ANASOC, noted that during his career in the Commandos he met every senior U.S. leader when they first deployed as majors and lieutenant colonels. He maintained connections and friendships with them as they rose in rank and authority, with many of them reaching senior positions at the three-star rank in USASOC and U.S. Special Operations Command. Wafa felt, "that helped me because I knew that guy already. I knew how he works. I knew what his strategy was. I knew what his priority for the Afghan SOF forces was and . . . how he's going to help me."[76] U.S. advisors echoed this sentiment, noting that building rapport is normally a long and drawn-out process that could take weeks or even months, so returning to the same area and Commando kandak was "instant rapport" and meant saving considerable time and effort toward that end. Coming back to the same kandak "is like seeing your relatives again."[77]

The deleterious effects were often clear when consistency was not possible. A contractor mentoring ANASOC logistics at the kandak level noted, "Every time they [military advisors] rotate out, you just start over again. It is like *Groundhog Day*."[78] Others pointed out that six-month deployments without returning to the same partner force sometimes created "mentor fatigue" among the Commandos who were dealing with a constant influx of new advisors. "There is reluctance on part of Afghans to really open up to you because they get tired [of constantly building new relationships]."[79] Another advisor with multiple rotations to Afghanistan found it difficult to overcome cultural and bureaucratic inertia, and repeated rotations helped advisors identify both problems that needed to be solved as well as strategies to overcome them. "You had to know where the bodies were buried" to be truly effective in Afghanistan, he said.[80] Some Afghans would wait out advisors who were attempting to limit corruption and graft, knowing that in six to twelve months they would be able to act with relative impunity: Afghans might delay any proposals for change that they didn't like until new advisors arrived and then use their lack of experience to kill the proposals. If the advisors had been deployed previously, they would have had experience with the tactic and would have been more circumspect in addressing motives.[81]

Few advisors downplayed the importance of consistency. Those who did felt other factors contributed to the calculus of whether or not a team should be rematched with the same partner force: Team leadership could change out, impacting the interpersonal relationships or the level of aggression needed for an area of operations. The area of operations could change from relatively peaceful to extremely violent—or vice versa—requiring a team with a different set of personalities, skills, and experiences. Returning the same team to the same area could build hubris and overconfidence or even stunt creativity or delay action. One officer with considerable experience in Afghanistan noted that on one rotation a 1st Group ODA on their first rotation did better than some 3rd or 7th Group teams on their fourth or fifth rotation who were too bitter, too tired, or too burned out to try new things. He felt previous experience was certainly helpful in understanding the tribes and challenges of Afghan roads, but it was not critical.[82]

Advisor Ability to Organize Host-Nation Unit

The first years after the fall of the Taliban were, in the words of one CJSOTF-A commander, "the Wild, Wild West."[83] There were few rules, and the United States had considerable ability to influence and organize Afghan forces. However, the Commandos were not formed until 2007, nearly six years after the initial invasion and regime change.[84] During that time lapse, Afghan sovereignty grew tremendously, meaning U.S. advisors were allowed to take the lead on fewer key decisions than they had in Iraq. Their ability to influence the direction of the Commandos only decreased as time progressed.

Initial Stand-Up of the Commandos: It Had "Everything to Do with the Human Capital that Was Provided"

Compared to the rigorous selection, assessment, and training process set up by Special Forces advisors in Iraq and the Philippines, initial selection and training of the Afghan Commandos was haphazard. ANA soldiers who had only just completed a six-week basic-training course formed the core of the first Commando kandak, and there was no selection and assessment phase as there had been with the Light Reaction Regiment in the Philippines or with the Iraqi Special Operations Forces. Many of the new recruits had no other military experience, and some were barely able to zero a rifle. This first group began the twelve-week Commando course, and SF trainers made the first week physically challenging, which weeded out roughly a quarter of the class. The remaining eleven weeks focused on individual and collective skills training, and nearly all the prospective Commandos passed that phase and graduated.[85] None of the next few classes was specially selected or recruited; most were regular ANA infantry battalions ordered to report for Commando training at Camp Morehead. Few prospective Commandos failed, a far cry from the control advisors exerted in Iraq where they had the final say on who joined the unit.[86]

Afghanistan's baseline education level made recruitment into the Commandos particularly challenging. The country's education system was barely functional, and adult literacy sat at 43 percent in 2020, the ninth lowest rate in the world.[87]

Many Commandos could not read, and it was nearly impossible to instill minimum standards for entry. Other skills were also weak, and one advisor noted that during his indirect-fire mortar class none of the Afghans could add or multiply—baseline prerequisites for that training. Another noted that over half of the students in his long-range radio class washed out before training even started because they could not read numbers and were therefore unable to correctly tune the radio dials to the right frequency.[88] During another exercise, one Commando candidate who already passed the physical requirements for entry ingested batteries because he thought they were food and could power him. Few Commando candidates had even baseline driving skills.[89] As Maj. Gen. Patrick Roberson contended, the effectiveness of the Commandos had "everything to do with the human capital that was provided."[90]

Over time, the recruitment process evolved, and replacement soldiers generally volunteered individually from regular ANA battalions or from basic training. Some new battalions were also formed via this individual-selection method, but others were created by sending entire ANA infantry battalions through Commando training as had been done for the first kandak. Many SF advisors noted that the failure rate decreased dramatically in later Commando classes, with one officer who ran the training program estimating it to be in the 1 to 2 percent range, with many of the failures recycling into later classes.[91] These statistics frustrated many advisors, some of whom argued that Commando training was the Afghan equivalent of "no kid left behind."[92]

Leadership selection was another problematic issue for SF advisors. While SF advisors were able to handpick key leaders for the first kandak, many reported that after that initial success it became difficult if not impossible to personally select or fire Commando leadership, particularly at the kandak level and above.[93] Such positions, they felt, were often political appointments based on nepotism or connections rather than leadership or combat skills.[94] Navigating these complexities was particularly challenging. For example, to replace an Uzbek in a key position would usually require replacing him with another Uzbek to keep the balance of power and status quo. If an Uzbek was not available locally, reassigning an Uzbek from another location to that role could set off power struggles that involved negotiations with the second location and likely reassigning an Uzbek to backfill that role also. In such cases, tribe and ethnic background trumped experience and capability. For the high-profile national counterterrorism force 6th Commando Kandak, not only did the commander have to be Uzbek, but he also had to be politically connected with the current Afghan president. U.S. advisors simply could not make changes on their own, and even suggesting a change created unwanted drama.[95]

The United States did have considerable leverage over how to equip the Commandos and what their organizational structure should be. In both cases, SF advisors made the most important decisions. The troop structure of the Commandos mirrored the structure of U.S. Ranger battalions, with some notable exceptions due to the insistence of Afghan leaders. These exceptions included that the Commando battalion headquarters include a religious affairs officer, a mullah or imam, and an Islamic education officer.[96] In terms of equipment, U.S. advisors selected what the Commando battalions would use, settling on American weapons and gear.

Yet even in the realm of equipping the Commandos there were challenges. Some units ended up with an ad hoc set of weapons and equipment because what they were assigned had been poached by other Afghan officers to give to their own units or to be sold on the black market. Winter clothing, communications equipment, and crew-served weapons were particularly susceptible to reappropriation. As one advisor noted, "what entered on the left side did not reach the ride side" of the supply warehouse.[97]

Concerns over Afghan sovereignty meant that SF advisors were usually not able to directly control Commando pay. At times they were able to step in and personally manage the funds to guard against corruption, but their intervention was far from uniform. Like in Iraq, SF advisors lobbied for the Commandos to be eligible for a special-incentive pay, and in the end they received an extra $50 per month as well as double rations.[98] The increase of Commando pay over ANA base pay, while nowhere near as significant as the ISOF's pay over the Iraqi Army's, was enough to create a different lifestyle for the Commandos.[99]

The scope of the U.S. effort to build such a large SOF element as well as its comparably late start made it more difficult to properly screen Commando candidates. Some Afghan military and political leaders saw it as a violation of sovereignty when U.S. advisors insisted that detailed background checks be run on every Commando. As a result, prospective Commandos only received a basic counterintelligence screening and provided biometric information that was then compared against insurgent databases.[100] Because of the limited screening, SF advisors faced an insider threat, and on multiple occasions they were shot or killed by their partners.[101] This altered the advisory relationship, and many units required an armed "guardian angel" to be present at training who would watch over the Afghans and stood ready to shoot them if they presented a threat.

Chapter 5

Stand-Up of Afghan National Army Special Operations Command Headquarters: Misuse Redux

When the Commandos were first organized, they worked directly for Afghan National Army corps commanders and received their logistics from them. Such a construct, in the words of one advisor, meant that the Commando command-and-control structure "was not clean-cut," and they suffered from unity of effort challenges and misuse.[102] Conducting any sort of operation with the Commandos first required approval from the conventional ANA brigade or division leadership, most of whom did not understand how to properly employ those elite forces. Rather than assigning them special-operations missions, conventional leaders often used the Commandos for checkpoints or to serve as a quick-reaction force because they were more reliable and willing to fight than conventional ANA soldiers.[103]

Sometimes when the Commandos or their SF advisors pushed back against the misuse, the conventional commander withheld Commando pay or even food until they agreed to carry out his orders. In at least one case an ANA conventional leader broke up Commando elements by picking the best fighters from the kandak to serve as his personal security detachment. In another case an ODA was moved from one location in Afghanistan at great expense—flown on limited fixed-wing resources—to link up with a Commando kandak for an operation. Upon arrival they discovered that the conventional ANA commander had sent the entire kandak to serve as checkpoint security over one hundred kilometers away, meaning the ODA left empty-handed.[104] On top of all of this, conventional ANA control of Commando logistics created additional problems when many officers skimmed money from the better-funded elite forces.[105]

To address these myriad problems, in 2012 U.S. and Afghan SOF leaders decided to stand up a brigade-sized headquarters to be led by a one-star general. This would become the Afghan National Army Special Operations Command (ANASOC). Unfortunately, even though the Commando kandaks fell under this new headquarters for institutional support, operationally they were still employed by ANA conventional commanders in the military districts. ANA leadership had insisted on this structure, which resulted in persistent misuse of the Commandos after the new headquarters was formed.[106] The effectiveness of the new headquarters was also hindered because it was challenging to find officers to fill the new organization who understood Commando capabilities.[107] Unable to perform command-and-control functions, the ANASOC headquarters performed functions that more closely paralleled the organize, train, and equip functions of U.S. Title 10 institutional headquarters.

Recognizing that the ANASOC commander's rank was lower than ANA corps and division commanders, the position was elevated to two-star rank in an attempt to offset the imbalance.[108] In addition, the brigade headquarters was expanded to division size with two subordinate Commando brigades in Shindand and Khost Districts that split responsibility for the country geographically between east and west. Even after that change, command and control was still difficult and misuse continued. Explaining these challenges, one advisor posited that each kandak had three bosses—first the ANASOC chain of command, second the ANA conventional battlespace commander, and third the U.S. CJSOTF advisors.[109]

From 2015 to 2020 ANASOC headquarters expanded again in another attempt to resolve the continuing misuse and command-and-control problems. Rather than a division headquarters led by a two-star general, ANASOC was elevated to a corps headquarters led by a three-star general.[110] It was thought that the higher rank would increase ANASOC clout relative to other conventional ANA units, as the ANASOC commander would be a peer to other ANA corps commanders after this promotion. No additional intermediate level of command was inserted, but two additional brigades were added to split the country geographically based on compass cardinal directions. A new organic logistics component was included to reduce Commando reliance on ANA conventional logistics.[111]

Unfortunately command-and-control issues endured as well as ANA mismanagement of the Commandos. During one crisis, recently elected President Ashraf Ghani was under pressure from Taliban advances in Kunduz. During meetings, the president directed the ANA chief of staff to move the 207th ANA Corps into the fight, but the unit was incapable or unwilling. The senior SF commander, sensing the political danger to the new president, lobbied to have the Commandos moved into the fight, later recalling that ANA corps commanders were putting Commandos pointlessly on checkpoints and to fix it. "I guess I have to go to the president of the country, but that's kind of what it takes here."[112]

The stand-up of ANASOC headquarters did lead to some improvements. As the war ground on and Commando casualties mounted, senior U.S. advisors helped the Afghans stand up a wounded warrior program. At first when Commandos were seriously wounded or lost limbs, they were forced to leave the military. This created problems with morale and retention when Afghan soldiers realized that if they became seriously wounded they would not be able to hold a job or earn money to support their family. ANASOC command Sergeant Major Faiz Wafa wondered, "how can we expect the younger generation to come into the army if they see the guys that lost their leg . . . and nobody took care of him?"[113] To address this issue, a program was created where seriously wounded Commandos would be retrained into office jobs within the military. Assisted by SF advisors, senior ANASOC leaders fought for four years to push the program through ANA bureaucracy and the Ministry of Health before ultimately succeeding.

Operation Freedom's Sentinel and the Never-Ending War

As the conflict progressed, the ability of SF advisors to organize the Commandos decreased further still. Some of the reduction was because of decreased U.S. authorities caused by the shift from Operation Enduring Freedom to Operation Freedom's Sentinel. With the end of U.S. offensive operations and the enhanced push to have Afghans take the lead in security operations, some advisors felt that the United States had grown casualty-averse, which in turn made Afghan partners less willing to take American advice and recommendations. After the shift to Operation Freedom's Sentinel, one advisor noted that his ODA had only three offensive missions over four months, which approximated their weekly rate before the change. Even then, such missions required extensive justification, with one advisor noting that he wrote a 117-page mission order with his Afghan partner to justify a kill/capture mission.[114] Others noted there was intense pressure to avoid ground movement due to improvised explosive devices, a result of which meant Americans were unable to attend many meetings where Afghans made decisions about the future of the Commandos and ANASOC.[115]

Some changes were a result of the duration of the conflict. Several advisors noted that even by 2015 many Afghans had begun looking toward what would happen after the United States had left and thus began making political calculations when deciding whether or not they should conduct a mission, weighing whom they would anger or what vendetta they might create. One advisor noted that his partner, a Commando company commander, refused to do anything other than checkpoint operations. "They knew we were leaving. Why would they do an operation if the United States was leaving?"[116] With a potential U.S. withdrawal looming, many ANASOC units became less—or not at all—responsive to requests from the coalition to make changes. Instead each request was assessed transactionally and evaluated for its political and tribal impact. "If Afghans didn't see that it [the mission] was in their own interest, they would not do it."[117] Even some missions were disapproved that the senior U.S.

SOF commander had felt were so important that the case was pled to the ANASOC commander directly. This marked a significant difference from earlier in the war.

At the tactical level, Commandos also pushed back against entreaties made by their U.S. partners. By 2016, many Commandos had been in combat longer than many of their advisors. These grizzled soldiers were jaded and less willing to take risks and had even begun to treat the SF groups differently according to previous combat experience. One Commando told his advisors, "You guys are from Colorado rather than North Carolina, so you know what mountains look like. That is good. But what might have worked in Iraq won't work here."[118]

Assessment

SF advisors stood up the first Commando unit more than six years after the fall of the Taliban. In the interim a new Afghan government was created as well as an accompanying military structure with its own bureaucracy. When U.S. advisors tried to organize the Commandos in the way they thought most effective, the Afghan government and surrounding bureaucracy interceded and blocked many of the proposals. Some decisions regarding force organization were set by the SF advisors, such as the general construct of the unit and its equipping as well as the establishment of a special-operations headquarters; but others, such as selection of unit members and leaders, were mostly made by the Afghans themselves. The "sovereignty clock" U.S. advisors had noted in the Philippines and in Iraq had run out. Standing up the ANASOC headquarters only partially alleviated these challenges, and by 2015 SF advisor ability to influence Commando units had decreased further still. For all these reasons the advisors' ability to organize host-nation forces is rated to be medium.

Combat Advising: "I Speak 556 and Footprints in the Sand"

After the Taliban were overthrown, the new Hamid Karzai government was extremely willing to have U.S. soldiers participate in combined combat operations with Afghan soldiers. SF advisors working with the Commandos had few restrictions placed on what they could do and trained with their partners, ate meals with them, and then fought shoulder to shoulder with them. No prohibitions were put in place determining how close they could get to combat operations, and many advisors were wounded or killed performing their mission. As a result, the degree of combat advising that was allowed with the Commandos is rated as high.

While there were few restrictions from the Afghans, U.S. advisors had vastly different interpretations as to what constituted combat advising. At the beginning of the mission there was a tendency by some ODAs to focus more on conducting combat operations themselves rather than on advising the Commandos. Some teams even balked at providing reports on the training levels of their partner kandaks, claiming that they were too busy with their own missions.[119] This trend might have occurred because ODAs had grown accustomed to unilateral or near-unilateral operations during the six years of war before the Commandos had been created. At the same time, a desire to focus on unilateral direct-action missions rather than on foreign internal defense has long been a preference for some factions within U.S. Special Forces.[120] One SF senior leader of the Afghan mission, Brig. Gen. Don Bolduc, reportedly told his subordinates "I don't need to speak the language, I speak 556," implying that shooting skills and killing the enemy were more important than teaching host-nation partners to do the same. ODAs inclined to follow such a methodology often conducted operations with the bare minimum number of Afghans required and only made nominal efforts to train the Commandos.[121]

Different interpretations of combat advising persisted, and later in the conflict some SF advisors who had deployed on numerous rotations concluded that their efforts were having little impact on the war. Teams with such a view became cautious when deciding on which missions they would accompany their partner force and questioned whether certain operations were worth risking their lives. As one SF battalion commander noted, some advisors had been "running on the hamster wheel" for years and had not seen significant progress, so they were not interested in conducting missions just for the sake of conducting missions. They had come to believe that their actions were only making footprints in the sand at the beach and the next tide would wipe out any progress they had made.[122] With such a perspective, risking lives while combat advising makes little sense.

Assessment: "Shoulder to Shoulder"

There was near-universal faith in the principle that combat advising was critical to producing effective partners. Command Sergeant Major Faiz Wafa, former ANASOC command sergeant major, noted that new advisors had to earn his trust to really build rapport, and the best way to do that was by fighting shoulder to shoulder as partners.[123] Maj. Gen. Ed Reeder reiterated this: "Their U.S. counterpart standing shoulder to shoulder with them, sharing the same burdens of combat," is what kept them going.[124] To him, embedded role models made a huge difference to combat advising because it showed that the advisors were willing to endure the same dangers as the Commandos. In a virtuous cycle, sharing those risks was seen as the best means to demonstrating commitment and dedication, something that would result in host-nation soldiers working to mirror that commitment themselves.

Others saw the practical benefits of combat advising. Having Americans fighting as partners meant that the Commandos were likely to get high-level medical care through helicopter evacuation as well as be treated by highly trained Special Forces medics. In addition, a U.S. presence meant air support and/or artillery would be available. Those factors seemingly made a huge impact on Commando willingness to fight, according to some advisors.[125]

EVALUATING COMBAT EFFECTIVENESS

In August 2017 Gen. John Nicholson, commander of U.S. and NATO forces, said, "The [Commandos] have never lost a battle.... The Taliban have never won against the Commandos.... They never will."[126] Unfortunately his optimistic prediction proved inaccurate—even before the United States had departed from Afghanistan. Even so, the Commandos were far more capable than other Afghan units and were relied upon extensively by ANA and U.S. senior leadership. Although the Commandos comprised only 7 percent of Afghan National Security Forces, they conducted 70 to 80 percent of all fighting.[127] Some U.S. advisors thought so highly of the Commandos that they argued individual soldiers from the unit could have served with distinction in U.S. Ranger battalions.[128] While there is little doubt that the Commandos were among the most effective forces that Americans had built in Afghanistan, we will assess their true capabilities against the same factors used to evaluate other case studies in this book.

Night Fighting

The Commandos were equipped similarly to their SF advisors. Each soldier was issued a PVS-7 night-vision goggle and PEQ-2 laser pointer, but they generally were not given the more technologically advanced PVS-14 or -15 goggles issued to the Iraqi Special Operations Forces and to SF CIF companies. Still, these capabilities gave the Commandos considerable advantage over almost all their opponents.[129]

Advisors provided mixed reviews on the Commandos' night-fighting skills. Most awarded high marks, noting that the Commandos hated daytime operations and preferred to conduct operations after dark when their skills outmatched most threats. By late in the war, Afghan National Army Special Operations Command had obtained thirty-five Mi-17 Hip helicopters whose pilots could conduct night infiltrations using goggles, further tipping the balance in their favor.[130] One advisor who worked with ANASOC noted that from a systemic level there were voracious requirements for the batteries used in night-vision equipment, seemingly indicating they were being used extensively. Others noted that Commandos rarely turned down nighttime missions.[131]

At the same time, some advisors commented negatively. One noted that while the Commandos routinely fought at night and were successful, he did not believe that they "owned" the night because sometimes periods of darkness would cause them to lose momentum and stall on an objective.[132] Another noted that his partner-force Commando kandak simply would not use their night-vision goggles, which effectively negated the value of the equipment and their training.[133] Others noted that some Commando units were capable of fighting at night but did not prefer to because they were not confident in their skills.[134]

Assessment

The varied appraisals of the Commandos' night-fighting skills warrant a medium rating. They were properly equipped to conduct operations, had no cultural disinclination to fight at night, and were suitably trained. Despite all those factors, advisor reviews of their skills reflect mixed capabilities on actual operations, resulting in a lower rating.

Conducting Multiday Combat Operations

When the Commandos were first stood up, the Combined Joint Special Operations Task Force and Afghan National Army leadership decided that they would obtain logistics support from regional ANA conventional units. This was in part because U.S. SF leaders wanted to focus first on developing the unit's combat capabilities and also because Afghan leaders preferred to not create a separate logistics system. Unfortunately, this construct proved extremely problematic. On numerous occasions ANA conventional commanders refused to resupply Commando units, at times even when elements were in contact with the enemy, such as during the politically sensitive battle to recapture Kunduz in 2015.[135] Under such conditions, some advisors noted that the Commandos could carry out operations for at most twenty-four hours and reported that they were even sometimes forced to rely on villagers for water and food resupply.[136] The Commandos were especially reliant on U.S. trauma care and casualty evacuation, seriously limiting their unilateral capabilities. Several advisors noted that because ANA units were not consistently providing logistics support and casualty evacuation, some Commando units became dependent on their U.S. advisors for those resources, a habit they found hard to break even after ANASOC added their own limited internal logistics capabilities.[137]

Because the original system proved deficient, SF advisors pursued multiple strategies to overcome those challenges. Some farsighted leaders, such as Col. Fred Dummar, implemented reforms so that the Commandos could sustain themselves through a helicopter-transportable "chuck wagon" vehicle that could provide hot meals for extended operations. Recognizing that U.S. casualty evacuation would not always be available to them, he pushed for the purchase of tactical ambulances that could provide forward medical care.[138] Other leaders focused on building a more-institutional logistics structure within ANASOC, and an entire support kandak was added to the headquarters.[139] A special-operations helicopter wing was created, partly to give the Afghans an organic infiltration capability, but also partly in recognition that the distances and infrastructure involved made ground resupply unrealistic for most missions. The skilled pilots were also capable of performing night casualty evacuations.

To ensure long-term sustainability of the force, significant energy was put toward preparing the Afghans to run the Commando Training Center, and by 2019 they were mostly running courses with little U.S. assistance. SF advisors trained Commando logisticians to preposition supplies where battles were anticipated, to have resupply bundles ready to drop to besieged forces, and to leapfrog units during long battles, where an initial Commando force would fight for forty-eight to seventy-two hours and then be extracted by the same helicopters that had just dropped off their replacements who would continue the fight. After these reforms, the Commandos could conduct combat operations for seventy-two hours or more, although not consistently. Afghan logistics trains were simply not robust enough to address the needs of the force, and at times the United States had to provide emergency resupplies of food and ammunition.[140]

U.S. reforms were significantly hampered by corruption, nepotism, and a general lack of understanding of logistics matters. One advisor noted that there was a common notion that, "If I'm not stealing fuel, I'm not being a good Afghan" because I'm not taking care of my family.[141] This often resulted in a negotiation over how much fuel was really needed for missions because the Afghans would request more than was required so they could resell the excess and pocket the difference. Another senior advisor recalled that in 2015 an SF team was trying to convince their partner kandak to deploy their amber-cycle (training) company to support the green-cycle (operations) company in a larger operation. The Afghan battalion commander refused, citing that he did not have enough fuel. Desperate to get the unit moving, the Americans called their headquarters, whose commander then engaged the three-star commander of ANASOC. Only after that general personally called the Commando battalion commander and told him that he knew he was selling part of his fuel ration to the fuel station across the street was the second company freed for the operation.[142]

Problems with corruption extended far beyond fuel supplies. The Afghan logistics system was so dysfunctional that during the 2018–2019 period of Commando growth, to ensure the supplies for the new units were properly distributed, U.S. SF advisors waited at airfields for key shipments (such as M4 rifles). If they did not, the equipment would almost certainly be stolen.[143] Other advisors noted how difficult it was getting uniforms for the Commandos because ANASOC logistics warehouses reported no uniforms were available. When the advisors visited the warehouses, the logisticians were wearing Commando uniforms, and the shelves were stocked. Issue boots were so bad due to graft and corruption that many Commandos preferred to fight in sandals rather than the unreliable boots that would fall apart after a few missions.[144]

The American premise of logistics also conflicted directly with Afghan cultural norms, which viewed a fully stocked shelf of equipment as a sign of success and plenty preferable to issuing equipment to tactical units and emptying warehouse shelves. Several advisors commented how critical issue items, such as crew-served weapon mounts for vehicles and mechanics' tool kits, were scarce in tactical units, but stocked in row after row of shelves in logistics warehouses.[145] Advisor attempts to change the culture had little impact, and they found that their best strategy to resolve shortages was to go to the warehouses themselves with empty trucks and take what their partners needed.

The shaky Afghan logistics systems came under even more pressure after the end of Operation Enduring Freedom in 2015, when U.S. forces withdrew over half of their troops and consolidated those remaining on fewer bases. The organic logistics system proved incapable of sustaining some Commando units, so they were moved to locations where Afghans could—with the occasional U.S. assist. Logistically supporting Farah and Herat Provinces was extremely challenging, as flying ANASOC rotary-wing assets to Commando bases there required setting up a forward arming and refueling point—which was beyond Afghan skills. Without constant U.S. support, the Commando logistics system faltered, presaging worse challenges to come when they would have to operate unilaterally.

Assessment

The model of relying on conventional forces for host-nation SOF logistics, which was adopted in both Iraq and Afghanistan, was unsuccessful and inhibited the ability of both countries' SOF units to conduct operations beyond seventy-two hours—at least until changes were made that increased organic SOF capabilities. Even after those policy shifts, ANASOC logistics struggled—partly from institutional problems, and partly from the challenges related to the size of Afghanistan, its terrain, and its lack of infrastructure.

At the tactical level, most Commando kandaks could conduct limited operations for seventy-two hours. That ability was more a testament to their resilience and acceptance of adversity than an indicator of their logistics capabilities. Even then, underlying cultural issues, endemic corruption, and the tyranny of Afghanistan's distances and infrastructure made operations extremely challenging. Conducting short-notice resupply missions for unexpected events was often beyond Commando ability because they lacked the necessary logistics force structure and equipment. At any level above tactical, the weakness of ANASOC's institutional logistics system came into focus. That fragility meant the Commandos could rarely conduct long-term resupply and were exceptionally challenged when units operated at any distance from their kandak headquarters or ANASOC logistics facilities. During some missions, desperate tactical commanders even resorted to social media appeals for supplies and food that their headquarters was unable to provide.[146] Considered as a whole, the Commandos have a medium capability to conduct extended combat operations—although at the low end of that rating.

Fighting without Advisors: A Collapse Waiting to Happen

While a select few Commando units performed superbly, most were challenged when transitioning from fighting while partnered with coalition forces to fighting independently—a precursor task to being able to conduct intelligence-driven operations. In fact, a 2019 study showed that ANASOC independent operations dropped nearly 20 percent from the year prior, an ongoing downward trend that reflected increasing—not decreasing—Commando reliance on U.S. support.[147] Many SF advisors confirmed this trend and expressed frustration at Commando inability to fight independently in the years before the final U.S. withdrawal. Several noted that at various points Commando units had considerable problems with discipline and drug addiction.[148] In 2015 the situation had grown so out of control in one kandak that SF medical personnel were deployed to perform drug testing on the Commandos, resulting in the cashiering of nearly an entire battalion.[149]

Describing the Commandos' ability to fight independently, one advisor noted, "they would generally be able to put in a support-by-fire position and go in and clear a compound, but under duress, when things got sporty, they tend to go to ground and let the Americans fight."[150] Others were less generous. "We had problems with elements that either wouldn't do their task, because they just didn't understand it somehow, or the minute that they got under gunfire, they would shut down to a degree, and no matter who told them that they needed to suppress or do whatever, they kind of did their own thing to protect their own little element."[151] Another bluntly noted that the Commandos could not conduct independent combat operations. "When the shooting started, they would hide. We would fight, then yell at them, and they would fight a little bit. Then they would stop fighting again and we would keep fighting. It wasn't worth the effort. We had to fend for ourselves."[152] Several SF advisors accurately predicted that the Commandos would collapse soon after the United States left Afghanistan.

Others noted that the Commandos had become reliant on U.S. fire support, intelligence, and logistics.[153] As soon as the United States withdrew these capabilities, the number of operations conducted by the Commandos dropped precipitously. In particular, if the United States did not provide the same enablers to the Commandos that they had provided to their own ODAs—such as AC-130 gunships, Predator drones for intelligence, surveillance, and reconnaissance, and local casualty evacuation—they would often refuse to conduct operations.[154] One advisor commented that those capabilities helped "strengthen the spine" of the Commandos when they had to close with the enemy and fight.[155] Without them, many Afghans were simply not willing to risk their lives.

But others had a more sanguine perspective on the Commandos. They argued that the Commandos could conduct independent operations, although carrying out intelligence-driven independent operations was more challenging. As evidence, the advisors pointed out that late in the war, Afghans became impatient with what they perceived to be U.S. risk avoidance and launched operations on their own with wheeled vehicles or Mi-17 helicopters. Others noted that if the Commandos were provided with U.S. intelligence they could launch unilateral operations but were not able to generate targetable intelligence and repeat the cycle themselves.[156]

Several advisors concluded that most Commando units could not perform the classic F3EAD model of intelligence-driven operations—find, fix, finish, exploit, analyze, and disseminate.[157] With the Commandos operating in ANA corps battlespace, they had to obtain targeting approval from those forces. The system was inherently dysfunctional, and few ANA divisions pushed intelligence down to the Commandos. These challenges could have been overcome from bottom-up targeting, but because the Commandos generally lived in cantonment areas and not among the people, they did not have good human intelligence—at least none responsive enough to enable intelligence-driven operations. Although the ANA SF were meant to fill that void, they usually proved incapable of the task.[158]

Additionally, there was little institutional-level intelligence sharing, and few Commando kandaks routinely shared intelligence with other ANA units or Ministry of Interior Affairs forces.[159] Some advisors noted that most actionable intelligence for the Commandos came from U.S. sources and capabilities.[160] When the United States began withdrawing its forces and limiting operations after the 2015 shift to Operation Freedom's Sentinel, the number of human-intelligence reports dropped significantly as there was not the same amount of American money to pay sources and contacts.[161] U.S. efforts to build an organic capability were often frustrated by rampant corruption, such as when low-profile civilian sedans purchased for use by human-intelligence agents in each kandak were taken over by Afghan general officers for their own personal use.[162]

Little effort was made to develop signals-intelligence assets because they were deemed beyond Afghanistan's technical and budgetary capabilities. ANASOC was given a rudimentary imagery-intelligence capability in the form of eighteen Pilatus PC-12 aircraft meant for intelligence, surveillance, and reconnaissance. Those aircraft were generally unable to provide real-time full-motion video-downlink capabilities and instead were used for photographic imagery, which was too slow for intelligence-driven operations. At times, the aircraft reflected the challenges of corruption, with U.S. advisors having to remind Afghan generals that the planes were not their personal means of transportation.[163]

At the tactical level, most kandaks could, however, do battlefield interrogation, and some could conduct follow-on operations based on intelligence garnered from those interrogations. Few, if any, Commando units were able to do detailed sensitive site exploitation of computers, documents, or phones that would lead to timely follow-on operations.[164] Some kandaks could perform close-target reconnaissance where Commandos used mobile GPS devices and cameras to identify a target and its location. But such capabilities were far from uniform.[165]

Assessment

While there is little doubt the Commandos were among the best Afghan forces, they struggled with many basic-level capabilities. Some kandaks were able to conduct unilateral operations, but many others simply refused to fight without U.S. advisors and their considerable enablers. The Commandos had limited human- and imagery-intelligence capabilities, but neither those skills nor the Commandos' operational abilities were sufficient to conduct true intelligence-driven operations. Combined, these factors result in a low rating for ability to fight without advisors present.

Performance against the Enemy in Combat

While U.S. forces remained in Afghanistan there were few engagements where the Commandos fought without the support of advisors or enablers. Afghanistan collapsed as the United States withdrew, making it challenging to determine how the Commandos would have performed independently. That said, the 2015 Battle of Kunduz provides some valuable insight, as do operations in 2021 when the United States had its smallest personnel footprint of the war and had shifted nearly all responsibility to the Afghans.

In late September 2015 the Taliban quickly and effortlessly took over the provincial capital of Kunduz. SF ODAs were given two hours to pack their equipment and load helicopters with as many Commandos as they could muster.[166] Despite being provided considerable support from AC-130 gunships, High Mobility Artillery Rocket Systems, and numerous airstrikes, the Commandos and their advisors made little progress in recapturing the city for the first two days. Additional U.S. and Afghan forces were surged into the battle, and fighting seesawed across the city for fifteen days before the Taliban were finally expelled, with the Commandos providing the bulk of the Afghan commitment.[167] The 6th Commando Kandak, part of the country's national mission force based in Kabul, fought fiercely, but the 10th Commando Kandak, based in Kunduz, refused to fight and instead only provided security at the nearby airfield.[168] Many saw this battle—the first time a major city had fallen to the Taliban—as first signs of how the ANA would perform by itself, as it occurred less than a year after the end of Operation Enduring Freedom. Despite hopes that the ANA (and the Commandos) could retake the city with little effort, the United States had to provide massive amounts of assistance. While Kunduz could not have been recaptured without the determined efforts of the Commandos, their reliance on extensive U.S. support shed doubt on their ability to handle the Taliban independently.

Combat actions in 2021 further confirmed that fear. As U.S. forces withdrew, Afghan forces—including the Commandos—lost large swaths of Afghanistan to the Taliban. From May to the end of June of that year, Taliban forces went from controlling 73 of Afghanistan's 407 districts to controlling 157.[169] The Commandos, in many cases the only forces staving off disaster after other Afghan units had dissolved, were pressed into service as conventional infantry and fought in twice as many battles as they had the previous year.[170] A select few Commando elements did continue to conduct special-operations nighttime heliborne kill/capture missions, but such capabilities and missions had become extremely rare.[171]

On June 19, a Commando unit that had been sent to relieve besieged ANA conventional forces in Faryab Province was defeated and then massacred. Twenty-two Commandos, including a famed commander who had received training in the United States, were executed after surrendering. At least one report indicates that the Commandos ran out of ammunition and the ANASOC headquarters could not resupply them or provide close air support.[172] Although the outpost was recaptured later that month with Commandos in the forefront of the battle, the incident highlights the unit's mixed performance in battle when left without U.S. assistance.

As the summer of 2021 progressed, the ANA made a series of desperate attempts to resist a complete Taliban takeover, yet province after province fell. As insurgent forces closed in on Kabul, the Commandos buckled and in some places collapsed in combat. Around the city of Kandahar, Commandos and other security forces battled the Taliban for more than a month.[173] When U.S.-contracted logistics withdrew and the Afghan supply system imploded, the Commando kandaks were not able to perform as they had been designed: reliant on the support of a heavy logistics footprint that could resupply them on demand. Commando elements began to run out of ammunition, food, and water. Some surrendered after extended sieges, putting themselves at the mercy of the Taliban. Another Commando element held the city of Mazar-i-Sharif until local warlords capitulated, leaving them surrounded.[174] After the fall of Kabul, several Commando units refused to give in and began the slow march to Panjshir Province, intent on joining a nascent resistance to the Taliban.[175] Other units moved to Hamid Karzai International Airport and helped secure the outer perimeter during the U.S.-led evacuation, which concluded on August 30, 2021.

Assessment

The Commandos were one of the most effective Afghan security forces built by the United States during its two-decade investment. That said, despite considerable publicity about the Commandos' performance in battle, the more often they fought without advisors or U.S. enablers, the more disappointing their performance became. Properly supported logistically and with air support, they often held their own against the Taliban and could defeat them. Unfortunately, those conditions were impossible for ANASOC and the ANA to consistently deliver, making the Commandos' performance in battle inconsistent at best. Based on a review of their performance during the Battle of Kunduz and operations in 2021, the Commandos earn a medium rating.

INITIAL ASSESSMENT

The Commandos received medium ratings in conducting multiday combat operations, night-fighting skills, and performance in combat and low scores in fighting without advisors present. When looking at those components as a whole, the Commandos have an overall ranking of low-moderate effectiveness. While they were one of the best Afghan government forces, their effectiveness in battle was erratic when they were not partnered with SF advisors and U.S. enablers. With an inadequate human-intelligence capability and nearly no imagery- or signals-intelligence resources, the Commandos had little ability to conduct intelligence-driven operations, the bellwether for fighting without advisors present. Many advisors also reported that the Commandos were often unwilling to fight without their advisors and enablers—an even lower and more basic standard than being able to conduct intelligence-driven operations. Logistically they could meet the standard of fighting for seventy-two hours but had significant institutional gaps and other supply challenges that made this capability unreliable. ANASOC Commandos were often capable night fighters, but at times they ignored their training and lacked confidence.

This chapter concludes the case studies, and in the next we will address overall observations, conclusions, and policy recommendations.

Special Forces soldiers wearing dress uniforms and green berets from each of the seven Special Forces Groups stand in a cordon and silently watch over the wreath-laying ceremony at the grave of President John F. Kennedy, Arlington National Cemetery, 2011. *DVIDS photo by Sgt. 1st Class Gonzalo (John) Gonzalez, 1st Special Forces Command (Airborne)*

Special Forces candidates move through a swamp during the Robin Sage culmination exercise of the Special Forces Qualification Course, near Hoffman, North Carolina, 2023. *DVIDS photo by K. Kassens, U.S. Army John F. Kennedy Special Warfare Center and School*

U.S. advisors train Salvadoran soldiers on counterambush drills, Cojutepeque, El Salvador, 1984. The presence of MSgt. Leamon (Lee) Ratterree, jumping down from the truck on the left, indicates how easy it would be for advisors to become engaged in combat. *Courtesy MSgt. Leamon Ratterree (Ret.)*

U.S. advisors attend peace talks between representatives from the Farabundo Martí National Liberation Front (FMLN) and Salvadoran government forces, Guazapa, 1992. Col. Mark Hamilton, then MILGRP commander, is on the left with sunglasses, then-major Francisco (Frank) Pedrozo is center with glasses, U.S. ambassador William G. Walker is in the checkered shirt with his back to the camera, and Fidel Recinos Alas, better known as Raul Hercules, commander of FMLN's National Resistance, is leaning back in his chair, right. *Courtesy Col. Frank Pedrozo (Ret.)*

The morning after their base had been nearly overrun, members of a Special Forces ODA, 3rd Battalion, 7th Special Forces Group, pose with a captured red FMLN armband, center, San Miguel, El Salvador, 1984. While conducting a mobile training team mission the soldiers had been drawn into the fighting, managing to block one of the guerrilla assaults from breaking through base defenses.
Courtesy Lt. Col. Cecil Bailey (Ret.)

Members of C Company, 1st Battalion, 1st Special Forces Group, train the Light Reaction Battalion (LRB) in close-quarters battle, Philippines, 2008. *Courtesy SF advisor*

LRB members conduct helicopter-infiltration training with Special Forces advisors, Fort Magsaysay, Philippines, 2008. *Courtesy SF advisor*

LRB members practice door-breaching techniques during training with Special Forces advisors in Cebu, Philippines, 2007. *Courtesy Sfc. Sean O'Connor (Ret.)*

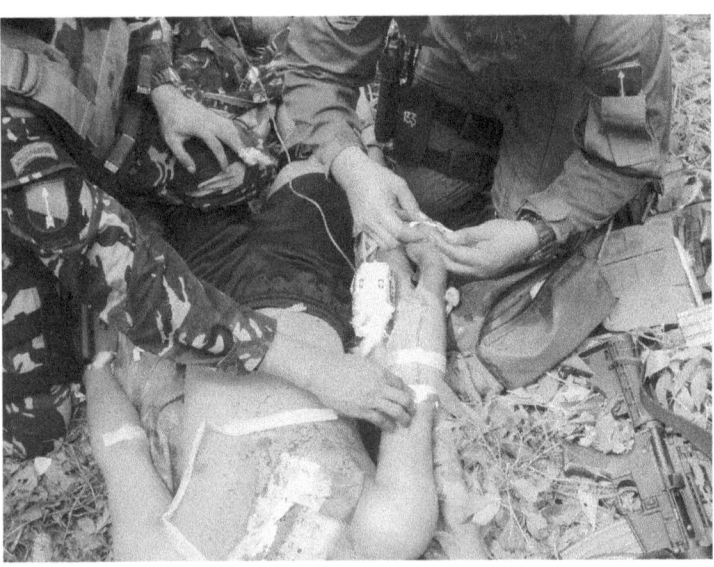

LRB elements conduct medical training on simulated battlefield casualties during joint training with 1st Special Forces Group, Cebu, Philippines, 2007. *Courtesy Sfc. Sean O'Connor (Ret.)*

AGLAN soldiers return from an operation against a FARC strongpoint, La Uribe, Colombia, 2006. *Courtesy the Official Colombian Military collection*

BACOA commandos await a high-altitude, low-opening parachute training jump, Colombia. *Courtesy the National Army of Colombia*

BACOA commandos conduct jungle-patrolling exercises, Colombia. *Courtesy the National Army of Colombia*

7th Special Forces Group advisors with a combined BACOA and AGLAN company train in Colombia for the unit's deployment to Afghanistan, 2010. Colombia went from being a nearly failed state that exported coca to a state that exported security forces globally and trained regional allies. *Courtesy Lt. Col. Joe Reagan*

Major General Fadhil al Barwari, commander of the 1st Iraqi Special Operations Forces Brigade, with Sgt. Maj. (Ret.) Ron McDaries, 2014 *Courtesy Sgt. Maj. Ron McDaries (Ret.)*

The Iraqi Counter Terrorism Service conducts fast-rope training, 2018. *DVIDS photo by Sgt. Dennis Glass, Combined Joint Task Force–Operation Inherent Resolve*

Iraqi Special Operations Forces conduct a night raid, 2007. *DVIDS photo by PO2 Brett Cote, Combined Joint Special Operations Task Force–Arabian Peninsula*

Iraqi Counter Terrorism Force (ICTF) operators depart for a mission, 2005. CW2 Travis Rolph is on the right. *Courtesy CW2 Travis Rolph (Ret.)*

An Iraqi soldier from the 36th Commando Battalion participates on a mission, Baghdad, 2007. *DVIDS photo, Combined Joint Special Operations Task Force–Arabian Peninsula*

The ICTF conducts a training exercise, 2018. *DVIDS photo by Pfc. Anthony Zendejas, Combined Joint Task Force–Operation Inherent Resolve*

A Special Forces advisor from A Company, 1st Battalion, 5th Special Forces Group (CIF) surveys a target with a member of the ICTF, 2005. *Courtesy CW2 Travis Rolph (Ret.)*

An Afghan commando engages Taliban fighters with an M249 Squad Automatic Weapon during a firefight, Kunar Province, 2012. *DVIDS photo by PO2 Clayton Weis, NATO Special Operations Component Command–Afghanistan*

Afghan Commandos with Special Forces advisors disembark a CH-47 Chinook helicopter during a combined raid against fortified insurgent positions, Uruzgan Province, 2009. *U.S. Army Combat Camera*

Afghan Commandos and Special Forces advisors fire an 81-mm mortar in support of troops in contact, Kandahar Province, 2009. *U.S. Army Combat Camera*

A Special Forces advisor on an all-terrain vehicle pairs with Afghan Commandos during combat operations in a built-up area, Helmand Province, 2009. *U.S. Army Combat Camera*

Special Forces advisors and Afghan Commandos conduct a combined multiday clearing operation, Kandahar Province, 2009. *U.S. Army Combat Camera*

An Afghan Commando sniper provides overwatch during a combat operation. *Courtesy the government of the Islamic Republic of Afghanistan*

Conclusions and Recommendations
Making Security Force Assistance Work

LEARNING THE RIGHT LESSONS

AFTER THE TWIN DISASTERS of the Iraq and Afghanistan wars, a widely accepted notion has developed that it is futile for the United States to conduct security force assistance. Such a sentiment has been echoed in most of the articles written as part of the postmortem of those failures. But many of those articles fail to capture the nuance of each operation, and others were more sensational than scholarly. The title of one otherwise-balanced and insightful essay in *Foreign Affairs* announces that the United States is incapable of building foreign militaries.[1] Another scholar bluntly concludes that the United States "should not build or rebuild foreign military institutions as part of a broader nation-building exercise, except in rare, unavoidable conditions."[2]

Such conventional wisdom is flawed for several reasons. First, it paints with too broad a brush, failing to note important outliers such as the Iraqi Special Operations Forces, the Colombian Special Operations Forces, the Philippines' Light Reaction Regiment, and other exceptions. Second, by convincing ourselves it is impossible to successfully build foreign militaries, we commit ourselves to repeating the same errors time after time when we have no choice but to conduct large-scale security-force assistance. We can—and must—draw valuable lessons from successful U.S. advisory missions, lessons that are transferable to other efforts.

Conclusions and Recommendations

Those who contend that it is impossible to perform security force assistance usually link their argument to the premise that the mission is not a part of great power competition; with the U.S. pivot from counterinsurgency and counterterrorism to squaring off against peer competitors of China and Russia, ditching security force assistance would seem to make some sense. Yet nothing could be further from the truth. The United States and its allies have gone to considerable lengths to equip and train the Ukrainian military during its existential struggle with Russia. In fact, some of Ukraine's original success in holding off the initial Russian invasion, such as employing Javelin antitank missiles, were a result of earlier Western train-and-assist efforts.

U.S. security force assistance successes such as in Ukraine are not black swan events—that is to say, rare or unpredictable—and the simplistic message that the United States cannot build foreign armies overlooks considerable evidence and nuance. Outside the scope of this study, it is generally acknowledged that U.S. efforts to help construct capable militaries were successful for South Korea, West Germany, and Japan. In the cases of Colombia and El Salvador, the United States helped build security forces that either achieved victory outright or successfully fought their opponents to a stalemate and allowed the government to remain in power. Both countries were in dire straits before the arrival of U.S. assistance, with Colombia teetering on the edge of state failure. While the overall security force assistance missions in Afghanistan and Iraq were gross failures, the United States still managed to construct elite forces that were much more capable than the remainder of the host nation's military forces. If not for the ISOF fighting doggedly and holding off ISIS in 2014, the Iraqi state probably would have disintegrated.

But the argument that the United States can't succeed at security force assistance isn't merely inaccurate; it is dangerous. Outside of U.S. Army Special Forces, security force assistance has always been peripheral for the U.S. military, receiving little to no funding, force structure, or preparation before major conflicts. When other parts of the military are forced to provide security force assistance during a crisis—often under the assumption that they can train themselves up to proficiency, seeing this as an "easier" skill to learn than combined-arms maneuver—they usually fail spectacularly. Scholars then claim that success is impossible because building foreign militaries is too difficult or because principal-agent theory predetermines that the United States will never be able to align our goals with those of our allies. Those failures, their specious explanations, and subsequent insistence that U.S.

foreign-advisory efforts are a hopeless endeavor then serve to prevent proper resourcing for security force assistance. But we have not failed because advising our allies is too hard; we've failed because we have never taken it seriously. We have refused to invest in either training or force structure and then muddled through it, making mistake after mistake. And then the next time we embark on building a foreign military, failure becomes a self-fulfilling prophecy.

Building foreign militaries is a difficult, long-term, and often thankless endeavor. But it is not impossible. A considerable part of U.S. failures stems from passively and actively avoiding learning the lessons that previous efforts should impart. Reversing that trend is one of the key objectives of this study. Lessons from the Special Forces missions included in this book can—and must—be transferred to future security force assistance efforts to improve their odds of success, and institutional security force assistance capabilities must be properly resourced.

KEY FINDINGS

In this study we have asked the question, *Under what conditions have U.S. Army Special Forces been successful in building a combat-effective partner force?* Perhaps the clearest finding is that there is no magic bullet, no single one-size-fits-all solution. Instead, a series of factors affect the creation of combat-effective partner forces: consistency in advisor pairing, the partner-to-advisor ratio, the ability to organize host-nation forces, advisor language training and cultural awareness, and the degree to which advisors can pair with their partners in combat. If, for example, the ratio of partner forces to advisors is too high or if advisor pairing is insufficiently consistent, then producing a combat-effective force becomes much more difficult, and other factors must align positively for the advisory effort to succeed. No single factor or set of factors is deterministic; rather, multiple permutations of these factors can produce combat-effective partners.

At the same time, some of those factors influence outcome more than others. Consistency in advisor pairing and a low partner-force-to-advisor ratio are both critical to producing combat-effective partners. Similarly critical to success is the advisor ability to organize host-nation forces, whether resulting from good advisor-partner rapport or openness of the host-nation forces to change. Neither combat advising nor proper advisor language and cultural-awareness skills have proven essential, although a vocal minority of interviewees disagree. A summary of the data reported across all five case studies is included in table 1.

TABLE 1 Advisory Factors

ADVISORY FACTOR	COUNTRY				
	AFGHANISTAN	EL SALVADOR	THE PHILIPPINES	IRAQ	COLOMBIA
Consistency in advisor pairing	low	medium	high	high	medium
Language training/ cultural awareness	low	high	high	low	high
Partner-to-advisor ratio	16.4	189.6	28.7	6.2	17.5
Ability to organize host-nation unit	medium	medium	low	high	high
Ability to combat advise	high	medium	medium	high	low
Overall host-nation combat effectiveness	*low-medium*	*low-medium*	*low-medium*	*medium-high*	*high*

How those factors affected the combat effectiveness of the five different host-nation SOF elements is illustrated in table 2. From most effective to least were the Colombian AGLAN and BACOA, the Iraqi Special Operations Forces, the LRR in the Philippines, the BIRIs in El Salvador, and the Afghan Commandos. As three of the units had the same overall effectiveness rating, I made subjective assessments to rank order them. Because the Afghan Commandos were often unable to function effectively without advisors present, realistically the most crucial consideration, they were assigned the lowest rating. The remaining tie between the Philippines and El Salvador was broken by the subjective assessment that ability to fight for seventy-two hours was more important than night-fighting skills. At the same time, it should be noted that all the units evaluated were assessed as being effective, with the lowest rating being low-medium. Colombia was a clear standout, with SOF elements as or more capable than those of many NATO allies. In other countries, such as El Salvador and Afghanistan, those forces more closely resembled elite infantry.

TABLE 2 Host-Nation Combat Effectiveness

HOST-NATION CAPABILITY	COUNTRY				
	AFGHANISTAN	EL SALVADOR	THE PHILIPPINES	IRAQ	COLOMBIA
Night fighting	medium	low	medium	high	high
Conducting multiday combat operations	medium	medium	low	medium	high
Fighting without advisors	low	low	low	medium	high
Performance against enemy	medium	medium	medium	high	high
Overall combat effectiveness	*low-medium*	*low-medium*	*low-medium*	*medium-high*	*high*
Rank	5	4	3	2	1

Consistency in Advisor Pairing

Greater consistency in advisor pairing resulted in more-effective host-nation units. It led to better rapport and trust, which then translated into the willingness of host-nation officials to share sensitive information, give greater authorities to SF advisors, and allow them more access to important events and leaders. Trust and rapport also allowed advisors to have difficult conversations with host-nation forces concerning performance and ways to improve, so consistency was helpful in overcoming some of the cultural barriers that affect bluntly honest conversations with the militaries of shame-honor societies. Over time, the impacts of consistency became exponential, as junior leaders in host-nation units were promoted to more-important positions of authority in which they were able to have an even greater impact on the trajectory of advised units. Personal relationships matter, and those built across multiple rotations proved important—even crucial at times—to overcoming bureaucratic inertia as well as resistance to changes recommended by advisors. When recommending that a host-nation leader be replaced, nothing helped U.S. advisors more than having long-standing connections and deep interpersonal bonds with senior host-nation officers.

Another advantage from consistency came in the familiarity advisors developed with the host-nation unit itself. Across multiple rotations, advisors came to understand the capabilities of their partner forces and were able to more quickly recognize their training needs. Consistency also shortened the period at the beginning of a mission in which soldiers of both nations get to know one another and build rapport. Further, when advisors were redeployed to the same units, they knew the key personnel and recognized where the unit was within its training cycle. With less wasted time, advisors were able to focus on critical training rather than on assessing the host-nation unit. These advantages were magnified when deployed advisors communicated with the next unit preparing to conduct the training mission, as was the case in the deployment cycle for SF units working with the Iraqi Counter Terrorism Force. In sum, consistency circumvented some of the information asymmetry in principal-agent theory that makes it so hard for advisors to achieve their objectives.

Consistency even helped when the relationship between the advisors and host-nation forces was more adversarial, as it was at times in Afghanistan and El Salvador. Advisors who had been on multiple rotations came to understand ways that host-nation forces might try to exploit or deceive them. As one advisor noted, returning to work with the same unit meant he "knew where the bodies were buried,"[3] enabling him to better uncover corruption or incompetence the host-nation forces may have been trying to hide. Consistency made it harder to pull the proverbial wool over the advisors' eyes.

Partner-to-Advisor Ratio

A lower partner-force-to-advisor ratio was also helpful in producing combat-effective partners. With a lower ratio, each advisor's span of control became smaller, meaning they were responsible for coaching, teaching, and mentoring fewer host-nation soldiers. This enabled advisors to monitor their partners more closely and spend more time with individual soldiers. In turn, troops received more individual attention and mentorship, meaning that fewer mistakes were made during training and in combat. But when mistakes *were* made, they were more easily identified and corrected because each advisor was carrying a lighter load.

Advisor Ability to Organize Host-Nation Units

Ensuring that advisors had the ability to organize host-nation forces was extremely important to producing effective partners. The less resistance advisors received from the partner force in making necessary changes, the more likely they were able to produce a combat-effective partner force. The amount of resistance depended on a variety of factors, such as the amount of financial assistance provided, the shared history between the two nations (problematic for the Philippines, positive for Colombia), rapport between advisors and host-nation forces, the degree of divergence in advisor and partner goals, and even whether significant incidents or scandals had occurred during the mission.[4] Of note, unlike the precepts of principal-agent theory, the advisors (the principal) could directly impact the performance of the host-nation forces (the agents) through the rapport they achieved, their actions, and other factors. Performance did not rely only on the degree of divergence between the advisors' and host nation's goals.

Organizing host-nation forces could be relatively easy, with some offering little resistance; or it could be transactional, wherein each action required some sort of restitution from advisors; or it could be nearly impossible, no matter what was offered in exchange or what threats were leveled. In addition, at the start of almost every mission the "sovereignty clock" began ticking, counting down the period in which the host nation was more amenable to change. During the early phases of a mission, a honeymoon period often saw partner forces willing to overlook issues of national sovereignty and accept reform. But as the mission stretched on, host-nation forces frequently tired of the advisors' presence, and implementing change became more difficult.

Combat Advising

While a large majority of interviewees reported that combat advising was important to outcomes, the most effective partner forces—BACOA and AGLAN in Colombia—were trained by U.S. advisors who were barred from combat. The worst, the Afghan Commandos, were advised shoulder to shoulder during intense combat. The Iraqi Special Operations Forces, the second-best force evaluated, partnered in conditions very similar to the Commandos. These conflicting results call into question the importance of combat advising, and it is likely that it provides some benefit but is not as important as other advisory factors. Despite intense anecdotal arguments that combat advising is critical, the evidence strongly suggests that it is not essential.

Those who stressed the importance of fighting alongside host-nation forces argued that trust and rapport were damaged when partners were sent into battle without their advisors. Not sharing the same risks can prove caustic to any relationship, impeding progress toward building effective combat units. In addition, a prohibition on combat advising prevented SF operators from observing how their partners performed in their most important test. With critical information on effectiveness only coming from the host-nation units themselves, advisors had difficulty ascertaining their partner's abilities.

A common refrain among those downplaying the importance of shoulder to shoulder combat was the assertion that SF soldiers permitted to advise their partners in combat are often more inclined to carry out the mission themselves rather than patiently coaching, teaching, and mentoring the host-nation unit. Lack of patience with the mentorship process or outsized desire to earn awards and accolades provided powerful incentives for U.S. advisors to step in and try to win the war themselves, resulting in partner forces missing out on valuable coaching and experience. In Afghanistan and Iraq, U.S. advisors sometimes commandeered operations—whether as an unintended byproduct of permission to accompany forces into combat or from a lack of partner progress.

Advisor Language Training and Cultural Awareness

The importance of language training and cultural awareness was highly contentious, with most respondents—particularly those with advisory experience in the Philippines, Iraq, or Afghanistan—indicating that it had little to do with building combat-effective partners. Advisors in El Salvador and Colombia generally felt the opposite, with most indicating that language skills and understanding local culture were essential to mission progress.

Those who stressed the importance of language training felt that speaking the language of the host nation was foundational to establishing rapport and earning trust.

> If you demonstrate competence in the language and culture, you become a trusted advisor. . . . Speaking the language . . . allows us to laugh together, discuss families [and] regional food, mock bordering countries, and make fun of yourself to help humanize us to the partner force. This creates a bond and often a friendship that translates through to operational effects. When it comes down to *Should I share this tidbit of intel, fuel, ammo, or gossip about internal*

office politics? it is the one who has gained rapport who gets it, and the one who doesn't never knows.[5]

Others noted that language skills were important in tactical scenarios: in the heat of combat communication has to be precise and timely. In addition, an advisor skilled in the host-nation language of a particular region was likely to either remain in that regionally oriented SF Group or return to it after other assignments. This made redeployment to the same set of countries more likely, increasing consistency in advisor pairing while building a deep roster of interpersonal connections and allowing a better understanding of the regional history and culture.

While few argued that language skills had no value whatsoever, most interviewees—including some with strong language skills—considered them to be more mission enhancing than mission essential. The explanations varied: Some noted that even though they did not speak the host-nation language, over a few weeks of their first deployment they were able to learn enough vocabulary to function in combat. Across multiple rotations, the value of language training became less important as individuals who were not regionally oriented picked up additional vocabulary and cultural awareness. Moreover, many host-nation soldiers spoke English or learned it during deployment, often obviating the need for advisor language capabilities. Some partners even asked their advisors to *not* speak the local language so the partners could practice their English—a critical skill with positive career and financial impacts.

In some countries where multiple languages were spoken, such as the Philippines and Afghanistan, it was particularly difficult to adequately staff advisor teams with linguists. Without the ability to communicate effectively, host-nation interpreters became the only viable option. Other SF soldiers opined that having the personality and temperament to serve as an advisor are more important than knowing the language, recalling incidents where poor linguists were able to establish rapport more effectively than native speakers. Empathy, patience, tolerance, humility, and a willingness to connect on a personal level proved more important than linguistic skills. Just as crucial are the advisor's knowledge of military skills relevant to the mission and their ability to teach them effectively. Language helped, but ultimately advisors had to be able to gain trust and provide value through training, advising, and delivering what they had promised.

It is worth noting that the divergence of opinion regarding the value of language split along a fault line of Spanish-speaking countries (El Salvador and Colombia) and all others. Several factors could explain this deviation. In El Salvador and Colombia, Spanish was the only official language, and few native dialects were spoken. English-speaking skills inside the Salvadoran military were limited, and one advisor reported that in his entire brigade only two soldiers spoke English.[6] Undoubtedly fluency in Spanish would have benefited any advisor in this scenario.

The relative difficulty of languages for an English speaker could also have played a role in diverging opinion. Spanish is a category I language according to the U.S. Interagency Language Round Table, meaning English speakers find it easiest to learn; Arabic, Dari, and Pashto are considerably more difficult to master.[7] The relative ease of learning Spanish as well as its primacy across Latin America makes it organizationally easier for 7th Group to focus on and train in that language. Another potential explanation for the divergence in opinion is that there was a larger supply of SF operators who had functional-level Spanish skills (more than double that of any other language, a fact likely linked to the heightened number of native speakers in the United States and the comparative ease of learning the language).[8]

Some advisors hypothesized that the high number of proficient Spanish speakers created an organizational norm to speak Spanish without an interpreter, which in turn became an expectation on the part of the host nation. "In our Latin American area of responsibility, *we* have set a precedent for being able to speak the language because we see it as important. The partner nation force/leadership doesn't require it. . . . This is apparent in [deployments to] Brazil as most of us arrive as Spanish speakers."[9]

POLICY IMPLICATIONS

Sovereignty Should Not Be Sacred

In general terms, this study evaluated two types of conflicts: one in which the United States conducted regime change and had nearly carte blanche to re-create the defense institutions of the defeated nation and a second in which the host nation requested assistance but maintained control over decisions made within its territory. While the two types of mission seem completely different from the standpoint of sovereignty, there are, in fact, similarities. In the first type, even when the United States initially had nearly unfettered ability to implement changes as it wished, the host nation demanded the return of its sovereignty relatively quickly, virtually switching the mission to the second type. In the second type, states calling for extensive U.S. assistance are usually fragile and desperate, and their governments are often on the edge of collapse. Either way, the issue of host-nation sovereignty should not be an excuse for overlooking corruption, incompetence, or other institutional rot, as in both cases the United States still has considerable leverage in trying to influence the host nation.

Despite the opportunity to make decisive cultural changes in states badly needing U.S. assistance, however, many U.S. advisors hamstrung themselves with the belief that sovereignty is binary—a state either has it or it doesn't. Sovereignty then became a pretense to avoid pushing too hard against states suffering problems with corruption, graft, and poor leadership. These problems especially manifested themselves in large-scale efforts to build the Iraqi and Afghan security forces that fell outside the control of SF advisors. One U.S. Army general noted that "the United States had the money and guns to try to influence Iraqi policy—including the selection of security force leaders—but often gave both away without caveat or condition."[10]

While respecting host-nation sovereignty has long been the foundation of U.S. foreign policy and a valuable component of its grand strategy to expand the pool of liberal democratic states, it should not be an excuse to blithely accept problematic issues within the culture of the host nation's military. Instead, the United States should require that the host nation appoint capable leaders and limit corruption. It must be willing to establish hard limits, the disregard for which result in the removal of host-nation leaders not passing muster. If not, the United States will simply dump money aimlessly into the mission and empower negative influences within the host nation's military, creating a downward spiral. In unstable states, the proverbial stick must be used as much as the carrot. Advisors must also be clear-eyed about the limited ability to purify fragile states and temper expectations that they can construct the equivalent of Switzerland in a single decade. Ultimately if the host nation is unwilling to make the necessary incremental changes, then the United States should simply pack up and leave rather than commit the sunk-cost fallacy.

To a degree, the United States managed the balance of sovereignty properly—and indirectly—in Colombia during the presidency of Ernesto Samper in the late 1990s. Cutting off $1 billion in aid sent a clear signal that helped empower reformers to use political pressure to implement changes and replace poor defense leaders. The newly emplaced officers brought their own capable subordinates, creating a virtuous cycle across the chain of command. While not a subject of this case study, in South Korea the United States used similar harsh tactics during the Korean War. Recognizing the extensive corruption and incompetence throughout the host-nation military, U.S. officers imposed their will, routinely firing Korean leaders who failed to perform to acceptable standards, making it clear to their partners that "they ignored advice, particularly in critical tactical situations, at their peril."[11] Even in the case of El Salvador, when U.S. advisors threatened to walk out and report their counterparts if they committed human-rights abuses, the Salvadorans complied—at least in the presence of their partners. In future conflicts, the United States must be able to draw a redline when necessary to accomplish its goals.

Such pressure tactics have expiration dates, and they are more effective earlier in a mission. To a certain degree, foreign advisors only have a limited amount of time before the host nation tires of their presence and domestic politics limit foreign influence—as happened in Iraq, Afghanistan, and the Philippines. At the beginning of an intervention, the "sovereignty clock" starts ticking, and when its time runs out, advisors will face intractable challenges to continued transformation of the host-nation military in any meaningful way. Recognizing this, in future advisory missions the United States should make changes as early as possible before their welcome wears out. The more that is accomplished early on, the better the odds that the changes will adhere, transforming the host nation's military culture. It is especially important to appoint key leaders who are capable and honest, as they—and their subordinates—often promote these values long after U.S. forces have left. While early change is not necessarily a determinant guaranteeing positive outcome, its impact can resound, especially in concert with firm U.S. resolve to limit corruption.

Leadership Matters, and Host-Nation Leadership Matters Even More

No host-nation factor is more important than who their leaders are. From a practical perspective, leaders selected during the early phases of a mission are likely to climb the ranks and eventually head organizations, thereby extending and intensifying their impact, either positive or negative. Having capable and supportive host-nation leaders has exponential effects as they are almost certain to be involved in the selection of their subordinates. Such a process is likely to result in a virtuous cycle where they pick skilled and sympathetic officers who in turn pick their own equally capable and supportive subordinates. Colombia was particularly blessed with a set of extremely talented and dedicated leaders, both political (President Álvaro Uribe Vélez and Minister of National Defense and President Juan Manuel Santos Calderón) and military (Generals Fernando Tapias, Jorge Enrique Mora Rangel, Carlos Ospina Ovalle, Freddy Padilla de León, and Alberto José Mejía Ferrero).[12] They not only were gifted in developing strategies to meet their nation's security needs but also knew when to accept and when to politely ignore U.S. suggestions. The ISOF in Iraq could neither have been constructed nor become as effective as it did without the larger-than-life figure of General Fadhil Jalil al Barwari. He continuously set the example for his subordinates in tactical performance and bravery, and showed little patience for officers who lacked courage or skill on the battlefield. At the same time, Barwari appears to have not been immune to the temptations of corruption; but his failings appear to be fewer than most other Iraqi officers and also offset by his combat effectiveness.

It is worthwhile to note that in both Colombia and Iraq, the United States directly or indirectly had a hand in the leader selection process. In Iraq, SF advisors installed Barwari as commander of the 36th Commandos both because of his leadership and bravery and also because of connections they had with him reaching back to Operation Provide Comfort in the 1990s. He rose through the ranks to become the ISOF commander. In Colombia, a more oblique case, U.S. pressure to implement reforms after the disastrous administration of Ernesto Samper helped lead to the sacking of many senior officers and the ascendance of competent leaders within the defense establishment. While not included as one of these cases, U.S. policy during the Korean War mirrored the heavy-handed tactics used with the ISOF, including selection of key leaders and replacement of any who proved incapable or ineffective. These tactics proved quite powerful.

For U.S. policymakers, this means identifying capable host-nation leaders early on in large-scale security force assistance missions and using whatever leverage possible to ensure those officers obtain and maintain positions of responsibility. Every case is different, and where nations have undergone regime change, such as Iraq and Afghanistan, the opportunity is greatest to exert external power to make critical personnel selections. But even in more traditional missions, leadership selection can be influenced, even if issues of sovereignty require that advisors be very circumspect. For it will be those leaders, or the subordinates they select, who will have to stand on their own when the United States and its allies eventually withdraw. The culture that those host-nation officers instill will help determine whether the partner military succeeds or fails.

Learn *a* Language, not *the* Language

Unfortunately the language capabilities of SF soldiers are often far from the hyped skills normally associated with the regiment. As of 2022 the graduation standard for the qualification course was only 1+ on the Defense Language Proficiency Test

(DLPT) or the oral proficiency interview (OPI), below the level-2 standard recognized as limited working proficiency where the student can "read with some misunderstandings straightforward, familiar, factual material but in general [is] insufficiently experienced with the language to draw inferences."[13] The five active-duty SF groups could barely maintain a 60 percent qualification rate for that 1+ standard, with the National Guard groups performing even worse.[14] As of April 2021, across all of Special Forces command, inclusive of the five active-duty and two National Guard groups and the large headquarters, there were 244 Special Forces branch personnel who scored at the 2/2 level on the DLPT or OPI in Spanish and 94 who scored at the 3/3 level. In other languages, the weakness was more acute. French had 74 at the 2/2 level and 31 at the 3/3 level, and Russian had 152 at the 2/2 level and 31 at the 3/3 level. For the more difficult languages, the situation was dire: Arabic had 45 at the 2/2 level and 12 at the 3/3 level, Farsi had 4 at 2/2 and none at 3/3, Mandarin had 9 at 2/2 and 5 at 3/3, and Korean had 5 at 2/2 and 10 at 3/3.[15]

Framed under those conditions, the Special Forces regiment should not return to pre-9/11 norms where it was sacrilegious for an SF group to deploy forces outside of its assigned region. Excepting 7th Special Forces Group, which focuses on Latin America, no other group has strong enough language skills to add significant value to an advisory mission. Moreover, most interviewees noted that they were able to successfully perform tactical-level advisory duties even if they did not speak the host nation's language.

In many ways, the fundamental challenge remains selecting which languages SF soldiers should learn. The U.S. Indo-Pacific Command's area of responsibility alone gives insight into these complexities. As 1st SF Group's focus, the region hosts over half the world's population, spread across thirty-six countries, sixteen time zones, and 52 percent of the Earth's surface. Over one thousand languages are spoken across its vastness, making it difficult if not impossible to match language skills with all the possible contingencies the Group could face.[16] While some other regions are less diverse, all face their own linguistic and cultural challenges in appropriately pairing linguistic talent with mission needs.

All things considered, language skills are important in advisory missions, and this study should not be interpreted as arguing against the value of language training and cultural awareness. To be crystal clear, it presents no such argument. There are considerable advantages that stem from being able to speak a foreign language in advisory efforts, and those advantages grow in concert as an individual's ability to converse grows. Knowing another language besides English—whether the language of the host nation or not—increases an advisor's ability to empathize with the force they are advising, to communicate clearly, and to build trust with their partners.

The conclusion that should be taken from this part of the study is that knowing a foreign language and having experience working with other cultures is more fungible and transferrable than what conventional wisdom assumes. Knowing the language of the host nation is not essential. SF soldiers trained in a language from one region can be deployed to another region and pick up important vocabulary and cultural knowledge after a rotation or two. Such deployments, however, should not impede maintaining consistency between advisors and host-nation SOF forces, which is much more important than language training and cultural awareness in building combat-effective partners. Language is not the be-all and end-all when producing capable, combat-effective partners.

Reconsider Doctrine for the Partner-to-Advisor Ratio

According to U.S. Army doctrine, Special Forces ODAs "can develop, organize, equip, train, and advise or direct indigenous forces up to battalion size."[17] With most battalions ranging in size from six hundred to nine hundred soldiers, the ratio of host-nation partners to advisors should be in the range of between sixty and seventy-five to one. Four of the five case studies we have explored had ratios far lower than that standard, usually by orders of magnitude, which calls into question current doctrine.[18] On these missions, rather than a single ODA advising a battalion-sized element, ratios were much closer to a single ODA advising a company-sized element. Given that all the units advised produced at least a medium level of combat effectiveness, ODAs were far more effective when training company-sized elements.

Given this reality, while technically the doctrinal statement is not incorrect, as an ODA *can* advise units up to battalion size, the guidance is still misleading. To clarify the true capabilities of an ODA, current doctrine should be revised to say that, *while an ODA can advise units up to battalion size, they are most successful when paired with host-nation units of company size, and efforts should be made to match forces at such a ratio.* Making this amendment would not be easy, as the premise that an ODA trains a battalion is nearly sacred in the SF planning process. Refocusing ODAs from battalions to the smaller companies could also generate an impression that the five Special Forces Groups, altogether, could only effectively advise a third of the forces that planners assumed they could. While not precisely accurate, such perception could trigger reviews of advisor management and the Special Forces Regiment's force structure at a time when the U.S. Army is trying to make a considerable cut to its special-operations forces. If anything, the Army needs more advisors, not fewer.

Special Operations Forces Cannot Be Mass-Produced

One of the five SOF "truths" holds that SOF cannot be mass-produced. These guidelines were originally intended to help U.S. policymakers construct the new U.S. SOF enterprise.[19] This particular truth was a caution against expanding the command beyond its ability to maintain elite capability and status. The evidence in this study confirms that the maxim also applies to the construction of foreign SOF elements.

Across the five case studies, the size of the partnered element differed vastly. In El Salvador, the six BIRIs constituted nearly 5,400 combatants. Although nearly a division's worth of Commandos was stood up in Afghanistan, only 2,600 fighters were normally available due to desertions, ghost soldiers, a small tooth-to-tail ratio of combat troops to support personnel, and a policy that had one-third of the force's combat power on leave at any given time. The remaining three missions we have studied were markedly smaller efforts: 750 troops paired with advisors in Iraq, 400 in the Philippines, and 370 in Colombia.

The efforts building the largest host-nation units, El Salvador and Afghanistan, produced the least-effective partners. While many factors contributed to the lackluster results, interviewees from both missions believed the lower quality was at least partially related to the mass production of host-nation forces. As the scale of the effort grew, quality control slipped, and screening and training emphases swung toward meeting production quotas. That shift occurred even though large numbers of advisors paired with the Commandos in Afghanistan, a force whose eventual collapse seemed to confirm advisor concerns about low-quality candidates being accepted into training.

Consistency Is Paramount

Perhaps one of the clearest conclusions, supported by qualitative anecdotal evidence from interviews across all five cases, was that consistency in advisor pairing helps produce combat effective partners. Regularly pairing the same advisors with the same host-nation forces provides a variety of advantages. First, it affords advisors a wellspring of knowledge concerning the performance and capabilities of the host-nation unit. Rather than having to reassess their partners at the beginning of each mission, repeat advisors were often able to restart training quickly and at the appropriate level. In some cases, as in Iraq with the ICTF, advisors worked on a back-to-back basis, with one unit deployed while the other rested. Such a construct, with the resting unit maintaining contact with the forward deployed unit and receiving updates on the partner force's progress, was ideal.

Consistency also led to increased rapport and stronger interpersonal connections. SF officers and NCOs gave examples of long-term relationships with host-nation leaders that began early in their careers and grew across multiple deployments as host-nation officers were promoted into positions of greater responsibility. Those connections helped the SF advisors make necessary changes, obtain important authorities, and overcome mission adversities.

Maintaining such an important factor did not prove to be easy, and either U.S. or host-nation decisions often affected consistency. In Afghanistan especially and Colombia to a degree, the consistently changing cadre of SF leaders led to a shifting focus that emphasized different host-nation units. Such "chasing shiny objects," as one interviewee described, should be avoided at all costs because it violates the principle of unity of effort and disrupts consistency in advisor pairing. At the tactical level, leaders should resist the temptation to change a policy focus just because it was implemented by the previous commander. To this end, it is unlikely that the United States will have sufficient time, money, or patience to be able to build more than one quality host-nation SOF organization properly. At the strategic level, SF leaders should refrain from giving every unit a chance to deploy to combat to "spread the wealth," as it also waters down the positive impacts of consistency. Similarly, efforts to prevent burnout by cycling different groups through combat missions have the unintended but consequential effect of reducing the critically important consistency.

In the Long, Hard Slog, "Culture Eats Strategy for Breakfast"

The comment "culture eats strategy for breakfast" was originally made in a business context, noting that to predict success, the culture of an organization matters more than detailed strategic plans.[20] If anything, culture matters as much in security force assistance as it does in business. Different components of culture, most of them difficult to quantify, all affect a host-nation unit's ability to change—among them, degree of ethnosectarian homogeneity, levels of corruption, and warrior spirit or martial attitude.

The United States and its allies usually do not conduct security force assistance in areas where governance is strong and corruption is low. As a result, changing the culture, which is necessary in many long-term SF advisory efforts, is slow, challenging, arduous, and frustrating. It requires great patience and consistency and near-constant contact. Much of the work is two steps forward and one step back. The missions in El Salvador, the Philippines, Colombia, Iraq, and Afghanistan lasted for eleven, fourteen, fifteen, eight, and fourteen years respectively.[21] Despite the duration of the missions, the involvement of high-quality advisors, and the expenditure of considerable economic and military assistance, most of the advisory efforts produced only a moderately capable partner force. Building foreign militaries takes decades, and uniformed leaders must be blunt and realistic when providing their best military advice about security force assistance to civilian leaders. In retrospect, the notion that we could construct host-nation armies in only a few years—central to the strategy in Iraq and Afghanistan—was nauseating.

Despite the length of the advisory efforts in these five cases, even some of the more-successful missions were not able to affect key elements of the host nation's culture. The United States was barely able to register an impact on the *tanda* system in El Salvador,[22] which promoted all Salvadoran Military Academy classmates of the same graduating year at the same time, regardless of circumstances, making no exceptions for ineptitude on the one hand or brilliant performance on the other. Seen as a cronyism that prevented capable officers from reaching positions of importance, the United States expended considerable effort toward rooting the practice out. Ultimately it was not successful, and in many ways the *tanda* system still flourishes today—though perhaps not to the same degree.[23] While the NCO corps in Colombia was the most capable of any of our case studies and better than some NATO allies, it still suffered from class issues. Some, if not many, officers often saw sergeants as part of the lower classes and therefore incapable of managing responsibility and autonomy, even if they had proven themselves proficient at taking charge.[24] Culture changes at a glacial pace, and even then some elements remain powerfully resistant to outside forces. In late 2003 then–secretary of defense Donald Rumsfeld predicted that the wars in Iraq and Afghanistan would be "a long, hard slog."[25] Changing host-nation military culture to enable their forces to stand on their own is perhaps the most difficult component of that drudgery.

CONCLUSIONS

For most of the current and last century, U.S. defense policy toward building foreign militaries has been erratic. During normal times, it is generally ignored in favor of focusing on fighting other nation-states in traditional conflicts. But during times of international turmoil when nation building becomes a crucial focus, the United States shifts its attention and money back onto large-scale security force assistance with a seemingly never-ending supply of resources often applied with little insight into what is effective. And when the crisis abates, security force assistance falls out of favor once again, and the traditionalists try to forget it ever happened. This cycle is dangerous, and we cannot keep repeating it.

Much of the current theory around security force assistance presupposes that there is nothing the advisory effort can do to change the outcome because it is in the hands of the host nation. But this is inaccurate: the host nation is not completely in the driver's seat, and the success or failure of the advisory effort is more accurately described as the product of shared input from both the advising force and the host nation. Without a doubt, the goals and objectives of the host nation have a significant—and perhaps dominant—impact. But at the same time, the decisions made by the advisory force have important consequences too. In the late 1990s Colombia was a failing state, on the verge of collapse. Without the U.S. advisory effort and monetary assistance, its trajectory might have mirrored Lebanon's, which has been in near-constant conflict for the past century and is well on the path to becoming a failed state. Moreover, Colombia's success was not just a consequence of its goals being in sync with those of the United States but also because U.S. advisors made a series of adept decisions that helped build superb Colombian forces.

Producing viable host-nation partners requires capable advisors employing effective tactics. Consistency in advisor pairing, a low partner-to-advisor ratio, long-term sustained presence, and the ability to organize the host-nation unit are all factors that most directly impact advisor ability to produce combat-effective partners. The advisor's language and cultural skills, as well as the ability to advise shoulder to shoulder in combat, also matter—although to a lesser degree. The appropriate mix of those factors, with strength in one factor counterbalancing weakness in another, is essential to successful security force assistance. To accomplish those ends requires a standing force of professional advisors, and the Special Forces regiment is neither sufficiently sized nor resourced to construct a sizeable foreign military on its own. Additional force structure must be committed to create a cadre of advisors, as trying to assemble a pickup team comprised of individuals with few skills and often even less desire will lead to the same results observed in Afghanistan and Iraq. The U.S. Army's Security Force Assistance Brigades are a step in the right direction. These new organizations are comprised of regionally aligned advisors focused on building the capabilities of U.S. allies' conventional forces. Even so, they would have to undergo significant changes to be most effective—that is, if they even remain a part of force structure as future cuts loom.

Conclusions and Recommendations

There are those who believe that the wars of Afghanistan and Iraq are conflicts of a dark past that should be forgotten because little of those experiences is relevant to the new strategic environment. Indeed, the U.S. Department of Defense has already shifted attention to peer and near-peer competitors such as China and Russia with expectations that those states could challenge the United States to the point that the outcome of a conflict would be in doubt. Some who herald this change believe that refocusing on the tactics required to face other armies requires abandoning "unnecessary" capabilities—such as advising allied forces—acquired during the post-9/11 emphasis on counterinsurgency. Yet the odds are that we will have to train another foreign military at some point in the near future. Such a mission will likely even be in the context of competition with a near-peer competitor and require the capacity to conduct security force assistance on a scale that parallels the missions in Iraq or Afghanistan. When it inevitably happens, we should be ready to implement the best strategies to give security force assistance the greatest chance of succeeding. Pretending a problem does not exist will not make it go away. Even in the type of conflicts they expect us to fight, we are still going to have to conduct security force assistance.

Appendix A

El Salvador Case Study, Calculating Partner-Force-to-Advisor Ratio

Year	Month	Number of advisors	Salvadorans advised	Monthly ratio
1981	January	130	5400	41.5
	February	130	5400	41.5
	March	130	6250	48.1
	April	130	6250	48.1
	May	130	6250	48.1
	June	130	6250	48.1
	July	130	6250	48.1
	August	130	6250	48.1
	September	130	6250	48.1
	October	130	6250	48.1
	November	130	6250	48.1
	December	130	6250	48.1
1982	January*	420	13350	31.8
	February*	420	13350	31.8
	March*	420	13350	31.8
	April	350	13350	38.1
	May	350	13350	38.1
	June	350	13350	38.1
	July	130	13350	102.7
	August	130	13350	102.7
	September	130	13350	102.7

Appendix A

Year	Month	Number of advisors	Salvadorans advised	Monthly ratio
	October	130	13350	102.7
	November	130	13350	102.7
	December	130	13350	102.7
1983	January	130	18750	144.2
	February	130	18750	144.2
	March	130	18750	144.2
	April	130	18750	144.2
	May	130	18750	144.2
	June	220	19600	89.1
	July	220	19600	89.1
	August	220	19600	89.1
	September	220	19600	89.1
	October*	300	20450	68.2
	November*	300	20450	68.2
	December*	300	20450	68.2
1984	January	210	25850	123.1
	February	210	25850	123.1
	March	210	25850	123.1
	April	130	25850	198.8
	May	130	25850	198.8
	June	130	25850	198.8
	July	130	25850	198.8
	August	130	25850	198.8
	September	130	25850	198.8
	October	130	25850	198.8
	November	130	25850	198.8
	December	130	25850	198.8
1985	January	130	31250	240.4
	February	130	31250	240.4
	March	130	31250	240.4
	April	130	31250	240.4
	May	130	31250	240.4

El Salvador Case Study, Calculating Partner-Force-to-Advisor Ratio

Year	Month	Number of advisors	Salvadorans advised	Monthly ratio
	June	130	31250	240.4
	July	130	31250	240.4
	August	130	31250	240.4
	September	130	31250	240.4
	October	130	31250	240.4
	November	130	31250	240.4
	December	130	31250	240.4
1986	January	130	31250	240.4
	February	130	31250	240.4
	March	130	31250	240.4
	April	130	31250	240.4
	May	130	31250	240.4
	June	130	31250	240.4
	July	130	31250	240.4
	August	130	31250	240.4
	September	130	31250	240.4
	October	130	31250	240.4
	November	130	31250	240.4
	December	130	31250	240.4
1987	January	130	31250	240.4
	February	130	31250	240.4
	March	130	31250	240.4
	April	130	31250	240.4
	May	130	31250	240.4
	June	130	31250	240.4
	July	130	31250	240.4
	August	130	31250	240.4
	September	130	31250	240.4
	October	130	31250	240.4
	November	130	31250	240.4
	December	130	31250	240.4
1988	January	130	31250	240.4

Appendix A

Year	Month	Number of advisors	Salvadorans advised	Monthly ratio
	February	130	31250	240.4
	March	130	31250	240.4
	April	130	31250	240.4
	May	130	31250	240.4
	June	130	31250	240.4
	July	130	31250	240.4
	August	130	31250	240.4
	September	130	31250	240.4
	October	130	31250	240.4
	November	130	31250	240.4
	December	130	31250	240.4
1989	January	130	31250	240.4
	February	130	31250	240.4
	March	130	31250	240.4
	April	130	31250	240.4
	May	130	31250	240.4
	June	130	31250	240.4
	July	130	31250	240.4
	August	130	31250	240.4
	September	130	31250	240.4
	October	130	31250	240.4
	November	130	31250	240.4
	December	130	31250	240.4
1990	January	130	31250	240.4
	February	130	31250	240.4
	March	130	31250	240.4
	April	130	31250	240.4
	May	130	31250	240.4
	June	130	31250	240.4
	July	130	31250	240.4
	August	130	31250	240.4
	September	130	31250	240.4

El Salvador Case Study, Calculating Partner-Force-to-Advisor Ratio

Year	Month	Number of advisors	Salvadorans advised	Monthly ratio
	October	130	31250	240.4
	November	130	31250	240.4
	December	130	31250	240.4
1991	January	130	31250	240.4
	February	130	31250	240.4
	March	130	31250	240.4
	April	130	31250	240.4
	May	130	31250	240.4
	June	130	31250	240.4
	July	130	31250	240.4
	August	130	31250	240.4
	September	130	31250	240.4
	October	130	31250	240.4
	November	130	31250	240.4
	December	130	31250	240.4
			Overall ratio	189.6

■ Indicates new BIRI operational

▭ Indicates training period for new BIRI (additional SF trainers)

* Indicates two BIRIs training

Appendix B

Philippines Case Study, Calculating Partner-Force-to-Advisor Ratio

Year	Month	Number of advisors	Number of soldiers in LR unit	Monthly ratio
2001	January	45	100	2.2
	February	45	100	2.2
	March	45	100	2.2
	April	45	100	2.2
	May	45	100	2.2
	June	45	100	2.2
	July	45	100	2.2
	August	2	100	50.0
	September	2	100	50.0
	October	2	100	50.0
	November	2	100	50.0
	December	2	100	50.0
2002	January	2	100	50.0
	February	14	100	7.1
	March	14	100	7.1
	April	14	100	7.1
	May	14	100	7.1
	June	14	100	7.1
	July	14	100	7.1
	August	14	100	7.1

Philippines Case Study, Calculating Partner-Force-to-Advisor Ratio

Year	Month	Number of advisors	Number of soldiers in LR unit	Monthly ratio
	September	14	100	7.1
	October	14	100	7.1
	November	12	100	8.3
	December	12	100	8.3
2003	January	12	100	8.3
	February	12	100	8.3
	March	12	100	8.3
	April	12	100	8.3
	May	12	100	8.3
	June	30	100	3.3
	July	30	100	3.3
	August	30	200	6.7
	September	30	200	6.7
	October	30	200	6.7
	November	30	200	6.7
	December	30	330	11.0
2004	January	6	330	55.0
	February	6	330	55.0
	March	6	330	55.0
	April	6	330	55.0
	May	6	330	55.0
	June	6	330	55.0
	July	6	330	55.0
	August	6	330	55.0
	September	6	330	55.0
	October	6	330	55.0
	November	6	330	55.0
	December	6	311	51.8
2005	January	6	311	51.8
	February	6	311	51.8
	March	6	311	51.8
	April	6	311	51.8

Appendix B

Year	Month	Number of advisors	Number of soldiers in LR unit	Monthly ratio
	May	6	311	51.8
	June	6	311	51.8
	July	6	311	51.8
	August	6	311	51.8
	September	6	311	51.8
	October	6	311	51.8
	November	6	311	51.8
	December	6	292	48.7
2006	January	6	292	48.7
	February	6	292	48.7
	March	6	292	48.7
	April	6	292	48.7
	May	6	292	48.7
	June	6	292	48.7
	July	6	292	48.7
	August	6	292	48.7
	September	6	292	48.7
	October	12	292	24.3
	November	12	292	24.3
	December	12	273	22.8
2007	January	12	273	22.8
	February	12	273	22.8
	March	12	273	22.8
	April	12	273	22.8
	May	12	273	22.8
	June	12	273	22.8
	July	12	273	22.8
	August	12	273	22.8
	September	12	273	22.8
	October	12	273	22.8
	November	12	273	22.8
	December	12	254	21.2

Philippines Case Study, Calculating Partner-Force-to-Advisor Ratio

Year	Month	Number of advisors	Number of soldiers in LR unit	Monthly ratio
2008	January	12	254	21.2
	February	12	254	21.2
	March	12	254	21.2
	April	12	254	21.2
	May	12	254	21.2
	June	12	254	21.2
	July	12	254	21.2
	August	12	254	21.2
	September	12	254	21.2
	October	12	254	21.2
	November	12	254	21.2
	December	12	235	19.6
2009	January	12	235	19.6
	February	12	235	19.6
	March	12	235	19.6
	April	12	235	19.6
	May	12	235	19.6
	June	12	235	19.6
	July	12	235	19.6
	August	12	235	19.6
	September	12	235	19.6
	October	12	235	19.6
	November	12	235	19.6
	December	12	216	18.0
2010	January	12	216	18.0
	February	12	216	18.0
	March	12	216	18.0
	April	12	216	18.0
	May	12	216	18.0
	June	12	216	18.0
	July	2	216	108.0
	August	2	216	108.0

Appendix B

Year	Month	Number of advisors	Number of soldiers in LR unit	Monthly ratio
	September	2	216	108.0
	October	2	216	108.0
	November	2	216	108.0
	December	2	197	98.5
2011	January	2	197	98.5
	February	12	197	16.4
	March	12	197	16.4
	April	12	197	16.4
	May	12	197	16.4
	June	12	197	16.4
	July	12	197	16.4
	August	12	197	16.4
	September	12	197	16.4
	October	12	197	16.4
	November	12	197	16.4
	December	12	178	14.8
2012	January	12	178	14.8
	February	12	178	14.8
	March	12	178	14.8
	April	12	178	14.8
	May	12	178	14.8
	June	12	178	14.8
	July	12	178	14.8
	August	12	178	14.8
	September	12	178	14.8
	October	12	178	14.8
	November	12	178	14.8
	December	12	159	13.3
2013	January	12	159	13.3
	February	12	159	13.3
	March	12	159	13.3
	April	12	159	13.3

Philippines Case Study, Calculating Partner-Force-to-Advisor Ratio

Year	Month	Number of advisors	Number of soldiers in LR unit	Monthly ratio
	May	12	159	13.3
	June	12	159	13.3
	July	12	159	13.3
	August	36	159	4.4
	September	36	139	3.9
	October	36	155	4.3
	November	36	170	4.7
	December	36	185	5.1
2014	January	36	200	5.6
	February	36	215	6.0
	March	36	230	6.4
	April	36	245	6.8
	May	36	260	7.2
	June	6	275	45.8
	July	6	290	48.3
	August	6	305	50.8
	September	6	320	53.3
	October	6	335	55.8
	November	6	350	58.3
	December	6	365	60.8
2015	January	6	380	63.3
	February	6	400	66.7
			Overall ratio	**28.7**

Appendix C

Colombia Case Study, Calculating Partner-Force-to-Advisor Ratio

Year	Month	Total advisors	Soldiers in BACOA	Soldiers in AGLAN	Total advised	Monthly ratio
2002	June	18	200		200	11.1
	July	18	200		200	11.1
	August	18	200		200	11.1
	September	18	200		200	11.1
	October	18	200		200	11.1
	November	18	200		200	11.1
	December	18	200		200	11.1
2003	January	21	200		200	9.5
	February	21	200		200	9.5
	March	21	200	170	370	17.6
	April	21	200	170	370	17.6
	May	21	200	170	370	17.6
	June	21	200	170	370	17.6
	July	21	200	170	370	17.6
	August	21	200	170	370	17.6
	September	21	200	170	370	17.6
	October	21	200	170	370	17.6
	November	21	200	170	370	17.6
	December	21	200	170	370	17.6
2004	January	30	200	170	370	12.3
	February	30	200	170	370	12.3

Colombia Case Study, Calculating Partner-Force-to-Advisor Ratio

Year	Month	Total advisors	Soldiers in BACOA	Soldiers in AGLAN	Total advised	Monthly ratio
	March	30	200	170	370	12.3
	April	30	200	170	370	12.3
	May	30	200	170	370	12.3
	June	30	200	170	370	12.3
	July	30	200	170	370	12.3
	August	30	200	170	370	12.3
	September	30	200	170	370	12.3
	October	30	200	170	370	12.3
	November	30	200	170	370	12.3
	December	30	200	170	370	12.3
2005	January	18	200	170	370	20.6
	February	18	200	170	370	20.6
	March	18	200	170	370	20.6
	April	18	200	170	370	20.6
	May	18	200	170	370	20.6
	June	18	200	170	370	20.6
	July	18	200	170	370	20.6
	August	18	200	170	370	20.6
	September	18	200	170	370	20.6
	October	18	200	170	370	20.6
	November	18	200	170	370	20.6
	December	18	200	170	370	20.6
2006	January	18	200	170	370	20.6
	February	18	200	170	370	20.6
	March	18	200	170	370	20.6
	April	18	200	170	370	20.6
	May	18	200	170	370	20.6
	June	12	200	170	370	30.8
	July	12	200	170	370	30.8
	August	12	200	170	370	30.8
	September	12	200	170	370	30.8
	October	18	200	170	370	20.6

Appendix C

Year	Month	Total advisors	Soldiers in BACOA	Soldiers in AGLAN	Total advised	Monthly ratio
	November	18	200	170	370	20.6
	December	18	200	170	370	20.6
2007	January	18	200	170	370	20.6
	February	18	200	170	370	20.6
	March	18	200	170	370	20.6
	April	18	200	170	370	20.6
	May	18	200	170	370	20.6
	June	18	200	170	370	20.6
	July	18	200	170	370	20.6
	August	18	200	170	370	20.6
	September	18	200	170	370	20.6
	October	18	200	170	370	20.6
	November	18	200	170	370	20.6
	December	18	200	170	370	20.6
2008	January	18	200	170	370	20.6
	February	18	200	170	370	20.6
	March	18	200	170	370	20.6
	April	18	200	170	370	20.6
	May	18	200	170	370	20.6
	June	18	200	170	370	20.6
	July	18	200	170	370	20.6
	August	18	200	170	370	20.6
	September	18	200	170	370	20.6
	November	18	200	170	370	20.6
	November	18	200	170	370	20.6
	December	18	200	170	370	20.6
2009	January	18	200	170	370	20.6
	February	18	200	170	370	20.6
	March	18	200	170	370	20.6
	April	18	200	170	370	20.6
	May	18	200	170	370	20.6
	June	18	200	170	370	20.6

Colombia Case Study, Calculating Partner-Force-to-Advisor Ratio

Year	Month	Total advisors	Soldiers in BACOA	Soldiers in AGLAN	Total advised	Monthly ratio
	July	18	200	170	370	20.6
	August	18	200	170	370	20.6
	September	18	200	170	370	20.6
	October	18	200	170	370	20.6
	November	18	200	170	370	20.6
	December	18	200	170	370	20.6
2010	January	18	200	170	370	20.6
	February	18	200	170	370	20.6
	March	18	200	170	370	20.6
	April	18	200	170	370	20.6
	May	18	200	170	370	20.6
	June	18	200	170	370	20.6
	July	18	200	170	370	20.6
	August	18	200	170	370	20.6
	September	18	200	170	370	20.6
	October	18	200	170	370	20.6
	November	18	200	170	370	20.6
	December	18	200	170	370	20.6
2011	January	18	200	170	370	20.6
	February	18	200	170	370	20.6
	March	18	200	170	370	20.6
	April	18	200	170	370	20.6
	May	18	200	170	370	20.6
	June	18	200	170	370	20.6
	July	18	200	170	370	20.6
	August	18	200	170	370	20.6
	September	18	200	170	370	20.6
	October	18	200	170	370	20.6
	November	18	200	170	370	20.6
	December	18	200	170	370	20.6
2012	January	18	200	170	370	20.6
	February	18	200	170	370	20.6

Appendix C

Year	Month	Total advisors	Soldiers in BACOA	Soldiers in AGLAN	Total advised	Monthly ratio
	March	18	200	170	370	20.6
	April	18	200	170	370	20.6
	May	18	200	170	370	20.6
	June	18	200	170	370	20.6
	July	18	200	170	370	20.6
	August	18	200	170	370	20.6
	September	18	200	170	370	20.6
	October	18	200	170	370	20.6
	November	18	200	170	370	20.6
	December	18	200	170	370	20.6
2013	January	30	200	170	370	12.3
	February	30	200	170	370	12.3
	March	30	200	170	370	12.3
	April	30	200	170	370	12.3
	May	30	200	170	370	12.3
	June	30	200	170	370	12.3
	July	30	200	170	370	12.3
	August	30	200	170	370	12.3
	September	30	200	170	370	12.3
	October	30	200	170	370	12.3
	November	30	200	170	370	12.3
	December	30	200	170	370	12.3
2014	January	30	200	170	370	12.3
	February	30	200	170	370	12.3
	March	30	200	170	370	12.3
	April	30	200	170	370	12.3
	May	30	200	170	370	12.3
	June	30	200	170	370	12.3
	July	30	200	170	370	12.3
	August	30	200	170	370	12.3
	September	30	200	170	370	12.3
	October	30	200	170	370	12.3

Colombia Case Study, Calculating Partner-Force-to-Advisor Ratio

Year	Month	Total advisors	Soldiers in BACOA	Soldiers in AGLAN	Total advised	Monthly ratio
	November	30	200	170	370	12.3
	December	30	200	170	370	12.3
2015	January	30	200	170	370	12.3
	February	30	200	170	370	12.3
	March	30	200	170	370	12.3
	April	30	200	170	370	12.3
	May	30	200	170	370	12.3
	June	30	200	170	370	12.3
	July	30	200	170	370	12.3
	August	30	200	170	370	12.3
	September	30	200	170	370	12.3
	October	30	200	170	370	12.3
	November	30	200	170	370	12.3
	December	30	200	170	370	12.3
2016	January	30	200	170	370	12.3
	February	30	200	170	370	12.3
	March	30	200	170	370	12.3
	April	30	200	170	370	12.3
	May	30	200	170	370	12.3
	June	30	200	170	370	12.3
					Overall ratio	**17.5**

┆┄┄┄┄┄┆ Creation of BACOA/AGLAN

Appendix D

Iraq Case Study, Calculating Partner-Force-to-Advisor Ratio

Year	Month	Number of advisors with ICTF	Number of soldiers in ICTF	Number of advisors with Commandos*
2003	October	24	44	34
	November	24	44	34
	December	24	44	34
2004	January	24	44	34
	February	24	44	34
	March	24	44	34
	April	24	44	34
	May	24	44	34
	June	24	44	34
	July	24	44	46
	August	24	44	46
	September	24	44	46
	October	24	44	46
	November	24	44	46
	December	24	44	46
2005	January	24	44	24
	February	24	44	24
	March	24	44	24
	April	24	44	24
	May	24	44	24

Iraq Case Study, Calculating Partner-Force-to-Advisor Ratio

Number of Commandos**	Total ISOF soldiers (per month)	Total advisors (per month)	Monthly ratio (for both elements)
240	284	58	4.9
240	284	58	4.9
240	284	58	4.9
240	284	58	4.9
240	284	58	4.9
240	284	58	4.9
240	284	58	4.9
240	284	58	4.9
240	284	58	4.9
240	284	70	4.1
240	284	70	4.1
240	284	70	4.1
240	284	70	4.1
240	284	70	4.1
240	284	70	4.1
240	284	48	5.9
240	284	48	5.9
240	284	48	5.9
240	284	48	5.9
240	284	48	5.9

Appendix D

Year	Month	Number of advisors with ICTF	Number of soldiers in ICTF	Number of advisors with Commandos*
	June	24	44	24
	July	24	44	24
	August	24	44	24
	September	24	44	24
	October	24	44	24
	November	24	44	24
	December	24	44	24
2006	January	24	44	24
	February	24	44	24
	March	24	44	24
	April	24	44	24
	May	24	44	24
	June	24	44	24
	July	24	44	24
	August	24	44	24
	September	24	44	24
	October	24	44	24
	November	24	44	24
	December	24	44	24
2007	January	24	44	24
	February	24	44	24
	March	24	44	24
	April	24	44	24
	May	24	44	24
	June	24	44	24
	July	24	44	24
	August	24	44	24
	September	24	44	24
	October	24	44	24
	November	24	44	24
	December	24	44	24

Iraq Case Study, Calculating Partner-Force-to-Advisor Ratio

Number of Commandos**	Total ISOF soldiers (per month)	Total advisors (per month)	Monthly ratio (for both elements)
240	284	48	5.9
240	284	48	5.9
240	284	48	5.9
240	284	48	5.9
240	284	48	5.9
240	284	48	5.9
240	284	48	5.9
240	284	48	5.9
240	284	48	5.9
240	284	48	5.9
240	284	48	5.9
240	284	48	5.9
240	284	48	5.9
240	284	48	5.9
240	284	48	5.9
240	284	48	5.9
240	284	48	5.9
240	284	48	5.9
240	284	48	5.9
240	284	48	5.9
240	284	48	5.9
240	284	48	5.9
240	284	48	5.9
240	284	48	5.9
240	284	48	5.9
240	284	48	5.9
240	284	48	5.9
240	284	48	5.9
240	284	48	5.9
240	284	48	5.9

Appendix D

Year	Month	Number of advisors with ICTF	Number of soldiers in ICTF	Number of advisors with Commandos*
2008	January	24	44	24
	February	24	44	48
	March	24	44	48
	April	24	44	48
	May	24	44	48
	June	24	44	48
	July	24	44	48
	August	24	44	48
	September	24	44	48
	October	24	44	48
	November	24	44	48
	December	24	44	48
2009	January	24	44	48
	February	24	44	60
	March	24	44	60
	April	24	44	60
	May	24	44	60
	June	24	44	60
	July	24	44	60
	August	24	44	60
	September	24	44	60
	October	24	44	60
	November	24	44	60
	December	24	44	60
2010	January	24	44	60
	February	24	44	60
	March	24	44	72
	April	24	44	72
	May	24	44	72
	June	24	44	72
	July	24	44	72
	August	24	44	72

Iraq Case Study, Calculating Partner-Force-to-Advisor Ratio

Number of Commandos**	Total ISOF soldiers (per month)	Total advisors (per month)	Monthly ratio (for both elements)
240	284	48	5.9
420	464	72	6.4
420	464	72	6.4
420	464	72	6.4
420	464	72	6.4
420	464	72	6.4
420	464	72	6.4
420	464	72	6.4
420	464	72	6.4
420	464	72	6.4
420	464	72	6.4
420	464	72	6.4
420	464	72	6.4
510	554	84	6.6
510	554	84	6.6
510	554	84	6.6
510	554	84	6.6
510	554	84	6.6
510	554	84	6.6
510	554	84	6.6
510	554	84	6.6
510	554	84	6.6
510	554	84	6.6
510	554	84	6.6
510	554	84	6.6
510	554	84	6.6
510	644	96	6.7
510	644	96	6.7
510	644	96	6.7
600	644	96	6.7
600	644	96	6.7
600	644	96	6.7

Appendix D

Year	Month	Number of advisors with ICTF	Number of soldiers in ICTF	Number of advisors with Commandos*
	September	24	44	72
	October	24	44	72
	November	24	44	72
	December	24	44	72
2011	January	24	44	72
	February	24	44	72
	March	24	44	72
	April	24	44	72
	May	24	44	72
	June	24	44	72
	July	24	44	72
	August	24	44	72
	September	24	44	72
	October	24	44	72
	November	24	44	72
	December	24	44	72

* This is the total number of advisors with both the Commando unit in Baghdad and the regional units.

** This is the total number of Iraqis with both the Commando unit in Baghdad and the regional units.

Iraq Case Study, Calculating Partner-Force-to-Advisor Ratio

Number of Commandos**	Total ISOF soldiers (per month)	Total advisors (per month)	Monthly ratio (for both elements)
660	704	96	7.3
660	704	96	7.3
660	704	96	7.3
660	704	96	7.3
660	704	96	7.3
660	704	96	7.3
690	734	96	7.6
690	734	96	7.6
690	734	96	7.6
690	734	96	7.6
690	734	96	7.6
700	744	96	7.8
700	744	96	7.8
700	744	96	7.8
700	744	96	7.8
700	744	96	7.8
			Overall ratio 6.2

Appendix E

Afghanistan Case Study, Calculating Partner-Force-to-Advisor Ratio

Year	Month	Number of advisors	Number of Commandos	Monthly ratio
2007	August	12	236	19.7
	September	12	231	19.3
	October	12	226	18.8
	November	24	457	19.0
	December	24	447	18.6
2008	January	24	437	18.2
	February	36	663	18.4
	March	36	648	18.0
	April	36	633	17.6
	May	36	618	17.2
	June	48	839	17.5
	July	48	819	17.1
	August	48	799	16.6
	September	48	779	16.2
	October	48	759	15.8
	November	60	975	16.3
	December	60	950	15.8
2009	January	60	925	15.4
	February	60	905	15.1
	March	60	885	14.8
	April	60	865	14.4

Afghanistan Case Study, Calculating Partner-Force-to-Advisor Ratio

Year	Month	Number of advisors	Number of Commandos	Monthly ratio
	May*	84	1086	12.9
	June	84	1071	12.8
	July	84	1056	12.6
	August	84	1046	12.5
	September	84	1036	12.3
	October	84	1026	12.2
	November	84	1016	12.1
	December	84	1011	12.0
2010	January	84	1006	12.0
	February	96	1237	12.9
	March	96	1227	12.8
	April	96	1217	12.7
	May	96	1212	12.6
	June	96	1207	12.6
	July	96	1202	12.5
	August	96	1197	12.5
	September	108	1428	13.2
	October	108	1418	13.1
	November	108	1408	13.0
	December	108	1398	12.9
2011	January	108	1388	12.9
	February	108	1378	12.8
	March	192	1368	7.1
	April	192	1358	7.1
	May	192	1348	7.0
	June	216	1574	7.3
	July	216	1559	7.2
	August	216	1549	7.2
	September	216	1539	7.1
	October	216	1529	7.1
	November	216	1519	7.0
	December	216	1509	7.0

Appendix E

Year	Month	Number of advisors	Number of Commandos	Monthly ratio
2012	January	216	1499	6.9
	February	216	1489	6.9
	March	120	1484	12.4
	April	120	1479	12.3
	May	120	1474	12.3
	June	120	1469	12.2
	July	120	1464	12.2
	August	120	1459	12.2
	September	120	1454	12.1
	October	120	1449	12.1
	November	120	1445	12.0
	December	120	1439	12.0
2013	January	120	1439	12.0
	February	120	1439	12.0
	March	120	1439	12.0
	April	120	1439	12.0
	May	120	1439	12.0
	June	216	1439	6.7
	July	216	1439	6.7
	August	216	1439	6.7
	September	216	1439	6.7
	October	216	1439	6.7
	November	216	1439	6.7
	December	216	1439	6.7
2014	January	216	1439	6.7
	February	216	1439	6.7
	March	216	1439	6.7
	April	216	1439	6.7
	May	216	1439	6.7
	June	216	1439	6.7
	July	216	1439	6.7

Afghanistan Case Study, Calculating Partner-Force-to-Advisor Ratio

Year	Month	Number of advisors	Number of Commandos	Monthly ratio
	August	216	1439	6.7
	September	216	1439	6.7
	October	216	1439	6.7
	November	80	1439	18.0
	December	80	1439	18.0
2015	January	80	1675	20.9
	February	80	1670	20.9
	March	80	1665	20.8
	April	80	1660	20.8
	May	80	1655	20.7
	June	80	1650	20.6
	July	80	1645	20.6
	August	80	1640	20.5
	September	80	1635	20.4
	October	80	1630	20.4
	November	80	1625	20.3
	December	80	1620	20.3
2016	January	80	1615	20.2
	February	80	1610	20.1
	March	80	1605	20.1
	April	80	1600	20.0
	May	80	1595	19.9
	June	80	1595	19.9
	July	80	1595	19.9
	August	80	1595	19.9
	September	80	1595	19.9
	October	80	1595	19.9
	November	80	1595	19.9
	December	80	1595	19.9
2017	January	80	1595	19.9
	February	80	1595	19.9

Appendix E

Year	Month	Number of advisors	Number of Commandos	Monthly ratio
	March	80	1595	19.9
	April	80	1595	19.9
	May	80	1595	19.9
	June	80	1595	19.9
	July	80	1595	19.9
	August	80	1595	19.9
	September	80	1595	19.9
	October	80	1595	19.9
	November	80	1595	19.9
	December	80	1595	19.9
2018	January	80	1713	21.4
	February	80	1711	21.4
	March	80	1827	22.8
	April	80	1823	22.8
	May	80	1937	24.2
	June	80	1931	24.1
	July	80	2043	25.5
	August	80	2035	25.4
	September	80	2145	26.8
	October	80	2135	26.7
	November	80	2243	28.0
	December	80	2231	27.9
2019	January	80	2337	29.2
	February	80	2323	29.0
	March	80	2427	30.3
	April	80	2411	30.1
	May	80	2513	31.4
	June	80	2495	31.2
	July	80	2597	32.5
	August	80	2579	32.2
	September	80	2563	32.0

Afghanistan Case Study, Calculating Partner-Force-to-Advisor Ratio

Year	Month	Number of advisors	Number of Commandos	Monthly ratio
	October	80	2547	31.8
	November	80	2533	31.7
	December	80	2521	31.5
			Overall ratio	**16.4**

■ Indicates new kandak operational

▨ Indicates new company operational (post-2017 growth)

⌇ Indicates surge period, where two ODAs are paired per kandak (one per company)

┆ Indicates drawdown: not every kandak has ODA support (half intermittent, half full-time ODA)

* The stand-up of 6th Kandak National Force occurred in May 2009. It was consistently advised by two ODAs and generally remained full strength because it was the national-level counterterrorism force and had priority for replacements.

Notes

INTRODUCTION

1. George W. Bush, Iraq speech, Fort Bragg, NC, June 28, 2005, text archived at "Full Text: George Bush's Iraq Speech," World News, *The Guardian*, June 29, 2005, https://www.theguardian.com/world/2005/jun/29/iraq.usa. Many military bases have changed names since this book was written; I use the base name at the time of reference.
2. Thomas Edward Lawrence was a British army officer and diplomat whose storied life inspired the 1962 film *Lawrence of Arabia*. While working for Britain's Arab Bureau, he began publishing in the *Arab Bulletin*, a daily dispatch to counsel British generals serving in the Arabian Peninsula. The issue of August 20, 1917, famously itemized Lawrence's twenty-seven "commandments" for successful operations in the region. They are quoted in U.S. Department of the Army, *Tactics in Counterinsurgency*, Field Manual no. 3-24.2 (FM 90-8, FM 7-98) (Washington, DC: U.S. Department of the Army, April 21, 2009), D1-4, archived online at https://irp.fas.org/doddir/army/fm3-24-2.pdf. Article 15 serves as the heading for chapter 8 in the Army manual, "Support to Host Nation Security Forces."
3. Jeremy Stöhs, "Built to Fail: The Iraqi Army from Invasion to the Rise of the Islamic State," *Journal for Intelligence, Propaganda, and Security Studies* 11, no. 2 (Spring 2017): 145, 152.
4. Sean McFate, "Shifting the Blame: How the Pentagon Lost Afghanistan," Opinion, *The Hill*, August 17, 2021, https://thehill.com/opinion/national-security/568102-shifting-the-blame-how-the-pentagon-lost-afghanistan.
5. By 2014 the ISOF was comprised of three maneuver brigades and a training brigade.
6. U.S. doctrine considers a unit as combat ineffective when it takes 30 percent casualties. Michael Knights and Alex Mello, "The Best Thing America Built in Iraq: Iraq's Counter-terrorism Service and the Long War against Militancy," *War on the Rocks*, July 19, 2017, https://warontherocks.com/2017/07/the-best-thing-america-built-in-iraq-iraqs-counter-terrorism-service-and-the-long-war-against-militancy/.

7. Carter Malkasian, "How the Good War Went Bad: America's Slow-Motion Failure in Afghanistan," *Foreign Affairs* 99, no. 2 (March/April 2020), https://www.foreignaffairs.com/articles/afghanistan/2020-02-10/how-good-war-went-bad.
8. Thomas Gibbons-Neff, Fahim Abed, and Jim Huylebroek, "On Afghanistan's Front Line, There Are No Good Choices," World, *New York Times*, August 9, 2021, https://www.nytimes.com/2021/08/09/world/asia/Afghanistan-taliban-kandahar.html.
9. Lieutenant Aldo Raine, the unit leader in the film *Inglourious Basterds*, is also a fictitious member of the First Special Service Force.
10. Tim Ball, "Talking the Talk: Language Capabilities for U.S. Army Special Forces," *War on the Rocks*, May 26, 2021, https://warontherocks.com/2021/05/talking-the-talk-language-capabilities-for-u-s-army-special-forces/.
11. One unit that has since grown in considerable renown, Detachment A, was part of a formerly highly classified project that based nearly one hundred Special Forces soldiers in Berlin. They wore civilian clothes and spoke fluent German or Eastern European languages so that in the event of a Soviet invasion they could disappear into urban and rural areas and lead partisans in guerrilla warfare.
12. President Kennedy is revered by Special Forces soldiers, who served as an honor guard at his funeral. His name also graces their training institution, the John F. Kennedy Special Warfare Center and School.
13. The Special Forces motto is *De oppresso liber*, a Latin phrase that roughly translates as "to free the oppressed."
14. In homage to these Vietnam missions, many homemade patches worn during Special Forces deployments to Iraq and Afghanistan mimicked the famous MACV-SOG patch, which depicts a skull with razor-sharp teeth, wearing a green beret.
15. This includes language training and other mandatory courses.
16. From 2007 to 2014 active-duty SF Groups grew from three to four battalions to meet the nearly insatiable personnel demands of the post-9/11 wars. Considerable resourcing challenges existed at least initially, with some units more shells than combat-capable organizations.
17. By 2001 U.S. force structure included five active-duty Special Forces Groups and two in the Army National Guard, a part-time reserve force.
18. U.S. Special Operations Command was budgeted for $51 million for language training in fiscal year 2021. U.S. Special Operations Command, U.S. Department of Defense, *Fiscal Year (FY) 2021 Budget Estimates: Operation and Maintenance, Defense-Wide United States Special Operations Command* (Washington, DC: U.S. Department of Defense, February 2020), TF36, https://comptroller.defense

.gov/Portals/45/Documents/defbudget/fy2021/budget_justification/pdfs/01_Operation_and_Maintenance/O_M_VOL_1_PART_1/SOCOM_OP-5.pdf.
19. The Mos Eisley Cantina in *Star Wars* was a gathering spot filled with a tremendous diversity of alien cultures, creatures, and races.
20. Also referred to as the Sons of Iraq or by its Arabic name, the Sahwa.
21. As discussed in Robert D. Ramsey III, *Advice for Advisors: Suggestions and Observations from Lawrence to the Present*, Global War on Terrorism Occasional Paper 19 (Fort Leavenworth, KS: Combat Studies Inst. Press, 2006), 3.
22. Kyle Rempfer, "New Force Generation Model Aims to Regionally Align Army Units, Give Troops Predictability," *Army Times*, October 19, 2020, https://www.armytimes.com/news/your-army/2020/10/14/new-force-generation-model-aims-to-regionally-align-army-units-give-troops-predictability/.
23. See, for example, Rusty Bradley's memoir, with Kevin Maurer, *Lions of Kandahar: The Story of a Fight against All Odds*, 1st ed. (New York: Bantam, 2011); and see Frank Antenori and Hans Halberstadt, *Roughneck Nine-One: The Extraordinary Story of a Special Forces A-Team at War*, 1st ed. (New York: St. Martin's Press, 2006).
24. U.S. Department of the Army, *Special Forces Operations*, Field Manual 3-05.20 (FM 31-20) (Washington, DC: U.S. Department of the Army, June 2001), 3–30, archived online at https://irp.fas.org/doddir/army/fm3-05-20.pdf.
25. See, for example, Matthew M. Chingos and Grover J. "Russ" Whitehurst, "Class Size: What Research Says and What It Means for State Policy," *Brookings* (blog), May 11, 2011, https://www.brookings.edu/research/class-size-what-research-says-and-what-it-means-for-state-policy/.
26. Douglass C. North, John Joseph Wallis, and Barry R. Weingast, *Violence and Social Orders: A Conceptual Framework for Interpreting Recorded Human History*, repr. ed. (Cambridge: Cambridge University Press, 2012), 18–26.
27. Principal-agent theory and its application to SFA are well explained in Stephen Biddle, Julia Macdonald, and Ryan Baker, "Small Footprint, Small Payoff: The Military Effectiveness of Security Force Assistance," *Journal of Strategic Studies* 41, nos. 1–2 (February 23, 2018): 89–142, https://doi.org/10.1080/01402390.2017.1307745.
28. For a good overview of this debate see Robert Tollast, "SOF, COIN, and the Question of Host Nation Viability: An Interview with Dick Couch," *Small Wars Journal*, July 1, 2013, https://smallwarsjournal.com/jrnl/art/sof-coin-and-the-question-of-host-nation-viability-an-interview-with-dick-couch.
29. John Dryer, "A Brief History of the Military Advising Mission," *Small Wars Journal*, May 20, 2018, https://smallwarsjournal.com/jrnl/art/brief-history-military-advising-mission.

30. U.S. Department of the Army, *Tactics in Counterinsurgency*, Field Manual 3-24.2, 5-2.
31. U.S. Department of the Army, *Security Force Assistance*, Field Manual 3-07.1 (Washington, D.C: U.S. Department of the Army, May 2011).
32. Richard H. Shultz Jr. and Joseph L. Votel, *Transforming US Intelligence for Irregular War: Task Force 714 in Iraq*, repr. ed. (Washington, DC: Georgetown University Press, 2020), 109–11, 125–31.
33. Stanley McChrystal, *My Share of the Task: A Memoir* (New York: Portfolio, 2014), 153–57.
34. Roger Trinquier, *Modern Warfare: A French View of Counterinsurgency*, 1st ed. (Westport, CT: Praeger, 2006 [1961]), 45.
35. U.S. Department of the Army, *Tactics in Counterinsurgency*, Field Manual 3-24.2, 5-25, 6-15, A-4; U.S. Joint Chiefs of Staff, *Counterinsurgency*, Joint Publication 3-24 (Washington, DC: U.S. Department of Defense, April 25, 2018), II-24–25, archived online at https://irp.fas.org/doddir/dod/jp3_24.pdf.
36. The origins of this quotation are unclear as it has been attributed variously to Napoleon Bonaparte, General Omar Bradley, and Commandant of the Marine Corps General Robert Barrow. See Barry Popik, "Amateurs Talk Strategy. Professionals Talk Logistics," BarryPopik.com, June 19, 2019, https://www.barrypopik.com/index.php/new_york_city/entry/amateurs_talk_strategy.
37. U.S. Army, *Security Force Assistance Brigade*, Army Techniques Publication 3-96.1 (Fort Benning, GA: U.S. Department of the Army, September 2, 2020), 4-6–4-9, https://armypubs.army.mil/epubs/DR_pubs/DR_a/ARN30336-ATP_3-96.1-000-WEB-1.pdf.
38. For theorists who discuss the importance of cohesion to combat effectiveness see Charles McMoran Wilson (Lord Moran), *The Anatomy of Courage: The Classic WWI Account of the Psychological Effects of War*, 1st ed. (New York: Carroll and Graf, 2007), 158–60, 171–74; Carl von Clausewitz, *On War*, trans. Michael Eliot Howard and Peter Paret, rev. ed. (Princeton: Princeton University Press, 1989), 184–86; Ben Connable et al., *Will to Fight: Analyzing, Modeling, and Simulating the Will to Fight of Military Units* (Washington, DC: RAND Corporation, 2018), 10–12; and Anthony King, "On Combat Effectiveness in the Infantry Platoon: Beyond the Primary Group Thesis," *Security Studies* 25, no. 4 (2016): 699–728, https://doi.org/10.1080/09636412.2016.1220205.
39. Lauren Fish and Paul Scharre, "The Soldier's Heavy Load," report, Center for a New American Security, September 26, 2018, https://www.cnas.org/publications/reports/the-soldiers-heavy-load-1.
40. Connable et al., *Will to Fight*, 47.

41. Henry A. Kissinger, "The Viet Nam Negotiations," *Foreign Affairs* 47, no. 2 (January 1969): 214, https://www.foreignaffairs.com/articles/asia/1969-01-01/viet-nam-negotiations (paywall).
42. David Galula, *Counterinsurgency Warfare: Theory and Practice*, new ed. (Westport, CT: Praeger Security International, 2006), 64.
43. Mao Tse-tung and Samuel B. Griffith, *On Guerrilla Warfare*, 2nd rev. edition (Urbana: University of Illinois Press, 2000 [1937]), 73, 77–78.

CHAPTER 1. "THE ONLY WAR WE HAD"

1. I chose 1991 as the ending of this case study rather than 1992 because the Chapultepec Peace Accords were signed on January 16, 1992. The last complete month of advising before the end of the war, therefore, was December 1991.
2. Patrick Paterson, *Training Surrogate Forces in International Humanitarian Law: Lessons from Peru, Colombia, El Salvador, and Iraq* (Tampa, FL: Joint Special Operations University, 2016), 61–64.
3. Brian D'Haeseleer, *The Salvadoran Crucible: The Failure of U.S. Counterinsurgency in El Salvador, 1979–1992* (Lawrence: University Press of Kansas, 2017), 59.
4. Interview, Frank Sobchak with Lt. Col. Ted Mataxis, January 15, 2021. There is some indication that the idea for the fifty-five total advisors came from the speed limit then common across the United States, which was fifty-five miles per hour. The ranks cited for the subjects interviewed across this book were accurate as of the date of interview. Some have since been promoted, which may result in other references showing a different rank.
5. D'Haeseleer, *The Salvadoran Crucible*, 70.
6. Paterson, *Training Surrogate Forces*, 67.
7. Charles H. Briscoe, "El Paraiso and the War in El Salvador (1981–1983)," *Veritas* 3, no. 1 (Summer 2007): 12. https://arsof-history.org/articles/v3n1_paraiso_page_1.html.
8. D'Haeseleer, *The Salvadoran Crucible*, 68–70. The Reagan administration was especially concerned that more-extensive support would trigger the 1973 War Powers Act, which could potentially prompt a congressional vote to shut down funding for the mission and end U.S. involvement.
9. Richard D. Downie, *Learning from Conflict: The U.S. Military in Vietnam, El Salvador, and the Drug War* (Westport, CT: Praeger, 1998), 133.
10. Briscoe, "El Paraiso and the War in El Salvador."
11. Limited numbers (perhaps 10 percent) of advisors were not Special Forces personnel, but those cases have been excluded from this study. At first the

military intelligence officers came from within that branch, but after one rotation they were mostly replaced with Operations and Intelligence–qualified Special Forces NCOs.

12. Interview, Frank Sobchak with Lt. Col. Ted Mataxis, January 15, 2021.
13. James S. Corum, "The Air War in El Salvador," *Airpower Journal* (Summer 1998): 30, archived online at https://apps.dtic.mil/sti/pdfs/ADA356597.pdf.
14. Interview, Frank Sobchak with Dr. David Spencer, January 22, 2021.
15. Interview, Frank Sobchak with Col. John Waghelstein, January 25, 2021.
16. Briscoe, "El Paraiso and the War in El Salvador."
17. Interview, Frank Sobchak with Dr. David Spencer, January 22, 2021.
18. Charles H. Briscoe, "San Miguel: The Attack on *El Bosque*," *Veritas* 3, no. 3 (Summer 2007), https://arsof-history.org/articles/v3n3_san_miguel_page_1.html.
19. Downie, *Learning from Conflict*, 142.
20. César A. Chelala, "Central America's Health Plight," *Christian Science Monitor*, March 22, 1990, https://www.csmonitor.com/1990/0322/echel.html.
21. Far more NCOs returned for multiple tours than officers, although some officers did deploy multiple times.
22. Interview, Frank Sobchak with Lt. Col. Cecil Bailey, September 21, 2020.
23. Interview, Frank Sobchak with Lt. Col. Ted Mataxis, January 15, 2021. Several interviewees (both within and outside 3/7) estimated that roughly half of the advisors were from 3/7 across the entire mission.
24. USSOCOM was created in 1987 and had no impact on the selection process until that time; even then their impact was negligible. While a Special Operations Forces coordination cell existed in all the unified combatant commands, it was led by a colonel, which was the same rank as the 7th Group commander, and he had little political clout as a result.
25. Lt. Col. (later Lt. Gen.) Geoffrey Lambert as quoted in "Interview: Special Forces in El Salvador," with Lt. Col. Geoffrey Lambert, Lt. Col. Frank Pedrozo, and Col. J. S. Roach, *Special Warfare* 6, no. 4 (October 1993): 34, https://www.dvidshub.net/publication/issues/8284.
26. Interview, Frank Sobchak with Col. Wayne (Pat) Richardson, January 20, 2021. At the time each SF Group had only nine maneuver companies, and with one committed full time to Honduras only eight remained in the pool for potential commitment to El Salvador.
27. Interview, Frank Sobchak with Maj. Gen. Ed Reeder, December 17, 2020.
28. Interview, Frank Sobchak with Col. Francisco (Frank) Pedrozo, September 8, 2020.

29. Interview, Frank Sobchak with Col. Kevin Higgins, September 30, 2020.
30. Army.mil/News, "3rd Special Forces Group," Military.com, June 12, 2013, https://www.military.com/special-operations/3rd-special-forces-group.html; J. M. Simpson, "1st Special Forces Group (Airborne) Celebrates 30th Anniversary of Unit Reactivation," NorthwestMilitary.com, September 5, 2014, http://www.northwestmilitary.com/news/news-front/2014/09/1st-Special-Forces-Group-Airborne-celebrates-30th-anniversary-of-unit-reactivation-at-Joint-Base-Lew/.
31. Interview, Frank Sobchak with Col. Wayne (Pat) Richardson, January 20, 2021.
32. Interview, Frank Sobchak with Lt. Col. Mike Hennelly, January 14, 2021.
33. Interview, Frank Sobchak with Col. Wayne (Pat) Richardson, January 20, 2021.
34. Interview, Frank Sobchak with Brig. Gen. Hector Pagan, January 5, 2021.
35. Interview, Frank Sobchak with Col. Francisco (Frank) Pedrozo, September 8, 2020.
36. Interview, Frank Sobchak with Lt. Col. Mike Hennelly, January 14, 2021.
37. Interview, Frank Sobchak with Lt. Col. Ted Mataxis, January 15, 2021.
38. Interview, Frank Sobchak with Col. Kevin Higgins, September 30, 2020.
39. Robert D. Ramsey, *Advising Indigenous Forces: American Advisors in Korea, Vietnam, and El Salvador* (Leavenworth, KS: Combat Studies Institute Press, 2012), 93.
40. Interview, Frank Sobchak with MSgt. Leamon (Lee) Ratterree, January 5, 2021.
41. Interview, Frank Sobchak with Col. Wayne (Pat) Richardson, January 20, 2021.
42. Interview, Frank Sobchak with Lt. Col. Cecil Bailey, September 21, 2020.
43. Interview, Frank Sobchak with MSgt. Leamon (Lee) Ratterree, January 5, 2021.
44. D'Haeseleer, *The Salvadoran Crucible*, 72–73.
45. As quoted in Ramsey, *Advising Indigenous Forces*, 90. Pickering was U.S. ambassador to El Salvador from 1983 to 1985. Some of his frustration came from the disparity to State Department diplomatic tours, which ranged from two to four years in length.
46. Interview, Frank Sobchak with Col. Francisco (Frank) Pedrozo, September 8, 2020.
47. Interview, Frank Sobchak with Lt. Col. Ted Mataxis, January 15, 2021.
48. Interview, Frank Sobchak with Maj. Gen. Simeon Trombitas, September 15, 2020.
49. Ramsey, *Advising Indigenous Forces*, 89. DLPT ratings range from zero to five and measure listening and reading, with five equating to functional native

proficiency and zero equating to barely survival communication skills. A plus would be added after the numeric score for those who scored close to the next-higher level.

50. Interagency Language Roundtable, "Interagency Language Roundtable Language Skill Level Descriptions—Reading," GovILR.org, U.S. Government, n.d. https://www.govtilr.org/Skills/ILRscale4.htm.
51. Interview, Frank Sobchak with Lt. Col. Ted Mataxis, January 5, 2021; interview, Frank Sobchak with Maj. Gen. Simeon Trombitas, September 15, 2020; Ramsey, in *Advising Indigenous Forces*, also confirms this change.
52. Interagency Language Roundtable, "Interagency Language Roundtable Language Skill Level Descriptions—Reading."
53. Interview, Frank Sobchak with CW3 Dave Hulsey, January 4, 2021.
54. Interview, Frank Sobchak with Col. Wayne (Pat) Richardson, January 20, 2021.
55. Interview, Frank Sobchak with Brig. Gen. Hector Pagan, January 5, 2021.
56. Interview, Frank Sobchak with Col. Wayne (Pat) Richardson, January 20, 2021.
57. Interview, Frank Sobchak with Col. Wayne (Pat) Richardson, January 20, 2021.
58. Interview, Frank Sobchak with Brig. Gen. Hector Pagan, January 5, 2021.
59. Interview, Frank Sobchak with Col. Francisco (Frank) Pedrozo, September 8, 2020.
60. Interview, Frank Sobchak with Col. John Waghelstein, January 25, 2021.
61. Interview, Frank Sobchak with Col. Francisco (Frank) Pedrozo, September 8, 2020.
62. Interview, Frank Sobchak with Col. Hy Rothstein, October 12, 2020.
63. Interview, Frank Sobchak with Lt. Col. Ted Mataxis, January 15, 2021.
64. Interview, Frank Sobchak with MSgt. Leamon (Lee) Ratterree, January 5, 2021.
65. Interview, Frank Sobchak with Lt. Col. Mike Hennelly, January 14, 2021.
66. Interview, Frank Sobchak with Brig. Gen. Hector Pagan, January 5, 2021; interview, Frank Sobchak with Col. Francisco (Frank) Pedrozo, September 8, 2020.
67. Most evidence indicates the cutoff to be counted against the fifty-five-advisor limit was ten days of duty in country. Interview, Frank Sobchak with Col. Roy Trumble, September 18, 2020.
68. Downie, *Learning from Conflict*, 145. Downie indicates that individuals on temporary duty for under fourteen days in El Salvador were not counted.
69. Interview, Frank Sobchak with Lt. Col. Ted Mataxis, January 15, 2021.
70. Interview, Frank Sobchak with Col. John Waghelstein, January 25, 2021.

71. Interview, Frank Sobchak with MSgt. Leamon (Lee) Ratterree, January 5, 2021.
72. Email, Command Sgt. Maj. Chris Zets to Frank Sobchak, December 23, 2020.
73. Interview, Frank Sobchak with Lt. Col. Cecil Bailey, September 21, 2020, email, Command Sgt. Maj. Chris Zets to Frank Sobchak, December 26, 2020.
74. Ramsey, *Advising Indigenous Forces*, 84.
75. Interview, Frank Sobchak with Lt. Col. Cecil Bailey, September 21, 2020.
76. Briscoe, "El Paraiso and the War in El Salvador."
77. Interview, Frank Sobchak with Col. Wayne (Pat) Richardson, January 20, 2021. A company headquarters plus five ODAs would likely result in the Atonal being trained by approximately seventy advisors.
78. Interview, Frank Sobchak with CW3 Dave Hulsey, January 4, 2021.
79. Briscoe, "San Miguel: The Attack on *El Bosque*."
80. Interview, Frank Sobchak with MSgt. Leamon (Lee) Ratterree, January 5, 2021; interview, Frank Sobchak with Lt. Col. Mike Hennelly, January 14, 2021.
81. Briscoe, "San Miguel: The Attack on *El Bosque*"; interview, Frank Sobchak with Col. Kevin Higgins, September 30, 2020.
82. Interview, Frank Sobchak with MSgt. Leamon (Lee) Ratterree, January 5, 2021; World Bank, "El Salvador Literacy Rate 1992–2021," archived online at Macrotrends, Macrotrends.net, n.d., https://www.macrotrends.net/countries/SLV/el-salvador/literacy-rate, accessed October 6, 2021.
83. Email, Command Sgt. Maj. Chris Zets to Frank Sobchak, December 23, 2020.
84. Kenneth Finlayson, "OPATT to PATT: El Salvador to Colombia and the Formation of the Planning and Assistance Training Teams," *Veritas* 2, no. 4 (2006), https://arsof-history.org/articles/v2n4_patt_page_1.html. Many advisors recalled BIRI strength in the range of 900 to 1,100 men. One advisor noted that the Belloso battalion was 950 soldiers. Email, Command Sgt. Maj. Chris Zets to Frank Sobchak, December 27, 2020.
85. Briscoe, "San Miguel: The Attack on *El Bosque*." AWOL soldiers were known as iguanas because they usually crawled under the base fence line to leave and return.
86. Email, Lt. Col. Cecil Bailey to Frank Sobchak, "El Salvadoran Brigade Size," September 12, 2021.
87. Email, Kevin Higgins to Frank Sobchak, "BACOA, AGALAN, and El Salvador Photos," September 17, 2023.
88. The personnel strength of each BIRI does not grow or change over time, but the number of BIRIs increases over time as each unit is stood up and begins training.
89. Paterson, *Training Surrogate Forces*, 67–69.
90. Email, Lt. Col. Cecil Bailey to Frank Sobchak, September 13, 2021.

91. See appendix A for calculations.
92. Doctrinally one Special Forces ODA of twelve personnel should be allotted to train a single host-nation battalion, equating to a ratio of fifty or seventy-five to one.
93. Interview, Frank Sobchak with Brig. Gen. Hector Pagan, January 5, 2021.
94. Interview, Frank Sobchak with Col. John Waghelstein, January 25, 2021.
95. Interview, Frank Sobchak with Maj. Gen. Simeon Trombitas, September 15, 2020.
96. Interview, Frank Sobchak with Col. Wayne (Pat) Richardson, January 20, 2021.
97. Interview, Frank Sobchak with Col. Francisco (Frank) Pedrozo, September 8, 2020.
98. Interview, Frank Sobchak with Col. Wayne (Pat) Richardson, January 20, 2021.
99. Interview, Frank Sobchak with MSgt. Leamon (Lee) Ratterree, January 5, 2021.
100. Interview, Frank Sobchak with Lt. Col. Ted Mataxis, January 15, 2021.
101. Interview, Frank Sobchak with Brig. Gen. Hector Pagan, January 5, 2021.
102. Interview, Frank Sobchak with CW3 Dave Hulsey, January 4, 2021.
103. Interview, Frank Sobchak with Brig. Gen. Hector Pagan, January 5, 2021.
104. Briscoe, "El Paraiso and the War in El Salvador."
105. As quoted in Ramsey, *Advising Indigenous Forces*, 89.
106. Interview, Frank Sobchak with MSgt. Leamon (Lee) Ratterree, January 5, 2021.
107. Interview, Frank Sobchak with Col. John Waghelstein, January 25, 2021.
108. Steve Balestrieri, "The Special Forces Branch Is Created April 9, 1987," Special Operations Forces Report, SOFREP.com, April 9, 2018, https://sofrep.com/specialoperations/special-forces-branch-is-created-april-9-1987/.
109. Interview, Frank Sobchak with Lt. Col. Mike Hennelly, January 14, 2021.
110. Belisario Betancur, Reinaldo Figueredo Planchart, and Thomas Buergenthal, "From Madness to Hope: The 12-Year War in El Salvador; Report of the Commission on the Truth for El Salvador," United Nations Security Council, April 1, 1993, available online at https://archive.org/details/S25500EN.
111. Interview, Frank Sobchak with MSgt. Leamon (Lee) Ratterree, January 5, 2021.
112. Interview, Frank Sobchak with Col. Wayne (Pat) Richardson, January 20, 2021.
113. Interview, Frank Sobchak with Col. Jim (Ranger) Roach, September 22, 2020.
114. Interview, Frank Sobchak with MSgt. Leamon (Lee) Ratterree, January 5, 2021.
115. Interview, Frank Sobchak with Lt. Col. Ted Mataxis, January 15, 2021.
116. Interview, Frank Sobchak with Col. Jim (Ranger) Roach, September 22, 2020.
117. Interview, Frank Sobchak with MSgt. Leamon (Lee) Ratterree, January 5, 2021; interview, Frank Sobchak with Lt. Col. Kalev (Gunner) Sepp, August 11, 2020.

118. Interview, Frank Sobchak with Col. Wayne (Pat) Richardson, January 20, 2021.
119. "Interview: Special Forces in El Salvador," *Special Warfare*, 36.
120. Interview, Frank Sobchak with Col. Francisco (Frank) Pedrozo, September 8, 2020.
121. Interview, Frank Sobchak with Lt. Col. Ted Mataxis, January 15, 2021.
122. Interview, Frank Sobchak with Col. Wayne (Pat) Richardson, January 20, 2021.
123. Bradley Graham, "Public Honors for Secret Combat," *Washington Post*, May 6, 1996.
124. Interview, Frank Sobchak with Col. Wayne (Pat) Richardson, January 20, 2021.
125. Interview, Frank Sobchak with Lt. Col. Mike Hennelly, January 14, 2021.
126. James Lemoyne, "Rebels Kill 43 Salvador Troops and U.S. Adviser," *New York Times*, April 1, 1987, sec. A1, A10, https://www.nytimes.com/1987/04/01/world/rebels-kill-43-salvador-troops-and-us-adviser.html.
127. Steve Balestrieri, "March 13, 1981, US to Send 15 Green Beret Advisors to El Salvador," Special Operations Forces Report, SOFREP.com, March 13, 2021, https://sofrep.com/specialoperations/march-13-1981-us-agrees-send-15-green-beret-advisors-el-salvador/.
128. U.S. Army Special Forces Command, "El Salvador Awards Ceremony," event program, June 12, 1998, author's private collection.
129. Interview, Frank Sobchak with Lt. Col. Ted Mataxis, January 15, 2021.
130. Interview, Frank Sobchak with Col. Wayne (Pat) Richardson, January 20, 2021.
131. Interview, Frank Sobchak with Col. Francisco (Frank) Pedrozo, September 8, 2020.
132. Interview, Frank Sobchak with Lt. Col. Cecil Bailey, September 21, 2020; interview, Frank Sobchak with Col. Wayne (Pat) Richardson, January 20, 2021.
133. Interview, Frank Sobchak with Maj. Gen. Ed Reeder, December 17, 2020.
134. Interview, Frank Sobchak with Lt. Col. Kalev (Gunner) Sepp, August 11, 2020.
135. Interview, Frank Sobchak with Lt. Col. Ted Mataxis, January 15, 2021.
136. Interview, Frank Sobchak with Brig. Gen. Hector Pagan, January 5, 2021.
137. Interview, Frank Sobchak with MSgt. Leamon (Lee) Ratterree, January 5, 2021.
138. Interview, Frank Sobchak with Col. Wayne (Pat) Richardson, January 20, 2021.
139. Interview, Frank Sobchak with Col. Francisco (Frank) Pedrozo, September 8, 2020.
140. Interview, Frank Sobchak with Maj. Gen. Ed Reeder, December 17, 2020.
141. Interview, Frank Sobchak with Col. John Waghelstein, January 25, 2021. Two other advisors, Col. Francisco Pedrozo and Col. Wayne Richardson, both concurred that only some of the BIRIs had become capable by the end of the war.
142. This section's subtitle is taken from interview, Frank Sobchak with Lt. Col. Mike Hennelly, January 14, 2021.

143. Interview, Frank Sobchak with CW3 Dave Hulsey, January 4, 2021.
144. Interview, Frank Sobchak with MSgt. Leamon (Lee) Ratterree, January 5, 2021; interview, Frank Sobchak with Col. Francisco (Frank) Pedrozo, September 8, 2020.
145. Interview, Frank Sobchak with Lt. Col. Mike Hennelly, January 14, 2021.
146. Interview, Frank Sobchak with Col. Wayne (Pat) Richardson, January 20, 2021.
147. Interview, Frank Sobchak with MSgt. Leamon (Lee) Ratterree, January 5, 2021.
148. Interview, Frank Sobchak with Col. Francisco (Frank) Pedrozo, September 8, 2020.
149. Interview, Frank Sobchak with Lt. Col. Ted Mataxis, January 15, 2021.
150. Interview, Frank Sobchak with Col. Jim (Ranger) Roach, September 22, 2020.
151. Interview, Frank Sobchak with Maj. Gen. Ed Reeder, December 17, 2020.
152. Interview, Frank Sobchak with MSgt. Leamon (Lee) Ratterree, January 5, 2021.
153. Interview, Frank Sobchak with Col. Francisco (Frank) Pedrozo, September 8, 2020.
154. Interview, Frank Sobchak with Col. Jim (Ranger) Roach, September 22, 2020.
155. Interview, Frank Sobchak with CW3 Dave Hulsey, January 4, 2021.
156. Interview, Frank Sobchak with Col. Francisco (Frank) Pedrozo, September 8, 2020.
157. Interview, Frank Sobchak with MSgt. Leamon (Lee) Ratterree, January 5, 2021.
158. Interview, Frank Sobchak with Col. John Waghelstein, January 25, 2021.
159. Interview, Frank Sobchak with Col. Wayne (Pat) Richardson, January 20, 2021.
160. Interview, Frank Sobchak with Lt. Col. Ted Mataxis, January 15, 2021.
161. Humberto Corado Figueroa, *En Defensa de la Patria: Historia del Conflicto Armado en El Salvador, 1980–1992* (San Salvador, El Salvador: Universidad Tecnológica de El Salvador, 2008), 385–86. Corado Figueroa's work is undoubtedly biased, made clear especially in his disparaging perspective of FMLN behavior. However, he does record government human-rights abuses, such as of BIRI Atlácatl, and how poorly the Salvadoran Army performed initially.
162. Interview, Frank Sobchak with MSgt. Leamon (Lee) Ratterree, January 5, 2021.
163. Interview, Frank Sobchak with Col. Wayne (Pat) Richardson, January 20, 2021. In terms of political reprisal, regular Army officers were often afraid that if they pursued enemy forces into another unit's sector it might reflect negatively on that commander and if that commander outranked the leader of the pursuing force it could then impact their own promotion.
164. Interview, Frank Sobchak with Col. Francisco (Frank) Pedrozo, September 8, 2020.

165. Interview, Frank Sobchak with Col. John Waghelstein, January 25, 2021.
166. Which is the definition of fighting without advisors present, per the introductory chapter.
167. Email, MSgt. Leamon Ratterree to Frank Sobchak, January 5, 2021.
168. Joel D. Rayburn and Frank K. Sobchak, eds., *The U.S. Army in the Iraq War, Volume 1: Invasion, Insurgency, Civil War, 2003–2006* (Carlisle, PA: Strategic Studies Institute, U.S. Army War College, 2019), 300.

CHAPTER 2. MARKSMEN OF DEATH

1. Linda Robinson, Patrick Johnston, and Gillian Oak, *U.S. Special Operations Forces in the Philippines, 2001–2014* (Washington, DC: RAND Corporation, 2016), 12.
2. Interview, Frank Sobchak with Col. Joseph Felter, July 20, 2020.
3. Thomas G. Mahnken, ed., *Learning the Lessons of Modern War*, 1st ed. (Stanford, CA: Stanford University Press, 2020), 199.
4. David S. Maxwell, "Foreign Internal Defense: An Indirect Approach to Counter-insurgency/Counter Terrorism; Lessons from Operation Enduring Freedom–Philippines for Dealing with Non-existential Threats to the United States," presentation given at Irregular Warfare Challenges and Opportunities, conference of the Foreign Policy Research Institute, Washington, DC, December 6, 2011, https://www.phibetaiota.net/wp-content/uploads/2016/10/Maxwell-OEF-P-Final-.pdf, p. 6.
5. Joint U.S. Military Assistance Group, "Republic of the Philippines Security Assistance Program Update," PowerPoint briefing, June 9, 2004.
6. Robinson, Johnston, and Oak, *U.S. Special Operations Forces*, 18.
7. Robinson, Johnston, and Oak, xvi–xvii.
8. For simplicity I will generally refer to the unit as the Light Reaction Regiment (LRR) unless it is in reference to the unit at a specific time.
9. U.S. Government Accountability Office, "Special Operations Forces: Opportunities Exist to Improve Transparency of Funding and Assess Potential to Lessen Some Deployments," GAO 15-571, report to congressional committees, Washington, DC, July 2015, https://www.gao.gov/assets/680/671920.pdf, p. 67.
10. Interview, Frank Sobchak with Col. David Maxwell, July 9, 2020.
11. Shahzad Bashir, "How Many Languages Are Spoken in Philippines?" Mars Translation, May 22, 2018, https://www.marstranslation.com/blog/how-many-languages-are-spoken-in-philippines.
12. Interview, Frank Sobchak with Col. David Maxwell, July 9, 2020.
13. Interview, Frank Sobchak with Lt. Col. Bob Boone, July 13, 2020.

14. Angie Slattery, "Interview with LTC Eric Walker," Combat Studies Institute, Fort Leavenworth, KS, April 20, 2010, available for download at https://cgsc.contentdm.oclc.org/digital/api/collection/p4013coll13/id/1902/download.
15. Interview, Frank Sobchak with Col. David Maxwell, July 9, 2020.
16. Jack Murphy, "Special Forces to Disband the Commanders-in-Extremis Force," *Jack Murphy Writes*, March 5, 2020, https://jackmurphywrites.com/153/special-forces-commanders-in-extremis-force-no-more/. CIF originally stood for "CINC's in-Extremis Force," or "Commander in Chief's in-Extremis Force." In October 2002 then-secretary of defense Donald Rumsfeld changed the title of commander in chief for all unified combatant commands to simply "commander" arguing that the United States has only one commander in chief—the president. For simplicity's sake, I use "Commander's in-Extremis Force" throughout this work.
17. Interview, Frank Sobchak with Sfc. John Mory, July 21, 2020.
18. Interview, Frank Sobchak with Col. David Maxwell, July 9, 2020.
19. Interview, Frank Sobchak with Col. David Maxwell, July 9, 2020; interview, Frank Sobchak with Lt. Col. Scott Malone, July 23, 2020; and interview, Frank Sobchak with Lt. Gen. David Fridovich, July 16, 2020.
20. Interview, Frank Sobchak with Lt. Col. Leo Liebreich, July 21, 2020.
21. Interview, Frank Sobchak with Col. David Maxwell, July 9, 2020.
22. Mahnken, *Learning the Lessons of Modern War*, 199.
23. Interview, Frank Sobchak with Col. David Maxwell, July 9, 2020.
24. Interview, Frank Sobchak with Lt. Col. Leo Liebreich, July 21, 2020.
25. Interview, Frank Sobchak with Maj. Noel Sioson, June 26, 2020.
26. Interview, Frank Sobchak with Lt. Col. Leo Liebreich, July 21, 2020.
27. Interview, Frank Sobhcak with Lt. Col. Leo Liebreich, July 21, 2020.
28. Interview, Frank Sobchak with Maj. Noel Sioson, June 26, 2020.
29. Slattery, "Interview with LTC Eric Walker."
30. Email, Col. Dennis Downey to Frank Sobchak, July 11, 2020.
31. Francis U. Villanueva, *Tiradores: Missions and the Men of the Philippine's Light Reaction Regiment* (New York: CreateSpace Independent Publishing Platform, 2020), 39–41.
32. Joint U.S. Military Assistance Group, "Republic of the Philippines."
33. Jack Murphy, "SOFREP Exclusive: Inside the Operations of the Light Reaction Regiment (Part 3)," Special Operations Forces Report, SOFREP.com, June 16, 2017, https://sofrep.com/news/sofrep-exclusive-inside-operations-light-reaction-regiment-part-3/.
34. U.S. Special Operations Command, U.S. Department of Defense, "SOF Truths," [1987?], archived online at https://www.socom.mil/about/sof-truths.

35. Robinson, Johnston, and Oak, *U.S. Special Operations Forces*, 15; email, Col. Dennis Downey to Frank Sobchak, July 15, 2020, Deputy Cdr. 1st Special Forces Group and Operations Officer SOCPAC. Although I do not have access to the personnel data of the LRB/LRR, several interviewees, including Lt. Col. Bob Boone, Lt. Col. Scott Malone, and Lt. Col. Ken Gleiman, indicated a steady decrease in the unit's strength, averaging about nineteen operators per year. This approximation is also supported by Villanueva in *Tiradores*.
36. Villanueva, *Tiradores*, 13.
37. Villanueva, 217.
38. Villanueva, 44–45.
39. Interview, Frank Sobchak with Col. Max Carpenter, July 17, 2020.
40. Maxwell, "Foreign Internal Defense," 5–6.
41. David [S.] Maxwell, "Commander's Summary of Operations OEF-P," Col. David Maxwell, Cdr., 1st Battalion, 1st Special Forces Group, May 5, 2002.
42. Robinson, Johnston, and Oak, *U.S. Special Operations Forces*, 28.
43. Interview, Frank Sobchak with Col. Max Carpenter, July 17, 2020; Robinson, Johnston, and Oak, *U.S. Special Operations Forces*, 36–37.
44. Maxwell, "Commander's Summary of Operations OEFP."
45. Email, Col. Dennis Downey to Frank Sobchak, July 15, 2020; Robinson, Johnston, and Oak, *U.S. Special Operations Forces*, 36.
46. Dennis Downey, "JTF 510/JSOTF-P 2002–2003 Locations," PowerPoint presentation, Col. Dennis Downey, July 12, 2003.
47. Juliana Gittler, "Philippine Soldiers Show Off What They Learned from the Green Berets," *Stars and Stripes*, December 14, 2003, https://www.stripes.com/news/philippine-soldiers-show-off-what-they-learned-from-the-green-berets-1.14479.
48. Robinson, Johnston, and Oak, *U.S. Special Operations Forces*, 38.
49. Interview, Frank Sobchak with Maj. Shawn Boyer, July 10, 2020.
50. Robinson, Johnston, and Oak, *U.S. Special Operations Forces*, 48.
51. Richard Swain, *Case Study: Operation Enduring Freedom Philippines* (Fort Belvoir, VA: Defense Technical Information Center, October 1, 2010), 23.
52. Interview, Frank Sobchak with Col. David Maxwell, July 9, 2020.
53. Robinson, Johnston, and Oak, *U.S. Special Operations Forces*, 48.
54. Robinson, Johnston, and Oak, 80.
55. Interview, Frank Sobchak with Maj. Noel Sioson, June 26, 2020.
56. Interview, Frank Sobchak with Col. Max Carpenter, July 17, 2020.
57. Interview, Frank Sobchak with Col. Erik Brown, October 5, 2020; interview, Frank Sobchak with Maj. Noel Sioson, June 26, 2020.
58. Villanueva, *Tiradores*, 11–12.

59. Villanueva, 27.
60. Interview, Frank Sobchak with Command Sgt. Maj. Brian Johnson, September 16, 2020.
61. Mahnken, *Learning the Lessons of Modern War*, 199–200.
62. Villanueva, *Tiradores*, 24–25.
63. Interview, Frank Sobchak with MSgt. Joe Morley, July 22, 2020.
64. Interview, Frank Sobchak with MSgt. Joe Morley, July 22, 2020.
65. Interview, Frank Sobchak with Col. David Maxwell, July 9, 2020.
66. Robinson, Johnston, and Oak, *U.S. Special Operations Forces*, 28.
67. David S. Maxwell, "Operation Enduring Freedom–Philippines: What Would Sun Tzu Say?" *Military Review* 84, no. 3 (May–June 2004): 20, https://www.armyupress.army.mil/Portals/7/military-review/Archives/English/100-Landing/Topics-Interest/Deployments/docs/Operation%20Enduring%20Freedom-2004.pdf.
68. Mahnken, *Learning the Lessons of Modern War*, 200.
69. Email, Col. Dennis Downey to Frank Sobchak, July 11, 2020.
70. Email, Col. Dennis Downey to Frank Sobchak, July 15, 2020.
71. Joint Task Force Comet, Western Mindanao Command, Armed Forces of the Philippines, "Plan Ultimatum: An Overview," after-action review, headquarters, undated (November 2007?).
72. Robinson, Johnston, and Oak, *U.S. Special Operations Forces*, 52.
73. Maxwell, "Foreign Internal Defense," 6.
74. Villanueva, *Tiradores*, 462.
75. Robinson, Johnston, and Oak, *U.S. Special Operations Forces*, 84.
76. Email, Col. Denis Downey to Frank Sobchak, July 15, 2020.
77. Prashanth Parameswaran, "What's in the New Philippines Special Operations Command?" *The Diplomat*, April 13, 2018, https://thediplomat.com/2018/04/whats-in-the-new-philippines-special-operations-command/.
78. Email, Col. Dennis Downey to Frank Sobchak, July 11, 2020. Some mutineers called themselves "The Rebels" and even flew the flag of the Confederate States of America.
79. Villanueva, *Tiradores*, 36–38.
80. Email, Col. Dennis Downey to Frank Sobchak, July 11, 2020.
81. Interview, Frank Sobchak with Lt. Col. John Moria, July 24, 2020.
82. Interview, Frank Sobchak with Lt. Col. Ken Gleiman, August 13, 2020.
83. Interview, Frank Sobchak with Lt. Col. John Moria, July 24, 2020.
84. David Maxwell, "Joint Special Operations Task Force Philippines (JSOTF-P): A Special Warfare Approach to Counterinsurgency and Counterterrorism," PowerPoint briefing, September 24, 2008, emphasis original.

85. Combined Joint Task Forces led the war efforts in Iraq (CJTF-7) and Afghanistan (CJTF-180 and -76) for several years.
86. Maxwell, "Foreign Internal Defense," 10.
87. Interview, Frank Sobchak with Col. Dennis Downey, July 20, 2020.
88. Interview, Frank Sobchak with Col. David Maxwell, July 9, 2020.
89. Swain, *Case Study*, 16–17.
90. Robinson, Johnston, and Oak, *U.S. Special Operations Forces*, 22–25.
91. Robinson, Johnston, and Oak, 36–38.
92. Robinson, Johnston, and Oak, 53.
93. Robinson, Johnston, and Oak, xvi.
94. Interview, Frank Sobchak with Col. Bill Coultrup, July 14, 2020.
95. Mahnken, *Learning the Lessons of Modern War*, 207.
96. Swain, *Case Study*, 17–20.
97. Interview, Frank Sobchak with Lt. Gen. David Fridovich, July 16, 2020.
98. Robinson, Johnston, and Oak, *U.S. Special Operations Forces*, 27.
99. Robinson, Johnston, and Oak, 53.
100. Interview, Frank Sobchak with Command Sgt. Maj. Brian Johnson, September 16, 2020.
101. Interview, Frank Sobchak with Col. Erik Brown, October 5, 2020.
102. Interview, Frank Sobchak with Maj. Joe Harosky, September 24, 2020.
103. Robinson, Johnston, and Oak, *U.S. Special Operations Forces*, 41.
104. Villanueva, *Tiradores*, 27.
105. Slattery, "Interview with LTC Eric Walker."
106. Interview, Frank Sobchak with Col. Erik Brown, October 5, 2020.
107. Interview, Frank Sobchak with Lt. Col. Max Carpenter, July 17, 2020.
108. Interview, Frank Sobchak with Sgt. Maj. Stephen Durfee, July 14, 2020; interview, Frank Sobchak with Lt. Col. Leo Liebreich, July 21, 2020.
109. Interview, Frank Sobchak with Lt. Col. John Moria, July 24, 2020.
110. Robinson, Johnston, and Oak, *U.S. Special Operations Forces*, 27.
111. Interview, Frank Sobchak with Lt. Gen. David Fridovich, July 16, 2020.
112. Interview, Frank Sobchak with Col. Erik Brown, October 5, 2020.
113. Interview, Frank Sobchak with Maj. Shawn Boyer, July 10, 2020; interview, Frank Sobchak with Command Sgt. Maj. Brian Johnson, September 16, 2020.
114. James Lewis, "The Battle of Marawi: Small Team Lessons Learned for the Close Fight," *Small Wars Journal*, January 23, 2019, https://smallwarsjournal.com/blog/battle-marawi-small-team-lessons-learned-close-fight; interview, Frank Sobchak with Col. Bill Coultrup, July 14, 2020.
115. Interview, Frank Sobchak with Col. Bill Coultrup, July 14, 2020.
116. Email, Col. Dennis Downey to Frank Sobchak, July 15, 2020.

117. Robert D. Kaplan, *Imperial Grunts: On the Ground with the American Military from Mogadishu to the Philippines to Iraq and Beyond* (New York: Random House, 2005), 155–56.
118. Maxwell, "Commander's Summary of Operations OEF-P."
119. Kaplan, *Imperial Grunts*, 157.
120. Interview, Frank Sobchak with Lt. Col. Leo Liebreich, July 21, 2020.
121. Interview, Frank Sobchak with Col. Dennis Downey, July 20, 2020.
122. Interview, Frank Sobchak with Lt. Col. Jim Keating, July 15, 2020.
123. Interview, Frank Sobchak with Col. Erik Brown, October 5, 2020.
124. Interview, Frank Sobchak with Lt. Col. John Moria, July 24, 2020; interview, Frank Sobchak with Maj. Noel Sioson, July 3, 2020.
125. Robinson, Johnston, and Oak, *U.S. Special Operations Forces*, 30–31.
126. Mahnken, *Learning the Lessons of Modern War*, 210.
127. Interview, Frank Sobchak with Lt. Gen. David Fridovich, July 16, 2020; interview, Frank Sobchak with Maj. Noel Sioson, July 3, 2020.
128. Interview, Frank Sobchak with Col. Bill Coultrup, July 14, 2020.
129. Email, Col. Dennis Downey to Frank Sobchak, July 11, 2020.
130. Interview, Frank Sobchak with Lt. Col. Scott Malone, July 23, 2020.
131. Interview, Frank Sobchak with Col. David Maxwell, July 9, 2020.
132. Interview, Frank Sobchak with Col. Bill Coultrup, July 14, 2020.
133. Interview, Frank Sobchak with Col. David Maxwell, July 9, 2020.
134. Interview, Frank Sobchak with Lt. Col. Leo Liebreich, July 21, 2020; interview, Lt. Col. Scott Malone, July 23, 2020; interview, Frank Sobchak with CDR James Marvin, July 23, 2020.
135. Villanueva, *Tiradores*, 213–40, 349–65.
136. Maxwell, "Foreign Internal Defense," 17.
137. Murphy, "SOFREP Exclusive: Inside the Operations."
138. Alan Taylor, "Bloody Philippine Siege Brought to an End," *The Atlantic*, September 30, 2013, https://www.theatlantic.com/photo/2013/09/bloody-philippine-siege-brought-to-an-end/100599/.
139. Robinson, Johnston, and Oak, *U.S. Special Operations Forces*, 100.
140. Robinson, Johnston, and Oak, 99. The JSOTF used force-protection clauses to allow the sharing of intelligence.
141. Villanueva, *Tiradores*, 230.
142. Villanueva, 281.
143. Villanueva, 223.
144. Villanueva, 285.
145. Agence France-Presse, "Marawi: City Destroyed in Philippines' Longest Urban War," *Inquirer News*, October 19, 2017, https://newsinfo.inquirer.net/939202/marawi-war-maute-terrorism-duterte-isnilon-hapilon-is-islamic-state.

146. Villanueva, *Tiradores*, 300–309, 415.
147. Kyodo News, "Lessons Learned from Marawi Siege, Government Officials Say," ABS-CBN News, May 24, 2018, https://news.abs-cbn.com/news/05/24/18/lessons-learned-from-marawi-siege-govt-officials-say.
148. Indo-Pacific Defense Forum staff, "Lessons from Marawi: Retired Lt. Gen. Danilo G. Pamonag Shares What He Learned from the Philippines' Largest Military Engagement since World War II," *Indo-Pacific Defense Forum* (blog), March 23, 2020, https://ipdefenseforum.com/2020/03/lessons-from-marawi/.
149. Villanueva, *Tiradores*, 451.
150. Lewis, "The Battle of Marawi," *Small Wars Journal*.
151. Villanueva, *Tiradores*, 430–32.
152. Lewis, "The Battle of Marawi," *Small Wars Journal*.
153. Interview, Frank Sobchak with Maj. Noel Sioson, July 3, 2020.
154. Jack Murphy, "SOFREP Exclusive: Marawi Commander Details What Really Happened in His Country's Largest Terrorist Attack and How His Men Fought Back," Special Operations Forces Report, SOFREP.com, December 14, 2017, https://sofrep.com/news/sofrep-exclusive-marawi-commander-details-what-really-happened-in-his-countrys-largest-terrorist-attack-and-how-his-men-fought-back/.
155. Stavros Atlamazoglou, "Best Non-US Special Operations Forces from around the World," *Business Insider*, updated November 24, 2022, https://www.businessinsider.com/best-non-us-special-operations-forces-from-around-the-world-2020-8.

CHAPTER 3. "THE DREAM ALLIES"

1. Kieran Duffy, "The Korean Connection, Colombia in the Korean War," *Bogotá Post*, February 17, 2016.
2. Jon Guttman, "Columbia [sic] in the Korean War," *HistoryNet*, May 28, 2013, https://www.historynet.com/seeking-information-on-columbia-in-the-korean-war.htm.
3. Duffy, "The Korean Connection."
4. Charles H. Briscoe, "Barbula and Old Baldy, March 1953: Colombia's Heaviest Combat in Korea," *Veritas* 2, no. 4 (Winter 2006), https://arsof-history.org/articles/v2n4_barbula_old_bardy_page_1.html.
5. Interview, Frank Sobchak with Tom Marks, January 20, 2021.
6. Charles H. Briscoe, "Colombian Lancero School Roots," *Veritas* 2, no. 4 (Winter 2006), https://arsof-history.org/articles/v2n4_lancero_page_1.html.
7. Jane Crichton, "U.S. Army Military Personnel Exchange Program in Colombia Strengthens Armies," Army.mil, May 25, 2011, https://www.army.mil/article/58119/u_s_army_military_personnel_exchange_program_in_colombia_strengthens_armies.

8. Nicholas Naquin, "Learning the Lancero Way: U.S. Helped Develop Elite Colombian Training," AUSA, March 2, 2020, https://www.ausa.org/articles/learning-lancero-way-us-helped-develop-elite-colombian-training.
9. Ambassador Kevin Whitaker in Daphne McCurdy and Nick Lopez, "Institution Building as a Counterinsurgency Tool: The Case of Colombia," *Irregular Warfare Podcast*, Modern War Institute, January 29, 2021. https://mwi.westpoint.edu/institution-building-as-a-counterinsurgency-tool-the-case-of-colombia/.
10. Ambassador Kevin Whitaker as quoted in McCurdy and Lopez, "Institution Building as a Counterinsurgency Tool."
11. Interview, Frank Sobchak with Lt. Col. Augustin Dominguez, February 11, 2021.
12. Robert D. Ramsey, *From El Billar to Operations Fenix and Jaque: The Colombian Security Force Experience, 1998–2008* (Fort Leavenworth, KS: Combat Studies Institute Press, 2009), 29.
13. Patrick Paterson, *Training Surrogate Forces in International Humanitarian Law: Lessons from Peru, Colombia, El Salvador, and Iraq* (Tampa, FL: Joint Special Operations University, 2016), 54.
14. Dana Priest, "Covert Action in Colombia," *Washington Post*, December 21, 2013.
15. Ramsey, *From El Billar to Operations Fenix and Jaque*, 30.
16. Interview, Frank Sobchak with Tom Marks, January 20, 2021.
17. Mark Moyar, Hector Pagan, and Wil R. Griego, *Persistent Engagement in Colombia* (Tampa, FL: Joint Special Operations University, 2019), 16. Plan Colombia would reach a total of $4.5 billion in assistance by the end of FY 2005.
18. Interview, Frank Sobchak with Tom Marks, January 20, 2021.
19. Moyar, Pagan, and Griego, *Persistent Engagement in Colombia*, 20.
20. Ramsey, *From El Billar to Operations Fenix and Jaque*, 23, 80.
21. Interview, Frank Sobchak with Tom Marks, January 20, 2021.
22. Interview, Frank Sobchak with Col. Carlos Berrios, January 12, 2021.
23. Carlos G. Berrios, "Critical Ingredient: US Aid to Counterinsurgency in Colombia," *Small Wars and Insurgencies* 28, no. 3 (May 4, 2017): 546–75, https://doi.org/10.1080/09592318.2017.1307610.
24. Interview, Frank Sobchak with Dr. David Spencer, January 22, 2021.
25. Paterson, *Training Surrogate Forces*, 54.
26. Moyar, Pagan, and Griego, *Persistent Engagement in Colombia*, 30.
27. Interview, Frank Sobchak with Col. Mike Brown, February 11, 2021.
28. Email, General Carlos Ospina Ovalle to Frank Sobchak, February 16, 2021.
29. Interview, Frank Sobchak with Dr. David Spencer, January 22, 2021.

30. Email, General Carlos Ospina Ovalle to Frank Sobchak, February 16, 2021. In an interesting parallel, after the units helped tamp down insurgents during the period of La Violencia, they were disbanded by conventional officers who believed they had limited utility—matching the dissolution of U.S. Army Ranger companies in the 1950s and 1960s.
31. Moyar, Pagan, and Griego, *Persistent Engagement in Colombia*, 30.
32. Interview, Frank Sobchak with Dr. David Spencer, January 22, 2021.
33. Charles H. Briscoe, "Operation Willing Spirit (OWS): Setting Conditions for Operación Jaque," *Veritas* 14, no. 3 (Fall 2018), https://arsof-history.org/articles/v14n3_op_willing_spirit_page_1.html.
34. Linda Robinson et al., *Improving the Understanding of Special Operations: A Case History Analysis* (Santa Monica, CA: RAND Corporation, 2018).
35. David Spencer, "The Sword of Honor Campaign in the Cauca Valley: 2011–2013 Colombian Conflict Focus of Effort," *Small Wars Journal*, May 31, 2013, p. 17, https://smallwarsjournal.com/jrnl/art/the-sword-of-honor-campaign-in-the-cauca-valley-2011-2013-colombian-conflict-focus-of-effor
36. Berrios, "Critical Ingredient."
37. Priest, "Covert Action in Colombia."
38. Priest.
39. Ambassador Kevin Whitaker as quoted in McCurdy and Lopez, "Institution Building as a Counterinsurgency Tool."
40. As quoted in Moyar, Pagan, and Griego, *Persistent Engagement in Colombia*, 36.
41. These were Col. Kevin Higgins, Command Sgt. Maj. Chris Zets, CW3 Dave Hulsey, Lt. Gen. Charles Cleveland, Maj. Gen. Ed Reeder, and Maj. Gen. Simeon Trombitas.
42. Kenneth Finlayson, "OPATT to PATT: El Salvador to Colombia and the Formation of the Planning and Assistance Training Teams," *Veritas* 2, no. 4 (2006), https://arsof-history.org/articles/v2n4_patt_page_1.html.
43. Interview, Frank Sobchak with Col. Kevin Higgins, October 6, 2020.
44. Interview, Frank Sobchak with Lt. Gen. Charles Cleveland, October 19, 2020.
45. Interview, Frank Sobchak with Col. Mike Brown, February 11, 2021.
46. Interview, Frank Sobchak with Command Sgt. Maj. Amil Alvarez, February 10, 2021.
47. Interview, Frank Sobchak with Lt. Col. Joe Reagan, February 8, 2021.
48. Interview, Frank Sobchak with Col. Carlos Berrios, January 12, 2021.
49. Interview, Frank Sobchak with Col. Carlos Berrios, January 12, 2021.
50. Interview, Frank Sobchak with Lt. Col. Douglas Judice, February 1, 2021.

51. Interview, Frank Sobchak with Command Sgt. Maj. Amil Alvarez, February 10, 2021. While 7th Group focused on Afghanistan, their Commander's in-Extremis Force, C/3/7, regularly deployed to Iraq to advise the Iraqi Counter Terrorism Force.
52. Interview, Frank Sobchak with Command Sgt. Maj. Amil Alvarez, February 10, 2021.
53. Interview, Frank Sobchak with Col. Barbara Fick, January 28, 2021.
54. Deployments to Afghanistan, by comparison, were nine months. Colombian missions were purposely shortened to increase the number and length of the missions to Afghanistan.
55. As discussed in Moyar, Pagan, and Griego, *Persistent Engagement in Colombia*, 46.
56. Interview, Frank Sobchak with Lt. Col. Kevin Key, February 8, 2020.
57. Interview, Frank Sobchak with Command Sgt. Maj. Amil Alvarez, February 10, 2021.
58. Interview, Frank Sobchak with Lt. Col. Joe Reagan, February 8, 2021.
59. Interview, Frank Sobchak with Col. Mike Brown, February 11, 2021.
60. Interview, Frank Sobchak with Command Sgt. Maj. Amil Alvarez, February 10, 2021.
61. Interview, Frank Sobchak with CW3 Dave Hulsey, January 4, 2021.
62. Interview, Frank Sobchak with Lt. Col. Kevin Key, February 8, 2020.
63. Austin Long et al., *Building Special Operations Partnerships in Afghanistan and Beyond: Challenges and Best Practices from Afghanistan, Iraq, and Colombia* (Santa Monica, CA: RAND Corporation, 2015), 71.
64. Interview, Frank Sobchak with Col. Mike Brown, February 11, 2021.
65. Interview, Frank Sobchak with Command Sgt. Maj. Amil Alvarez, February 10, 2021.
66. Email, General Carlos Ospina Ovalle to Frank Sobchak, February 16, 2021.
67. Interview, Frank Sobchak with Lt. Col. Joe Reagan, February 8, 2021.
68. Interview, Frank Sobchak with Col. Greg Wilson, September 1, 2020.
69. Interview, Frank Sobchak with Lt. Col. Kevin Key, February 8, 2020.
70. Interview, Frank Sobchak with CW3 Dave Hulsey, January 4, 2021.
71. The U.S. Army National Guard's 19th and 20th Special Forces Groups contributed individual augmentees and a few detachments (ODAs) and even a company occasionally, but they were not a major force contributor. Those who did deploy were regionally oriented to Latin America.
72. Interview, Frank Sobchak with Maj. Gen. Ed Reeder, July 17, 2020.
73. Interview, Frank Sobchak with Lt. Col. Kevin Key, February 8, 2020.
74. Long et al., *Building Special Operations Partnerships*, 68.

75. Interview, Frank Sobchak with Lt. Col. Kevin Key, February 8, 2020.
76. Interview, Frank Sobchak with Lt. Col. Scott Morley, February 11, 2021.
77. Interview, Frank Sobchak with Command Sgt. Maj. Amil Alvarez, February 10, 2021.
78. Email, General Ospina Ovalle to Frank Sobchak, February 16, 2021.
79. Interview, Frank Sobchak with Lt. Col. Joe Reagan, February 8, 2021.
80. Interview, Frank Sobchak with Lt. Col. Scott Morley, February 11, 2021.
81. Interview, Frank Sobchak with Lt. Col. Kevin Key, February 8, 2020.
82. Interview, Frank Sobchak with Command Sgt. Maj. Amil Alvarez, February 10, 2021. Each Group had a total of four to five battalion commanders and command sergeant majors—some of the most important leaders in the organization.
83. Interview, Frank Sobchak with Col. Barbara Fick, January 28, 2021.
84. Interview, Frank Sobchak with Col. Carlos Berrios, January 12, 2021.
85. Moyar, Pagan, and Griego, *Persistent Engagement in Colombia*, 46.
86. U.S. Army Special Forces Command, "USASFC(A) Policy 350-1-14: Command Language Program," July 9, 2014.
87. Interview, Frank Sobchak with Command Sgt. Maj. Amil Alvarez, February 10, 2021.
88. Interview, Frank Sobchak with Lt. Col. Joe Reagan, February 8, 2021.
89. Interview, Frank Sobchak with Dr. David Spencer, January 22, 2021.
90. Interview, Frank Sobchak with Col. Barbara Fick, January 28, 2021.
91. Interview, Frank Sobchak with Lt. Col. Douglas Judice, February 1, 2021.
92. Interview, Frank Sobchak with Col. Mike Brown, February 11, 2021.
93. Interview, Frank Sobchak with Lt. Col. Augustin Dominguez, February 11, 2021.
94. Interview, Frank Sobchak with Col. Carlos Berrios, January 12, 2021.
95. Kenneth Finlayson, "Colombian Special Operations Forces," *Veritas* 2, no. 4 (Fall 2006), https://arsof-history.org/articles/v2n4_colombian_sof_page_1.html.
96. Pedro Vallejo, "Organización CCOES," PowerPoint presentation, Comando Conjunto de Operaciones Especiales (CCOES), February 15, 2021; interview, Frank Sobchak with Col. Mike Brown, February 11, 2021; interview, Frank Sobchak with Col. Carlos Berrios, January 12, 2021.
97. Finlayson, "Colombian Special Operations Forces."
98. Brian S. Petit, *Going Big by Getting Small: The Application of Operational Art by Special Operations in Phase Zero* (Denver: Outskirts Press, 2013), 130.
99. Interview, Frank Sobchak with Dr. David Spencer, January 22, 2021.
100. Moyar, Pagan, and Griego, *Persistent Engagement in Colombia*, 31.

101. Interview, Frank Sobchak with Maj. Gen. Ed Reeder, July 17, 2020; interview, Frank Sobchak with Lt. Col. Douglas Judice, February 1, 2021; interview, Frank Sobchak with CW3 Dave Hulsey, January 4, 2021. While only an AOB (company) remained of advisors, the battalion headquarters and staff (forward operating base or FOB) continued to be a part of the commitment to Colombia. The FOB served as the command element for the AOB that trained and advised Colombian forces as well as another AOB deployed to Latin America, but their primary focus was on the Operation Willing Spirit mission, which aimed to rescue the American hostages held by the FARC. That construct lasted until 2008, when the unilateral Colombian rescue of the hostages made such a large command-and-control element unnecessary. Interview, Frank Sobchak with Col. Carlos Berrios, January 12, 2021.
102. Interview, Frank Sobchak with Lt. Col. Joe Reagan, February 8, 2021.
103. Interview, Frank Sobchak with Lt. Gen. Charles Cleveland, October 19, 2020.
104. Moyar, Pagan, and Griego, *Persistent Engagement in Colombia*, 34; interview, Frank Sobchak with CW3 Dave Hulsey, January 4, 2021.
105. Interview, Frank Sobchak with Lt. Col. Joe Reagan, February 8, 2021; interview, Frank Sobchak with Lt. Col. Douglas Judice, February 1, 2021.
106. Interview, Frank Sobchak with Lt. Col. Kevin Key, February 8, 2020.
107. Finlayson, "Colombian Special Operations Forces."
108. Moyar, Pagan, and Griego, *Persistent Engagement in Colombia*, 45.
109. Interview, Frank Sobchak with Lt. Col. Douglas Judice, February 1, 2021.
110. Interview, Frank Sobchak with Dr. David Spencer, January 22, 2021.
111. Finlayson, "OPATT to PATT."
112. Interview, Frank Sobchak with Lt. Col. Douglas Judice, February 1, 2021.
113. Doctrinally one Special Forces ODA of twelve personnel should train a host-nation battalion, equating to a ratio between fifty and seventy-five to one. The partner-force-to-advisor ratio in Colombia was three to four times that ratio.
114. Interview, Frank Sobchak with Col. Mike Brown, February 11, 2021.
115. Interview, Frank Sobchak with Lt. Col. Kevin Key, February 8, 2020.
116. Interview, Frank Sobchak with Lt. Col. Douglas Judice, February 1, 2021.
117. Interview, Frank Sobchak with Lt. Col. Scott Morley, February 11, 2021.
118. Interview, Frank Sobchak with Lt. Col. Joe Reagan, February 8, 2021.
119. Interview, Frank Sobchak with Lt. Col. Douglas Judice, February 1, 2021.
120. Interview, Frank Sobchak with Tom Marks, January 20, 2021.
121. Interview, Frank Sobchak with CW3 Dave Hulsey, January 4, 2021.
122. Interview, Frank Sobchak with Lt. Col. Augustin Dominguez, February 11, 2021.
123. Berrios, "Critical Ingredient," 568–69. COESE and CCOPE, as they were known, were created in 2003 and 2005, respectively.

124. Interview, Frank Sobchak with Command Sgt. Maj. Amil Alvarez, February 10, 2021.
125. Interview, Frank Sobchak with Lt. Col. Kevin Key, February 8, 2020.
126. Interview, Frank Sobchak with Lt. Col. Douglas Judice, February 1, 2021.
127. Interview, Frank Sobchak with Col. Mike Brown, February 11, 2021.
128. This was because often they preferred to retain control of assets for operational reasons and to avoid fratricide.
129. Interview, Frank Sobchak with Command Sgt. Maj. Amil Alvarez, February 10, 2021. This phenomenon was similar to the justification that helped the United States stand up its national-level counterterrorism forces, which were not limited by the constraints of different geographic combatant commands.
130. Interview, Frank Sobchak with Lt. Col. Augustin Dominguez, February 11, 2021; quotation from interview, Frank Sobchak with Col. Mike Brown, February 11, 2021.
131. Interview, Frank Sobchak with Lt. Col. Douglas Judice, February 1, 2021.
132. Interview, Frank Sobchak with Col. Barbara Fick, January 28, 2021.
133. Interview, Frank Sobchak with Sgt. Maj. David Topejr, December 23, 2020.
134. Interview, Frank Sobchak with Command Sgt. Maj. Amil Alvarez, February 10, 2021.
135. Email, General Carlos Ospina Ovalle to Frank Sobchak, February 16, 2021.
136. Interview, Frank Sobchak with Col. Carlos Berrios, January 12, 2021; interview, Frank Sobchak with Dr. David Spencer, January 22, 2021; interview, Frank Sobchak with Tom Marks, January 20, 2021.
137. Email, Tom Marks to Frank Sobchak, January 7, 2021.
138. Interview, Frank Sobchak with Lt. Col. Douglas Judice, February 1, 2021.
139. Interview, Frank Sobchak with Dr. David Spencer, January 22, 2021.
140. Interview, Frank Sobchak with Col. Mike Brown, February 11, 2021.
141. Email, Tom Marks to Frank Sobchak, January 23, 2021.
142. Interview, Frank Sobchak with Col. Carlos Berrios, January 12, 2021.
143. Interview, Frank Sobchak with Tom Marks, January 20, 2021.
144. Interview, Frank Sobchak with Lt. Col. Scott Morley, February 11, 2021; interview, Frank Sobchak with Command Sgt. Maj. Amil Alvarez, February 10, 2021. Adm. Eric Olson, USSOCOM commander from 2007 to 2011, frequently called Major Force Program 11, the SOCOM acquisition authority, the "crown jewel" of the organization's strength.
145. Email, General Carlos Ospina Ovalle to Frank Sobchak, February 16, 2021.
146. Interview, Frank Sobchak with Lt. Col. Augustin Dominguez, February 11, 2021.
147. Interview, Frank Sobchak with Col. Barbara Fick, January 28, 2021.
148. Moyar, Pagan, and Griego, *Persistent Engagement in Colombia*, 33.

149. Briscoe, "Operation Willing Spirit."
150. Interview, Frank Sobchak with Col. Mike Brown, February 11, 2021.
151. Interview, Frank Sobchak with Command Sgt. Maj. Chris Zets, December 21, 2020.
152. Interview, Frank Sobchak with Col. Carlos Berrios, January 12, 2021.
153. U.S. Army Special Operations Command, "ARSOF and Operation Willing Sprit 2003–08, An Operational Analysis," white paper, May 2018. Note that ARSOF stands for U.S. Army Special Operations Forces.
154. Briscoe, "Operation Willing Spirit."
155. Interview, Frank Sobchak with Lt. Gen. Charles Cleveland, October 19, 2020; interview, Frank Sobchak with Col. Carlos Berrios, January 12, 2021.
156. Charles Cleveland and Daniel Egel, *The American Way of Irregular War: An Analytical Memoir* (Washington, DC: RAND Corporation, 2020), 136, https://doi.org/10.7249/PEA301-1.
157. Interview, Frank Sobchak with CW3 Dave Hulsey, January 4, 2021.
158. Interview, Frank Sobchak with Lt. Col. Douglas Judice, February 1, 2021.
159. Interview, Frank Sobchak with Lt. Col. Scott Morley, February 11, 2021.
160. Interview, Frank Sobchak with Lt. Col. Kevin Key, February 8, 2020; interview, Frank Sobchak with Lt. Col. Douglas Judice, February 1, 2021; interview, Frank Sobchak with Col. Mike Brown, February 11, 2021.
161. Moyar, Pagan, and Griego, *Persistent Engagement in Colombia*, 33.
162. Interview, Frank Sobchak with Command Sgt. Maj. Amil Alvarez, February 10, 2021; interview, Frank Sobchak with Lt. Col. Douglas Judice, February 1, 2021.
163. As quoted in Moyar, Pagan, and Griego, *Persistent Engagement in Colombia*, 33.
164. Interview, Frank Sobchak with Maj. Gen. Ed Reeder, July 17, 2020.
165. As quoted in Moyar, Pagan, and Griego, *Persistent Engagement in Colombia*, 33.
166. Interview, Frank Sobchak with Command Sgt. Maj. Chris Zets, December 21, 2020.
167. Interview, Frank Sobchak with Command Sgt. Maj. Amil Alvarez, February 10, 2021.
168. Interview, Frank Sobchak with Lt. Col. Joe Reagan, February 8, 2021.
169. As quoted in Donald Stoker, ed., *Military Advising and Assistance*, 1st ed. (London: Routledge, 2008), 178.
170. Interview, Frank Sobchak with Command Sgt. Maj. Chris Zets, December 21, 2020.
171. Interview, Frank Sobchak with Col. Kevin (Duke) Christie, October 19, 2020.
172. Interview, Frank Sobchak with Lt. Col. Joe Reagan, February 8, 2021.

173. Interview, Frank Sobchak with CW3 Dave Hulsey, January 4, 2021; interview, Frank Sobchak with Col. Mike Brown, February 11, 2021; interview, Frank Sobchak with Lt. Col. Douglas Judice, February 1, 2021; interview, Frank Sobchak with Col. Carlos Berrios, January 12, 2021.
174. Interview, Frank Sobchak with Lt. Col. Kevin Key, February 8, 2020.
175. Also known as high-altitude, low-opening—or HALO—operations.
176. As recounted in email, Lt. Col. Augustin Dominguez to Frank Sobchak, February 4, 2021.
177. Interview, Frank Sobchak with Lt. Col. Scott Morley, February 11, 2021.
178. Interview, Frank Sobchak with Dr. David Spencer, January 22, 2021.
179. Interview, Frank Sobchak with Command Sgt. Maj. Amil Alvarez, February 10, 2021.
180. Interview, Frank Sobchak with Col. Mike Brown, February 11, 2021.
181. Interview, Frank Sobchak with CW3 Dave Hulsey, January 4, 2021.
182. Interview, Frank Sobchak with Lt. Col. Joe Reagan, February 8, 2021.
183. Interview, Frank Sobchak with Dr. David Spencer, January 22, 2021.
184. Interview, Frank Sobchak with Command Sgt. Maj. Amil Alvarez, February 10, 2021.
185. Interview, Frank Sobchak with Col. Mike Brown, February 11, 2021.
186. Interview, Frank Sobchak with Lt. Col. Kevin Key, February 8, 2020.
187. Cleveland and Egel, *American Way of Irregular War*, 136.
188. Interview, Frank Sobchak with Col. Mike Brown, February 11, 2021.
189. Interview, Frank Sobchak with Maj. Gen. Ed Reeder, July 17, 2020.
190. Interview, Frank Sobchak with Command Sgt. Maj. Chris Zets, December 21, 2020; interview, Frank Sobchak with Dr. David Spencer, January 22, 2021.
191. Interview, Frank Sobchak with Lt. Col. Kevin Key, February 8, 2020.
192. Interview, Frank Sobchak with Lt. Col. Douglas Judice, February 1, 2021.
193. Interview, Frank Sobchak with Command Sgt. Maj. Chris Zets, December 21, 2020.
194. Cleveland and Egel, *American Way of Irregular War*, 135.
195. Interview, Frank Sobchak with Col. Mike Brown, February 11, 2021.
196. Interview, Frank Sobchak with Dr. David Spencer, January 22, 2021.
197. Interview, Frank Sobchak with Command Sgt. Maj. Amil Alvarez, February 10, 2021.
198. Interview, Frank Sobchak with Lt. Col. Joe Reagan, February 8, 2021.
199. Interview, Frank Sobchak with Dr. David Spencer, January 22, 2021.
200. The assessment in this section does not include Operation Jaque (or "check," from "chess," in English), the highly successful deception mission in 2008 that saw fifteen hostages rescued, including former Colombian presidential

candidate Íngrid Betancourt and the three American contractors held since 2003. While Colombian SOF elements unwittingly played a support role to the mission through actions that discouraged FARC leaders from moving the hostages, current evidence indicates they were not part of the operation itself. Charles H. Briscoe and Daniel J. Kulich, "Operación Jaque: The Ultimate Deception," *Veritas* 14, no. 3 (2018), https://arsof-history.org/articles/v14n3_op_jaque_page_1.html.

201. Interview, Frank Sobchak with Lt. Col. Augustin Dominguez, February 11, 2021.
202. Interview, Frank Sobchak with Lt. Col. Scott Morley, February 11, 2021.
203. Interview, Frank Sobchak with Lt. Col. Augustin Dominguez, February 11, 2021. Operation Red Wings was a 2005 U.S. Navy SEAL reconnaissance mission in Afghanistan that aimed to find an insurgent leader and then kill or capture him. The team was quickly compromised by insurgent forces, and the helicopter bringing the quick-reaction force in to rescue them was shot down, killing all on board. Unable to escape, three of four members of the initial reconnaissance team were also killed.
204. As quoted in Gabriel Ángel, "El Yarí, la Selva de la Guerra contra las Disidencias de las FARC," Poder, *Las 2 Orillas*, February 11, 2019, https://www.las2orillas.co/el-yari-la-selva-de-la-guerra-contra-las-disidencias-de-las-farc/. A bloc is a FARC major regional subunit made up of one thousand to ten thousand guerrillas. The FARC subdivided the country into seven blocs, which were only subordinate to the Central High Command (Estado Mayor Central).
205. Gabriel Ángel reports the FARC side of the encounter, while the government side is recounted in email, General Carlos Ospina Ovalle to Frank Sobchak, February 16, 2021.
206. La Nueva Televisión del Sur C.A., "When Colombia Bombed Ecuador: The Killing of Raul Reyes," February 28, 2016, https://www.telesurenglish.net/news/When-Colombia-Bombed-Ecuador-The-Killing-of-Raul-Reyes-20160228-0009.html.
207. Priest, "Covert Action in Colombia."
208. Spencer, "The Sword of Honor Campaign."
209. Priest, "Covert Action in Colombia."
210. Interview, Frank Sobchak with Lt. Col. Scott Morley, February 11, 2021.
211. Jay Bouchard, "How 5 Kayakers Were Taken Hostage in Colombia by FARC Rebels," *Outside Online*, May 11, 2017, https://www.outsideonline.com/gallery/how-5-kayakers-were-taken-hostage-colombia-farc-rebels/.
212. Interview, Frank Sobchak with Lt. Col. Scott Morley, February 11, 2021.

213. Lt. Col. Will Griego, US SOF Advisor to Colombian SOF, as quoted in Berrios, "Critical Ingredient," 570.
214. Interview, Frank Sobchak with Lt. Col. Augustin Dominguez, February 11, 2021.
215. Steve Balestrieri, "Colombian SF Operators Win Fuerzas Commando 2019 Special Ops Competition," Special Operations Forces Report, SOFREP.com, June 30, 2019, https://sofrep.com/news/colombian-special-forces-operators-win-fuerzas-commando-2019-special-ops-competition/.
216. Interview, Frank Sobchak with Lt. Col. Joe Reagan, February 8, 2021.
217. CBS News, "Colombia to Aid US in Taliban Fight," CBSNews.com, July 27, 2009. Also see interview, Frank Sobchak with Dr. David Spencer, January 22, 2021.
218. Interview, Frank Sobchak with Lt. Col. Scott Morley, February 11, 2021.
219. Interview, Frank Sobchak with CW3 Dave Hulsey, January 4, 2021.
220. Interview, Frank Sobchak with Col. Carlos Berrios, January 12, 2021.

CHAPTER 4. "WE HAVE KILLED MANY MEN TOGETHER"

1. ISOF generally refers to all of Iraq's elite forces included in the Counter Terrorism Command, which include the ICTF, the Commandos, and other elite units.
2. David M. Witty, *The Iraqi Counter Terrorism Service* (Washington, DC: The Center for Middle East Policy at Brookings Institution, 2016), 7.
3. Austin Long et al., *Building Special Operations Partnerships in Afghanistan and Beyond: Challenges and Best Practices from Afghanistan, Iraq, and Colombia* (Santa Monica, CA: RAND Corporation, 2015), 45–46.
4. Interview, Frank Sobchak with Brigadier General Arkan Fadhil, September 8, 2020.
5. Witty, *Iraqi Counter Terrorism Service*, 12.
6. Interview, Frank Sobchak with CW2 Travis Rolph, October 29, 2020.
7. Interview, Frank Sobchak with MSgt. Scott Ford, October 29, 2020. Each CIF was comprised of two troops, and in many cases one troop deployed to advise the ICTF while one remained at home station, recovering or training.
8. Long et al., *Building Special Operations Partnerships*, 48.
9. CW Jade Anderson, "The 36th Commando Battalion Evolution to the 1/1st ISOF Commando Battalion of Today," unpublished article, December 6, 2019.
10. Interview, Frank Sobchak with Sgt. Maj. Ron McDaries, October 30, 2020; interview, Frank Sobchak with MSgt. Clay Morrow, November 2, 2020.
11. Interview, Frank Sobchak with Col. Erik Brown, October 5, 2020.

12. Please see appendix D for those calculations. Doctrinally one Special Forces ODA of twelve personnel should be allotted to train a single host-nation battalion, equating to a ratio of between fifty and seventy-five to one. The partner-force-to-advisor ratio in Iraq was an astronomical eight to twelve times the doctrinal ratio, representing a massive increase in effort.
13. The most common situation for multiple cases was deployment to both Iraq and Afghanistan. However, there were some advisors who advised SOF partners in Colombia, Afghanistan, and Iraq as well as a very small set of advisors who had done the same across the Philippines, Iraq, and Afghanistan.
14. Interview, Frank Sobchak with MSgt. Scott Ford, October 29, 2020.
15. Interview, Frank Sobchak with CW2 Travis Rolph, October 29, 2020.
16. Interview, Frank Sobchak with Col. Erik Brown, October 5, 2020.
17. Jack Murphy, "Special Forces to Disband the Commanders—in Extremis—Force (CIS)," *Jack Murphy Writes*, March 5, 2020, https://jackmurphywrites.com/153/special-forces-commanders-in-extremis-force-no-more/.CIF Companies.
18. Interview, Frank Sobchak with Sgt. Maj. Ron McDaries, October 30, 2020.
19. Anderson, "36th Commando Battalion Evolution."
20. Interview, Frank Sobchak with Maj. Gen. Michael Repass, September 21, 2020; U.S. Army Special Forces, Forward Operating Base 51, 1st Battalion, 5th Special Forces Group, "The 36th Commando Battalion," PowerPoint presentation, September 6, 2004.
21. Email, CW4 Jade Anderson to Frank Sobchak, October 28, 2020; interview, Frank Sobchak with Col. Erik Brown, October 5, 2020.
22. Interview, Frank Sobchak with CW2 Travis Rolph, October 29, 2020.
23. Email, CW4 Jade Anderson to Frank Sobchak, October 28, 2020.
24. Interview, Frank Sobchak with MSgt. Seaux Larreau, October 29, 2020.
25. Long et al., *Building Special Operations Partnerships*, 54.
26. Interview, Frank Sobchak with Maj. Gen. Patrick Roberson, December 22, 2020.
27. Interview, Frank Sobchak with MSgt. Seaux Larreau, October 29, 2020.
28. Interview, Frank Sobchak with MSgt. Scott Ford, October 29, 2020.
29. Interview, Frank Sobchak with Col. Max Carpenter, July 24, 2020.
30. Interview, Frank Sobchak with Col. Erik Brown, October 5, 2020.
31. Interview, Frank Sobchak with Sgt. Maj. Ron McDaries, October 30, 2020.
32. Interview, Frank Sobchak with CW4 Eric Brashears, October 29, 2020.
33. Interview, Frank Sobchak with Col. Erik Brown, October 5, 2020.
34. Interview, Frank Sobchak with Col. Erik Brown, October 5, 2020.
35. Interview, Frank Sobchak with Col. Mark Mitchell, September 29, 2014.

36. In that case, a 10th Special Forces Group soldier tried to romantically engage the sister of an ISOF Commando, who grew enraged, at which point the offender was sent back to the United States. Interview, Frank Sobchak with MSgt. Seaux Larreau, October 29, 2020.
37. Interview, Frank Sobchak with Col. Erik Brown, October 5, 2020. A 3/3 score on the Defense Language Proficiency Test for listening and reading equates to general proficiency.
38. Email, CW4 Jade Anderson to Frank Sobchak, October 28, 2020.
39. Interview, Frank Sobchak with Sgt. Maj. Ron McDaries, October 30, 2020.
40. Interview, Frank Sobchak with MSgt. Seaux Larreau, October 29, 2020.
41. Interview, Frank Sobchak with CW4 Eric Brashears, October 29, 2020.
42. Interagency Language Roundtable, "Interagency Language Roundtable Language Skill Level Descriptions—Reading," GovILR.org, U.S. Government, n.d., https://www.govtilr.org/Skills/ILRscale4.htm.
43. Robert R. Greene Sands, *Assessing Special Operations Forces Language, Region, and Culture Needs: Leveraging Digital and LRC Learning to Reroute the "Roadmap" from Human Terrain to Human Domain* (MacDill Air Force Base, FL: The JSOU Press, 2016), 62–63.
44. Email, Department of the Army Civilian Francis Restituyo, USASOC Language, Regional Expertise, and Culture director, to Frank Sobchak, April 12, 2021.
45. Long et al., *Building Special Operations Partnerships*, 49–50.
46. Interview, Frank Sobchak with Sgt. Maj. Ron McDaries, October 30, 2020.
47. Interview, Frank Sobchak with MSgt. Scott Ford, October 29, 2020.
48. Interview, Frank Sobchak with Brigadier General Arkan Fadhil, September 8, 2020.
49. Email, CW4 Jade Anderson, to Frank Sobchak, October 28, 2020.
50. Interview, Frank Sobchak with Sgt. Maj. Ron McDaries, October 30, 2020.
51. Interview, Frank Sobchak with Col. Erik Brown, October 5, 2020; interview, Frank Sobchak with Sgt. Maj. Ron McDaries, October 30, 2020.
52. David M. Witty, "Remembering Maj. Gen. Fadhil Barwari—ISOF Commander," *SOF News*, September 25, 2018, https://sof.news/iraq/mg-fadhil-al-barwari/. While Barwari's tactical prowess and leadership were seen unequaled in Iraq, in 2017 he was accused of paying two U.S. contractors (who were not part of my interview list) hundreds of thousands of dollars in a kickback land-rental scheme. No charges were brought, however, and he died of a heart attack the following year.
53. Interview, Frank Sobchak with Maj. Gen. Patrick Roberson, December 22, 2020.
54. Witty, *Iraqi Counter Terrorism Service*, 7–9.

55. Joel D. Rayburn and Frank K. Sobchak, eds., *The U.S. Army in the Iraq War: Volume 1, Invasion, Insurgency, Civil War, 2003–2006* (Carlisle, PA: Strategic Studies Institute, U.S. Army War College, 2019), 342.
56. Interview, Frank Sobchak with MSgt. Clay Morrow, November 2, 2020.
57. Rayburn and Sobchak, *U.S. Army in the Iraq War: Volume 1*, 341.
58. Interview, Frank Sobchak with Sgt. Maj. Ron McDaries, October 30, 2020.
59. Interview, Frank Sobchak with Col. Erik Brown, October 5, 2020.
60. Witty, *Iraqi Counter Terrorism Service*, 26.
61. Combined Joint Special Operations Task Force–Arabian Peninsula, briefing on the 36th Iraqi Civil Defense Corps Battalion, c. January 2004.
62. Witty, *Iraqi Counter Terrorism Service*, 8.
63. Interview, Frank Sobchak with Brigadier General Arkan Fadhil, September 8, 2020.
64. Interview, Frank Sobchak with Brigadier General Arkan Fadhil, September 8, 2020.
65. Interview, Frank Sobchak with Col. Erik Brown, October 5, 2020.
66. Interview, Frank Sobchak with Sgt. Maj. Ron McDaries, October 30, 2020.
67. Witty, *Iraqi Counter Terrorism Service*, 13.
68. Interview, Frank Sobchak with Maj. Gen. Patrick Roberson, December 22, 2020.
69. Interview, Frank Sobchak with Col. Erik Brown, October 5, 2020.
70. Email, Col. Dennis Downey to Frank Sobchak, July 11, 2020.
71. Long et al., *Building Special Operations Partnerships*, 50.
72. Interview, Frank Sobchak with Col. Chris Conner, July 13, 2020.
73. Witty, *Iraqi Counter Terrorism Service*, 9.
74. Interview, Frank Sobchak with Rear Adm. Edward Winters, October 22, 2015.
75. Interview, Frank Sobchak with Col. Mark Mitchell, September 29, 2014.
76. Witty, *Iraqi Counter Terrorism Service*, 10.
77. Interview, Frank Sobchak with Brigadier General Arkan Fadhil, September 8, 2020.
78. The CTC commander would later be advanced to be a three-star general.
79. Interview, Frank Sobchak with Lt. Col. (Ret.) Patrick Morrison, September 22, 2014.
80. Email, CW4 Jade Anderson to Frank Sobchak, October 28, 2020.
81. Interview, Frank Sobchak with MSgt. Clay Morrow, November 2, 2020.
82. Interview, Frank Sobchak with Lt. Col. (Ret.) Patrick Morrison, September 22, 2014.
83. Email, CW4 Jade Anderson to Frank Sobchak, October 28, 2020.

84. Marisa Sullivan, *Maliki's Authoritarian Regime*, Middle East Security Report 10 (Washington, DC: Institute for the Study of War, April 2013), 12, https://www.understandingwar.org/sites/default/files/Malikis-Authoritarian-Regime-Web.pdf.
85. Shane Bauer, "Iraq's New Death Squad," *The Nation*, June 3, 2009, https://www.thenation.com/article/archive/iraqs-new-death-squad/.
86. Joel D. Rayburn and Frank K. Sobchak, eds., *The U.S. Army in the Iraq War: Volume 2, Surge and Withdrawal, 2007–2011* (Carlisle, PA: Strategic Studies Institute, U.S. Army War College, 2019), 417.
87. Michael Knights and Alex Mello, "The Best Thing America Built in Iraq: Iraq's Counter-Terrorism Service and the Long War against Militancy," *War on the Rocks*, July 19, 2017, https://warontherocks.com/2017/07/the-best-thing-america-built-in-iraq-iraqs-counterterrorism-service-and-the-long-war-against-militancy/.
88. Witty, *Iraqi Counter Terrorism Service*, 26.
89. David M. Witty, *Iraq's Post-2014 Counter Terrorism Service*, Policy Focus 157 (Washington, DC: The Washington Institute for Near East Policy, October 2018), 5, https://www.washingtoninstitute.org/media/1293.
90. Interview, Frank Sobchak with CW2 Travis Rolph, October 29, 2020.
91. Interview, Frank Sobchak with CW2 Travis Rolph, October 29, 2020.
92. Interview, Frank Sobchak with CW4 Eric Brashears, October 29, 2020.
93. Interview, Frank Sobchak with Col. Erik Brown, October 5, 2020.
94. Interview, Frank Sobchak with Sgt. Maj. Ron McDaries, October 30, 2020.
95. Interview, Frank Sobchak with CW4 Eric Brashears, October 29, 2020.
96. Witty, *Iraq's Post-2014 Counter Terrorism Service*, 5.
97. Interview, Frank Sobchak with Maj. Gen. Michael Repass, September 21, 2020.
98. Interview, Frank Sobchak with MSgt. Clay Morrow, November 2, 2020.
99. Witty, *Iraq's Post-2014 Counter Terrorism Service*, 24.
100. Interview, Frank Sobchak with Col. Chris Conner, July 13, 2020.
101. Mitch Utterback, "What the Fight against ISIS Is Actually Like on the Iraqi Frontlines," *Athlon Outdoors* (blog), May 13, 2020, https://www.athlonoutdoors.com/article/frontlines-fight-against-isis/.
102. Louisa Loveluck and Mustafa Salim, "Hunting ISIS: On a Nighttime Raid with Iraqi Special Forces," *Washington Post*, February 3, 2021, https://www.washingtonpost.com/world/2021/02/03/iraq-isis-american-troops-counterterrorism/.
103. Email, CW4 Jade Anderson to Frank Sobchak, October 28, 2020.
104. Interview, Frank Sobchak with Col. Kevin (Duke) Christie, October 19, 2020.
105. Witty, *Iraqi Counter Terrorism Service*, 20.
106. Interview, Frank Sobchak with Col. Erik Brown, October 5, 2020.

107. Interview, Frank Sobchak with Brigadier General Arkan Fadhil, September 8, 2020.
108. Hannah Allam and Mitchell Prothero, "Islamists Have Cornered Commandos Defending Iraq's Largest Refinery," McClatchy Washington Bureau, July 9, 2014, https://www.mcclatchydc.com/news/nation-world/world/article24770242.html.
109. Knights and Mello, "The Best Thing America Built in Iraq."
110. Utterback, "What the Fight against ISIS Is Actually Like."
111. Interview, Frank Sobchak with Sgt. Maj. Ron McDaries, October 30, 2020.
112. Interview, Frank Sobchak with CW2 Travis Rolph, October 29, 2020; interview, Frank Sobchak with MSgt. Seaux Larreau, October 29, 2020.
113. Witty, *Iraqi Counter Terrorism Service*, 14.
114. Interview, Frank Sobchak with Maj. Gen. Michael Repass, September 21, 2020.
115. Knights and Mello, "The Best Thing America Built in Iraq."
116. Interview, Frank Sobchak with Brigadier General Arkan Fadhil, September 8, 2020.
117. Interview, Frank Sobchak with Col. Ken Gleiman, July 13, 2020.
118. Mitch Utterback, "Up to the Sniper Line," *Mitch Utterback: A Veteran in Transition*, April 30, 2017, https://mitchutterback.wordpress.com/2017/04/30/up-to-the-sniper-line/.
119. Interview, Frank Sobchak with Lt. Col. David Witty, September 3, 2020.
120. Loveday Morris and Mustafa Salim, "Chaos in Iraqi Forces Contributed to Islamic State's Biggest Win This Year," Middle East, *Washington Post*, May 23, 2015.
121. Witty, *Iraq's Post-2014 Counter Terrorism Service*, 6–7.
122. Loveday Morris, "The Force Leading the Iraq Army's Fight against ISIS Went from 'Dirty Division' to Golden Boys," Middle East, *Washington Post*, July 26, 2016.
123. Witty, *Iraq's Post-2014 Counter Terrorism Service*, 6–10.
124. Loveluck and Salim, "Hunting ISIS."

CHAPTER 5. "CHASING BRIGHT AND SHINY OBJECTS"

1. Interview, Frank Sobchak with anonymous active-duty 3rd SF Group member, January 8, 2021.
2. "Q&A: Brigadier General Edward M. Reeder Jr.," Game Changers, *Special Warfare* 24, no. 4 (October–December 2011): 20, https://www.dvidshub.net/publication/issues/9449.
3. Interview, Frank Sobchak with Maj. Gen. Ed Reeder, December 17, 2020.
4. Interview, Frank Sobchak with Col. Fred Dummar, December 16, 2020.

5. Email, Col. Fred Dummar to Frank Sobchak, December 26, 2020.
6. The title of this subsection comes from U.S. Special Operations Command, U.S. Department of Defense, "SOF Truths," n.d., archived online at https://www.socom.mil/about/sof-truths.
7. Interview, Frank Sobchak with Command Sargeant Major Faiz Wafa, January 8, 2021.
8. Interview, Frank Sobchak with Col. Fred Dummar, December 16, 2020.
9. Soraya Sarhaddi Nelson, "New Afghan Commandos Take to the Frontlines," *Morning Edition*, NPR.org, July 23, 2007, https://www.npr.org/2007/07/23/12127848/new-afghan-commandos-take-to-the-frontlines.
10. Interview, Frank Sobchak with Maj. Gen. Ed Reeder, December 17, 2020.
11. "Afghan National Army (ANA)—Order of Battle," Military, GlobalSecurity.org, n.d., https://www.globalsecurity.org/military/world/afghanistan/ana-orbat.htm, accessed June 16, 2021.
12. Interview, Frank Sobchak with Maj. Gen. Ed Reeder, December 17, 2020.
13. Interview, Frank Sobchak with Sgt. Maj. Stephen Durfee, September 2, 2020; and U.S. Special Operations Command, "SOF Truths."
14. Interview, Frank Sobchak with Sgt. Maj. David Topejr, December 23, 2020.
15. Interview, Frank Sobchak with MSgt. Scott Ford, October 29, 2020.
16. Dan Lamothe, "Afghanistan Is Building Up Its Commando Force to Fight the Taliban. But at What Cost?" Asia and Pacific, *Washington Post*, April 28, 2018, https://www.washingtonpost.com/world/asia_pacific/afghanistan-is-building-up-its-commando-force-to-fight-the-taliban-but-at-what-cost/2018/04/27ddıc0c1c-44cd-11e8-b2dc-b0a403e4720a_story.html.
17. Interview, Frank Sobchak with Col. Larry Niedringhaus, January 7, 2021.
18. Susannah George, "With Less U.S. Tactical Support, Afghanistan's Elite Forces Are Struggling to Roll Back Taliban Advances," Asia and Pacific, *Washington Post*, March 7, 2021, https://www.washingtonpost.com/world/asia_pacific/afghanistan-taliban-battles-kandahar/2021/03/05/2d88fea4-777e-11eb-9489-8f7dacd51e75_story.html. By 2021 ANASOC included ANA Special Forces and other SOF units, as well as the Commandos.
19. Interview, Frank Sobchak with MSgt. Scott Ford, October 29, 2020.
20. Interview, Frank Sobchak with Col. Fred Dummar, December 16, 2020; interview, Frank Sobchak with Maj. Gen. Ed Reeder, December 17, 2020; email, CW5 J. P. Guidry to Frank Sobchak, January 8, 2021.
21. Austin Long et al., *Building Special Operations Partnerships in Afghanistan and Beyond: Challenges and Best Practices from Afghanistan, Iraq, and Colombia* (Santa Monica, CA: RAND Corporation, 2015), 33.

22. Interview, Frank Sobchak with Valentin Swegle, December 22, 2020; interview, Frank Sobchak with Col. Larry Niedringhaus, January 7, 2021.
23. Interview, Frank Sobchak with Col. Fred Dummar, December 16, 2020; interview, Frank Sobchak with Col. Bill Carty, January 6, 2021.
24. As quoted in Long et al., *Building Special Operations Partnerships*, 33–34.
25. Long et al., 34; interview, Frank Sobchak with Col. Bill Carty, January 6, 2021; interview, Frank Sobchak with Col. Larry Niedringhaus, January 7, 2021.
26. Interview, Frank Sobchak with Maj. Gen. Ed Reeder, December 17, 2020.
27. Interview, Frank Sobchak with Col. Larry Niedringhaus, January 7, 2021.
28. Interview, Frank Sobchak with CW4 Eric Brashears, November 2, 2020.
29. Interview, Frank Sobchak with MSgt. Joshua Stephen, January 5, 2021.
30. Interview, Frank Sobchak with MSgt. Joshua Stephen, January 5, 2021; interview, Frank Sobchak with Col. Brian Petit, December 21, 2020. The authorized strength number comes from the ANASOC modification table of organization and equipment (MTOE), "ANA 1398 v2," n.d., provided by Col. Fred Dummar.
31. Interview, Frank Sobchak with Valentin Swegle, December 22, 2020. Although it was roughly half of the annual ANA desertion rate, which was a dismal 40 percent, it was still significant enough to mean many Commando tactical units became combat ineffective.
32. Interview, Frank Sobchak with Col. Larry Niedringhaus, January 7, 2021.
33. "ANA Commandos," Military, Global Security, n.d., accessed June 16, 2021, https://www.globalsecurity.org/military/world/afghanistan/comando.htm. The numbers cited on the website match what at least one advisor notes were being produced annually.
34. Interview, Frank Sobchak with MSgt. Scott Ford, October 29, 2020.
35. Interview, Frank Sobchak with Col. Bill Carty, January 6, 2021.
36. Interview, Frank Sobchak with MSgt. Joshua Stephen, January 5, 2021.
37. U.S. Central Intelligence Agency, "Afghanistan: People and Society," *The World Factbook*, CIA.gov, last updated January 17, 2024, https://www.cia.gov/the-world-factbook/countries/afghanistan/#people-and-society.
38. Interview, Frank Sobchak with Valentin Swegle, December 22, 2020.
39. Interview, Frank Sobchak with Col. Bill Carty, January 6, 2021.
40. Interview, Frank Sobchak with Valentin Swegle, December 22, 2020.
41. Interview, Frank Sobchak with Col. Fred Dummar, December 16, 2020.
42. Association of the United States Army. "DLI's Language Guidelines," AUSA.org, August 1, 2010, https://www.ausa.org/articles/dlis-language-guidelines.
43. Interview, Frank Sobchak with Maj. Gen. Ed Reeder, December 17, 2020.
44. Interview, Frank Sobchak with CW4 Eric Brashears, November 2, 2020.
45. Interview, Frank Sobchak with Maj. Gen. Ed Reeder, December 17, 2020.

46. Interview, Frank Sobchak with Sgt. Maj. David Topejr, December 23, 2020.
47. Interview, Frank Sobchak with MSgt. Joshua Stephen, January 5, 2021.
48. Interview, Frank Sobchak with Col. Bill Carty, January 6, 2021.
49. Interview, Frank Sobchak with Sgt. Maj. David Topejr, December 23, 2020.
50. Interview, Frank Sobchak with Col. Bill Carty, January 6, 2021.
51. Interview, Frank Sobchak with Col. Bill Carty, January 6, 2021.
52. Interview, Frank Sobchak with Maj. Gen. Ed Reeder, December 17, 2020.
53. Interview, Frank Sobchak with Sgt. Maj. David Topejr, December 23, 2020.
54. Interview, Frank Sobchak with Sgt. Maj. David Topejr, December 23, 2020.
55. Interview, Frank Sobchak with Maj. Gen. Jim Linder, December 21, 2020.
56. Interview, Frank Sobchak with Valentin Swegle, December 22, 2020.
57. Long et al., *Building Special Operations Partnerships*, 39.
58. Interview, Frank Sobchak with MSgt. Joshua Stephen, January 5, 2021.
59. Interview, Frank Sobchak with Col. Bill Carty, January 6, 2021.
60. Long et al., *Building Special Operations Partnerships*, 39–40.
61. Interview, Frank Sobchak with anonymous active-duty 3rd SF Group member, January 8, 2021.
62. Between 2008 and 2012, Groups grew from three to four organic SF battalions. The fourth battalion was focused more on operational preparation of the environment and nicknamed the "Jedburgh Battalion," a throwback to the OSS pilot team mission during World War II when Allied operatives were air-dropped into Nazi-occupied territories to commit sabotage and lead guerilla warfare ahead of the D-Day invasion. Excluding that battalion, which was rarely used for Commando advisory missions, three battalions remained, each with three companies. Subtracting the CIF company from each group resulted in the availability of eight companies.
63. Interview, Frank Sobchak with MSgt. Joshua Stephen, January 5, 2021.
64. Jessica Donati, *Eagle Down: The Last Special Forces Fighting the Forever War* (New York: PublicAffairs, 2021), 270.
65. Interview, Frank Sobchak with Maj. Gen. Ed Reeder, December 17, 2020.
66. Many advisors commented on this trend, including Col. Fred Dummar, December 16, 2020; CW4 Eric Brashears, November 2, 2020; and Col. Brian Petit, December 21, 2020, all in interview with the author.
67. Interview, Frank Sobchak with MSgt. Scott Ford, October 29, 2020.
68. Interview, Frank Sobchak with anonymous active-duty 3rd SF Group member, January 8, 2021.
69. There was considerable frustration with ANASF, with some interviewees calling its objectives unclear and others feeling it was meant to lend "boutique SOF

capability" to Afghanistan, a country that neither needed nor could maintain such a capability.
70. Interview, Frank Sobchak with Command Sergeant Major Faiz Wafa, January 8, 2021.
71. Interview, Frank Sobchak with anonymous active-duty 3rd SF Group member, January 8, 2021.
72. Interview, Frank Sobchak with Col. Bill Carty, January 6, 2021.
73. Interview, Frank Sobchak with Sgt. Maj. David Topejr, December 23, 2020.
74. Interview, Frank Sobchak with MSgt. Joshua Stephen, January 5, 2021.
75. Interview, Frank Sobchak with Maj. Gen. Jim Linder, December 21, 2020.
76. Interview, Frank Sobchak with Command Sergeant Major Faiz Wafa, January 8, 2021.
77. Interview, Frank Sobchak with anonymous active-duty 3rd SF Group member, January 8, 2021.
78. Long et al., *Building Special Operations Partnerships*, 40. In the 1993 film *Groundhog Day* a man is trapped in a time loop and must relive the same day over and over again.
79. Todd C. Helmus, *Advising the Command: Best Practices from the Special Operation's Advisory Experience in Afghanistan* (Santa Monica, CA: RAND, 2015), 10.
80. Interview, Frank Sobchak with Col. Fred Dummar, December 16, 2020.
81. Interview, Frank Sobchak with Col. Fred Dummar, December 16, 2020.
82. Interview, Frank Sobchak with Col. Brian Petit, December 21, 2020.
83. Interview, Frank Sobchak with Maj. Gen. Ed Reeder, December 17, 2020.
84. By contrast, SF advisors were organizing Iraqi Special Operations Forces less than six months after the 2003 fall of Baghdad.
85. Interview, Frank Sobchak with Col. Fred Dummar, December 16, 2020.
86. Interview, Frank Sobchak with Command Sergeant Major Faiz Wafa, January 8, 2021.
87. UNESCO Institute for Statistics, "Literacy Rate, Adult Total (% of People Ages 15 and Above)—Afghanistan," The World Bank, September 2020, https://data.worldbank.org/indicator/SE.ADT.LITR.ZS?end=2018&locations=AF&start=1979.
88. Interview, Frank Sobchak with Valentin Swegle, December 22, 2020. The radios were long-range Harris high-frequency equipment, which could have helped make the Commandos more independent by allowing them to unilaterally call for logistics support or intelligence updates.
89. Interview, Frank Sobchak with MSgt. Scott Ford, October 29, 2020.

90. Interview, Frank Sobchak with Maj. Gen. Patrick Roberson, December 22, 2020. Roberson noted that the educational backgrounds and personal experiences of Afghans were different from many of the other cases in this study.
91. Interview, Frank Sobchak with Col. Larry Niedringhaus, January 7, 2021.
92. Interview, Frank Sobchak with anonymous active-duty 3rd SF Group member, January 8, 2021.
93. Interview, Frank Sobchak with Col. Tim Williams, October 16, 2020.
94. Interview, Frank Sobchak with MSgt. Scott Ford, October 29, 2020.
95. Interview, Frank Sobchak with Col. Fred Dummar, December 16, 2020.
96. ANASOC MTOE, "ANA 1398 v2," n.d., provided by Col. Fred Dummar.
97. Interview, Frank Sobchak with CW4 Eric Brashears, November 2, 2020.
98. Interview, Frank Sobchak with Maj. Gen. Ed Reeder, December 17, 2020; email, Command Sergeant Major Faiz Wafa to Frank Sobchak, June 14, 2021.
99. Interview, Frank Sobchak with Maj. Gen. Patrick Roberson, December 22, 2020.
100. Interview, Frank Sobchak with Col. Fred Dummar, December 16, 2020.
101. Haley Britzky, "Casualties Reported after US Special Forces Team Ambushed in Afghanistan," *Task & Purpose*, February 8, 2020, https://taskandpurpose.com/news/afghanistan-nangarhar-attack-casualties/. Also see interview, Frank Sobchak with Maj. Gen. Patrick Roberson, December 22, 2020.
102. Interview, Frank Sobchak with Maj. Gen. Ed Reeder, December 17, 2020.
103. Interview, Frank Sobchak with MSgt. Scott Ford, October 29, 2020.
104. Interview, Frank Sobchak with CW4 Eric Brashears, November 2, 2020.
105. Interview, Frank Sobchak with Col. Fred Dummar, December 16, 2020.
106. Interview, Frank Sobchak with Maj. Gen. Ed Reeder, December 17, 2020.
107. Interview, Frank Sobchak with Sgt. Maj. David Topejr, December 23, 2020.
108. Interview, Frank Sobchak with Col. Fred Dummar, December 16, 2020.
109. Interview, Frank Sobchak with Col. Brian Petit, December 21, 2020.
110. Interview, Frank Sobchak with Command Sergeant Major Faiz Wafa, January 8, 2021.
111. "ANA Special Operations Command (ANASOC)," Military, GlobalSecurity.org, n.d., https://www.globalsecurity.org/military/world/afghanistan/anasoc.htm, accessed December 18, 2020.
112. Interview, Frank Sobchak with Maj. Gen. Ed Reeder, December 17, 2020.
113. Interview, Frank Sobchak with Command Sergeant Major Faiz Wafa, January 8, 2021.
114. Interview, Frank Sobchak with MSgt. Joshua Stephen, January 5, 2021.
115. Interview, Frank Sobchak with Sgt. Maj. David Topejr, December 23, 2020.
116. Interview, Frank Sobchak with Sgt. Maj. David Topejr, December 23, 2020.
117. Interview, Frank Sobchak with Col. Brian Petit, December 21, 2020.

118. Interview, Frank Sobchak with CW4 Eric Brashears, November 2, 2020. A relative newcomer to the Afghan theater due to its focus on Iraq until 2011, 10th Special Forces Group has its headquarters and most of its units in Colorado, while 3rd and 7th Special Forces Groups, which shouldered most of the burden of advising the Commandos, had been based in North Carolina (until 7th Group moved to Florida in 2011).
119. Interview, Frank Sobchak with Col. Larry Niedringhaus, January 7, 2021.
120. Direct-action missions usually focus on offensive operations such as prepared attacks, ambushes, or raids.
121. Here "556" refers to the cartridge size (5.56 mm) of the standard U.S. Army rifle. As recalled by Sgt. Maj. David Topejr, quoting Brig. Gen. Bolduc; interview, Frank Sobchak with Sgt. Maj. David Topejr, December 23, 2020. This quotation closely matches the words of Brig. Gen. Frank Toney, a previous U.S. Army Special Forces Command commanding general and Special Operations Command Central commanding general, who once stated, "556 is the only language you need to speak." The source for Brig. Gen. Toney's remark is the author, who heard it in 1999 during a command visit to Fort Campbell.
122. Interview, Frank Sobchak with Col. Brian Petit, December 21, 2020.
123. Interview, Frank Sobchak with Command Sergeant Major Faiz Wafa, January 8, 2021.
124. Interview, Frank Sobchak with Maj. Gen. Ed Reeder, December 17, 2020.
125. Interview, Frank Sobchak with Col. Brian Petit, December 21, 2020.
126. Resolute Support Public Affairs Office, "Press Conference Statement by General John Nicholson, Commander, NATO Resolute Support Mission and Resolute Support Public Affairs Office," press release, U.S. Central Command, August 24, 2017, https://www.centcom.mil/MEDIA/PRESS-RELEASES/Press-Release-View/Article/1287992/press-conference-statement-by-general-john-nicholson-commander-nato-resolute-su/.
127. Helene Cooper, "Afghan Forces Are Praised, Despite Still Relying Heavily on U.S. Help," World, *New York Times*, August 20, 2017, https://www.nytimes.com/2017/08/20/world/asia/afghanistan-military-strategy.html.
128. Interview, Frank Sobchak with Col. Fred Dummar, December 16, 2020.
129. Interview, Frank Sobchak with Col. Fred Dummar, December 16, 2020.
130. Interview, Frank Sobchak with Maj. Gen. Ed Reeder, December 17, 2020.
131. Interview, Frank Sobchak with Col. Larry Niedringhaus, January 7, 2021.
132. Interview, Frank Sobchak with Col. Brian Petit, December 21, 2020.
133. Interview, Frank Sobchak with MSgt. Joshua Stephen, January 5, 2021.
134. Interview, Frank Sobchak with Col. Martin (Marty) Schmidt, September 9, 2020.

135. Donati, *Eagle Down*, 74.
136. Interview, Frank Sobchak with Sgt. Maj. David Topejr, December 23, 2020.
137. Interview, Frank Sobchak with CW4 Eric Brashears, November 2, 2020.
138. Interview, Frank Sobchak with Valentin Swegle, December 22, 2020.
139. Interview, Frank Sobchak with Command Sergeant Major Faiz Wafa, January 8, 2021.
140. Interview, Frank Sobchak with Col. Brian Petit, December 21, 2020.
141. Interview, Frank Sobchak with Valentin Swegle, December 22, 2020.
142. Interview, Frank Sobchak with Col. Fred Dummar, December 16, 2020.
143. Interview, Frank Sobchak with Col. Larry Niedringhaus, January 7, 2021.
144. Interview, Frank Sobchak with Valentin Swegle, December 22, 2020.
145. Interview, Frank Sobchak with Col. Fred Dummar, December 16, 2020.
146. Pamela Constable, "Death of Famed Afghan Commander in Taliban Massacre Highlights the Country's Struggles and Fears," Asia and Pacific, *Washington Post*, June 19, 2021. https://www.washingtonpost.com/world/asia_pacific/afghanistan-taliban-commando-killed/2021/06/19/ebd748fc-d03e-11eb-a224-bd59bd22197c_story.html.
147. Shawn Snow, Leo Shane III, and Joe Gould, "Afghan Special Operators Partnering with US Forces More Often, Still Reliant on American Support," *Military Times*, February 5, 2020, https://www.militarytimes.com/flashpoints/2020/02/05/afghan-special-operators-partnering-with-us-forces-more-often-still-reliant-on-american-support/.
148. Interview, Frank Sobchak with MSgt. Joshua Stephen, January 5, 2021; interview, Frank Sobchak with Col. Larry Niedringhaus, January 7, 2021.
149. Interview, Frank Sobchak with Valentin Swegle, December 22, 2020.
150. Interview, Frank Sobchak with Col. Fernando Lujan, August 11, 2020.
151. Interview, Frank Sobchak with MSgt. Scott Ford, October 29, 2020.
152. Interview, Frank Sobchak with MSgt. Joshua Stephen, January 5, 2021.
153. Interview, Frank Sobchak with Col. Bill Carty, January 6, 2021.
154. Interview, Frank Sobchak with Maj. Gen. Ed Reeder, December 17, 2020.
155. Interview, Frank Sobchak with Col. Brian Petit, December 21, 2020.
156. Interview, Frank Sobchak with Col. Fred Dummar, December 16, 2020; interview, Frank Sobchak with Sgt. Maj. David Topejr, December 23, 2020.
157. Interview, Frank Sobchak with MSgt. Joshua Stephen, January 5, 2021.
158. Interview, Frank Sobchak with Col. Brian Petit, December 21, 2020.
159. Helmus, *Advising the Command*, 29.
160. Interview, Frank Sobchak with MSgt. Joshua Stephen, January 5, 2021.
161. Interview, Frank Sobchak with Maj. Gen. Ed Reeder, December 17, 2020.
162. Interview, Frank Sobchak with Valentin Swegle, December 22, 2020.

163. Interview, Frank Sobchak with Maj. Gen. Ed Reeder, December 17, 2020; interview, Frank Sobchak with Col. Fred Dummar, December 16, 2020.
164. Interview, Frank Sobchak with Col. Larry Niedringhaus, January 7, 2021.
165. Interview, Frank Sobchak with anonymous active-duty 3rd SF Group member, January 8, 2021.
166. Interview, Frank Sobchak with MSgt. Joshua Stephen, January 5, 2021.
167. Rod Nordland, "Taliban End Takeover of Kunduz after 15 Days," *New York Times*, October 13, 2015, https://www.nytimes.com/2015/10/14/world/asia/taliban-afghanistan-kunduz.html.
168. Donati, *Eagle Down*, 70–75.
169. Bill Roggio, "Taliban Doubles Number of Controlled Afghan Districts since May 1," *Long War Journal*, June 29, 2021, https://www.longwarjournal.org/archives/2021/06/taliban-doubles-number-of-controlled-afghan-districts-since-may-1.php.
170. George, "With Less U.S. Tactical Support."
171. Jim Huylebroek, "On the Front Line: A Night with Afghan Commandos," World, *New York Times*, June 25, 2021, https://www.nytimes.com/2021/06/25/world/asia/afghan-commandos-helmand.html.
172. Anna Coren, Sandi Sidhu, Tim Lister, and Abdul Basir Bina, "Taliban Fighters Execute 22 Afghan Commandos as They Try to Surrender," CNN.com, last updated July 14, 2021, https://www.cnn.com/2021/07/13/asia/afghanistan-taliban-commandos-killed-intl-hnk/index.html.
173. Thomas Gibbons-Neff, Fahim Abed, and Jim Huylebroek, "On Afghanistan's Front Line, There Are No Good Choices," World, *New York Times*, August 9, 2021, https://www.nytimes.com/2021/08/09/world/asia/Afghanistan-taliban-kandahar.html.
174. Hollie McKay, "Exclusive: Embedded with the Last Afghan Special Forces Team in Mazar-i-Sharif," Intel, *Coffee or Die Magazine* (blog), August 22, 2021, https://coffeeordie.com/afghan-special-forces-mazar/.
175. Sami Sahak, Wali Arian, and Jim Huylebroek, "Taliban Claim Control over Panjshir Valley, but Resistance Vows to Fight On," World, *New York Times*, September 6, 2021, https://www.nytimes.com/2021/09/06/world/asia/afghanistan-panjshir-taliban-resistance.html.

CONCLUSIONS AND RECOMMENDATIONS

1. Rachel Tecott, "Why America Can't Build Allied Armies," *Foreign Affairs*, August 26, 2021, https://www.foreignaffairs.com/articles/united-states/2021-08-26/why-america-cant-build-allied-armies.

2. Robert Farley, "Can the U.S. Military Build an Army for a Foreign Country? Here Is What History Says," 1945.com, August 31, 2021. https://www.19fortyfive.com/2021/08/can-the-u-s-military-build-an-army-for-a-foreign-country-here-is-what-history-says/.
3. Interview, Frank Sobchak with Col. Fred Dummar, December 16, 2020.
4. While financial assistance was usually helpful in obtaining host-nation support for changes (the proverbial carrot), assistance without strings (the stick) often proved to be counterproductive by unintentionally increasing corruption.
5. Email, Col. Scott Morley to Frank Sobchak, August 5, 2021.
6. Interview, Frank Sobchak with Maj. Gen. Simeon Trombitas, September 15, 2020.
7. Association of the United States Army, "DLI's Language Guidelines," AUSA.org, August 1, 2010, https://www.ausa.org/articles/dlis-language-guidelines.
8. U.S. Army Special Operations Command, 1st Special Forces Command, "Language, Regional Expertise, and Culture Capability (LREC) Executive Summary," PowerPoint presentation, November 21, 2022.
9. Email, Col. Scott Morley to Frank Sobchak, August 5, 2021, emphasis original.
10. As quoted in Joel D. Rayburn and Frank K. Sobchak, eds., *The U.S. Army in the Iraq War: Volume 2, Surge and Withdrawal, 2007–2011* (Carlisle, PA: Strategic Studies Institute, U.S. Army War College, 2019), 631.
11. Robert D. Ramsey, *Advising Indigenous Forces: American Advisors in Korea, Vietnam, and El Salvador* (Leavenworth, KS: Combat Studies Institute Press, 2012), 18–19.
12. Thomas A. Marks, "A Model Counterinsurgency: Uribe's Colombia (2002–2006) vs. FARC," *Military Review* (March–April 2007): 41–56. https://www.armyupress.army.mil/Portals/7/military-review/Archives/English/MilitaryReview_20070430_art010.pdf.
13. Interagency Language Roundtable, "Interagency Language Roundtable Language Skill Level Descriptions—Reading," GovILR.org, U.S. Government, n.d., https://www.govtilr.org/Skills/ILRscale4.htm, accessed April 6, 2021.
14. U.S. Army Special Operations Command, 1st Special Forces Command, "Language, Regional Expertise, and Culture Capability."
15. Email, U.S. Department of the Army, USASOC Language, Regional Expertise, and Culture director, to Frank Sobchak, April 12, 2021.
16. "USPACOM Area of Responsibility," *Special Warfare* (January–March 2014): 8–9, https://www.dvidshub.net/publication/issues/14790.
17. U.S. Department of the Army, *Field Manual 3-05.20, Special Forces Operations* (Washington, DC: U.S. Department of the Army, 2011), 3–30. An ODA is comprised of twelve SF-qualified personnel.

18. The ratio for Iraq was 6.2 to 1, Afghanistan 16.4 to 1, Colombia 17.5 to 1, and the Philippines 28.7 to 1. Only El Salvador (189.6 to 1) met or exceeded the doctrinal amount.
19. U.S. Special Operations Command, U.S. Department of Defense, "SOF Truths," [1987?], archived online at https://www.socom.mil/about/sof-truths.
20. Jacob M. Engel, "Why Does Culture 'Eat Strategy For Breakfast'?" *Forbes*, November 20, 2018, https://www.forbes.com/sites/forbescoachescouncil/2018/11/20/why-does-culture-eat-strategy-for-breakfast/. The maxim itself was coined by Peter Drucker, a management consultant and business management scholar.
21. This is based on the years measured in this study. Technically the advisory effort in El Salvador lasted through 1992, although with the peace accords signed in January of that year, there was no need to further evaluate the combat effectiveness of the BIRIs.
22. *Tanda* roughly translates as "class year," and by the start of the Salvadoran Civil War its meaning had become the equivalent of a caste system, wherein longevity mattered far more than skill. Promotional upward mobility to jump classes for either command or rank was nearly impossible.
23. Ramsey, *Advising Indigenous Forces*, 94, 98–99.
24. Donald Stoker, ed., *Military Advising and Assistance*, 1st ed. (London: Routledge, 2008), 184–85.
25. In October 2003, *USA Today* leaked Rumsfeld's memo admonishing civilian deputies and senior military officers to bring fresh strategic thinking to the wars being fought in the Middle East. Julian Borger, "Leaked Memo Exposes Rumsfeld's Doubts about War on Terror," World news, *The Guardian*, October 22, 2003, https://www.theguardian.com/world/2003/oct/23/usa.julianborger.

Bibliography

SOURCES CITED

Agence France-Presse. "Marawi: City Destroyed in Philippines' Longest Urban War." *Inquirer News*, October 19, 2017. https://newsinfo.inquirer.net/939202/marawi-war-maute-terrorism-duterte-isnilon-hapilon-is-islamic-state.

Allam, Hannah, and Mitchell Prothero. "Islamists Have Cornered Commandos Defending Iraq's Largest Refinery." McClatchy Washington Bureau, July 9, 2014. https://www.mcclatchydc.com/news/nation-world/world/article24770242.html.

Anderson, Jade. "The 36th Commando Battalion Evolution to the 1/1st ISOF Commando Battalion of Today." Unpublished article, December 6, 2019.

Ángel, Gabriel. "El Yarí, La Selva de La Guerra Contra Las Disidencias de Las FARC." *Poder, Las 2 Orillas*, February 11, 2019. https://www.las2orillas.co/el-yari-la-selva-de-la-guerra-contra-las-disidencias-de-las-farc/.

Antenori, Frank, and Hans Halberstadt. *Roughneck Nine-One: The Extraordinary Story of a Special Forces A-Team at War*. 1st edition. New York: St. Martin's Press, 2006.

Army.mil/News. "3rd Special Forces Group." Military.com, June 12, 2013. https://www.military.com/special-operations/3rd-special-forces-group.html.

Association of the United States Army. "DLI's Language Guidelines." AUSA.org, August 1, 2010. https://www.ausa.org/articles/dlis-language-guidelines.

Atlamazoglou, Stavros. "Best Non-US Special Operations Forces from around the World." *Business Insider*, updated November 24, 2022. https://www.businessinsider.com/best-non-us-special-operations-forces-from-around-the-world-2020-8.

Ball, Tim. "Talking the Talk: Language Capabilities for U.S. Army Special Forces." War on the Rocks, May 26, 2021. https://warontherocks.com/2021/05/talking-the-talk-language-capabilities-for-us-army-special-forces/.

Balestrieri, Steve. "Colombian SF Operators Win Fuerzas Commando 2019 Special Ops Competition." Special Operations Forces Report, SOFREP.com, June 30, 2019. https://sofrep.com/news/colombian-special-forces-operators-win-fuerzas-commando-2019-special-ops-competition/.

———. "March 13, 1981, US to Send 15 Green Beret Advisors to El Salvador." Special Operations Forces Report, SOFREP.com, March 13, 2021. https://sofrep

.com/specialoperations/march-13-1981-us-agrees-send-15-green-beret-advisors-el-salvador/.

———. "The Special Forces Branch Is Created April 9, 1987." Special Operations Forces Report, SOFREP.com, April 9, 2018. https://sofrep.com/specialoperations/special-forces-branch-is-created-april-9-1987/.

Bashir, Shahzad. "How Many Languages Are Spoken in Philippines?" Mars Translation, May 22, 2018. https://www.marstranslation.com/blog/how-many-languages-are-spoken-in-philippines.

Bauer, Shane. "Iraq's New Death Squad." The Nation, June 3, 2009. https://www.thenation.com/article/archive/iraqs-new-death-squad/.

Berrios, Carlos G. "Critical Ingredient: US Aid to Counterinsurgency in Colombia." *Small Wars and Insurgencies* 28, no. 3 (May 4, 2017): 546–75. https://doi.org/10.1080/09592318.2017.1307610.

Betancur, Belisario, Reinaldo Figueredo Planchart, and Thomas Buergenthal. "From Madness to Hope: The 12-Year War in El Salvador; Report of the Commission on the Truth for El Salvador." United Nations Security Council, April 1, 1993. Available online at https://archive.org/details/S25500EN.

Biddle, Stephen, Julia Macdonald, and Ryan Baker. "Small Footprint, Small Payoff: The Military Effectiveness of Security Force Assistance." Journal of Strategic Studies 41, nos. 1–2 (February 23, 2018): 89–142. https://doi.org/10.1080/01402390.2017.1307745.

Borger, Julian. "Leaked Memo Exposes Rumsfeld's Doubts about War on Terror." World news, *The Guardian*, October 22, 2003. https://www.theguardian.com/world/2003/oct/23/usa.julianborger.

Bouchard, Jay. "How 5 Kayakers Were Taken Hostage in Colombia by FARC Rebels." *Outside Online*, May 11, 2017. https://www.outsideonline.com/gallery/how-5-kayakers-were-taken-hostage-colombia-farc-rebels/.

Bradley, Rusty, and Kevin Maurer. *Lions of Kandahar: The Story of a Fight against All Odds*. 1st edition. New York: Bantam, 2011.

Briscoe, Charles H. "Barbula and Old Baldy, March 1953: Colombia's Heaviest Combat in Korea." *Veritas* 2, no. 4 (Winter 2006). https://arsof-history.org/articles/v2n4_barbula_old_bardy_page_1.html.

———. "Colombian Lancero School Roots." *Veritas* 2, no. 4 (Winter 2006). https://arsof-history.org/articles/v2n4_lancero_page_1.html.

———. "El Paraiso and the War in El Salvador: Part I (1981–1983)." *Veritas* 3, no. 1 (Summer 2007): 12. https://arsof-history.org/articles/v3n1_paraiso_page_1.html.

———. "Operation Willing Spirit (OWS): Setting Conditions for Operación Jaque." Veritas 14, no. 3 (Fall 2018). https://arsof-history.org/articles/v14n3_op_willing_spirit_page_1.html.

———. "San Miguel: The Attack on *El Bosque*." *Veritas* 3, no. 3 (Summer 2007). https://arsof-history.org/articles/v3n3_san_miguel_page_1.html.

Briscoe, Charles H., and Daniel J. Kulich. "Operación Jaque: The Ultimate Deception." *Veritas* 14, no. 3 (2018). https://arsof-history.org/articles/v14n3_op_jaque_page_1.html.

Britzky, Haley. "Casualties Reported after US Special Forces Team Ambushed in Afghanistan." *Task and Purpose*, February 8, 2020. https://taskandpurpose.com/news/afghanistan-nangarhar-attack-casualties/.

Burton, Janice. "1st Special Forces Group in the PACOM AOR." *Special Warfare* (January–March 2014.): 8–9. https://www.dvidshub.net/publication/issues/14790.

Bush, George W. Iraq speech, Fort Bragg, NC, June 28, 2005. Text archived at "Full Text: George Bush's Iraq Speech," World News, *The Guardian*, June 29, 2005. https://www.theguardian.com/world/2005/jun/29/iraq.usa.

CBS News. "Colombia to Aid US in Taliban Fight." CBS News.com, July 27, 2009.

Chelala, C'esar A. "Central America's Health Plight." *Christian Science Monitor*, March 22, 1990. https://www.csmonitor.com/1990/0322/echel.html.

Chingos, Matthew M., and Grover J. "Russ" Whitehurst. "Class Size: What Research Says and What It Means for State Policy." *Brookings* (blog), May 11, 2011. https://www.brookings.edu/research/class-size-what-research-says-and-what-it-means-for-state-policy/.

Clausewitz, Carl von. *On War*. Translated by Michael Eliot Howard and Peter Paret. Revised edition. Princeton, NJ: Princeton University Press, 1989.

Cleveland, Charles, and Daniel Egel. *The American Way of Irregular War: An Analytical Memoir*. Washington, DC: RAND Corporation, 2020. https://doi.org/10.7249/PEA301-1.

Combined Joint Special Operations Task Force Arabian Peninsula. Briefing on the 36th Iraqi Civil Defense Corps Battalion. Circa January 2004.

Connable, Ben, Michael McNerney, William Marcellino, Aaron Frank, Henry Hargrove, Marek Posard, S. Zimmerman, Natasha Lander, Jasen Castillo, and James Sladden. *Will to Fight: Analyzing, Modeling, and Simulating the Will to Fight of Military Units*. Washington, DC: RAND Corporation, 2018.

Constable, Pamela. "Death of Famed Afghan Cdr. in Taliban Massacre Highlights the Country's Struggles and Fears." Asia and Pacific, *Washington Post*, June 19, 2021. https://www.washingtonpost.com/world/asia_pacific/afghanistan-taliban-commando-killed/2021/06/19/ebd748fc-d03e-11eb-a224-bd59bd22197c_story.html.

Cooper, Helene. "Afghan Forces Are Praised, Despite Still Relying Heavily on U.S. Help." World, *New York Times*, August 20, 2017. https://www.nytimes.com/2017/08/20/world/asia/afghanistan-military-strategy.html.

Corado Figueroa, Humberto. *En Defensa de la Patria: Historia del Conflicto Armado en El Salvador, 1980–1992*. San Salvador, El Salvador: Universidad Tecnológica de El Salvador, 2008.

Coren, Anna, Sandi Sidhu, Tim Lister, and Abdul Basir Bina. "Taliban Fighters Execute 22 Afghan Commandos as They Try to Surrender." CNN.com, last updated July 14, 2021. https://www.cnn.com/2021/07/13/asia/afghanistan-taliban-commandos-killed-intl-hnk/index.html.

Corum, James S. "The Air War in El Salvador." *Airpower Journal* (Summer 1998): 27–44. Archived online at https://apps.dtic.mil/sti/pdfs/ADA356597.pdf.

Crichton, Jane. "U.S. Army Military Personnel Exchange Program in Colombia Strengthens Armies." Army.mil, May 25, 2011. https://www.army.mil/article/58119/u_s_army_military_personnel_exchange_program_in_colombia_strengthens_armies.

D'Haeseleer, Brian. *The Salvadoran Crucible: The Failure of U.S. Counterinsurgency in El Salvador, 1979–1992*. Lawrence: University Press of Kansas, 2017.

Donati, Jessica. *Eagle Down: The Last Special Forces Fighting the Forever War*. New York: PublicAffairs, 2021.

Downey, Dennis. "JTF 510/JSOTF-P 2002–2003 Locations." PowerPoint presentation, July 12, 2003.

Downie, Richard D. *Learning from Conflict: The U.S. Military in Vietnam, El Salvador, and the Drug War*. Westport, CT: Praeger, 1998.

Dryer, John. "A Brief History of the Military Advising Mission." *Small Wars Journal*, May 20, 2018. https://smallwarsjournal.com/jrnl/art/brief-history-military-advising-mission.

Duffy, Kieran. "The Korean Connection, Colombia in the Korean War." *Bogotá Post*, February 17, 2016.

Engel, Jacob M. "Why Does Culture 'Eat Strategy For Breakfast'?" *Forbes*, November 20, 2018. https://www.forbes.com/sites/forbescoachescouncil/2018/11/20/why-does-culture-eat-strategy-for-breakfast/.

Farley, Robert. "Can the U.S. Military Build an Army for a Foreign Country? Here Is What History Says." 1945.com, August 31, 2021. https://www.19fortyfive.com/2021/08/can-the-u-s-military-build-an-army-for-a-foreign-country-here-is-what-history-says/.

Finlayson, Kenneth. "Colombian Special Operations Forces." *Veritas* 2, no. 4 (Fall 2006). https://arsof-history.org/articles/v2n4_colombian_sof_page_1.html.

———. "OPATT to PATT: El Salvador to Colombia and the Formation of the Planning and Assistance Training Teams." *Veritas* 2, no. 4 (2006). https://arsof-history.org/articles/v2n4_patt_page_1.html.

Fish, Lauren and Paul Scharre. "The Soldier's Heavy Load." Report, Center for a New American Security, September 26, 2018. https://www.cnas.org/publications/reports/the-soldiers-heavy-load-1.

Galula, David. *Counterinsurgency Warfare: Theory and Practice.* New edition. Westport, CT: Praeger Security International, 2006.

George, Susannah. "With Less U.S. Tactical Support, Afghanistan's Elite Forces Are Struggling to Roll Back Taliban Advances." Asia and Pacific. *Washington Post*, March 7, 2021. https://www.washingtonpost.com/world/asia_pacific/afghanistan-taliban-battles-kandahar/2021/03/05/2d88fea4-777e-11eb-9489-8f7dacd51e75_story.html.

Gibbons-Neff, Thomas, Fahim Abed, and Jim Huylebroek. "On Afghanistan's Front Line, There Are No Good Choices." World, *New York Times*, August 9, 2021. https://www.nytimes.com/2021/08/09/world/asia/Afghanistan-taliban-kandahar.html.

Gittler, Juliana. "Philippine Soldiers Show Off What They Learned from the Green Berets." *Stars and Stripes*, December 14, 2003. https://www.stripes.com/news/philippine-soldiers-showoff-what-they-learned-from-the-green-berets-1.14479.

GlobalSecurity.org. "Afghan National Army (ANA)—Order of Battle." Military, GlobalSecurity.org, n.d. https://www.globalsecurity.org/military/world/afghanistan/ana-orbat.htm. Accessed June 16, 2021.

———. "ANA Commandos." Military, GlobalSecurity.org, n.d. https://www.globalsecurity.org/military/world/afghanistan/comando.htm. Accessed June 16, 2021.

———. "ANA Special Operations Command (ANASOC)." Military, GlobalSecurity.org, n.d. https://www.globalsecurity.org/military/world/afghanistan/anasoc.htm.

Graham, Bradley. "Public Honors for Secret Combat." *Washington Post*, May 6, 1996.

Guttman, Jon. "Seeking information on Columbia [sic] in the Korean War." *HistoryNet*, May 28, 2013. https://www.historynet.com/seeking-information-on-columbia-in-the-korean-war.htm.

Helmus, Todd C. *Advising the Command: Best Practices from the Special Operation's Advisory Experience in Afghanistan.* Santa Monica, CA: RAND, 2015.

Huylebroek, Jim. "On the Front Line: A Night with Afghan Commandos." World, *New York Times*, June 25, 2021. https://www.nytimes.com/2021/06/25/world/asia/afghan-commandos-helmand.html.

Indo-Pacific Defense Forum staff. "Lessons from Marawi: Retired Lt. Gen. Danilo G. Pamonag Shares What He Learned from the Philippines' Largest Military Engagement since World War II." *Indo-Pacific Defense Forum* (blog), March 23, 2020. https://ipdefenseforum.com/2020/03/lessons-from-marawi/.

Interagency Language Roundtable. "Interagency Language Roundtable Language Skill Level Descriptions—Reading." GovILR.org, U.S. Government, n.d. https://www.govtilr.org/Skills/ILRscale4.htm. Accessed April 6, 2021.

Joint Task Force Comet, Western Mindanao Command, Armed Forces of the Philippines. "Plan Ultimatum: An Overview." After-action review, headquarters, undated (November 2007?).

Joint U.S. Military Assistance Group. "Republic of the Philippines Security Assistance Program Update." PowerPoint briefing, June 9, 2004.

Kaplan, Robert D. *Imperial Grunts: On the Ground with the American Military from Mogadishu to the Philippines to Iraq and Beyond.* New York: Random House, 2005.

King, Anthony. "On Combat Effectiveness in the Infantry Platoon: Beyond the Primary Group Thesis." *Security Studies* 25, no. 4 (2016): 699–728. https://doi.org/10.1080/09636412.2016.1220205.

Kissinger, Henry A. "The Viet Nam Negotiations." *Foreign Affairs* 47, no. 2 (January 1969): 211–34. https://www.foreignaffairs.com/articles/asia/1969-01-01/viet-nam-negotiations (paywall).

Knights, Michael, and Alex Mello. "The Best Thing America Built in Iraq: Iraq's Counter-Terrorism Service and the Long War against Militancy." *War on the Rocks*, July 19, 2017. https://warontherocks.com/2017/07/the-best-thing-america-built-in-iraq-iraqs-counter-terrorism-service-and-the-long-war-against-militancy/.

Kyodo News. "Lessons Learned from Marawi Siege, Government Officials Say." ABS-CBN News, May 24, 2018. https://news.abs-cbn.com/news/05/24/18/lessons-learned-from-marawi-siege-govt-officials-say.

La Nueva Televisión del Sur C.A. "When Colombia Bombed Ecuador: The Killing of Raul Reyes," February 28, 2016. https://www.telesurenglish.net/news/When-Colombia-Bombed-Ecuador-The-Killing-of-Raul-Reyes-20160228-0009.html.

Lamothe, Dan. "Afghanistan Is Building Up Its Commando Force to Fight the Taliban. But at What Cost?" Asia and Pacific, *Washington Post*, April 28, 2018. https://www.washingtonpost.com/world/asia_pacific/afghanistan-is-building-up-its-commando-force-to-fight-the-taliban-but-at-what-cost/2018/04/27/dd1c0c1c-44cd-11e8-b2dc-b0a403e4720a_story.html.

Lemoyne, James. "Rebels Kill 43 Salvador Troops and U.S. Adviser." *New York Times*, April 1, 1987, sec. A1, A10. https://www.nytimes.com/1987/04/01/world/rebels-kill-43-salvador-troops-and-us-adviser.html.

Lewis, James. "The Battle of Marawi: Small Team Lessons Learned for the Close Fight." *Small Wars Journal*, January 23, 2019. https://smallwarsjournal.com/blog/battle-marawi-small-team-lessons-learned-close-fight.

Long, Austin, Todd Helmus, S. Zimmerman, Christopher Schnaubelt, and Peter Chalk. *Building Special Operations Partnerships in Afghanistan and Beyond: Challenges and Best Practices from Afghanistan, Iraq, and Colombia*. Santa Monica, CA: RAND Corporation, 2015.

Loveluck, Louisa, and Mustafa Salim. "Hunting ISIS: On a Nighttime Raid with Iraqi Special Forces." *Washington Post*, February 3, 2021. https://www.washingtonpost.com/world/2021/02/03/iraq-isis-american-troops-counterterrorism/.

Mahnken, Thomas G., ed. *Learning the Lessons of Modern War*. 1st edition. Stanford, CA: Stanford University Press, 2020.

Malkasian, Carter. "How the Good War Went Bad: America's Slow-Motion Failure in Afghanistan." *Foreign Affairs* 99, no. 2 (March/April 2020). https://www.foreignaffairs.com/articles/afghanistan/2020-02-10/how-good-war-went-bad.

Mao, Tse-tung, trans. by Samuel B. Griffith. *On Guerrilla Warfare*. 2nd revised edition. Urbana: University of Illinois Press, 2000 [1937].

Marks, Thomas A. "A Model Counterinsurgency: Uribe's Colombia (2002–2006) vs FARC." *Military Review* (March–April 2007): 41–56. https://www.armyupress.army.mil/Portals/7/military-review/Archives/English/MilitaryReview_20070430_art010.pdf.

Maxwell, David S. "Commander's Summary of Operations OEF-P." Col. David Maxwell, Cdr., 1st Battalion, 1st Special Forces Group. May 5, 2002.

———. "Foreign Internal Defense: An Indirect Approach to Counter-insurgency/Counter Terrorism; Lessons from Operation Enduring Freedom–Philippines for Dealing with Non-existential Threats to the United States," presentation given at Irregular Warfare Challenges and Opportunities, conference of the Foreign Policy Research Institute, Washington, DC, December 6, 2011. https://www.phibetaiota.net/wp-content/uploads/2016/10/Maxwell-OEF-P-Final-.pdf.

———. "Joint Special Operations Task Force Philippines (JSOTF-P): A Special Warfare Approach to Counterinsurgency and Counterterrorism." PowerPoint briefing, September 24, 2008.

———. "Operation Enduring Freedom–Philippines: What Would Sun Tzu Say?" *Military Review* 84, no. 3 (May–June 2004): 20–23. https://www.armyupress.army.mil/Portals/7/military-review/Archives/English/100-Landing/Topics-Interest/Deployments/docs/Operation%20Enduring%20Freedom-2004.pdf.

McChrystal, Stanley. *My Share of the Task: A Memoir*. New York: Portfolio, 2014.

McCurdy, Daphne, and Nick Lopez. "Institution Building as a Counterinsurgency Tool: The Case of Colombia." *Irregular Warfare Podcast*, Modern War Institute, January 29, 2021. https://mwi.westpoint.edu/institution-building-as-a-counterinsurgency-tool-the-case-of-colombia/.

McFate, Sean. "Shifting the Blame: How the Pentagon Lost Afghanistan." Opinion, *The Hill*, August 17, 2021. https://thehill.com/opinion/national-security/568102-shifting-the-blame-how-the-pentagon-lost-afghanistan.

McKay, Hollie. "Exclusive: Embedded with the Last Afghan Special Forces Team in Mazar-i-Sharif." Intel, *Coffee or Die Magazine* (blog), August 22, 2021. https://coffeeordie.com/afghan-special-forces-mazar/.

Moran, Charles McMoran Wilson. *The Anatomy of Courage: The Classic WWI Account of the Psychological Effects of War.* 1st edition. New York: Carroll and Graf, 2007.

Morris, Loveday. "The Force Leading the Iraq Army's Fight against ISIS Went from 'Dirty Division' to Golden Boys." Middle East, *Washington Post*, July 26, 2016. https://www.washingtonpost.com/world/middle_east/the-force-leading-the-iraqi-militarys-fight-against-isis-went-from-dirty-division-to-golden-boys/2016/07/25/8e6b0164-389e-11e6-af02-1df55f0c77ff_story.html.

Morris, Loveday, and Mustafa Salim. "Chaos in Iraqi Forces Contributed to Islamic State's Biggest Win This Year." Middle East, *Washington Post*, May 23, 2015. https://www.washingtonpost.com/world/middle_east/chaos-in-iraqi-forces-contributed-to-islamic-states-biggest-win-this-year/2015/05/22/cf4e000e-ffd4-11e4-8c77-bf274685e1df_story.html.

Moyar, Mark, Hector Pagan, and Wil R. Griego. *Persistent Engagement in Colombia.* Tampa, FL: Joint Special Operations University, 2019.

Murphy, Jack. "SOFREP Exclusive: Inside the Operations of the Light Reaction Regiment (Part 3)." Special Operations Forces Report, Special Operations Forces Report, SOFREP.com, June 16, 2017. https://sofrep.com/news/sofrep-exclusive-inside-operations-light-reaction-regiment-part-3/.

———. "SOFREP Exclusive: Marawi Commander Details What Really Happened in His Country's Largest Terrorist Attack and How His Men Fought Back." Special Operations Forces Report, SOFREP.com, December 14, 2017. https://sofrep.com/news/sofrep-exclusive-marawi-commander-details-what-really-happened-in-his-countrys-largest-terrorist-attack-and-how-his-men-fought-back/.

———. "Special Forces to Disband the Commanders—in-Extremis—Force (CIF)." *Jack Murphy Writes*, March 5, 2020. https://jackmurphywrites.com/153/special-forces-commanders-in-extremis-force-no-more/.

Naquin, Nicholas. "Learning the Lancero Way: U.S. Helped Develop Elite Colombian Training." AUSA, March 2, 2020. https://www.ausa.org/articles/learning-lancero-way-us-helped-develop-elite-colombian-training.

Nordland, Rod. "Taliban End Takeover of Kunduz after 15 Days." Asia Pacific, *New York Times*, October 13, 2015. https://www.nytimes.com/2015/10/14/world/asia/taliban-afghanistan-kunduz.html.

North, Douglass C., John Joseph Wallis, and Barry R. Weingast. *Violence and Social Orders: A Conceptual Framework for Interpreting Recorded Human History*. Reprint edition. Cambridge: Cambridge University Press, 2012.

Parameswaran, Prashanth. "What's in the New Philippines Special Operations Command?" *The Diplomat*, April 13, 2018. https://thediplomat.com/2018/04/whats-in-the-new-philippines-special-operations-command/.

Paterson, Patrick. *Training Surrogate Forces in International Humanitarian Law: Lessons from Peru, Colombia, El Salvador, and Iraq*. Tampa, FL: Joint Special Operations University, 2016.

Petit, Brian S. *Going Big by Getting Small: The Application of Operational Art by Special Operations in Phase Zero*. Denver: Outskirts Press, 2013.

Priest, Dana. "Covert Action in Colombia." *Washington Post*, December 21, 2013. https://www.washingtonpost.com/sf/investigative/2013/12/21/covert-action-in-colombia/.

Popik, Barry. "Amateurs Talk Strategy. Professionals Talk Logistics." BarryPopik.com, June 19, 2019. https://www.barrypopik.com/index.php/new_york_city/entry/amateurs_talk_strategy.

Ramsey, Robert D., III. *Advice for Advisors: Suggestions and Observations from Lawrence to the Present*. Global War on Terrorism Occasional Paper 19. Fort Leavenworth, KS: Combat Studies Inst. Press, 2006.

———. *Advising Indigenous Forces: American Advisors in Korea, Vietnam, and El Salvador*. Leavenworth, KS: Combat Studies Institute Press, 2012.

———. *From El Billar to Operations Fenix and Jaque: The Colombian Security Force Experience, 1998–2008*. Fort Leavenworth, KS: Combat Studies Institute Press, 2009.

Rayburn, Joel D., and Frank K. Sobchak, eds. *The U.S. Army in the Iraq War, Volume 1: Invasion, Insurgency, Civil War, 2003–2006*. Carlisle, PA: Strategic Studies Institute, U.S. Army War College, 2019.

———. eds. *The U.S. Army in the Iraq War: Volume 2, Surge and Withdrawal, 2007–2011*. Carlisle, PA: Strategic Studies Institute, U.S. Army War College, 2019.

Rempfer, Kyle. "New Force Generation Model Aims to Regionally Align Army Units, Give Troops Predictability." *Army Times*, October 19, 2020. https://www.armytimes.com/news/your-army/2020/10/14/new-force-generation-model-aims-to-regionally-align-army-units-give-troops-predictability/.

Resolute Support Public Affairs Office. "Press Conference Statement by General John Nicholson, Commander, NATO Resolute Support Mission and Resolute Support Public Affairs Office." Press release, U.S. Central Command, August 24, 2017. https://www.centcom.mil/MEDIA/PRESSRELEASES/Press-Release-View/Article/1287992/press-conference-statement-by-general-john-nicholson-commander-nato-resolute-su/.

Robinson, Linda, Patrick Johnston, and Gillian Oak. *U.S. Special Operations Forces in the Philippines, 2001–2014*. Washington, DC: RAND Corporation, 2016.

Robinson, Linda, Austin Long, Kimberly Jackson, and Rebeca Orrie. *Improving the Understanding of Special Operations: A Case History Analysis*. Santa Monica, CA: RAND Corporation, 2018.

Roggio, Bill. "Taliban Doubles Number of Controlled Afghan Districts since May 1." *Long War Journal*, June 29, 2021. https://www.longwarjournal.org/archives/2021/06/taliban-doubles-number-of-controlled-afghan-districts-since-may-1.php.

Sahak, Sami, Wali Arian, and Jim Huylebroek. "Taliban Claim Control over Panjshir Valley, but Resistance Vows to Fight On." World, *New York Times*, September 6, 2021. https://www.nytimes.com/2021/09/06/world/asia/afghanistan-panjshir-taliban-resistance.html.

Sands, Robert R. Greene. *Assessing Special Operations Forces Language, Region, and Culture Needs: Leveraging Digital and LRC Learning to Reroute the "Roadmap" from Human Terrain to Human Domain*. MacDill Air Force Base, FL: The JSOU Press, 2016.

Sarhaddi Nelson, Soraya. "New Afghan Commandos Take to the Frontlines." *Morning Edition*, NPR.org, July 23, 2007. https://www.npr.org/2007/07/23/12127848/new-afghan-commandos-take-to-the-frontlines.

Shultz, Richard H., Jr., and Joseph L. Votel. *Transforming US Intelligence for Irregular War: Task Force 714 in Iraq*. Reprint edition. Washington, DC: Georgetown University Press, 2020.

Simpson, J. M. "1st Special Forces Group (Airborne) Celebrates 30th Anniversary of Unit Reactivation." NorthwestMilitary.com, September 5, 2014. http://www.northwestmilitary.com/news/news-front/2014/09/1st-Special-Forces-Group-Airborne-celebrates-30th-anniversary-of-unit-reactivation-at-Joint-Base-Lew/.

Slattery, Angie. "Interview with LTC Eric Walker." Combat Studies Institute, Fort Leavenworth, KS, April 20, 2010. Available for download at https://cgsc.contentdm.oclc.org/digital/api/collection/p4013coll13/id/1902/download.

Snow, Shawn, Leo Shane III, and Joe Gould. "Afghan Special Operators Partnering with US Forces More Often, Still Reliant on American Support." *Military Times*, February 5, 2020. https://www.militarytimes.com/flashpoints/2020/02/05/afghan-special-operators-partnering-with-us-forces-more-often-still-reliant-on-american-support/.

Special Warfare. "Interview: Special Forces in El Salvador." With Lt. Col. Geoffrey Lambert, Lt. Col. Frank Pedrozo, and Col. J. S. Roach. *Special Warfare* 6, no. 4 (October 1993): 34–38. https://www.dvidshub.net/publication/issues/8284.

———. "Q&A: Brigadier General Edward M. Reeder Jr." *Special Warfare* 24, no. 4 (October–December 2011): 20–21. https://www.dvidshub.net/publication/issues/9449.

———. "USPACOM Area of Responsibility." *Special Warfare* (January–March 2014): 8–9. https://www.dvidshub.net/publication/issues/14790.

Spencer, David. "The Sword of Honor Campaign in the Cauca Valley: 2011–2013 Colombian Conflict Focus of Effort." *Small Wars Journal*, May 31, 2013. https://smallwarsjournal.com/jrnl/art/the-sword-of-honor-campaign-in-the-cauca-valley-2011-2013-colombian-conflict-focus-of-effor.

Stöhs, Jeremy. "Built to Fail: The Iraqi Army from Invasion to the Rise of the Islamic State." *Journal for Intelligence, Propaganda, and Security Studies* 11, no. 2 (Spring 2017): 145–56.

Stoker, Donald, ed. *Military Advising and Assistance*. 1st edition. London: Routledge, 2008.

Sullivan, Marisa. *Maliki's Authoritarian Regime*. Middle East Security Report 10. Washington, DC: Institute for the Study of War, April 2013. https://www.understandingwar.org/sites/default/files/Malikis-Authoritarian-Regime-Web.pdf.

Swain, Richard. *Case Study: Operation Enduring Freedom Philippines*: Fort Belvoir, VA: Defense Technical Information Center, October 1, 2010.

Taylor, Alan. "Bloody Philippine Siege Brought to an End." In Focus. *The Atlantic*, September 30, 2013. https://www.theatlantic.com/photo/2013/09/bloody-philippine-siege-brought-to-an-end/100599/.

Tecott, Rachel. "Why America Can't Build Allied Armies." *Foreign Affairs*, August 26, 2021. https://www.foreignaffairs.com/articles/united-states/2021-08-26/why-america-cant-build-allied-armies.

Tollast, Robert. "SOF, COIN, and the Question of Host Nation Viability: An Interview with Dick Couch." *Small Wars Journal*, July 1, 2013. https://smallwarsjournal.com/jrnl/art/sof-coin-and-the-question-of-host-nation-viability-an-interview-with-dick-couch.

Trinquier, Roger. *Modern Warfare: A French View of Counterinsurgency*. 1st edition. Westport, CT: Praeger, 2006 [1961].

UNESCO Institute for Statistics. "Literacy Rate, Adult Total (% of People Ages 15 and above)—Afghanistan." The World Bank, September 2020. https://data.worldbank.org/indicator/SE.ADT.LITR.ZS?end=2018&locations=AF&start=1979.

U.S. Army. *Security Force Assistance Brigade*. Army Techniques Publication 3-96.1. Fort Benning, GA: U.S. Department of the Army, September 2, 2020. https://armypubs.army.mil/epubs/DR_pubs/DR_a/ARN30336-ATP_3-96.1-000-WEB-1.pdf.

U.S. Army Special Forces Command. "El Salvador Awards Ceremony." Original pamphlet, June 12, 1998. Author's private collection.

———. "USASFC(A) Policy 350–1–14: Command Language Program." July 9, 2014.

U.S. Army Special Forces, Forward Operating Base 51, 1st Battalion, 5th Special Forces Group. "The 36th Commando Battalion." PowerPoint presentation, September 6, 2004.

U.S. Army Special Operations Command. "ARSOF and Operation Willing Spirit 2003–08, An Operational Analysis." White paper, May 2018.

U.S. Army Special Operations Command, 1st Special Forces Command. "Language, Regional Expertise, and Culture Capability (LREC) Executive Summary." PowerPoint presentation, November 21, 2022.

U.S. Central Intelligence Agency. "Afghanistan: People and Society." *The World Factbook*, CIA.gov, last updated January 17, 2024. https://www.cia.gov/the-world-factbook/countries/afghanistan/#people-and-society.

U.S. Department of the Army. *Security Force Assistance*. Field Manual 3-07.1. Washington, DC: U.S. Department of the Army, May 2011.

———. *Special Forces Operations*. Field Manual 3-05.20 (FM 31-20). Washington, DC: U.S. Department of the Army, June 2001. Archived online at https://irp.fas.org/doddir/army/fm3-05-20.pdf.

———. *Tactics in Counterinsurgency*. Field Manual no. 3-24.2 (FM 90-8, FM 7-98). Washington, DC: Department of the Army, April 21, 2009. Archived online at https://irp.fas.org/doddir/army/fm3-24-2.pdf.

U.S. Government Accountability Office. "Special Operations Forces: Opportunities Exist to Improve Transparency of Funding and Assess Potential to Lessen Some Deployments." GAO 15-571, report to congressional committees, Washington, DC, July 2015. https://www.gao.gov/assets/680/671920.pdf.

U.S. Joint Chiefs of Staff. *Counterinsurgency*. Joint publication 3-24. Washington, DC: U.S. Department of Defense, April 25, 2018. Archived online at https://irp.fas.org/doddir/dod/jp3_24.pdf.

U.S. Special Operations Command, U.S. Department of Defense. *Fiscal Year (FY) 2021 Budget Estimates: Operation and Maintenance, Defense-Wide United States Special Operations Command*. Washington, DC: U.S. Department of Defense, February 2020. https://comptroller.defense.gov/Portals/45/Documents/defbudget/fy2021/budget_justification/pdfs/01_Operation_and_Maintenance/O_M_VOL_1_PART_1/SOCOM_OP-5.pdf.

———. "SOF Truths." N.d. Archived online at https://www.socom.mil/about/sof-truths.

Utterback, Mitch. "Up to the Sniper Line." *Mitch Utterback: A Veteran in Transition*, April 30, 2017. https://mitchutterback.wordpress.com/2017/04/30/up-to-the-sniper-line/.

———. "What the Fight against ISIS Is Actually like on the Iraqi Frontlines." *Athlon Outdoors* (blog), May 13, 2020. https://www.athlonoutdoors.com/article/frontlines-fight-against-isis/.

Vallejo, Pedro. "Organización CCOES." PowerPoint presentation, Comando Conjunto de Operaciones Especiales (CCOES), February 15, 2021.

Witty, David [M]. *The Iraqi Counter Terrorism Service*. Washington, DC: The Center for Middle East Policy at Brookings Institution, 2016.

———. *Iraq's Post-2014 Counter Terrorism Service*. Policy Focus 157. Washington, DC: The Washington Institute for Near East Policy, October 2018. https://www.washingtoninstitute.org/media/1293.

———. "Remembering Maj. Gen. Fadhil Barwari—ISOF Commander" *SOF News*, September 25, 2018. https://sof.news/iraq/mg-fadhil-al-barwari/.

World Bank. "El Salvador Literacy Rate 1992–2021." Archived online at Macrotrends, Macrotrends.net, n.d. https://www.macrotrends.net/countries/SLV/el-salvador/literacy-rate. Accessed October 6, 2021.

ADDITIONAL SOURCES CONSULTED

Abbas, Yasir, and Dan Trombly. "Inside the Collapse of the Iraqi Army's 2nd Division." *War on the Rocks*, July 1, 2014. https://warontherocks.com/2014/07/inside-the-collapse-of-the-iraqi-armys-2nd-division/.

Adamsky, Dima. *The Culture of Military Innovation: The Impact of Cultural Factors on the Revolution in Military Affairs in Russia, the US, and Israel*. 1st edition. Stanford, CA: Stanford University Press, 2010.

Amon, Robert R. *Rice Roots: The Vietnam War; True Stories from the Diary of a U.S. Combat Advisor*. St. Augustine, FL: Legacies and Memories, 2020.

Bacevich, Andrew J., James Hallums, Richard White, and Thomas Young. *American Military Policy in Small Wars: The Case of El Salvador*. Washington, DC: Pergamon-Brassey's, 1988.

Bailey, Cecil. "OPATT: The U.S. Army SF Advisers in El Salvador." *Special Warfare* 17, no. 2 (December 2004): 18–29. https://www.dvidshub.net/publication/issues/8230.

Barnett, Paul. "If What Gets Measured Gets Managed, Measuring the Wrong Thing Matters." *Corporate Finance Review* 19, no. 4 (2015): 5–10.

Bendickson, Josh, Jeff Muldoon, Eric W. Liguori, and Phillip E. Davis. "Agency Theory: Background and Epistemology." *Journal of Management History* 22, no. 4 (2016): 437–49.

Betts, Richard K. *Military Readiness: Concepts, Choices, Consequences*. Washington, DC: Brookings Institution Press, 1995.

Biddle, Stephen. *Military Power: Explaining Victory and Defeat in Modern Battle*. Princeton, NJ: Princeton University Press, 2006.

Blanken, Leo J., Hy Rothstein, and Jason J. Lepore, eds. *Assessing War: The Challenge of Measuring Success and Failure*. Washington, DC: Georgetown University Press, 2015.

Bolton, Stephan R. "Partners of Choice and Necessity: Special Operations Forces and the National Security Imperatives of Building Partner Capacity." Master's thesis, U.S. Army Command and General Staff College, 2015. Available online at https://apps.dtic.mil/sti/tr/pdf/AD1001244.pdf.

Boot, Max, and Richard Bennet. "Treading Softly in the Philippines." *The Weekly Standard* 14, no. 16 (2009): 22–28.

Bosse, Douglas A., and Robert A. Phillips. "Agency Theory and Bounded Self-Interest." *Academy of Management Review* 41, no. 2 (2016): 276–97.

Bovens, Mark, Robert E. Goodin, and Thomas Schillemans, eds. *The Oxford Handbook of Public Accountability*. Reprint edition. Oxford: Oxford University Press, 2016.

Brady, Adam R., and Terence L. Satchell. "Security Force Assistance and the Concept of Sustainable Training as a Role for the U.S. Military in Today's World." *Military Review*, online exclusive, January 22, 2016. https://www.armyupress.army.mil/Journals/Military-Review/Online-Exclusive/2016-Online-Exclusive-Articles/Security-Force-Assistance/.

Briscoe, Charles H. "Balikatan Exercise Spearheaded ARSOF Operations in the Philippines." *Special Warfare* 17, no. 1 (September 2004): 16–25. https://www.dvidshub.net/publication/issues/8225.

———. "*Los Artefactos Explosivos*: Improvised Explosive Devices in El Salvador." *Veritas* 2, no. 1 (2006): 7. https://arsof-history.org/articles/v2n1_artefactos_explosivos_page_1.html.

———. "Reflections and Observations on ARSOF Operations during Balikatan 02-1." *Special Warfare* 17, no. 1 (September 2004): 55–57. https://www.dvidshub.net/publication/issues/8225.

Briscoe, Charles H., Kenneth Finlayson, Robert W. Jones, Cherilyn Walley, Dwayne Aaron, Michael Mullins, and James A. Schroder. *All Roads Lead to Baghdad: Army Special Operations Forces in Iraq*. Fort Bragg, NC: USASOC History Office, 2007.

Briscoe, Charles H., Richard L. Kiper, James A. Schroder, and Kalev I. Sepp. *Weapon of Choice: U.S. Army Special Operations Forces in Afghanistan*. Leavenworth, KS: Combat Studies Institute Press, 2003.

Bruneau, Thomas. "Challenges in Building Partner Capacity: Civil-Military Relations in the United States and New Democracies." *Small Wars and Insurgencies* 26, no. 3 (2015): 429–45.

Burton, Janice. "ARSOF in Colombia: 50 Years of Persistent Engagement." *Special Warfare* 25, no. 4 (December 2012): 24–33. https://www.dvidshub.net/publication/issues/10975.

Buswell, Philip A. "Keeping Special Forces Special: Regional Proficiency in Special Forces." Master's thesis, Naval Postgraduate School, 2011.

Cachero, Paulina. "US Taxpayers Have Spent Over $2 Trillion for the Iraq War, Report Says." *Business Insider*, February 6, 2020. https://www.businessinsider.com/us-taxpayers-spent-8000-each-2-trillion-iraq-war-study-2020-2.

Campbell, Jason, Richard Girven, Ben Connable, Jonah Blank, Raphael Cohen, Larry Hanauer, William Young, Linda Robinson, and Sean Mann. *Implications of the Security Cooperation Office Transition in Afghanistan for Special Operations Forces: An Abbreviated Report of the Study's Primary Findings*. Santa Monica, CA: RAND Corporation, 2017. https://doi.org/10.7249/RR1201.1.

Carlton, Charles A. Interview with Col. Joseph S. Stringham, Cdr., U.S. Military Group–El Salvador, Carlisle Barracks, PA, May 29, 1985. Archived by the U.S. Army Military History Institute, Oral History Program.

Castillo, Jasen J. *Endurance and War: The National Sources of Military Cohesion*. 1st edition. Stanford, CA: Stanford Security Studies, 2014.

Childress, Michael. *The Effectiveness of U.S. Training Efforts in Internal Defense and Development: The Cases of El Salvador and Honduras*. Washington, DC: RAND, 1995. https://www.rand.org/pubs/monograph_reports/MR250.html.

Clarke, Duncan L., Jason D. Ellis, and Daniel B. O'Connor. *Send Guns and Money: Security Assistance and U.S. Foreign Policy*. Westport, CT: Praeger, 1997.

Collins, Patrick. "Cdr.'s Summary of the Joint Special Operations Task Force Philippines (JSOTF-P) 2006–2007." Joint Special Operations Task Force Philippines, December 31, 2009.

Cordesman, Anthony H. *Iraqi Security Forces: A Strategy for Success*. 1st edition. Westport, CT: Praeger, 2005.

Crandall, Russell. *The Salvador Option: The United States in El Salvador, 1977–1992*. New York: Cambridge University Press, 2016.

Crocker, George. Interview of Lt. Col. Peter E. Reilly, Cdr. Salvadoran Training Center, 1987. US Army Military History Institute.

Csicsila, Michael A. "Using BATs, CATs, and RATs to Defeat Transnational Terrorists and Control Ungoverned Space." Monograph, School of Advanced Military Studies, 2006. https://apps.dtic.mil/sti/tr/pdf/ADA449943.pdf.

Dear, Keith Patrick. "Beheading the Hydra? Does Killing Terrorist or Insurgent Leaders Work?" *Defence Studies* 13, no. 3 (September 2013): 293–337.

D'Haeseleer, Brian. "'Drawing the Line' in El Salvador: Washington Confronts Insurgency in El Salvador, 1979–92." *Cold War History* 18, no. 2 (2018): 131–48.

Donovan, David. *Once a Warrior King: Memories of an Officer in Vietnam*. New York: Ballantine Books, 1986.

Dorn, Nancy. "El Salvador Training." January 10, 1990. Digital National Security Archive, El Salvador 1980–1994. http://search.proquest.com/docview/1679115717/.

Eisenhardt, Kathleen. "Agency Theory: An Assessment and Review." *The Academy of Management Review* 14, no. 1 (1989): 57–74.

Faint, Charles, and Michael Harris. "F3EAD: Opsintel-Fusion 'Feeds' the SOF Targeting Process." *Small Wars Journal*, January 31, 2012. https://smallwarsjournal.com/jrnl/art/f3ead-opsintel-fusion-%E2%80%9Cfeeds%E2%80%9D-the-sof-targeting-process.

Farris, Stuart L. "Joint Special Operations Task Force–Philippines." Monograph, School of Advanced Military Studies, 2009. https://apps.dtic.mil/sti/pdfs/ADA505075.pdf.

Faunce, John. "A History of Assessment and Selection." *Special Warfare* 29, no. 2 (July–December 2016): 12–18. https://www.dvidshub.net/publication/issues/46546.

Finlayson, Kenneth. "Army Special Operations Forces (ARSOF) in Colombia: Introduction." *Veritas* 2, no. 4 (2006). https://arsof-history.org/articles/v2n4_colombia_page_1.html.

———. "'Conducting the Orchestra': AOB 740 in Colombia." *Veritas* 2, no. 4 (Fall 2006). https://arsof-history.org/articles/v2n4_conducting_orchestra_page_1.html.

Forero, Juan. "In Colombia Jungle Ruse, U.S. Played A Quiet Role." *Washington Post*, July 9, 2008.

Gordon, Michael R., and Bernard E. Trainor. *The Endgame: The Inside Story of the Struggle for Iraq, from George W. Bush to Barack Obama*. Reprint edition. New York: Vintage, 2013.

Grauer, Ryan. *Commanding Military Power: Organizing for Victory and Defeat on the Battlefield*. Cambridge: Cambridge University Press, 2016.

Gray, Wesley. *Embedded: A Marine Corps Adviser Inside the Iraqi Army*. First edition. Annapolis, MD: Naval Institute Press, 2009.

Hamilton, Donald R. "El Salvador in the 1980s: War by Other Means." Newport, RI: U.S. Naval War College, June 2015.

Hanlon, Querine, and Richard H. Shultz. *Prioritizing Security Sector Reform: A New U.S. Approach*. Washington, DC: United States Institute of Peace, 2016.

Hastings, Jonathan P, and Krishnamurti Mortela. "The Strategy-Legitimacy Paradigm: Getting It Right in the Philippines." Naval Postgraduate School, 2008.

Herd, Walter M. "Current Unconventional Warfare Capability versus Future War Requirements." Fort Belvoir, VA: Defense Technical Information Center, April 9, 2002.

Hitt, Michael A., Kai Xu, and Christina Matz Carnes. "Resource Based Theory in Operations Management Research." *Journal of Operations Management* 41, no. 1 (January 2016): 77–94. https://doi.org/10.1016/j.jom.2015.11.002.
Jayamaha, Buddhika B., and Jahara W. Matisek. "The Crisis of Security Sector Reform in Fragmented States: Oligopolies, Duopolies, and Monopolies of Violence." Political Science working paper, Northwestern University, January 16, 2018. https://polisci.northwestern.edu/documents/Matisek-ESOC-paper.pdf.
Jenkins, Derek C. "Distinguishing between Security Force Assistance and Foreign Internal Defense: Determining a Doctrine Road-Ahead." *Small Wars Journal*, December 10, 2008. https://smallwarsjournal.com/blog/journal/docs-temp/146-jenkins.pdf.
Jensen, Michael C., and William H. Meckling. "Theory of the Firm: Managerial Behavior, Agency Costs and Ownership Structure." *Journal of Financial Economics* 3, no. 4 (October 1976): 305–60. https://doi.org/10.1016/0304-405X(76)90026-X.
Jones, Robert W., Jr. "Plan Colombia and Plan Patriota: The Evolution of Colombia's National Strategy." *Veritas* 2, no. 4 (2006). https://arsof-history.org/articles/v2n4_plan_colombia_page_1.html.
Karlin, Mara E. *Building Militaries in Fragile States: Challenges for the United States*. Philadelphia: University of Pennsylvania Press, 2018.
Kelly, Terrence K., Nora Bensahel, and Olga Oliker. *Security Force Assistance in Afghanistan: Identifying Lessons for Future Efforts*. Santa Monica, CA: RAND Corporation, 2011.
Kilcullen, David. *The Accidental Guerrilla: Fighting Small Wars in the Midst of a Big One*. 1st edition. Oxford: Oxford University Press, 2009.
Kirila, Robert M. "Ahead of the Guns: SOF in Central America." *Special Warfare* 25, no. 4 (October–December 2012): 15–21. https://www.dvidshub.net/publication/issues/10975.
Kirsch, Christina, John Chelliah, and Parry Warren. "The Impact of Cross-cultural Dynamics on Change Management." *Cross Cultural Management: An International Journal* 19, no. 2 (2012). https://doi.org/10.1108/13527601211219865.
Knarr, William. *Village Stability Operations and the Evolution of SOF Command and Control in Afghanistan: Implications for the Future of Irregular Warfare*. Tampa, FL: Joint Special Operations University, 2020.
Knox, MacGregor, and Williamson Murray, eds. *The Dynamics of Military Revolution, 1300–2050*. 1st edition. Cambridge: Cambridge University Press, 2001.
Koven, Barnett S. "Competing with Great Powers through Competitive Strategy and Unconventional Warfare." *Special Operations Journal* 7, no. 1 (January 2, 2021): 68–86. https://doi.org/10.1080/23296151.2021.1905227.

Krivdo, Michael E. "CJSOTF-A: Combined Joint Special Operations Task Force–Afghanistan, A Short History, 2002–2014." *Veritas* 12, no. 2 (Winter 2016): 7. https://arsof-history.org/articles/v12n2_cjsotf_page_1.html.

Ladwig, Walter C. "Influencing Clients in Counterinsurgency: U.S. Involvement in El Salvador's Civil War, 1979–92." *International Security* 41, no. 1 (Summer 2016): 99–146. https://doi.org/10.1162/ISEC_a_00251.

Lane, Jan-Erik. "The Principal-Agent Approach to Politics: Policy Implementation and Public Policy-Making." *Open Journal of Political Science* 3, no. 2 (2013): 85–89. https://www.scirp.org/pdf/OJPS_2013042915421321.pdf.

Lawrence, T. E. *Seven Pillars of Wisdom*. New edition. Ware, Hertfordshire: Wordsworth Editions Ltd., 1999.

Leech, Garry M. "The Battle for Colombia's 'Little Sarajevo.'" *NACLA Report on the Americas* 36, no. 5 (2003): 19–25. https://doi.org/10.1080/10714839.2003.11722474.

Leival, Tim C. "Combat Advising the ANA 205th Commandos: An Operational Perspective." *Small Wars Journal*, December 27, 2010.

Lewis, James. "The Battle of Marawi: Small Team Lessons Learned for the Close Fight." *The Cove*, November 27, 2018. https://cove.army.gov.au/article/battle-marawi-small-team-lessons-learned-close-fight.

Liston, Mark R. "Seven Counterinsurgency Principles for Tactical Leaders: A Primer for Company-Level Counterinsurgency Operations with Operational and Strategic Benefits." Master's thesis, USMC Command and Staff College, 2011. https://apps.dtic.mil/sti/pdfs/ADA600781.pdf.

Long, Austin. *The Soul of Armies*. 1st edition. Ithaca, NY: Cornell University Press, 2016.

Long, Joseph E. "Framing Indigenous Leadership." *Advances in Social Sciences Research Journal* 4, no. 6 (March 25, 2017). https://doi.org/10.14738/assrj.46.2936.

Luján, Fernando M. *Light Footprints: The Future of American Military Intervention*. Washington, DC: Center for a New American Security, 2013.

Mansoor, Peter R., and Williamson Murray, eds. *The Culture of Military Organizations*. New York: Cambridge University Press, 2019.

Manwaring, Max G., and Court Prisk. *El Salvador at War: An Oral History of Conflict from the 1979 Insurrection to the Present*. Washington, DC: National Defense University, 1988.

———. "A Strategic View of Insurgencies: Insights from El Salvador." McNair paper no. 8, Institute for National Strategic Studies, National Defense University Press, May 1990. https://apps.dtic.mil/sti/pdfs/ADA271343.pdf.

Marr, Phebe. *The Modern History of Iraq*. 4th edition. New York: Routledge, 2018.

Matisek, Jahara. "Pathways to Military Effectiveness: Armies and Contemporary African States." PhD diss., Northwestern University, June 2018. Available for download at https://arch.library.northwestern.edu/downloads/9880vr17q.

Maxwell, David S. "Commander's Summary of the Joint Special Operations Task Force Philippines (JSOTF-P) 2006–2007." Col. David Maxwell. October 2007.

———. "Is the OSS Contribution to Special Forces a Result of Disinformation?" *Small Wars Journal*, December 3, 2018. https://smallwarsjournal.com/jrnl/art/oss-contribution-special-forces-result-disinformation.

———. "Operation Enduring Freedom–Philippines." In *Routledge Handbook of U.S. Counterterrorism and Irregular Warfare Operations*. 1st edition. New York: Routledge, 2021.

———. Testimony before the U.S. House Committee on Armed Services, House Armed Services Committee. 2012.

McWhirter, William. "El Salvador: Low Profile." *Time*, no. 8 (May 4, 1981): 41. https://time.com/vault/issue/1981-05-04/page/57/.

Menjivar, Milton. "Response to Congressional Inquiry (Rep. Moakley)—Atlacatl Training." Memorandum, U.S. Southern Command, March 20, 1990. http://search.proquest.com/docview/1679117235/.

Meyer, Christina. *Underground Voices: Insurgent Propaganda in El Salvador, Nicaragua, and Peru*. Washington, DC: RAND Corporation, 1991.

Miller, Judith. "15 U.S. Green Berets to Aid Salvadorans in Combat Training." *New York Times*, March 14, 1981. https://www.nytimes.com/1981/03/14/world/15-us-green-berets-to-aid-salvadorans.html.

Millett, Allan R., and Williamson Murray, eds. *Military Effectiveness: Volume 1, The First World War*. 2nd edition. New York: Cambridge University Press, 2010.

———. *Military Effectiveness: Volume 3, The Second World War*. 2nd edition. New York: Cambridge University Press, 2010.

Millett, Allan R., Williamson Murray, and Kenneth H. Watman. "The Effectiveness of Military Organizations." *International Security* 11, no. 1 (Summer 1986): 37–71. https://doi.org/10.2307/2538875.

Mines, Keith W. *Why Nation-Building Matters: Political Consolidation, Building Security Forces, and Economic Development in Failed and Fragile States*. Lincoln, NE: Potomac Books, 2020.

Montes, Julio A. "El Salvador: The Last Battlefield in Central America." *International Defense Review* 24, no. 9 (September 1991): 915–18.

Moroney, Jennifer D. P., David E. Thaler, and Joe Hogler. *Review of Security Cooperation Mechanisms Combatant Commands Utilize to Build Partner Capacity*. Santa Monica, CA: RAND Corporation, 2013.

Mosier, Duane L. "The Road to Al Amarah: Operation Yarborough and U.S. Army Special Forces in Southern Iraq (January–June 2008)." *Small Wars Journal*, November 4, 2010. https://smallwarsjournal.com/blog/journal/docs-temp/593-mosier.pdf.

Mott, William H. *United States Military Assistance: An Empirical Perspective*. Westport, CT: Praeger, 2002.

Mott, William H., IV. *Military Assistance: An Operational Perspective.* Westport, CT: Praeger, 1999.

Moyo, Dambisa. *Dead Aid: Why Aid Is Not Working and How There Is a Better Way for Africa.* Reprint edition. New York: Farrar, Straus and Giroux, 2010.

Mulroy, Mick, and Eric S. Oehlerich. "A Tale of Two Partners: Comparing Two Approaches for Partner Force Operations." Middle East Institute, January 29, 2020. https://www.mei.edu/publications/tale-two-partners-comparing-two-approaches-partner-force-operations.

Murphy, Jack. "Inside the Light Reaction Regiment, the Philippines Answer to Delta Force." Special Operations Forces Report, SOFREP.com, June 13, 2017. https://sofrep.com/news/sofrep-exclusive-inside-light-reaction-regiment-philippines-answer-delta-force-part-2/.

———. "Philippine Forces Still in for a Tough Fight in Marawi." Special Operations Forces Report, SOFREP.com, June 26, 2017. https://sofrep.com/news/philippine-forces-still-in-fora-tough-fight-in-marawi/.

———. "The Philippines Stands Up a True Special Operations Command for the First Time." SOFREP.com, April 17, 2018. https://sofrep.com/news/the-philippines-stands-up-a-true-special-operations-command-socom-for-the-first-time/

———. "SOFREP Exclusive: The Death-Dealing Philippine SOF Unit behind the Headlines." SOFREP.com, June 9, 2017. https://sofrep.com/news/sofrep-exclusive-death-dealing-philippine-sof-unit-behind-headlines-part-1/.

Murray, Williamson, and Allan R. Millett, eds. *Military Innovation in the Interwar Period.* Revised edition. Cambridge: Cambridge University Press, 1998.

Nagl, John A. *Learning to Eat Soup with a Knife: Counterinsurgency Lessons from Malaya and Vietnam.* 1st edition. Chicago: The University of Chicago Press, 2005.

Nasr, Vali. *The Shia Revival: How Conflicts within Islam Will Shape the Future.* 1st edition. New York: W. W. Norton, 2006.

NBC News. "Iraq Issues Arrest Warrants in $1 Billion Scam." NBCNews.com, October 7, 2005. https://www.nbcnews.com/id/wbna9618533.

North, Douglass C., John Joseph Wallis, Steven B. Webb, and Barry R. Weingast. *Limited Access Orders in the Developing World: A New Approach to the Problems of Development.* Policy Research Working Papers. Washington, DC: The World Bank, 2007.

Outzen, Richard. "Language, Culture, and Army Culture: Failing Transformation." *Small Wars Journal,* 2012. https://smallwarsjournal.com/jrnl/art/language-culture-and-army-culture-failing-transformation.

Ovalle, Carlos Alberto Ospina. *A la Cima Sobre los Hombros del Diablo: Narrativa Histórica de como las FARC Alcanzaron su Máximo Desarrollo y se Convirtieron en la Mayor Amenaza en Colombia*. Saarbrücken, Germany: Editorial Académica Española, 2012.

———. *Batallas No Contadas*. Bogotá, Colombia: Editorial Oveja Negra LTDA, 2013.

———. "Colombia and the FARC: From Military Victory to Ambivalent Political Reintegration?" In *Impunity: Countering Illicit Power in War and Transition*, ed. Michelle Hughes and Michael Miklaucic, 150–169. Washington, DC: Center for Complex Operations, 2016.

———. *Los Años en que Colombia Recuperó la Esperanza. Cómo la Aplicación Coordinada de Política y Estrategia Logró la Recuperación Social, Económica y de Seguridad de la Nación Colombiana*. 1st edition. Medellín, Colombia: U. Pontificia Bolivariana, 2014.

Paddock, Alfred H. *U.S. Army Special Warfare: Its Origins*. Revised edition. Lawrence: University Press of Kansas, 2002.

Panganiban, Artemio V. "Visiting Forces Agreement, Mutual Defense Treaty Not Enforceable in U.S., Philippines." *Philippine Daily Inquirer*, June 7, 2020. https://opinion.inquirer.net/130548/vfa-mdt-not-enforceable-in-us-ph.

Pappalardo, Joe. "Looking Downrange." *Popular Mechanics* 189, no. 7 (July 2012): 76–83, 142–43. Archived online at https://ia902907.us.archive.org/31/items/PopularMechanics2012-07/Popular%20Mechanics%202012-07.pdf.

Parker, Russel Worth. "U.S. Foreign Advisory Missions: Rich History—Mixed Results." *Small Wars Journal*, April 27, 2017. https://smallwarsjournal.com/jrnl/art/us-foreign-advisory-missions-rich-history-mixed-results.

Paterson, Patrick. "Measuring Military Professionalism in Partner Nations: Guidance for Security Assistance Officials." *Journal of Military Ethics* 18, no. 2 (2019): 145–63. https://doi.org/10.1080/15027570.2019.1638461.

Pazdziorek, Przemyslaw. "Special Forces Transformation in the Face of Contemporary Conflicts Challenges." *Review of the Air Force Academy* 14 no. 1 (2016): 47–60. Archived online at https://www.afahc.ro/ro/revista/2016_1/Pazdziorek_2016_1.pdf.

Peifer, Jeremy L. "Coffee Beans and Rice Paddies—War on the Cheap: American Advisors in El Salvador and Vietnam:" Monograph, School of Advanced Military Studies, 2014. https://apps.dtic.mil/sti/tr/pdf/ADA611975.pdf.

Piasecki, Eugene G. "The History of Special Warfare." *Special Warfare* 28, no. 2 (April–June 2015): 8–13. https://www.dvidshub.net/publication/issues/26504.

Pollack, Kenneth M. *Arabs at War: Military Effectiveness, 1948–1991*. Lincoln: Bison Books, 2004.

———. *Armies of Sand: The Past, Present, and Future of Arab Military Effectiveness*. New York: Oxford University Press, 2019.

Potter, Joshua J. *American Advisors: Security Force Assistance Model in the Long War.* Leavenworth, KS: Combat Studies Institute Press, 2011.

Preston, Jason. "Culture Eats Strategy for Breakfast." *Harvard Business School Digital Initiative* (blog), September 6, 2017. https://digital.hbs.edu/managing-in-the-digital-economy/culture-eats-strategy-breakfast/.

Princeton University. "Philippines: Empirical Studies of Conflict." Empirical Studies of Conflict, n.d. https://esoc.princeton.edu/country/philippines. Accessed June 30, 2020.

Reiter, Dan, ed. *The Sword's Other Edge: Trade-Offs in the Pursuit of Military Effectiveness.* Cambridge: Cambridge University Press, 2017.

Rempe, Dennis M. *The Past as Prologue? A History of U.S. Counterinsurgency Policy in Colombia, 1958–66.* Carlisle, PA: Strategic Studies Institute, U.S. Army War College, 2002.

Reveron, Derek S. *Exporting Security: International Engagement, Security Cooperation, and the Changing Face of the US Military.* 2nd edition. Washington, DC: Georgetown University Press, 2016.

Reynolds, Phillip W. "Persistent Conflict and Special Operations Forces." *Military Review* 94, no. 3 (2014): 62–69. https://www.armyupress.army.mil/Portals/7/military-review/Archives/English/MilitaryReview_20140630_art014.pdf.

Richardson, J. L. "Performance Management Framework for Security Sector Assistance." U.S. Department of Defense, 2016. https://open.defense.gov/portals/23/Documents/foreignasst/SAA_PPD_Performance_Management_Framework.pdf.

Robinson, Eric. "The Missing, Irregular Half of Great Power Competition." Modern War Institute, September 8, 2020. https://mwi.usma.edu/the-missing-irregular-half-of-great-power-competition/.

Robinson, Linda. *One Hundred Victories: Special Ops and the Future of American Warfare.* 1st edition. New York: Public Affairs, 2013.

——. "The SOF Experience in the Philippines and the Implications for Future." *PRISM | National Defense University* 6, no. 3 (December 7, 2016): 150–67. https://ndupress.ndu.edu/Portals/68/Documents/prism/prism_6-3/prism_6-3.pdf.

——. "Warrior Class: Why Special Forces Are America's Tool of Choice in Colombia and around the Globe; Arauca, Colombia." *U.S. News and World Report* (February 2003): 34–46.

Robinson, Linda, Daniel Egel, and Ryan Brown. *Measuring the Effectiveness of Special Operations.* Santa Monica, CA: RAND Corporation, 2019.

Rogers, Clifford J., ed. *The Military Revolution Debate: Readings on the Military Transformation of Early Modern Europe.* 1st edition. Boulder, CO: Westview Press, 1995.

Rosello, Victor. "Lessons from El Salvador." *Parameters: U.S. Army War College Quarterly* 23, no. 1 (1993): 100–108. https://press.armywarcollege.edu/cgi/viewcontent.cgi?article=1676&.

Rosen, Jonathan D. *The Losing War: Plan Colombia and Beyond*. Reprint edition. New York: State University of New York Press, 2015.

Rosen, Stephen Peter. *Winning the Next War: Innovation and the Modern Military*. 6th edition. Ithaca, NY: Cornell University Press, 1994.

Rowen, Henry. "Atlacatl." Reply to questions submitted by Rep. Moakley to the Department of Defense on the history of the U.S. training activities involving the Atlacatl Battalion. February 9, 1990. Moakley Archive and Institute, Digital Collections, Suffolk University, Boston, MA. https://moakleyarchive.omeka.net/files/show/2111.

Russell, James. *Innovation, Transformation, and War: Counterinsurgency Operations in Anbar and Ninewa Provinces, Iraq, 2005–2007*. 1st edition. Stanford, CA: Stanford University Press, 2010.

Sacquety, Troy J. "The OSS Influence on Special Forces." *Veritas* 14, no. 2 (Winter 2018). https://arsof-history.org/articles/v14n2_oss_to_sf_page_1.html.

Saint Victor, Florent de. "Interview: About the Iraqi Counter Terrorism Service, with David M. Witty." *Mars Attaque* (blog), October 19, 2018. http://mars-attaque.blogspot.com/2018/10/interview-about-iraqi-counter-terrorism.html.

Saum-Manning, Lisa. "VSO/ALP: Comparing Past and Current Challenges to Afghan Local Defense." WR-936. Santa Monica, CA: RAND, December 2021. https://www.rand.org/pubs/working_papers/WR936.html.

Schneider, Paul. "The Plight of the Green Beret: Why Special Forces Is Still Losing Most of Its Junior Leaders and Its Survivors Are Forced to Contend with a Cultural Crisis." *Small Wars Journal*, January 20, 2022. https://smallwarsjournal.com/jrnl/art/plight-green-beret-why-special-forces-still-losing-most-its-junior-leaders-and-its.

Schoen, Fletcher. "Reorganization Is Imperative to Fixing Special Forces' Bent Unconventional Culture." *Small Wars Journal*, June 29, 2015. https://smallwarsjournal.com/jrnl/art/reorganization-is-imperative-to-fixing-special-forces%E2%80%99-bent-unconventional-culture.

Schwalm, Tony. *The Guerrilla Factory: The Making of Special Forces Officers, the Green Berets*. Reissue edition. New York: Simon and Schuster, 2013.

Schwarz, Benjamin C. "American Counterinsurgency Doctrine and El Salvador: The Frustrations of Reform and the Illusions of Nation Building." Santa Monica, CA: RAND Corporation, 1991. https://www.rand.org/content/dam/rand/pubs/reports/2006/R4042.pdf.

Sedra, Mark. *Security Sector Reform in Conflict-Affected Countries: The Evolution of a Model*. 1st edition. Philadelphia: Routledge, 2018.

Serafino, Nina M. "Security Assistance and Cooperation: Shared Responsibility of the Departments of State and Defense." Report, Congressional Research Service, May 26, 2016. https://crsreports.congress.gov/product/pdf/R/R44444.

Serena, Chad C. *A Revolution in Military Adaptation: The US Army in the Iraq War*. Original edition. Washington, DC: Georgetown University Press, 2011.

Shurkin, Michael, John Gordon IV, Bryan Frederick, and Christopher G. Pernin. *Building Armies, Building Nations: Toward a New Approach to Security Force Assistance*. Santa Monica, CA: RAND Corporation, 2018.

Smith, Rupert. *The Utility of Force: The Art of War in the Modern World*. Reprint edition. New York: Vintage, 2008.

Smyth, Frank. "Secret Warriors: U.S. Advisers Have Taken Up Arms in El Salvador." *The Village Voice*, Frank Smyth Independent Journalism, August 11, 1987. Archived online at https://franksmyth.com/the-village-voice/secret-warriors-u-s-advisers-have-taken-up-arms-in-el-salvador/.

Southard, Aaron. "Security Force Assistance Metrics: Blood and Treasure." *Special Warfare* 28, no. 3 (July–September 2015): 26–28. https://www.dvidshub.net/publication/issues/26508.

Talmadge, Caitlin. *The Dictator's Army: Battlefield Effectiveness in Authoritarian Regimes*. 1st edition. Ithaca, NY: Cornell University Press, 2015.

Terzian, John. "SF Advisers in El Salvador: The Attack on El Paraiso." *Special Warfare* 14, no. 2 (Spring 2001): 18–25. https://www.dvidshub.net/publication/issues/8221.

Transparency.org. "Corruption Perceptions Index." 2020, Iraq. https://www.transparency.org/en/cpi/2020/index/irq

Tripp, Charles. *A History of Iraq*. 3rd edition. Cambridge: Cambridge University Press, 2007.

Ucko, David H. "Counterinsurgency in El Salvador: The Lessons and Limits of the Indirect Approach." *Small Wars and Insurgencies* 24, no. 4 (October 2013): 669–95. https://doi.org/10.1080/09592318.2013.857938.

Ugarriza, Juan Esteban, and Nathalie Pabón Ayala. *Militares y Guerrillas: La Memoria Histórica del Conflicto Armado en Colombia desde los Archivos Militares 1958–2016*. 1st edition. Bogota, Colombia: Editorial Universidad del Rosario, 2017.

U.S. Army Special Operations Command, 1st Special Forces Command. "Language, Regional Expertise, and Culture Capability (LREC) Executive Summary." PowerPoint presentation, November 21, 2022.

U.S. Congress Senate Committee on Foreign Relations. *"Plan Colombia": Elements for Success; Staff Trip Report to the Committee on Foreign Relations, United States Senate, One Hundred Ninth Congress, First Session, December 2005*. S. Prt. 109-43.

Washington, DC: U.S. Government Printing Office, 2005. https://www.govinfo.gov/content/pkg/CPRT-109SPRT25278/html/CPRT-109SPRT25278.htm.

U.S. Department of the Army. *Field Manual 3-24 Counterinsurgency*. Washington, DC: U.S. Department of the Army, 2006.

U.S. Department of Defense, Office of the Undersecretary for Personnel and Readiness. *Implementation Plan for Language Skills, Regional Expertise, and Cultural Capabilities*. Washington, DC: U.S. Department of Defense, 2014. https://dlnseo.org/sites/default/files/APPROVED%20Implementation%20Plan.pdf.

U.S. House of Representatives, Committee on Armed Services, Subcommittee on Oversight and Investigation. "Building Language Skills and Cultural Competencies in the Military: DOD's Challenge in Today's Educational Environment," November 2008. https://prhome.defense.gov/Portals/52/Documents/RFM/Readiness/DLNSEO/files/LanguageCultureReportNov08_HASC.pdf.

U.S. Joint Chiefs of Staff. *Joint Publication 3-20, Security Cooperation*. Washington, DC: U.S. Department of Defense, 2017.

Utterback, Mitch. "How a Retired Soldier Jason Bourned His Way to Mosul as a War Reporter." *Athlon Outdoors* (blog), July 27, 2020. https://www.athlonoutdoors.com/article/retired-soldier-war-reporter-mosul/.

Vallejo, Pedro. "Organización CCOES 2019." PowerPoint presentation, Comando Conjunto de Operaciones Especiales (CCOES), August 29, 2019.

Vasquez, Juan M. "Delays Cut Training Time at U.S. Base in Honduras; Boot Camp for Salvadorans." *Los Angeles Times*, 1983.

Waddell, Jeffrey D. "United States Army Special Forces Support to 'Plan Colombia.'" U.S. Army War College, Carlisle, PA, April 7, 2003. https://apps.dtic.mil/sti/tr/pdf/ADA414500.pdf.

Webb, Hershel. Interview of Col. John A. Cash, Defense attaché, El Salvador, 1988. U.S. Army Heritage and Education Center, U.S. Military History Institute.

West, Bing. *The Village*. 7th edition. New York: Pocket Books, 2003.

West, Owen. *The Snake Eaters: Counterinsurgency Advisors in Combat*. Reprint edition. New York: Simon and Schuster, 2013.

White, Troy, Joint Special Operations University (U.S.), and JSOU Press. *Growing SOLO: Expanding the Spectrum of SOF Advisory Capabilities*. Tampa, FL: Joint Special Operations University, 2018.

Wilson, Gregory. "Anatomy of a Successful COIN Operation: OEF-PHILIPPINES and the Indirect Approach." *Military Review* 86, no. 6 (November–December 2006): 38–49. https://www.armyupress.army.mil/Portals/7/PDF-UA-docs/Wilson-2008-UA.pdf.

Wilson, James Q. *Bureaucracy: What Government Agencies Do and Why They Do It*. 1st edition. New York: Basic Books, 1991.

Wright, Donald, and Combat Studies Institute Press. *A Different Kind of War: The US Army in Operation Enduring Freedom: October 2001–September 2005*. Fort Leavenworth, KS: Combat Studies Institute Press, 2010.

Yarger, Harry R. "Building Partner Capacity." JSOU report 15-1, Joint Special Operations University, February 1, 2015. https://apps.dtic.mil/sti/pdfs/ADA619818.pdf.

Yeo, Andrew. "President Duterte Wants to Scrap a Philippines-U.S. Military Agreement. This Could Mean Trouble." Monkey Cage. *Washington Post*, February 13, 2020. https://www.washingtonpost.com/politics/2020/02/13/president-duterte-wants-scrap-philippines-us-military-agreement-this-could-mean-trouble/.

Yildiz, Kerim. *The Kurds in Iraq: The Past, Present and Future*. 2nd edition. London: Pluto Press, 2007.

Zabriskie, Phil. "We're Here to Help the Philippines." Interview with Col. David Fridovich. *Time*, February 8, 2002. https://content.time.com/time/world/article/0,8599,201660,00.html.

ORIGINAL INTERVIEWS

El Salvador

Lt. Col. Cecil Bailey, MTT Advisor with 3/7 SFG 1981, MILGROUP Staff El Salvador 1984–1985, September 21, 2020.

Lt. Gen. Charles Cleveland, MTT advisor with 3/7 SFG 1987–1990, October 19, 2020.

Maj. Gen. Mark Hamilton, MILGROUP Cdr. 1990–1992, September 28, 2020.

Lt. Col. Mike Hennelly, J5 El Salvador Desk and other Staff Positions at SOUTHCOM 1986–1989, January 14, 2021.

Col. Kevin Higgins, MTT Advisor 1983–1984, OPATT Advisor (San Miguel) 1986–1988, September 30, 2020.

CW3 Dave Hulsey, 7 SFG advisor to BIRI training at CREM in Honduras 1984, January 4, 2021.

Lt. Col. Ted Mataxis, Chief of Advisor Program 1988–1990, January 15, 2021.

Brig. Gen. Hector Pagan, 7th SFG MILGRP Liaison 1989, January 5, 2021.

Col. Francisco (Frank) Pedrozo, El Salvador OCS Advisor 1982, OPATT advisor 5th Brigade 1985–1986, MLGRP Training Officer, Operations Officer, and Deputy Cdr. 1989–1992, September 8, 2020.

MSgt. Leamon (Lee) Ratterree, ODA NCO for BIRI Belloso training at Fort Bragg 1982, MTT Advisor 1984, OPATT Advisor 1985–1986, January 5, 2021.

Maj. Gen. Ed Reeder, National Civil Defense OPATT Advisor, 1987–1988, December 17, 2020.

Col. Wayne (Pat) Richardson, MTT Advisor from 3/7 SFG 1980–1984, OPATT Advisor 1988–1990, January 20 and 21, 2021.

Col. Jim (Ranger) Roach, SOUTCOM J3 Staff Officer 1983–1984, OPATT Brigade Advisor and Senior OPATT Advisor 1984–1986, September 22, 2020.

Col. Hy Rothstein, 7th SFG OPATT Advisor 1987–1989, 7 SFG DCO 1990–1993, October 12, 2020.

Maj. Kalev (Gunner) Sepp, OPATT Advisor 1989–1990 (1st Brigade in San Salvador and 2nd Brigade in Santa Ana), August 11, 2020.

Dr. David Spencer, National Defense University professor and author on El Salvador War, January 22, 2021.

Maj. Gen. Simeon Trombitas, OPATT Advisor (4th Brigade) 1989–1990, September 15, 2020.

Col. Roy Trumble, Company Cdr. and Battalion XO for 3/7 SFG (Panama) 1981–1984, Battalion Cdr. 1988–1990, September 18, 2020.

Col. John Waghelstein, Battalion Cdr. (7th SFG) 1981–1983, El Salvador MILGRP Cdr. 1983–1984, 7th SFG Cdr. 1985–1987, January 25, 2021.

Command Sgt. Maj. Chris Zets, ODA NCO for BIRI Belloso training at Fort Bragg 1982, December 21, 2020.

The Philippines

Lt. Col. Bob Boone, SOCPAC Chief of Staff 2010, July 13, 2020.

Maj. Shawn Boyer, Joint Intelligence Center and JSOTF-P J-2, 2004–2009, July 10, 2020.

Col. Erik Brown, JSTOF-P Cdr. 2014–2015, October 5, 2020.

Col. Max Carpenter, AOB Cdr. 2001–2002, Deputy Group Cdr. 2012–2014, July 17, 2020.

Col. Bill Coultrup, JSOTF-P Cdr. 2007–2010, July 14, 2020.

Col. Dennis Downey, JSTOTF-P Deputy Cdr. 2002–2004, JSTOTF-P Cdr. 2004, SOCPAC J35 2008–2010, July 20, 2020.

Sgt. Maj. Stephen Durfee, ODA Team Sergeant 2006–2008, Company Sgt. Maj. 2012–2013, July 14, 2020.

Lt. Col. Joseph Felter, Attaché in Embassy during OEFP 200–2002, July 20, 2020.

Lt. Gen. David Fridovich, JSOTF-P Cdr. 2002, SOCCENT CG, PACOM J3 2005–2008, July 16, 2020.

Col. Ken Gleiman, ODA Team Leader, Assistant Battalion S3, and AOB Cdr. (4 rotations from 2000–2009), August 13, 2020.

Maj. Joe Harosky, ODA Team Leader 2005–2008, September 24, 2020.

Command Sgt. Maj. Brian Johnson, ODA Team Sergeant 1999–2000, Company Sgt. Maj. 2004, Battalion Command Sgt. Maj. 2011, 1st SF Group Command Sgt. Maj. 2013–2014, September 16, 2020.

Lt. Col. Jim Keating, JSOTF-P Chief of Staff 2011, July 15, 2020.

Lt. Col. Leo Liebreich, ODA Team Leader 2006–2008, 1 SFG assigned to Embassy as JUSMAG Ground OIC 2013–2015, July 21, 2020.
Lt. Col. Scott Malone, ODA Team Leader, ODB Cdr., JSOTF-P J3, Chief of Current Operations SOCPAC 2003–2011, July 23, 2020.
Cdr. (SEAL) James Marvin, JSTOTF-P Deputy Cdr. 2006–2007, July 23, 2020.
Col. David Maxwell, 1st Battalion, 1st SFG Cdr. 2000–2002, JSOTF-P Cdr. 2006–2007, July 9, 2020.
Lt. Col. John Moria, Battalion Cdr. 2006–2008, July 24, 2020.
MSgt. Joe Morley, ODA Lead Assault Troop Trainer 2001, July 22, 2020.
Sfc. John Mory, ODA Assault Troop Trainer 2000–2002, July 21, 2020.
CW2 Duke Sawyer, ODA Team Warrant Officer 2001–2002, July 24, 2020.
Maj. Noel Sioson, ODA Team Leader 2010–2011, ODB Company Cdr. 2015–2017, June 26 and July 3, 2020.
Lt. Gen. Donald Wurster, SOCPAC Cdr. 2000–2003, JTF-510 Cdr. 2002, October 4, 2023.

Colombia

Command Sgt. Maj. Amil Alvarez, 7th SFG, Battalion Command Sgt. Maj. 2011–2013, 7th SFG Group Command Sgt. Maj. 2013–2016, SOCSOUTH Command Sgt. Maj. 2016–2018, February 10 and 24, 2021.
Col. Carlos Berrios, SOUTHCOM J5 2000–2003, Colombia MILGRP 2003–2006, Joint Staff Andean Ridge Desk 2006–2008, January 12, 2021.
Col. Mike Brown, 7th SFG, AFEU Colombia exchange officer 1996–1998, Army Chief Colombia MILGRP 2004–2007, USARSOUTH 2008–2009, MILGRP Chief Colombia 2009–2012, February 11, 2021.
Col. Kevin (Duke) Christie, Battalion Cdr. 3/7 SFG 2002–2003, October 19, 2020.
Lt. Gen. Charles Cleveland, SOCSOUTH CG 2005–2008, October 19, 2020.
Lt. Col. Agustin Dominguez, Joint Staff Colombia Desk 2014, Army Attaché Colombia 2016–2018, February 11, 2021.
Col. Barbara Fick, Colombia desk SOUTHCOM 2001–2004, SOUTHCOM CAG 2004–2008, Plans officer Colombia MILGRP 2008–2010, January 28, 2021.
Col. Kevin Higgins, MILGRP Cdr. Colombia 1999–2001, October 6, 2020.
CW3 Dave Hulsey, 7th SFG and SOCOM SOCSOUTH Desk 1993–1994, 2000, 2004–2020, January 4, 2021.
Lt. Col. Douglas Judice, 7th SFG, ODA Team Leader with AFEU 2001, Exchange Officer AFEU 2003–2005, Colombia PATT 2007–2010, SOUTHCOM J35 2010–2012, Army Mission Chief Embassy 2012–2015, February 1, 2021.
Lt. Gen. Ken Keen, Colombia MILGRP Cdr. 2001–2003, CG USARSOUTH 2005–2007, DCG SOUTHCOM 2009–2011, October 15, 2020.

Lt. Col. Kevin Key, ODA Team Leader 2006, AOB Cdr. 2013, 7th SFG S3 2014–2016, SOCSOUTH 2018–2020, February 8, 2020.
Tom Marks, Journalist and U.S. contractor in Colombia 1998–2015, January 20, 2021.
Lt. Col. Scott Morley, SOLO Colombia 2016–2018, February 11, 2021.
General Carlos Ospina Ovalle, National Army of Colombia, Commander of the Colombian Army, 2002–2004, Commander General of the Colombian Military Forces, 2004–2007, February 16, 2021.
Lt. Col. Joe Reagan, 7th SFG, ODA Team Leader 2010, AOB Cdr. 2015, SOCSOUTH J3 2017–2020, February 8, 2021.
Maj. Gen. Ed Reeder, 7th SFG, Battalion S-3 1998–1999, Cdr. 7th SFG 2006–2007, July 17, 2020.
Dr. David Spencer, Advisor to Colombian Armed Forces 1998–2018, Colombia Desk Officer OSD (P) 2012–2017, January 22, 2021.
Sgt. Maj. David Topejr, 7th SFG, ODA Team Sergeant, Company Sgt. Maj. 1999–2001 and 2004, December 23, 2020.
Maj. Gen. Simeon Trombitas, Colombia MILGRP Cdr. 2003–2005, September 15, 2020.
Col. Greg Wilson, J3 SOCSOUTH 2006, SOCFWD Cdr. 2007–2009, September 1, 2020.
Command Sgt. Maj. Chris Zets, 7th SFG Company Sgt. Maj. 1998–2000, Group Command Sgt. Maj. 2006–2008, December 21, 2020.

Iraq
CW4 Eric Brashears, ODA and ODB Warrant Officer (10th SFG) 2004–2005, October 29, 2020.
Col. Erik Brown, CJSOTF Chief of Staff (10th SFG) 2008–2009, Battalion Cdr. SOTF-C 2010–2011, October 5, 2020.
Col. Max Carpenter, Advisor to Gen. Kenani Iraqi CTS CG 2009–2010, July 24, 2020.
Col. Kevin (Duke) Christie, CJSOTF LNO to CFLCC 2005, CJSOTF Deputy Commander 2006–2007, October 19, 2020.
Col. Chris Conner, Battalion Cdr. (5th SFG) for 4 rotations 2003–2007, CJSOTF Cdr. 2008–2009, July 13, 2020.
Sfc. Tom Disburg, ODA NCO (10th SFG) 2007, October 28, 2020.
Col. Dennis Downey, MNFNW Staff 2005, MNFI Staff 2007, October 29, 2020.
Sgt. Maj. Stephen Durfee, ODA Team Sergeant (1st SFG) 2007, August 12, 2020.
Brigadier General Arkan Fadhil, Iraqi ISOF Commando 2003–present, current Cdr. ISOF Academy, September 8, 2020.
MSgt. Scott Ford, ODA Team Sergeant (B/2/3 SFG) 2004–2005, October 29, 2020.
Col. Ken Gleiman, ODB Company Cdr. (1st SFG) 2008–2009, July 13, 2020, August 13, 2020.

Col. Burton Glover, ODA Team Leader, ODB Company Cdr., other staff positions in 5th SFG 2003–2011, July 20 and 23, 2020.
Maj. Joe Harosky, ODA Team Leader (1st SFG) 2007, September 24, 2020.
Command Sgt. Maj. Brian Johnson, Battalion Command Sgt. Maj. 2009 (1st SFG), September 16, 2020.
MSgt. Seaux Larreau, ODA NCO (5th and 10th SFG) 2003–2006, October 29, 2020.
Col. Derek Lipson, AOB Cdr. 2006–2007, SOITT Senior Advisor 2008, Battalion Cdr. SOTF-N (20th SFG) 2010–2011, September 24, 2020.
Sgt. Maj. Ron McDaries, ODA Team Sergeant, ODB Company Sgt. Maj. (5th SFG) 2003–2004, October 30, 2020.
Col. Mark Mitchell, CJSOTF Battalion Cdr., 2005–2006, Cdr., 2009–2011, September 29, 2014.
Lt. Col. (Ret.) Patrick Morrison, Iraqi Special Operations Forces, Brigade Senior Advisor, Iraqi National Counter Terrorism Force Transition Team, 2005–2007, 2009, September 22, 2014.
MSgt. Clay Morrow, ODA Team Sgt. (5th SFG) 2005, November 2, 2020.
Maj. Gen. Michael Repass, CJOSTF Cdr. (10th SFG) 2004–2005, September 21, 2020.
Maj. Gen. Patrick Roberson, AOB Cdr., Battalion Cdr. (10th SFG) multiple tours, 2003–2009, December 22, 2020.
CW2 Travis Rolph, ODA Warrant Officer (A/1/5 SFG) 2005–2006 ODA, October 29, 2020.
Lt. Gen. Ken Tovo, Battalion Cdr. 2003–2004, CJSOTF Cdr. (10th SFG) 2006–2007, October 5, 2020.
Maj. Gen. Simeon Trombitas, INCTFTT CG 2008–2009 (7th SFG background), September 15, 2020.
Col. Tim Williams, Battalion Cdr. 2002–2004 (5th SFG), CJSOTF Chief of Staff 2005, MNFI Staff 2011, October 16, 2020.
Rear Adm. Edward Winters, Iraqi National Counterterrorism Force Transition Team Commander, 2007–2008, October 22, 2015.
Lt. Col. David Witty, Senior Advisor to ICTS 2007–2008 and 2013–2014, September 3, 2020.

Afghanistan

Anonymous 3rd SF Group member, deployments in 2006–2007, 2010, 2011–2012, January 8, 2021.
CW4 Eric Brashears, Battalion Warrant Officer (10th SFG) 2010–2012 and 2016–2017, November 2, 2020.
Col. Bill Carty, CJSOTF Chief of Staff (3rd SFG) 2009, Battalion Cdr. of SOTF-S (Kandahar) 2011–2012, January 6, 2021.

Col. Kevin (Duke) Christie, ISAF SOF Cdr. 2011–2013, October 19, 2020.

Col. Fred Dummar, 7th SFG CJSOTF XO 2006–2007, CJSOTF-A Chief of Staff 2013–2014, Cdr. ANASOC 2014–2015, contractor ANASOC HQ 2015–2016, December 16, 2020.

Sgt. Maj. Stephen Durfee, Camp Morehead SOAG NCO (1st SFG) 2010–2011, September 2, 2020.

MSgt. Scott Ford, ODA Team Sgt. (3rd SFG) 2007–2008, October 29, 2020.

Col. Burton Glover, Battalion Cdr. of SOTF-A (7th SFG) 2016–2017, July 23, 2020.

Col. Jack Hastings, ODA Team Leader (1st SFG) 2004, Staff Officer SOTFS 2009–2011, September 9, 2020.

Maj. Gen. Jim Linder, SOJTF-A CG 2017–2018, NTMA SOF DCG 2011–2012, December 21, 2020.

Col. Fernando Lujan, Deputy Cdr. Camp Morehead (SOAG) 2013–2014, August 11, 2020.

Col. Larry Niedringhaus, AOB Cdr. (7th SFG) 2008–2009, Camp Morehead SOAG Deputy Cdr. 2014–2015, Camp Morehead SOAG Cdr. 2017–2018, January 7, 2021.

Col. Brian Petit, Battalion Cdr. of SOTF-S (Kandahar) 2010, ANASOC SOAG Cdr. 2013–2014, December 21, 2020.

Maj. Gen. Ed Reeder, CJSOTF-A Cdr. (7th SFG) 2006–2007, CG CFSOCC-A 2009–2010, CG SOJTF-A 2014–2015, December 17, 2020.

Maj. Gen. Patrick Roberson, CJSOTF-A Cdr. (3rd SFG) 2013, December 22, 2020.

Col. Martin (Marty) Schmidt, AOB Cdr. (7th SFG) 2002, SOTF Cdr. 2013–2014, SOAG Cdr. 2017–2018, September 9, 2020.

MSgt. Joshua Stephen, ODA Team Sgt. (3rd SFG) Kandahar 2010–2011, Jalalabad 2012, Battle of Kunduz 2015, January 5, 2021.

Valentin Swegle, Center for Army Analysis ORSA attached to SOAG 2014–2015, December 22, 2020.

Sgt. Maj. David Topejr, ODA Team Sgt. and Company Sgt. Maj. (7th SFG) 2006–2007 and 2013, December 23, 2020.

Command Sergeant Major Faiz Wafa, Afghan Commando Battalion Command Sergeant Major (Gardez) 2007–2008, ANASOC Command Sergeant Major 2008–2015, January 8, 2021.

Col. Tim Williams, J3 SOCCENT Staff Officer 2006–2008, October 16, 2020.

Index

Note: page numbers in italics refer to figures.

Abu Sayyaf Group (ASG): American hostages taken by, 48, 49, 60; area of operation, 59; attacks in Philippines, 48; and Battle of Marawi, 73–74; Philippines' capture of Abu Sulaiman, 71; poor use of Light Reaction units against, 60

advisor pairing consistency: conventional views on, 11; evaluation of impact, 11; of five case studies, compared, *178*; importance to success, 177, 179–80, 190–91

advisor pairing consistency, in Afghanistan, 153–57; advisors on advantages of, 155–56; advisors on disadvantages of, 156–57; lack of policy to support, 153–54; range of units trained and, 154–55; reasons for lack of, 153–55

advisor pairing consistency, in Colombia, 82–85; benefits of, 86; demands of Afghanistan and Iraq wars and, 83–84; and development of trust, 86; efforts to improve, 85; history of U.S.-Colombia cooperation and, 76, 82; and long-term relationships with Colombian counterparts, 84–85; policy changes with leadership changes, 83; stability in Colombian units and, 85–86; U.S. rotation of personnel and, 82–83; varying opinions on importance of, 83–84

advisor pairing consistency, in El Salvador, 23–27; benefits of extended pairings, 26–27; factors negatively affecting, 25–26; factors positively affecting, 23–25; overall medium level, 23

advisor pairing consistency, in Iraq, 114–19; advantages of, 118–19; Commando battalions and, 116–17; exceptional cases of disadvantages from, 119; and friendships with Iraq soldiers, 117–19; Iraqi Counter Terrorism Force (ICTF) and, 114–16

advisor pairing consistency, in Philippines: benefits of, 53–54; high level of, 51–53

Afghan Army Special Forces (ANASF), decision to create, 154–55

Afghan Commandos: advisors killed by, 159; as best of Afghan forces, 173; combat effectiveness of, 165–74; diminished capacity after U.S. force reduction, 169–73; expansion of Commandos, 142, 143–44; helicopter support capability, 165, 167; logistical problems after U.S. force reduction, 168, 173; number of personnel, 190; special incentive pay for, 159; structure of, 143; successful operations, 2; training by U.S. Army Special Forces, 2; U.S. motives for creating, 141–42. *See also* Afghanistan, SF training in (2007–21); combat effectiveness, of Afghan Commandos; fighting without advisor present, by Afghan Commandos; performance against enemy forces, of Afghan Commandos

Afghan National Army (ANA): dysfunctional personnel system,

146–47; and summer offensive of 2015, 2; U.S. training for, 154

Afghan National Army Special Operations Command (ANASOC): addition of logistics structure, 167; and advisor pairing consistency, 156; ANASF and, 154; benefits of, 161–62, 163; creation of, 160; helicopter support capability, 165, 167; logistics and, 167–68, 169, 173, 174; percentage of Afghan security forces under control of, 144; problems with, 160–61; reconnaissance aircraft, 171; training of forces under, 143; U.S. loss of control over, 162–63

Afghanistan: banking system, lack of, 145; Commando Training Center, 143, 144, 146, 167; U.S. final evacuation, 173; U.S. goal of creating centralized Afghan national military force, 141–42; Village Stability Operations (VSO) program, 155

Afghanistan, SF training in (2007–21): and absurdity of plan to rapidly create new army, 192; advisors killed by Commandos, 159; and Afghan Army Special Forces (ANASF), 154–55; and Afghan Commandos, structure of, 143; combat effectiveness of Afghan Commandos, 165–74; Commandos as best of Afghanistan forces, 173; cost of, 2; delay in creating Afghanistan SOF, 141, 159, 163, 164; expansion of Commandos and, 142, 143–44; failure to address corruption and incompetence, 185; high desertion rates, reasons for, 146–47; lack of control over quality of recruits, 143–44; length of mission, 192; lessons from Iraq and, 142; as moderate success within larger failure, 176; and multiple bosses for units, 161; overview of, 9; risk from infiltrators, 126, 159; special incentive pay for Commandos, 159; Special Operations Command Headquarters, creation of, 160–62; theft of equipment and supplies, 159, 167–68; U.S. motives for creating Commandos, 141–42; U.S. Special Forces Groups involved in, 148–49, 154; and wounded warrior program, 161–62. *See also* advisor pairing consistency, in Afghanistan; Afghan Commandos; authority to organize host-nation unit, in Afghanistan; combat operations, advisor's ability to join, in Afghanistan; fighting without advisor present, by Afghan Commandos; language and cultural training of U.S. Special Forces, in Afghanistan; partner-to-advisor ratio, in Afghanistan; performance against enemy forces, of Afghan Commandos

Afghanistan, U.S. reduced force in (Operation Freedom's Sentinel), 142–43; and Afghan forces' inability to operate independently, 171; and Commando logistical problems, 168, 173; and Commandos' diminished capacity, 169–73; as Obama administration plan, 142; and Taliban gains, 142–43; and U.S. loss of influence, 162–63

Afghanistan War: Afghan forces' ineffectiveness against Taliban, 142–43; Battle of Bunduz, 172; cause of, 140; installation of Karzai government, 140; lack of U.S. progress in, 142; Operation Red Wings, 106; shift of forces to Iraq War, 140–41, 145; Taliban victory in, 143; U.S. conventional forces' takeover of, 141; U.S. special forces' role in initial invasion, 140; U.S. turn from fighting to training Afghan forces, 142; variations in U.S. strategy, 141. *See also* Taliban

AGLAN (Agrupación de Lanceros) [Colombia]: capacities and types of missions, 80; creation of, 80, 90; equipment given to, 102; high level of performance, 108–9; low levels of corruption or desertion, 90, 102; multiday operation capacity, 102–4; number of commandos in, 90; ongoing training of, 91–92; performance against enemy forces, 106–8; role in victory over FARC, 81

Agrupación de Lanceros. *See* AGLAN (Agrupación de Lanceros) [Colombia]
Alvarez, Amil, 84, 86
ANASOC. *See* Afghan National Army Special Operations Command
Army Special Warfare Center and School, and changing language education needs, 149
Arroyo, Gloria, 61–62, 65
authority to organize host-nation unit: employment decisions and, 13; evaluation of impact, 12–13; of five case studies, compared, *178*; force equipping decisions and, 13; force structure decisions and, 13; importance to success, 177, 181; measures of, 13; personnel decisions and, 13; resistance to change as norm in, 12
authority to organize host-nation unit, in Afghanistan, 157–63; decay over time, 157, 162–63; existing Afghanistan units sent for retraining, 157, 158; inability to run security checks on recruits, 159; inability to stop misuse of Commando units, 160; initial wide latitude, 157; leadership selection constraints, 158–59; loss of, with impending U.S. departure, 162–63; low quality of applicant pool, 157–58; medium rating of, 163; selection of equipment and, 159; Special Operations Command Headquarters creation and, 160; unit organization and, 159; wounded warrior program and, 161–62
authority to organize host-nation unit, in Colombia, 92–98; Colombia's receptive attitude, 92–95, 97; limits to Colombian compliance, 96–97; SOF headquarters creation and, 94–95; strong influence on Colombia SOF, 97–98; trust built through long relationship and, 95; U.S. experience in Afghanistan and Iraq and, 95–96
authority to organize host-nation unit, in El Salvador, 33–37; cases of failed influence, 36–37; earned respect for abilities and, 35; on human rights and civilian relations, 36–39; influence of U.S. resources and, 35–36; issues of rank and, 36; medium rating of, 39; rapport with partner and, 35; small number of advisors and, 37; on treatment of troops, 38
authority to organize host-nation unit, in Iraq, 123–30; control of recruit selection and training, 125–26; creation of Counter Terrorism Command and, 127–28; creation of Counter Terrorism Service and, 127–28; creation of non-sectarian units, 125, 128; equipment selection and, 124–25; initial complete control, 123–27; leadership selection and, 124; Maliki's takeover of control, 128–29; resilience of U.S. standards over time, 129–30; return of control to Iraqi government (2008), 123, 126–27; SOF headquarters creation and, 127; special protections for family members, 126
authority to organize host-nation unit, in Philippines, 57–63; decline in influence over time, 62–63; early successes, 57–59, 63; government fear of coup and, 61–62, 63; misuse of units against U.S. advice, 60–61, 63; Philippines' sensitivity to sovereignty issues and, 57, 59; previous U.S.-Philippines relationship and, 57; resistance to SOF headquarters creation, 59–60, 61

BACOA (Batallón de Comandos Ambrosio Almeyda) [Colombia]: capacities and types of missions, 79–80; creation of, 79, 90, 96; criteria for troop selection, 80; equipment given to, 102; exchange officer assigned to, 91; high level of performance, 108–9; long-term U.S.-Columbian friendships developed in, 85; low levels of corruption or desertion, 90, 102; multiday operation capacity, 102–4; number of commandos in, 90; ongoing training of, 91–92; performance against enemy forces, 106–8

305

Index

Balikatan 02-1, 64
Barwari, Fardhil Jalil al-, 117–19, 124, 128, 187
Batallón de Comandos Ambrosio Almeyda. *See* BACOA (Batallón de Comandos Ambrosio Almeyda) [Colombia]
Batallones de Infantería de Reacción Inmediata. *See* BIRIs (Batallones de Infantería de Reacción Inmediata) [El Salvador]
Betancourt, Ingrid, 79
Biden, Joe, 143
BIRIs (Batallones de Infantería de Reacción Inmediata) [El Salvador]: ability to conduct multiday operations, 43–45; and corruption in logistical system, 44–45; creation of, 22, 30–31; disbandment at war's end, 39; inability to conduct intelligence-driven operations, 45–46; lack of separate command, 37; low to moderate effectiveness of, 47; modest success in training of, 47; night-fighting ability, 42–43; number of personnel, 190; performance against enemy forces, 46–47; training of, 22, 30–31, 32–33
Blackman, Donald, 3
Blair, Dennis, 52
Bolduc, Don, 164
Brown, Erik, 66
Bush, George W., 1, 110

Cano, Alfonso, 107
CIF. *See* Commander's in-Extremis Force (CIF) companies
CJSOTF. *See* Combined Joint Special Operations Task Force
CJSOTF-AP. *See* Combined Joint Special Operations Task Force–Arabian Peninsula
Colombia: civil war (La Violencia), U.S. assistance in, 76–77; history of military cooperation with U.S., 76, 82; and Korean War, 76; leadership, high quality of, 186–87; U.S. cutting of ties with Samper administration, 78; U.S. pressure to install effective leaders, 187; U.S.'s effective pressure to address corruption and incompetence, 78, 185, 193
Colombia, battle against FARC rebels: Battle of El Billar, 77; Colombian military's early losses, 77; Operation Willing Spirit, 81, 99, 103, 104–5; Plan Colombia and, 78–79, 80, 81, 96–97; Plan Patriota and, 81–82; and sensitive site exploitation (SSE), 99, 104, 107; splinter groups' ongoing after peace agreement, 82, 107–8; turnover to police, in final stage, 105; U.S. assistance in, 78; U.S. hostages taken by FARC, 80–81; U.S. spending in, 78; victory in, 81–82. *See also* Grupos Armados Organizados (GAOs)
Colombia, SF training in (2002–16): advisors sent on permanent-change-of-station orders, 91–92; Colombian special operations unit prior to, 79, 80; FARC targeting of advisors, 98; length of mission, 192; lessons from El Salvador and, 82; misuse of newly-formed SOF elements, 94; other training in addition to SF work, 82–83, 91; overview of, 8; personnel shortages during Iraq War, 81; as Planning and Assistance Advisory Team (PATT), 82; post-9/11 removal of barriers between counterterrorism and counternarcotics operations, 77; SOF headquarters creation, Colombian cooperation with, 94–95; sovereignty issues as never of concern, 97; success of, 176; targeting of FARC leadership, 81–82; turning points in, 77–78. *See also* advisor pairing consistency, in Colombia; AGLAN (Agrupación de Lanceros); authority to organize host-nation unit, in Colombia; BACOA (Batallón de Comandos Ambrosio Almeyda);

306

combat effectiveness, of Colombia SOF; combat operations, advisor's ability to join, in Colombia; language and cultural training of U.S. Special Forces, in Colombia deployment; partner-to-advisor ratio, in Colombia; performance against enemy forces, by Colombian SOF

Colombian Army: class-based discrimination in, 192; as low capability conscript force, 79

Colombia's Lancero commando school: exchange officer assigned to, 92; founding of, 77; long-term U.S.-Columbian friendships developed in, 85; and training of BACOA and AGLAN troops, 77; U.S. advisors attendance, to build rapport, 95

combat effectiveness: effect of advisor factors in five case studies, compared, 178, *179*; of five case studies, compared, *177*, *178*; four capacities used to measure, 14–17; grading of, 17. *See also* fighting without advisor present; multiday combat capacity; night-fighting ability; performance against enemy forces

combat effectiveness, of Afghan Commandos, 165–74; ability to fight without advisors, 168, 169–74; drug use and discipline problems, 169–70; initial assessment, 174; as low to moderate, 174; multiday combat capacity, 166–69; night-fighting ability, 165–66, 173; performance against enemy forces, 172–74

combat effectiveness, of Colombia SOF, 101–8; ability to fight without advisors, 99, 104–6; aggressiveness and, 101; combat operations, advisor's ability to join in, 80–81, 84; initial assessment, 108–9; logistics systems, 102–3, 104; medical evacuation capacities, 103, 104; multiday combat capacity, 102–4; night-fighting ability, 101–2, 103; performance against enemy forces, 106–8; toughness of troops, 102–3, 104

combat effectiveness, of El Salvador's SOF, 42–47; ability to fight without advisors, 45–46; focus on, in second phase of training, 21; initial assessment, 47; multiday combat capacity, 43–45; night-fighting ability, 42–43; performance against enemy forces, 46–47

combat effectiveness, of Iraqi SOF, 132–39; ability to conduct intelligence-driven operations, 136–37; ability to fight without advisors, 136–37; initial assessment, 139; misuse during fight against ISIS, 138; modest intelligence capacities, 136–37; multiday combat capacity, 133–35; night-fighting ability, 132–33; overall high-moderate rating, 139; performance against enemy, 137–39

combat effectiveness, of Philippines' Light Reaction forces, 67–75; ability to fight without advisors, 69–72; initial assessment, 75; multiday combat capacity, 68–69; night-fighting ability, 67–68, 74; performance against enemy forces, 72–75

combat operations, advisor's ability to join: conventional views on, 13; evaluation of impact, 13–14; of five case studies, compared, *178*; importance to success, 177, 181–82; as necessary to gain influence, 131–32, 164–65

combat operations, advisor's ability to join, in Afghanistan, 163–65; Afghanistan government's lack of restrictions on, 163; better medical support accompanying, 165; and loss of faith in progress, 164; as necessary for gaining influence, 164–65; some advisors' lack of faith in Afghan Commandos, 163–64

combat operations, advisor's ability to join, in Colombia, 98–101; change after capture of U.S. hostages, 98–99; clash with rules in Afghanistan and Iraq, 84; and confusion created by Afghanistan deployments, 100; impact on mission effectiveness, 100–101; prohibition on self-defense, 98; as strictly forbidden, 98–101; and technology tracking their movements, 98; temporary changes in rules on, 80–81, 98

combat operations, advisor's ability to join, in El Salvador: importance for advisors, 42; medium rating of, 42; rules vs. reality of, 40–42

combat operations, advisor's ability to join, in Iraq, 130–32; advisors' immersion within units trained, 131; as necessary for credibility, 131–32

combat operations, advisor's ability to join, in Philippines, 63–67; Philippines' constitutional prohibition on, 63–64, 65; restrictions' damage to mission, 66–67; U.S. restrictions on, 65–66

Combined Joint Special Operations Task Force (CJSOTF): and Afghanistan War, 141, 145; Reeder as commander of, 151; standing down of, 145

Combined Joint Special Operations Task Force–Arabian Peninsula (CJSOTF-AP), 111, 112, 114, 116, 119–20, 126–27, 129; and Maliki's abuse of ISOF, 128

Commander's in-Extremis Force (CIF) companies: as model for Iraqi Counter Terrorism Force (ICTF), 111, 114; in SF training in Iraq, 113, 114–16, 117, 120; in SF training in Philippines, 51, 59, 67

Counter Terrorism Command (CTC) [Iraq]: and Battle of Ramadi, 138; capability after U.S. withdrawal, 136; creation of, 127–28; disloyal elements in, 129; intelligence issues in, 137; and ISOF logistics, 134, 135

Counter Terrorism Service (CTS) [Iraq]: and command of ISOF, 134; creation of, 127–28; disloyal elements in, 129; and logistical issues, 134; political capture of, 129; and saving of Iraq, 130

CTC. *See* Counter Terrorism Command (CTC) [Iraq]

CTS. *See* Counter Terrorism Service (CTS) [Iraq]

Devil's Brigade, The (film), 3
Dummar, Fred, 167
Duterte, Rodrigo, 62

El Salvador: *tanda* system of promotion in armed forces, 192; troops in Afghanistan and Iraq, 47; U.S.'s effective pressure to address corruption and incompetence, 186

El Salvador, civil war in: and Army's lack of counterinsurgency capacity, 21; Chapultepec Peace Accords, 22, 39; combat medals awarded to U.S. troops, 41; Congress's resistance to U.S. engagement in, 20; corruption in logistical system, 44; destruction caused by, 22; lack of Salvadoran special forces and, 37; logistical inadequacies of Salvadoran army, 44–45; and medical evacuation, limited capacity for, 44; origin of insurgency in, 19; Soviet Union and, 19–20, 22; U.S. achievement of strategic goals in, 47; U.S. soldiers killed in, 41; Woerner Report on, 20. *See also* FMLN (Frente Farabundo Martí para la Liberación Nacional)

El Salvador, SF training in (1981–91): achievement of U.S. strategic objective in, 22; advisors' preference for, 24–25; brigade-advisor phase, 20, 21; career consequences for advisors, 25–26; *cazador* (hunter) units and, 21–22; first phase focus on growth of armed forces, 20; length of mission, 192; limit on number of U.S. advisors, 20, 28, 29–30; mobile training team (MTT) period, 20, 21, 27, 28; Operational Planning and Assistance Training Teams (OPATTs) phase, 21, 28, 32–33; overview of, 8; second phase focus on increasing effectiveness, 21; success of, 176; and two-year cycle of conscription, 26. *See also* advisor pairing consistency, in El Salvador; authority to organize host-nation unit, in El Salvador; BIRIs (Batallones de Infantería de Reacción Inmediata); combat effectiveness, of El Salvadors SOF; combat operations, advisor's ability to join, in El Salvador; language and cultural training of U.S. Special Forces, in El Salvador; partner-to-advisor ratio, in El Salvador

Enduring Freedom, Operation (Afghanistan), 141; replacement with Operation Freedom's Sentinel, 142, 162. *See also* Afghanistan War

Estrada, Joseph, 61–62

F3EAD cycle: Afghan Commandos and, 170–71; Colombian SOF and, 104, 105; definition of, 15; as measure of independent fighting ability, 15

Farabundo Martí National Liberation Front. *See* FMLN

FARC (Fuerzas Armadas Revolucionarias de Colombia): Colombian SOF's killing of leadership, 106–8; funds from narcotrafficking, 77; large number of hostages held by, 79; splinter groups continuing to fight after Colombian peace agreement (Grupos Armados Organizados, GAOs), 82, 107–8. *See also* Colombia, battle against FARC rebels

Felter, Joseph, 48

Fertig, Wendell, 3

fighting without advisor present: criteria for measurement of, 15; of five case studies, compared, *178*; as measure of combat effectiveness, 14, 15

fighting without advisor present, by Afghan Commandos, 168, 169–74; collapse after U.S. withdrawal, 172–73; collapses under fire, 170; lack of intelligence-gathering capacity, 170–72; logistical problems and, 168, 169, 173, 174; rampant theft of equipment and supplies and, 171

fighting without advisor present, by Colombia SOF: ability to conduct intelligence-driven operations, 104–6; and sensitive site exploitation, 99, 104, 107; signals- and imagery-intelligence capabilities, 104

fighting without advisor present, by El Salvadoran SOF, 45–46

fighting without advisor present, by Iraqi SOF, 136–37

fighting without advisor present, by Philippines' Light Reaction forces, 69–72; poor logistical capacity, 68–69, 72; weak intelligence-gathering capacity, 69–73

First Special Services Force, 3

FMLN (Frente Farabundo Martí para la Liberación Nacional): fear of BIRI units, 46; and peace agreement, demand for U.S. advisors to remain, 39; support from Soviets and Soviet proxies, 19–20, 22; targeting of U.S. soldiers, 40; transition to political party after peace accords, 22; as well-organized and well-armed, 21–22

Freedom's Sentinel, Operation. *See* Afghanistan, U.S. reduced force in (Operation Freedom's Sentinel)

Frente Farabundo Martí para la Liberación Nacional. *See* FMLN

Fridovich, David, 66

Fuerzas Commando competition, Colombian SOF's success in, 108–9

Galula, David, 17

Galvin, John, 77

Ghani, Ashraf, 161

Golden Division. *See* Iraqi Special Operations Forces

great power competition, current emphasis on, 176, 194

Green Beret. *See* U.S. Army Special Forces (Green Beret, SF)

Grupos Armados Organizados (GAOs), 107–8

Gulf War of 1990–91, 110

Index

Hapilon, Isnilon, 73–74
Honduras: 7th Special Forces Group in, 23; Football War with El Salvador, 21; training of Salvadoran BIRIs in, 31
Hussein, Saddam, 9, 110, 129

ICTF. *See* Iraqi Counter Terrorism Force
International Security Assistance Force, in Afghanistan, 141
Iraq, SF training in (2003–11), 112–14, *115*; and absurdity of plan to rapidly create new army, 192; advisors' immersion within units trained, 131; cost of, 1–2; and failure of Iraqi Army, 2; failure to address corruption and incompetence, 185; friendships with Iraq soldiers, 117–19; high pay of SF units, loyalty gained by, 126; and Iraqi soldiers' adoption of Western habits, 121; Iraqi Special Operations Forces as central focus of SF training, 111; length of mission, 192; need to replace disbanded Iraqi security forces, 111; overview of, 9; and sovereignty clock, 130; as success within larger failure, 176; and U.S. exit, 1; and U.S. selection of leadership, 187; U.S. SF groups involved in, 111. *See also* advisor pairing consistency, in Iraq; authority to organize host-nation unit, in Iraq; combat effectiveness, of Iraqi SOF; combat operations, advisor's ability to join, in Iraq; Counter Terrorism Command (CTC) [Iraq]; Counter Terrorism Service (CTS) [Iraq]; Iraqi Army Commando Battalions; Iraqi Counter Terrorism Force (ICTF); Iraqi Special Operations Forces (Golden Division, ISOF); language and cultural training of U.S. Special Forces, in Iraq; partner-to-advisor ratio, in Iraq
Iraq War: Battle of Baiji, 134–35, 137–38; Battle of Mosul, 135, 138; Battle of Tikrit, 138; insurgency, coalition errors leading to, 111; reasons for, 110; U.S. Army's rebuilding of Iraqi army, 111; U.S. special forces in, 110–11

Iraqi Army: Commando Battalions, creation of, 111; destruction in Gulf War, 110; lack of advisor pairing consistency, 118; U.S. rebuilding of, 111
Iraqi Army Commando Battalions: ability to replace casualties, 134–35; addition of second battalion with regional companies, 112, 129; advisor pairing consistency, 116–17; combat effectiveness, 132–33; creation of initial 36th Battalion, 111; language and cultural training of SF trainers, 120; as part of Iraqi Special Operations Forces (ISOF), 111; partner-to-advisor ratio, 113–14; structure and missions of, 111
Iraqi Counter Terrorism Force (ICTF): ability to replace casualties, 134–35; advisor pairing consistency, 114–15; combat effectiveness, 132–33; creation of, 111; equipment selected for, 124–25, 132, 134; grueling pace of missions, 116; language and cultural training of SF trainers, 119–20; missions of, 111; as part of Iraqi Special Operations Forces (ISOF), 111; partner-to-advisor ratio, 113; structure of, 114
Iraqi Freedom, Operation, 110
Iraqi Special Operations Forces (Golden Division, ISOF): as central focus of U.S.'s SF training, 111; difficulty filling units, 111; good leadership of, 187; growth of, 112; Maliki's misuse for political ends, 128–29; misuse of, after U.S. withdrawal, 133; SOF headquarters creation, 127; Special Warfare Center and School associated with, 112; success against ISIS, 130; successful operations, 2; units in, 111, 112
Iraqi Special Warfare Center and School, 112
ISIS. *See* Islamic State of Iraq and Syria
Islamic State of Iraq and Syria (ISIS), ISOF success against, 130, 134–35, 137–38
Islamic terrorists, attacks in Philippines, 48. *See also* Abu Sayyaf Group (ASG)
ISOF. *See* Iraqi Special Operations Forces

Japan, U.S. success in constructing military of, 176
JCETs. *See* Joint Combined Exchange Training Teams
Joint Combined Exchange Training Teams (JCETs), 5, 7
Joint Special Operations Task Force-Philippines (JSOTF-P): number of personnel, 49, 55, 56; and Philippines' sensitivity to U.S. presence, 64–65; political oversight of, 64–65; renaming of, to reduce political impact in Philippines, 64; as response to September 11th terrorist attacks, 49; and siege of Zamboanga City, 72–73

Karimi, Sher Mohammad, 142
Karzai, Hamid, 140, 141, 163
Keen, Ken, 79
Kennedy, John F., 3–4
Kissinger, Henry, 17
Korean War, and U.S. pressure to install effective leaders, 185, 187

language and cultural training of U.S. Special Forces: conventional views on, 6, 10; cost of, 6, 10; countries with multiple languages and, 183; difficult languages and, 184, 188; evaluation of impact, 10–11; of five case studies, compared, *178*; greater importance of cultural knowledge *vs.* language, 152; importance to success, 177, 182–84; questionable need for, 2–3; recommendations on, 187–89; regional orientations and, 188; and rigidity of deployment, 10
language and cultural training of U.S. Special Forces, in Afghanistan, 147–53; advisors' views on importance of, 150; cultural differences and, 150; difficulty of languages and, 151; importance of building rapport, 152–53; languages spoken by Commandos, 150; and multiple languages spoken in Afghanistan, 150–51; mutual understanding developed over time, 151–52; need for interpreters of language and culture, 151; small number trained in native languages, 147–50
language and cultural training of U.S. Special Forces, in Colombia deployment, 86–90; 7th SF Group's proficiency in Spanish, 86–87; decline in, with deployments to Afghanistan and Iraq, 87, 88–89; equal importance of personality, 89–90; importance of cultural component, 89; views on importance of, 87–88
language and cultural training of U.S. Special Forces, in El Salvador, 25, 27–29
language and cultural training of U.S. Special Forces, in Iraq, 119–23; ability to build rapport as most important skill, 121–22; advisors' opinions on importance of, 120–23; availability of interpreters and, 121; demands on U.S. Special Forces and, 119; and difficulty of mastering Arabic, 122; rare cases of cultural errors, 121; and small vocabulary needed for combat, 123
language and cultural training of U.S. Special Forces, in Philippines, minimal effects of, 49–51; large number of English speakers in Philippines and, 50–51; number of languages spoken in Philippines and, 50
Lawrence, T. E., 1, 10
leadership: of host nation, importance of high quality of, 186–87; inept or corrupt, importance of demanding replacement of, 185–86; and virtuous cycle in selecting subordinates, 186
lessons learned from U.S. security force assistance efforts: culture changes in host nations as lengthy, difficult process, 191–92; futility of assistance efforts as false conclusion, 175–77; importance of addressing host-nation corruption and incompetence, 184–86, 193; importance of advisor's ability to join combat operations, 177,

181–82; importance of analyzing, 175; importance of authority to organize host-nation unit, 177, 181; importance of consistency in advisor pairing, 177, 179–80, 190–91; importance of good leadership of host nation forces, 186–87; importance of language and cultural training, 177, 182–84; importance of partner-to-adviser ratio, 177, 180; importance of training and preparation, 176–77, 193–94; mass-production of SOF, impossibility of, 190; need for both carrot and stick, 185; need for larger number of U.S. Special Forces, 189–90, 193–94; number of successful cases, 176; partner-to-advisor ratio, most effective, 189–90; recommendations on language and cultural training, 187–89; relevance to current great power competition, 176, 194

Liebreich, Leo, 53

Light Reaction counterterrorism force [Philippines]: Battle of Marawi, 62, 71, 73–74; conventional-force commanders' resistance to, 54; creation of, 48–49; decline in equipment theft *vs.* regular army units, 69; expansion to regiment strength, 54; improvements in equipment maintenance *vs.* regular army units, 69; lack of dedicated training center, 54; loss of personnel through casualties and dissatisfaction, 54–55; low rating of, 63; naming of, 57; Operation Ultimatum, 60–61; personnel strength, 54; Philippines Army's misuse of, 60–61, 63; poor logistical capacity, 68–69, 72; poor medical evacuation capacity, 67–68; recruiting difficulties, 54; siege of Zamboanga City, 54, 71, 72–73; U.S. equipment given to, 67, 68; weak intelligence-gathering capacity, 69–73, 74. *See also* Philippines, SF training in (2001–15)

Linder, Jim, 155

Maliki, Nouri al-, 127, 128–30
Mao Zedong, 17
Maxwell, David, 52, 53, 66–67
McChrystal, Stanley, 15
McDaries, Ron, 118–19
McDowell, Robert, 56–57
Mejía Ferrero, Alberto José, 83, 95, 186
Mobile Training Teams (MTTs): in El Salvador, 20, 21, 27, 28; introduction of, 5
Modern Warfare (Trinquier), 15
Mohammed, Khalid Sheikh, 48
Mora Rangel, Jorge Enrique, 79, 186
Morley, Joe, 52
Moro National Liberation Front (MNLF), 72–73
Mulholland, Sean, 85
multiday combat capacity: definition of, 16; of five case studies, compared, *179*; logistics and, 16; as measure of combat effectiveness, 14, 16; unit cohesion and, 16
multiday combat capacity, of Afghan Commandos, 166–69; logistical problems and, 166–69; rampant theft of equipment and supplies and, 167–68; weak medical evacuation capacity, 167
multiday combat capacity, of Colombia SOF, 102–4; logistics systems, 102–3, 104; medical evacuation capacities, 103, 104
multiday combat capacity, of Iraqi SOF, 133–35; logistical issues and successes, 133–35
multiday combat capacity, of Philippines Light Reaction units, 68–69
multiday combat capacity, of Salvadoran SOF, 43–45

National Guard units: language standards and, 188; in SF training in Iraq, 122; in SF training in Philippines, 50
Navarro Jiménez, Luis Fernando, 108
Nicholson, John, 165
night-fighting ability: of Afghan Commandos, 165–66, 173; of

Colombian SOF, 101–2, 103; of five case studies, compared, *179*; heavy jungle and, 68, 101; of Iraqi SOF, 132–33; as measure of combat effectiveness, 14, 15–16; of Philippines' Light Reaction units, 67–68, 74; of Salvadoran units in civil war, 42–43
North, Douglass, 12

Obama, Barack, 142
Office of Strategic Services (OSS), 3
Operation Enduring Freedom-Philippines (EF-P): cost to U.S., 49. *See also* Joint Special Operations Task Force-Philippines (JSOTF-P)
Operation Red Wings (Afghanistan), 106
Ospina Ovalle, Carlos, 80, 86, 87, 95, 97–98, 186

Pamonag, Danilo, 53
partner-to-advisor ratio: advisors' views on importance of, 147; benefits of smaller ratios, 114; conventional views on, 11; evaluation of impact, 11–12; of five case studies, compared, *178*; importance to success, 177, 180; recommendations on, 189–90
partner-to-advisor ratio, in Afghanistan, 143–47; desertion and AWOL rates and, 146–47; expansion of Afghan SOF units, 143–44; fluctuation in advisor numbers, 144–46; by month, 147, *148*; as overly large, 190
partner-to-advisor ratio, in Colombia, 90–92; demands of Afghanistan and Iraq war and, 91; fluctuations in advisor numbers and, 90–91; by month, 92, *93*
partner-to-advisor ratio, in El Salvador, 29–33; and difficulty of adequate training, 33; difficulty of calculating, 29–30; and fictional Salvadoran unit strengths, 32; and fluctuations in Salvadoran unit strengths, 33; by month, 33, *34*; as overly large, 190; troops technically not included in U.S. troop cap and, 30–32

partner-to-advisor ratio, in Iraq, 112–14; demands on U.S. SF and, 113; in Iraqi commando battalions, 113–14; in Iraqi Counter Terrorism Force, 113; by month, *115*
partner-to-advisor ratio, in Philippines: fluctuations in number of advisors, 55–57; fluctuations in size of SF forces, 54–55; by month, 57, *58*
Pastrana, Andrés, 78
performance against enemy forces: of five case studies, compared, *179*; importance in counterinsurgency, 17; as measure of combat effectiveness, 15, 17
performance against enemy forces, by Colombian SOF, 106–8; successful missions, 106–8; willingness to take risks, 106
performance against enemy forces, by Philippines' Light Reaction forces, 72–75; in Battle of Marawi, 62, 71, 73–74; in siege of Zamboanga City, 54, 71, 72–73
performance against enemy forces, of Afghan Commandos, 172–74
performance against enemy forces, of Iraqi SOF, 137–39
performance against enemy forces, of Salvadoran SOF, 46–47
personality and rapport building, importance for SF advisors, 35, 89–90, 95, 121–22, 152–53
Philippines: Oakwood coup attempt, 61–62, 63. *See also* Operation Enduring Freedom-Philippines (EF-P)
Philippines, SF training in (2001–15): cap on number of advisors, 59; cost to U.S., 54, 57–59; creation of Philippines' Joint Special Operations Group (JSOG), 60–61; intelligence sharing, 53–54; Islamic terrorist attacks as impetus for, 48, 57; length of mission, 192; number of advisors, fluctuation in, 55–57; overview of, 8; previous U.S.-Philippines relationship and, 52–53, 57; ramped up training after September

11th terrorist attacks, 49, 55; reduced training after 2015, 49; and revival of lapsed U.S.-Philippines relations, 48. *See also* advisor pairing consistency, in Philippines; authority to organize host-nation unit, in Philippines; combat effectiveness, of Philippines' Light Reaction forces; combat operations, advisor's ability to join, in Philippines; language and cultural training of U.S. Special Forces, in Philippines; Light Reaction counterterrorism force [Philippines]; partner-to-advisor ratio, in Philippines

Pickering, Thomas, 26

Planning Assistance Training Team (PATT), 82

policy implications. *See* lessons learned from U.S. security force assistance efforts

principle-agent theory, and SF ability to influence host-nation units, 12

Provide Comfort, Operation, 110, 118, 124, 187

rapport building, importance for SF advisors, 35, 89–90, 95, 121–22, 152–53

Reagan administration, and Salvadoran counterinsurgency, 20

Reeder, Ed, 143, 151, 152, 164

Reyes, Raúl, 107

Roberson, Patrick, 117–18, 124, 158

Robin Sage guerrilla-warfare exercise, 153

Romero, Humberto, 19

Rumsfeld, Donald, 65–66, 192

Samper, Ernesto, 78, 185, 187

security force assistance (SFA), U.S.: erratic policy toward, 192–93; failure of most missions, 1; role in post 9/11 wars, 1; successes in, 176; Ukraine's war against Russia and, 176. *See also* Afghanistan, SF training in (2007–21); Colombia, SF training in (2002–16); El Salvador, SF training in (1981–91); Iraq, SF training in (2003–11); lessons learned from U.S. security force assistance efforts; Philippines, SF training in (2001–15)

Security Force Assistance Brigade (U.S. Army), 16

sensitive site exploitation (SSE): in Colombia's battle against FARC, 99, 104, 107; by Iraqi SOF, 137; Philippines' Light Reaction forces' weak capacity for, 71

September 11th Terrorist attacks: and Afghanistan War, 140; and change in U.S. policy on Iraq, 110; and demand for U.S. Special Forces, 6; and ramped up SF training in Philippines, 49, 55. *See also* Joint Special Operations Task Force-Philippines (JSOTF-P)

SF. *See* U.S. Army Special Forces

SFA. *See* security force assistance

Sioson, Noel, 53

South Korea: U.S. success in constructing military of, 176; U.S.'s effective pressure to address corruption and incompetence, 185, 187

sovereignty, addressing host-nation corruption and incompetence despite, 184–86, 193

sovereignty clock: and Colombia SF training, 97; and importance of addressing host-nation leadership problems early, 186; and Iraq SF training, 130; and Philippines SF training, 63

Soviet Union, and Salvadoran civil war, 19–20, 22

Special Operations Command, U.S. (USSOCOM): authorization by Congress, 37; equipment of, 134; Language Regional Expertise and Culture Strategy Report, 122; policy on consistency in advisor pairing, 153; and SF training in Philippines, 23; study on SF training in Colombia, 84

Stringham, Joseph, 47

Sulaiman, Abu, 71

Taliban: advances with U.S. withdrawals, 173; Afghan forces' ineffectiveness against, 142–43; and Battle of Bunduz, 172; gains after U.S. partial withdrawal, 142–43; initial defeat by U.S. forces, 140; U.S. counterinsurgency against, 141; U.S. inability to eradicate, 141, 142; U.S. special forces' initial defeat of, 140; victory in Afghanistan War, 143

Trinquier, Roger, 15

Trombitas, Simeon, 27

Trump, Donald J., 143

Ukraine, U.S. security force assistance in, 176

Uribe Vélez, Álvaro, 81, 186

U.S. Army Security Force Assistance Brigades, 193–94

U.S. Army Special Forces (Green Beret, SF): demand for, in post-9/11 wars, 6; factors influencing effectiveness of, 9–14; history of, 3–6; need for larger number of, 189–90, 193–94; number of groups in early 1980s, 24; organization of, 5–6; regional orientation of Groups, importance before 9/11, 6, 10; regional orientation of Groups, recommendations on, 188; training and types of missions, 4, 5–6; unit sizes and personnel, 5–6

U.S. Army Special Forces, 1st Group: in Afghanistan, 156–57; in Iraq, 116; in Philippines, 48–50, 51, 55–57, 59, 65; regional orientation of, 10, 49, 188

U.S. Army Special Forces, 3rd Group: in Afghanistan, 149–50, 154; in Iraq, 81, 111, 114, 116, 120, 131

U.S. Army Special Forces, 5th Group: in Afghanistan, 140–41, 147, 149; in Iraq, 81, 111, 114–17, 119, 120, 122, 131, 147–49; and language skills, 122; in Syria, 149

U.S. Army Special Forces, 7th Group: in Afghanistan, 83, 95, 149–50, 152, 154; areas of responsibility, 24; close relationships with Latin American militaries, 82; in Colombia, 79, 83, 84–85, 86–87, 90–91, 95; in El Salvador, 8, 20, 23–24, 28; high level of Spanish language proficiency, 27–28; in Iraq, 81, 116; regional orientation of, 10

U.S. Army Special Forces, 10th Group, in Iraq, 110, 111, 116, 117, 119, 120, 121, 124, 147–49

U.S. Army Special Forces, training of foreign SOF: cases selected for analysis of, 6–9; factors influencing effectiveness of, 9–10; successful training missions, importance of understand characteristics of, 2–3, 6, 18. *See also* advisor pairing consistency; Afghanistan, SF training in (2007–21); authority to organize host-nation unit; combat operations, advisor's ability to join; El Salvador, SF training in (1981–91); Iraq, SF training in (2003–11); language and cultural training of U.S. Special Forces; partner-to-advisor ratio; Philippines, SF training in (2001–15)

U.S. Pacific Command Augmentation Team (PAT), 49, 73

USSOCOM. *See* Special Operations Command, U.S.

Vietnam War: restrictions on advisors following, 40; U.S. Army Special Forces in, 4, 13

Volckmann, Russell, 3

Wafa, Faiz, 154, 155–56, 162, 164

Wallis, John, 12

Weingast, Barry, 12

West Germany, U.S. success in constructing military of, 176

Whitaker, Kevin, 77, 82

Woerner Report, 20, 21

Wolfowitz, Paul, 65–66

Yousef, Ramzi, 48

Zets, Chris, 100

About the Author

Frank K. Sobchak, PhD, is a retired Special Forces colonel who served in various assignments in war and peace during a twenty-six-year military career. He is chair of Irregular Warfare Studies at the Modern War Institute at the U.S. Military Academy, Senior Fellow at the Global and National Security Institute at the University of South Florida, and Fellow (contributor) for the MirYam Institute. He is coauthor of the acclaimed two-volume *The U.S. Army in the Iraq War* and has been published in the *Wall Street Journal, Foreign Policy, Newsweek, Time*, the *Jerusalem Post, Defense One, The Hill, War on the Rocks*, the *Modern War Institute*, and the *Small Wars Journal*. He has a PhD in international relations from Tufts University's Fletcher School of Law and Diplomacy. He is married to his West Point classmate, Lt. Col. Iris Sobchak (Ret.), and they live in Holliston, Massachusetts, with their four children.

The **Naval Institute Press** is the book-publishing arm of the U.S. Naval Institute, a private, nonprofit, membership society for sea service professionals and others who share an interest in naval and maritime affairs. Established in 1873 at the U.S. Naval Academy in Annapolis, Maryland, where its offices remain today, the Naval Institute has members worldwide.

Members of the Naval Institute support the education programs of the society and receive the influential monthly magazine *Proceedings* or the colorful bimonthly magazine *Naval History* and discounts on fine nautical prints and on ship and aircraft photos. They also have access to the transcripts of the Institute's Oral History Program and get discounted admission to any of the Institute-sponsored seminars offered around the country.

The Naval Institute's book-publishing program, begun in 1898 with basic guides to naval practices, has broadened its scope to include books of more general interest. Now the Naval Institute Press publishes about seventy titles each year, ranging from how-to books on boating and navigation to battle histories, biographies, ship and aircraft guides, and novels. Institute members receive significant discounts on the Press' more than eight hundred books in print.

Full-time students are eligible for special half-price membership rates. Life memberships are also available.

For more information about Naval Institute Press books that are currently available, visit www.usni.org/press/books. To learn about joining the U.S. Naval Institute, please write to:

Member Services
U.S. Naval Institute
291 Wood Road
Annapolis, MD 21402-5034
Telephone: (800) 233-8764
Fax: (410) 571-1703
Web address: www.usni.org

www.ingramcontent.com/pod-product-compliance
Ingram Content Group UK Ltd.
Pitfield, Milton Keynes, MK11 3LW, UK
UKHW041912140426
5217IPUK00001B/7